From the Library of
Fred Holland
Ashland Ohio 44805

COLLECTED PAPERS ON SOUTH ASIA

# RURAL INDIA

CENTRE OF SOUTH ASIAN STUDIES
SCHOOL OF ORIENTAL AND AFRICAN STUDIES
UNIVERSITY OF LONDON

*COLLECTED PAPERS ON SOUTH ASIA*

1. RULE, PROTEST, IDENTITY: Aspects of Modern South Asia
*Edited by Peter Robb and David Taylor*

2. POLITICAL IDENTITY IN SOUTH ASIA
*Edited by David Taylor and Malcolm Yapp*

3. THE CITY IN SOUTH ASIA
*Edited by Kenneth Ballhatchet and John Harrison*

4. BUDDHIST STUDIES
*Edited by Philip Denwood and Alexander Piatigorsky*

5. RURAL SOUTH ASIA
*Edited by Peter Robb*

6. RURAL INDIA
*Edited by Peter Robb*

7. INDIAN RELIGION
*Edited by Richard Burghart and Audrey Cantlie*

COLLECTED PAPERS ON SOUTH ASIA NO. 6

# RURAL INDIA

## *LAND, POWER AND SOCIETY UNDER BRITISH RULE*

*Edited by*
PETER ROBB

CURZON PRESS

First published 1983

Curzon Press Ltd : London and Dublin

© Centre of South Asian Studies, SOAS 1983

ISBN
0 7007 0161 3

ISSN
0141 0156

Printed in Great Britain by
Nene Litho, Wellingborough, Northants.

CONTENTS

# LIST OF CONTRIBUTORS

Dr *Ian Catanach*, Department of History, Canterbury (New Zealand)

Dr *Neil Charlesworth*, Department of Economic History, Glasgow

Professor *Dharma Kumar*, Centre for Advanced Study in Economic Development and Economic History, Delhi School of Economics, Delhi

Dr *Jacques Pouchepadass*, Centre d'Etudes de l'Inde et de l'Asie du Sud, Paris

Professor *Rajat K. Ray*, Presidency College, Calcutta

Dr *Peter Robb*, Department of History, School of Oriental and African Studies, London

Dr *Ian Talbot*, Department of History, Bangor

Professor *Burton Stein*, Department of History, Hawaii

Professor *Anand Yang*, Department of History, Utah

# PREFACE

In December 1980 a number of scholars came together under the auspices of the Centre of South Asian Studies at the London School of Oriental and African Studies, to discuss the 'external dimension in rural South Asia, linkages between localities and the wider world'. The scholars were drawn from Britain, Europe, India, New Zealand and the United States. A preliminary meeting had also been held in June 1980. Some of the papers given on these occasions bore particularly on the question of economic development and are published as a companion volume in this series, entitled *Rural South Asia: Linkages, Change and Development.* Some of the other papers, all of them historical in emphasis and relating to the period or the impact of British rule, have been included in the present volume. I have in both cases added introductory essays.

The title of this volume is not intended to imply pretensions of comprehensiveness. All books by several hands are bound to contain diverse and usually divergent views and approaches; part of their value is often the comparisons and debates implicit in these differences. All such books are bound too to offer specific studies and not a general survey. However, the socio-economic history of rural India in particular is in an interesting phase, and the papers in this volume can probably make a greater contribution together than if published separately. For all - social, or political too - provide pictures of Indian rural society from the standpoint of its relationships and exchanges: the village is seen not as an isolated entity but as one which exists in and reacts with a physical and cultural context. The cumulative effect of the papers, I argue, is therefore radical, not so much in themselves perhaps but in what they represent. The intention of my introductory essay in this volume is mainly to explain and justify this claim.

The conference, and hence this volume, would not have been possible without the financial assistance provided by the Projects Committee of the School of Oriental and African Studies; that assistance is gratefully acknowledged. I have also been assisted by the editorial committee of the Centre of South Asian Studies, and particularly by Professor Kenneth Ballhatchet and Dr David Taylor.

As in the previous volume, complete uniformity between papers has not been attempted, italics have been kept to a minimum, and no attempt has been made to 'correct' the transliteration of words current in Anglo-Indian usage and not, strictly speaking, employed directly from an Indian language. As a rule, also, such words are not italicized after their first appearance.

*P.G.R.*

# LAND AND SOCIETY: THE BRITISH 'TRANSFORMATION' IN INDIA

*Peter Robb*

'Cambridge had fields (*campos*) as the neighbouring villages had fields: vast, hedgeless, fenceless tracts of arable land ...'. So remarked F.W. Maitland in one of his Ford lectures at Oxford in 1897. He explained: 'through the crust of academic learning, through the crust of trade and craft, of municipality and urbanity, the rustic basis of Cambridge is displayed'; he concluded: 'those who would study the early history of our towns ... have fields and pastures on their hands.' 'We shall have,' he went on, 'to think away distinctions which seem to us as clear as the sunshine; we must think ourselves back into a twilight.'[1] By contrast most people - Emmanuel Le Roy Ladurie for example - define the town in opposition to the country, the townsman in opposition to the peasant, not just in the present day but in pre-industrial societies. A village, existing among other villages, is seen as dominated or surrounded by powers which are distinct from it, and thus as essentially stable, turned in on itself.[2] Maitland's perception would transform the history of land and society into one of exchange and connection, not only in revolutionary times but to explain continuities. Where towns have fields so villages have access to or relations with rulers, merchants and craftsmen. Instead of Ladurie's opposition we are offered ambiguities and a blurring of categories. We are invited to confront and assess our own assumptions.

I believe India under British rule invites a similar approach. There were supposedly changes in relations between the countryside and a wider world. They included improved communications and an increase in the number and range of the exchanges in which rural people took part. They included codifications of law, followed by greater recourse to the courts, some shifts in the basis for behaviour, and some changes in behaviour itself. They included the bureaucratization and enhanced activity of government, with in some areas significant inputs of capital, but eventually a reduction of the direct financial demands upon the countryside by the state: the British at first made high assessments along radical lines but later sought to weaken the impact of revenue policies at the same time as their interference through law, administration and public works became more effective. In the countryside cultivation expanded, the value of production grew, and holdings were increasingly subdivided or fragmented. Competition became more open, over land, in tenures and rents, and for labour; and there is at least the possibility that disparities in income widened. Attitudes also changed, or the expression of them did. People tried to improve status or defend religion; landlords complained of unruly tenants and tenants of rapacious landlords. People became readier to appeal to the government's 'duty' to look after 'rights', but also to resent its interventions.

The British in India were in at least two minds about change. They believed that major economic and social reforms were necessary and inevitable; in the later nineteenth century they were forced by serious famines to think in terms of development. At the same time a rival consensus held that it was dangerous to disturb rural India. An enhanced anthropological interest sapped the earlier European confidence in universal remedies. In the eyes of influential officials, British laws were proving inappropriate to India and the market economy was destroying social cohesion. The British were led to a confusion of belief which did not cripple their will but perhaps went some way towards neutralizing their impact. However, on the diagnosis of the Indian condition and on the long-term direction of change, both sides were fundamentally agreed, and their unanimity is the more seductive of the historian because it accords with powerful and almost unconscious assumptions within European thought. I have already remarked that the peasant is, in effect, regarded as a particular genus of humankind, and that such assumptions, as Maitland recognised, result from a way of looking at the world; they result from a philosophy and from empirical emphasis. Applied to India, they assert that the country was essentially rural, its social, economic and political institutions in the 'Asiatic' mode. People lived in relationships of unchanging dependence, fixed by birth and superstition. Monetary transactions and trade were peripheral to their activities; the power which was exercised over them was hierarchical and despotic. They were (it was often implied) at an earlier stage of social evolution.

The fundamental dichotomy, for example, is assumed to be between traditional, meaning 'stable', and modern, meaning 'dynamic', as in the discontinuity postulated by nineteenth-century officials in India (equally as confidently as by Ladurie) between subsistence and commercial agriculture or between country and town. The first contrast is repeated in more recent formulations such as the 'dual economy'; the second, of truly ancient origin, is reincarnated in fashionable notions such as the 'moral economy' of the peasant. But, we might ask, what does the dual economy mean when one and the same cultivator grows millets for consumption, sugar for local trade, and cotton and oilseeds for the international market? What does it mean when even a subsistence crop (one grown for food and not as surplus for marketing) may in fact be bought and sold by those who provide credit between harvests? How complete is the division between urban and rural when few economic or social activities are restricted to one arena or the other, and when the same trading, credit and social or religious networks pervade both? It becomes uncertain that discontinuity is a helpful concept.

At another level too it may be seen that the British in India thought in terms of categories. Perhaps inevitably, as aliens, they liked to deal in certainties, which survive to exaggerate the extent and rapidity of changes under their rule. They divided Indians into castes and tribes. Often enough, they mean separated and inflexible groupings according to birth or race, and occupation, *and* culture as well. There were 'martial' castes and 'agricultural' castes, regional 'tribes' (that is, the local or linguistic units such as Bengalis or Punjabis) and religious 'tribes' (Muslims,Hindus). Many statistics on economic conditions were taken and sorted into such groups rather than by economic criteria: they blurred social and economic disparities between caste-fellows so that castes might be treated as universal categories. The ritual hierarchy has thus come to be emphasized today at the expense of, say, economic ranking or political influence, and seldom because of any conscious and justified decision. Moreover those who employed such terms in the nineteenth century talked of 'good' agricultural castes, 'wily' Bengalis, 'sturdy' Sikhs, supposing in effect that in India certain qualities and abilities predominated in or were exclusive to particular groups. Of course caste is crucial in establishing status and affecting behaviour, even if it is not quite the institution nineteenth-century observers took it to be, and indeed is a different institution in different conditions; but it is only one of several variables, so that it must be proved to be the appropriate unit of analysis (for example, in setting out patterns of land-holding). More obviously, it must not be taken as implying an exclusive set of human qualities which are invariable. Indian social forms may be exceptionally effective in perpetuating themselves, but they are not wholly rigid. In examining their history one asks whether there was sufficient pressure to change them, and, if not, why not. I admit that attitudes and beliefs inhibit or enhance change, whether one considers culture to be a prime mover or, itself, to be a product of objective conditions. But I believe one must shake off the assumptions of the nineteenth-century British view of culture to a greater extent than has always been managed in the past. There were conservative and sentimental elements in that view, but also criticisms of India. Its people were poor, its agriculture relatively unproductive. In prevailing habits of thought it was too easy to believe that culture did more than help create or maintain the conditions, that it caused them or (when British failures were suggested) excused them. Owners and cultivators lost out to money-lenders, rural people to townsmen, peasants to politicians, it was thought, because they were ignorant, feckless or fatalistic. We need to know the determinants of poverty and of change more fully. It is the quintessential 'development' issue (discussed in the companion to this book).

The records of British India are also coloured by the crisis of confidence which beset late Victorians. No doubt their era was the apogee of empire, and of intellectual and cultural and economic imperialism as well, but, as I have already suggested, among the rulers there were also doubters. Nationalist and international critics were beginning to be heard, just as Britain's economic and political power was being challenged. British rule in India, faced with financial crises, famines and upheaval, and uncertain of improvement, no longer seemed an unqualified success even to its admirers. Some big, straight-forward jobs such as building railways or administrations had been undertaken, but underlying discrepancies between Britain and India in mores, living standards and productivity seemed to be ever-widening. And, whether rural uplift was to be tackled by systemic or particular reforms, it was a daunting and hugely various task, one no longer thought amenable to the available administrative or scientific remedies. The Utilitarian hopes for law had been challenged (as has been shown for the Punjab)[3] by that preference for historical over analytical jurism implied above. Where famine had been expected to disappear after the beneficent application of public works, it was now commonly attributed to climatic change, a force beyond contemporary understanding, or to lack of work, a cause embedded in economic and social structures which no one knew how to alter. Among agricultural experts too there was agreement that the Indian cultivator was after all rational, if only in choosing to minimize risks in marginal or unpredictable conditions. Naturally, the experts made more of this in their reports, to combat the ignorance of the popular assertions to the contrary, than in their practical work; but even so it was at one level a doctrine of despair. How much more comforting to believe that the peasant merely needed to be taught and persuaded by those who knew better, by the paternalist official and the European 'expert'.

From these different strands within the copious records, comes the intellectual equivalent of a sleight of hand. It was axiomatic that Asiatic ways were different; it was therefore convincing that the British were transforming India. Imperialists thought the changes were beneficial and justified empire; social conservatives worried about popular unrest. But everyone believed in cross-cultural influence: it was, I suggest, a *belief*. Consider, for example, the conservative reaction. Finally, in their failure of nerve, these latter-day imperialists rejected the economic optimism of earlier generations without trial. They justified legislation to curb land transfer, partly with the argument that the unbridled operation of the market economy had not led to prosperity. The low capitalization of Indian agriculture, and habits which militated against improvements by non-agriculturalists, supposedly prevented any economic benefits from the transfer of titles in land. The expropriation by foreclosure (often not accompanied by ejection of the former proprietor or cultivator) merely aided the accumulation of wealth by middlemen on the basis of existing agricultural practice and productivity. Yet this verdict is not proven. On the one hand, it might be argued, the expansion of cultivation which did take place did so as much on under-utilized plots within cultivated areas as through the breaking in of virgin land, and came about under the stimulus of price rises in advance of population pressure - for all the world as if entrepreneurial spirits had been at work. On the other hand it may be shown that the land market was not after all free and effective but inhibited by custom; it promised significant change only in the long run. The pessimists offer a picture of drastic change without improvement, and an optimist could counter with one of improvement without drastic change. The contemporary rhetoric, however, is very largely pessimistic in this sense, and most subsequent accounts have followed suit.

The historian is tempted above all perhaps because the records are so plausible. Government and technology were themselves changing, and bringing change. It is obvious that labour will be more mobile, for example, if communications are improved and new opportunities arise - abroad, in towns, plantations and factories, public works or the army. It is likely, too, that competition will be quickened if population rises or if the returns on crops leave a balance after rent and revenue payments to permit money wages for labour. But to locate such changes specifically in the nineteenth century in India and to attribute them wholly to British rule should not be so easy. Nor is it safe to characterise them too readily as a process leading towards economic modernity, or as a revolution from a society based on status to one based on contract. We need to understand better than we do the nature of the transactions the British observed and, because a benchmark is needed, of those supposedly being replaced.

The collection of essays in this book has been made as an attempt, therefore, to contribute to the debate about the nature of rural society which is implied by the comparison between the radical approach of Maitland and the more conventional interpretation (in this one area) of Ladurie. The book is substantially about land, its control and use, and about changes during British rule. The first papers consider ways of perceiving relations in land; others discuss, for example, the land market, commercial agriculture, rural credit, and local power and administration. Three final essays look mainly at other aspects of the countryside, or draw out themes which play minor roles in the first six. Together the papers are intended to provide studies which focus on linkages across a continuum, rather than on the separateness and self-sufficiency of rural affairs and institutions. A starting-point therefore is the definition of what is external and what is internal to the village, and the study of the interplay between the two. Burton Stein takes 'internal' to mean 'indigenous' and 'external' to mean 'exotic': the internal originated from a mix of influence within and outside village society but was able to persist for a time even when the mix had changed. Gradually, however, it transformed itself (in Stein's example) into a 'distinctive Madras presidency style', an amalgam of British and pre-British influences. In other papers the distinction which is made or implied is between levels of society or over geographical space (the village and the outside world) but it is clear that what is meant is in essence the same: the difference between what is at any one time native to a particular location or community and that which is foreign to it. It is clear too that the content of each category is in flux, and that therefore the dividing line is broad and indefinite.

Stein's contribution brings us at once to the ways land was held, a theme taken up also in the two following papers, by Dharma Kumar and Jacques Pouchepadass. I am not going to be able, without unreasonably extending this introduction, to discuss all the essays or all of the issues in this book, but the question of land is so central to the general field of interest that I wish to take it up here, to represent the others. It is an example with some important theoretical and methodological implications. In Stein's case, the critical assertion about land is that the prevailing Munro school of administration in Madras derived from a way of seeing and not something observed. There has been an idea that raiyatwari as a system was nearer than zamindari to some original form of Indian rural society. According to Stein this is yet another false legacy of the village republic ideal, and a forerunner of theories of single-line evolution represented by Maine (unqualified by Baden-Powell).[4] Stein makes us recognise the importance of external perceptions of internal arrangements: the suggestion is that these impinge on one another, and indeed that difficulties and short-comings in British institutions in India, as well as indigenous political developments, may be traced to the discontinuities between pre-British and British arrangements, or alternatively to the persistence of one under or within the other.

Dharma Kumar too is interested in the external dimension which is embodied in the perceptions and categorizations of outsiders. In discussing terminology, however, she is naturally concerned with establishing what it is that is to be described; in particular she looks at ownership of property. There has been a readiness, she implies, to seize upon glib and absolute distinctions in regard to relationships to land, as between for example, 'land to own' and 'land to rule'.[5] But, she claims, no ownership is absolute. In particular she challenges the idea that there was, before the nineteenth century, no effective transferable interest in land and hence no private property in it or several ownership of it, in India. The questioning here goes, in one sense, a stage further than Stein's, but the challenge is to the same orthodoxy. Denzil Ibbetson made one of the best statements of this, writing as a member of the Government of India's Revenue and Agriculture Department during the consultations which led to the Punjab Alienation of Land Act in 1900.[6] It was believed that British revenue policies introduced land property rights into India, with consequences in terms of debt and land alienation, and social and political control in rural areas. Ibbetson concluded, not that private land transfer was unknown before British laws, but that it was discouraged by the state, by joint proprietary and joint family customs, and by political and fiscal instability because it reduced the value of land: in all respects the tendency of British administration had been to reverse these conditions. There are really two points here, though this has not generally been stated. First, there is the argument that land was not normally transferred by sale. Second, there is the observation that there was no market in land, that is, that the price paid in any transfer was not freely and competitively established. Both of these points are derived from principle rather than evidence. They depend upon the pervading idea of the village republic as popularized by Sir Henry Maine, and on the expectation of social evolution away from closed custom and stability towards the free market and rapid change of modernity. Indeed the discussions in the 1890s pointed to Indian native states, where widely different practices prevailed in respect of land transfer, and attributed the difference to the degree of British interference, to an opening up of society that was inevitable in proportion as the state developed its resources or reduced its demands after the British example. Similarly the argument from value, seen as an incident of land in exclusive and secure possession and of agricultural surplus, depends upon definitions provided by classical economic theory, and on the rational economic man to be found therein.

By contrast, according to Kumar, land was bought

and sold in the south even in Chola times. Indeed I conclude that the Ibbetson point that pre-British landholders did not sell land but sold 'rights' (for example, a well) depends on an unreal distinction. Kumar also challenges the commercial argument: on the one hand in the nineteenth century the Madras and other governments in fact did take very high proportions of surplus as revenue and discouraged alienation of land. (This stopped after mid-century and by the 1900s revenue was probably below ten per cent of gross produce.) And, on the other hand, we do not know the basis or the extent of the effective taxation in pre-British times, whatever the assertions that it managed to corner all the surplus. I am sure that there must have been bargaining between payers and collectors, and that there were, moreover, 'proper' rates (and hence expectations?) which affected practice and in so far as they fell short of the entire surplus created value. There is evidence too in other normative indicators. In Bihar for example the terms for occupancy tenant are *maurūsi*, *kadimi*, *dehi* and *jaddi*, which mean hereditary, ancient, resident and ancestral, but they are contrasted with *pāhi*, *kharidgi*, *hāl upārjit*, meaning foreign or non-resident, acquiring by purchase, and newly-created.[7] My inference is that ancestral right was thought superior but also that other kinds of interest existed and had to be distinguished from it. Such interests may have been of recent creation in the nineteenth century, but it seems more likely that an indigenous notion of occupancy conferred by residence was always complemented by the idea of landholding achieved in other ways, including transfer if only, originally, from hereditary residents (claiming descent from a first settler or conqueror) to 'foreign' residents (who made no such claims or were not so recognised). In short, if all land rights were not fixed, resident and inherited, then some could be acquired and transferred.

Pouchepadass tackles the point directly. He takes the orthodox view and provides a lucid account which it will be useful to follow through, at the cost of some repetition, in order to clarify and enlarge upon the arguments I have just advanced. In talking of the land market in pre-British times, Pouchepadass is referring explicitly to Indian 'concepts' of land and rights in land (thus contributing to a major tendency of this book). He tends to accept the assertion that, though alienation used to be permissable, in practice it did not normally occur, because of political and economic inhibitions; and that in Mughal times what was transferred were specific rights (for example of revenue collection) but not land. (Thus he follows Ibbetson.) 'Tenant rights', Pouchepadass says categorically, 'remain untransferable', and the 'conception of property as an individual and exclusive right in the soil is unknown'. But then the permanent settlement in Bengal, he goes on to claim, did give transferable rights - indeed it did so, if only because transfer had been specifically forbidden by the British a few years before - and as a result of the change in law land was transferred. This had social consequences. Patnidars began to proliferate. The major impact, however, was to come with the economic change which followed the legal one and which reversed the previously low value of land. A market became practicable. That it did not arise at once was due to cultural restraints (here we reach Pouchepadass's main contention, one of considerable subtlety, which will speak for itself below). Now, except for the last point, this too is Ibbetson's case. In its broad outlines it is likely to carry conviction as a description of what was happening during the nineteenth century, but it is clearly controversial in the significance attributed to what it describes.

It depends, as Pouchepadass spells out, on certain other contentions. As already discussed, it depends on the Mughal intention (Pouchepadass's word) to take the entire surplus in tax: this, I argue, blurs the necessary distinction between aim and achievement, and perhaps between the revenue demand, the customary obligation and the realization; it is at least theoretically possible that in the interstices value in land might arise. Pouchepadass adds that in British times the right of sale was not recognised in princely states and, following the officials who first advanced that argument, he implies that this was the original situation. But he also makes it clear that he means only that sales were not officially recognized. Thus the point is not conclusive with regard to practice; while the idea that non-recognition was an 'original' form depends on what I have already implied is a glib, circular and unproven correlation between the differences in various princes' laws and customs, and the degree of modernization under British influence. Next, Pouchepadass assumes that patnidars - intermediary feeders on surplus, at once the proof and the product of the transferability of land - had been unknown before 1793. But Ratnalekha Ray has cast doubt upon their novelty,[8] and if subinfeudation is not to be blamed on British laws, then the entire argument begins to totter.

The point, I think, is that certainties have tended to be pushed beyond the point at which evidence is secure (which indeed is precisely Pouchepadass's argument when he relates indigenous perceptions to the growth of a free market in land). But when Pouchepadass asserts that it is everywhere a modern idea that a man can gain control of land by purchase, I would reply: it depends what you mean. It is true that Hindu concepts and indigenous custom do not encourage private sale or temporary alienation, and that legitimacy was founded habitually on settlement or conquest. But neither rules out other routes to the economic and political possession of land (which is what matters in practice). Indeed, becoming perhaps over-subtle, one might interpret strong and repeated assertions of custom as implying some contrary behaviour which society or the state was seeking to prevent. The idea that 'no coherent land market' existed during the nineteenth century is at once less and more than the assertion that land was inalienable or untransferable. It is a statement about a way in which land did not change hands - that it did not do so at prices freely regulated by supply and demand (or as nearly so as in the West today). Indeed pursuing our general theme, not that of Pouchepadass, we have to ask whether the right to transfer by sale in a free land market is really an essential attribute of private ownership in land, treated as an objective economic and political concept. (Denying inam was 'private', Stein substitutes possession of land as shares in a two-way system.) If our concept of ownership is culturally loaded we need to disentangle the essential features if we are to measure the changes in the nineteenth and twentieth centuries. My point here is not new, but it is worth restating because it is frequently forgotten. The fact is that proprietary rights are distinct from revenue-collecting rights, however much the two may be enjoyed by the same person in respect of the same land. The British tended to conflate them, it is true, but we should not fall into the same error and assume that proprietary rights were unknown before the British thus created them. We too often seem to talk of property, when we should be talking of proprietors. The implication of all this is that the legal possession created by British revenue policy cannot be of such general impact (creating or destroying 'rights') as is sometimes supposed, if the previous situation was one in which effective proprietorial rights were already being enjoyed, represented by rental income, labour services and control of village resources.[9] This is of course a rather different point from my argument about transfer - the one relates to the role of land in social and economic dominance, the other to the flexibility of the tenurial system. But the two meet in relation to the argument about exclusive individual possession, for which transferability is often supposed to be the indicator, and for which I am substituting proprietorial rights because in economic and social terms they come to the same thing.

That being said I am also interested in the question of transfer in its own right, because of its importance for understanding the impact of British rule. I believe that the orthodox interpretation is the product of an overly static view of rural society in the eighteenth century, and an exaggeratedly dynamic view of it in the nineteenth. We are forced particularly to consider the vexed question of the impact of British law; it will already be apparent that the conflict between normative rule and individual custom is a frequent visitor to the pages of this book. Why was it, for example, that purchasers at land sales early in the nineteenth century met resistance when taking possession? Was it that transfer was not recognised, even from one locally-powerful person to another, even by consent to redress, say, an imbalance between labour supply and access to land, or to redeem an acknowledged family debt? Or was it that the purchaser at British revenue sales was merely buying a piece of paper, an entry in the record, which was not synonymous with practical and locally-recognized 'ownership' of the land? It is only in an integrated system of law and administration that title necessarily carries with it in practice the rights it specifies; and conflicts over possession in nineteenth-century India may readily be attributed to the incomplete penetration of British law. The changes discussed by Pouchepadass and others are therefore of great importance - they chart the progress of that penetration and a transformation in the terms on which land is held - but they do not necessarily represent a shift from inflexible to transferable interests in land.

The argument from value may similarly be seen to be less conclusive and of different import than has been thought. It is clear that forced government sales, however interpreted, provide an imperfect measure of value in the early nineteenth century. Yet the evidence for the low value of land comes almost entirely from such sales.[10] We know almost nothing of value at private sales until the British start recording them late in the century (and at once discover quite large numbers). Earlier there are only hints at the price for property freely or unofficially transferred - merely suggestions that there *was* some such value, of which the courts were ignorant (to the advantage of moneylenders). Moreover, we might believe that private sales were rare before they began to be recorded - after all, in the Punjab (the Pouchepadass example) they were actively discouraged by the local government. But we may still quibble about definitions: is what the British recognised as private sale identical with all private land transfer? The infrequency of the one, as shown in revenue records, tells us little about the other, for the records were notoriously inaccurate as statements of actual holdings.

In general, in my view, the more one considers the nineteenth-century debates the less original and certain the current orthodoxies appear. With regard to property and land transfer, I argue that discouragement of sale and the lack of economic value in land do not prove that land was never transferred (even by sale), though they increase the likelihood of transfers being concealed, and must influence the nature and range of the mechanisms involved. Of course one cannot prove a negative, and the onus is therefore upon me to suggest why we should believe that transfers occurred, before the impact of British law. I believe there *are* indications: for example in the fluctuations of population, family size and the climate which must have occurred before British rule, or in the extent to which, in spite of joint inheritance, fragmentation of holdings was kept in check. Such factors suggest considerable annual or periodic flexibility in holdings between different units, to allow for example for infertility, or surplus labour, and expanding or contracting cultivation. But I cannot dwell on these points now, and in any case they must form part of that essential task, understanding the eighteenth century, rather than of my present purpose, to comment on the impact of the British. For the latter goal the crux is the attempt to be ever more precise about what was happening.

To take another example, legislation was applied to Bihar and Bengal in 1859 and 1885 providing certain privileges for tenants who had enjoyed continuous occupancy over a period of twelve years. Part of the argument about what was done in these acts refers back to supposed conditions before the permanent settlement of Bengal in 1793. As we have seen, it is said that the regulations at that time ignored the multiplicity of rights in land; they favoured those of exclusive 'landlords', at the expense of those formerly enjoyed by 'tenants'. If we are talking only about the law the matter is indeed simple. Tenants did have no rights under the 1793 regulations, and some of them were given an occupancy right in law in 1859 and 1885. But if we are talking about practice, matters are more complicated. After all the nineteenth-century Acts provided occupancy rights in law only for those who already enjoyed occupancy in practice, either before the Acts or afterwards. Those who look only at the laws can say that before the later nineteenth century all tenants in Bengal were tenants-at-will. But obviously they were nothing of the kind, in practice, or no-one would ever have been able to claim occupancy status even after the Acts. Indeed there are many indicators that certain classes of agriculturalist had long had recognised and heritable rights of cultivation in certain villages, if not on particular plots or holdings; and it is clear too that in some cases these rights were transferable, either with or even without the landlord's permission. The rights can be seen in the terminology already mentioned, and in land-holding records of various kinds. What did the British Acts do then, if not to create new rights? I think they had an impact, after a time, not of creating but of consolidating and protecting some tenants' position. Put briefly the 1793 provisions were introduced at a time when population and the availability of land and the high tax demands on landlords, all tended (relatively speaking) to favour the tenants, and when in any case British law hardly ran in the countryside. The nineteenth-century Acts were passed at a time when population pressure on the land and rising prices for agricultural produce and the increasing recourse by rural people to the courts, all meant that it had begun to matter that tenants had no protection under British law. The incentive was for landlords to reduce all tenants to tenants-at-will *in practice* as well as in law - 1885 made that more difficult.

Similarly when we turn to the presumed link between property ownership and debt, as discussed in some of the essays, and an important part of the orthodoxy about the consequences of newly-gained property rights, we find that the picture is not after all clear, again because law and practice tend to be confused. Debt was habitually taken to signify, almost to be a measure of, poverty; and indeed it still is, in spite of the efforts of Malcolm Darling in the 1920s to examine the real world behind the assumptions. Property comes into the debate because credit was always needed by cultivators, and, recognising this, the argument is that before the British gave property rights the maximum liability for each holding was the entire net produce and not the land itself. Doubt has been cast repeatedly on the extent to which nineteenth-century money-lenders did acquire their debtors' property, but, even more important, if we consider the practice and not the legal position, we may see that a cultivator forced to relinquish his entire surplus to finance his and his ancestors' debts is hardly distinguishable from the 'rack-rented tenant' of British record (the officials believed he had lost his title to his land and instead worked on it for the money-lender); and equally we see that a cultivator forced to relinquish more than the net produce (because allowed less than the appropriate return for his labour) is very similar to that other familiar British characterization, the former proprietor reduced to the level of a landless labourer. The implication is that if the latter conditions flourished after British impact, the former might as readily have flourished without it. And the reason people did not believe they did, was largely that they habitually saw the 'traditional' countryside as isolated from outside influence - though it is obvious that that picture is false if money-lending is to be regarded as an outside activity (not being within the grasp of the majority of cultivators). We might be on stronger ground suggesting that the gradual spread of a single enforceable law and the improvement of communications made it easier for non-local money-lenders to operate. This created new competition, and hence generated among local creditors a resentment which the British officials heard, though they supposed themselves to be responding to the needs of the debtors.

We see in these examples how the questioning of British rhetoric and the rethinking of their and our view of the countryside, are at the bottom the same task. Our concern is to discover the substance which lurks behind the form. Thus if I accept that land transfer was discouraged before the British, and that sale was regarded as less complete or privileged than other methods of land acquisition (such as settlement, conquest or inheritance), I do not therefore assert, in effect, that there were no transferable rights in property and that any change in the pattern of transfers during British rule was absolute - at the same time caused by, proved by and responsible for a weakening of social ties in the Indian countryside. The methodology has two main stages: the separation of law and practice, and the establishing of what the latter meant at different times in terms of production, tenure, authority or social relations.

The papers in this volume all address themselves directly or obliquely to this better understanding of change. The two further papers on Bihar, my own and that of Anand Yang, stress the limitation and unevenness of British impact, in contrast with the impression of omnipotence given by British activities. Neil Charlesworth, writing on land use in Western India, also questions contemporary interpretations of the rural economy. Ian Catanach on plague and Ian Talbot on Punjabi politics illustrate further aspects of the entanglement of the countryside with the wider environment. Rajat Ray provides a portrait of rural society in Bengal on the basis of internal or indigenous perceptions.

With my paper and with Charlesworth's we are still mainly concerned with land and with interpretations of rural institutions. My paper tries to re-interpret various aspects of Bihari rural life the better to assess the impact of British rule in the nineteenth century, concluding that it advantaged dominant groups in the shorter term and *hence* eventually disadvantaged them in comparison with those who prospered in other regions. Charlesworth similarly re-thinks explanations of scattering and subdivision of units of ownership or, as he prefers, fragmentation of units of cultivation: he sees debt as risk aversion rather as I do, and he attributes fragmentation to the desire to maximize labour and profit in regions where physical conditions were diverse and there was competition over the land most suitable for commercial agriculture. (His analysis requires a relatively free market to determine the effective possession of land, though not necessarily the legal titles: in tenancies or sub-tenancies for example.)

By contrast, Yang and Talbot are primarily interested in political control, the first comparing nineteenth-century local institutions with what is really an ideal of how the Mughal patwari and kanungo were supposed to work, the second at root considering how various sources of influence - in land, religion, British institutions - were mobilized in search for power in the new arena of provincial government. These two papers demonstrate that the approach adopted in this volume is not of relevance only to economic history. Indeed the overwhelming historiography of the development of nationalism in South Asia may more readily be digested if its past assumptions are recognised for what they are. The question of why mass support could be mobilized in the twentieth century, for example, becomes a quite different kind of problem once we re-examine the generally facile or misleading categorizations of India made by the British raj and Western thought in general. Nationalism itself, at the ideological level, comes to be regarded differently (as indeed many recent scholars have suggested). It is after all essentially the demand for political self-determination. In this century it apparently came to harness, or at least to act as an umbrella for, local grievances and local political networks. Clearly, therefore, people were both identifying themselves with broader communities and expecting that the communities would influence or control those who ruled over them. Either or both of these conditions were not present in the past, and nationalism (in the technical sense, opposed to identity) did not exist. Villages were indeed integrated with the wider world, in ways suggested in these papers, and the linkages could be modified to carry different and wider cultural or political messages once local supporters looked for regional or national leaders, and leaders wooed supporters. But, more than today, the unit with which people consistently identified was certainly the caste in its operative form of local jati, or the village; and moreover such people had no expectation of having a say in who ruled, or rather - for sovereignty was also fragmented - who governed over those aspects of life which were generally accepted as belonging to the zamindar, the raja or the emperor. This is not to say that there was no religious or cultural antagonism between peoples; it was merely that technology, communication, government and the popular consensus did not encourage the antagonisms to lead to political demands. Much of the terminology in which these issues were once debated, and are still, on such topics as the uprisings of 1857-8, is thus inappropriate: a Mughal or an Englishman could not be regarded as objectionably foreign if most people regarded rulers as 'foreign' by definition.

Ian Catanach extends the themes of the book further, into unfamiliar territory. He demonstrates the importance of indigenous perceptions and the way they are adapted in new situations, by describing the role of mythology in rendering plague comprehensible to its potential victims. He illustrates the continuities of town and countryside by, for example, describing the way that gerbils' warrens spread out under the soil or that rumour was disseminated in the villages. Rajat Ray also breaks relatively new ground, in using the writings of a Bengali novelist to enter the minds of rural people. In particular he finds inappropriate both the social categories in which they are usually grouped, and the psychological assessments made of them by outside observers. Rather, he portrays the self-perception of interdependent classes- gentry, caste peasants, dependents - all interacting in different ways. Ray eschews, in other words, any form of cultural or intellectual imperialism. All the papers thus share a picture of the rural world, as glimpsed by Catanach and surveyed in depth by Ray. Their verdicts rest upon a denial that the Indian rural world used to be static as a result of being isolated; they offer shades and mixtures rather than clear outlines. This is perhaps peculiarly appropriate to the Indian setting, in that Hindu thinking does tend towards emphasizing oneness, in contrast with that of Europeans who categorise and reify experience.[11] Moreover, in questioning the rigidity and certainty of Indian social institutions, we are sharing in a trend of thought currently to be observed in several fields. I have mentioned the implications for political study. Among anthropologists, too, M.N. Srinivas, for example, has recently suggested that varna position and hierarchical status should be regarded as ambiguous in practice; and dominant castes, with their tendency to faction and fission, as subtly and secretly proselytizing in order to maintain significant numbers.[12] Thus (or so I would interpret it) status is not so much a cause as a consequence of economic and political success. Like Dharma Kumar's idea of customs binding the controllers as well as the controlled, this suggests placing interdependence above dominance in discussing the Indian rural world. It also restores the temporal aspect to its proper place in our studies: if caste is as Srinivas describes it, then the system is flexible in content if not in form. Let us leave aside the case of the Brahmans which is complicated by their special role, and let us also disregard the possible normative pressure of modern education and communications. Then, if we accept that a group will tend over time to have high ritual status or esteem as a result of its having wealth or power, we are conceiving of hierarchy in a radical way: it will indeed tend to perpetuate itself but it will not necessarily be endlessly reproduced. We are therefore forced to consider changes over time as well as structures.

The present is a period of debate about directions being taken in historical studies.[13] Collectively the essays in this volume may have some small relevance. First, to those who reassert the validity of narrative, they say that personalities and incidents of the past *are* essentially trivial in themselves - or that they are if we wish to escape cultural arrogance. Narrative history is necessarily elitist and almost unavoidably Europe-centred. It is largely irrelevant to the student of non-Western societies. In my view the range of important historical topics has widened and ought to be widened still further. The concerns and methods of this symposium make a minor contribution to that end. Secondly, to those who object to an excess of detailed monographs, these essays reply that detailed studies may be so related to larger themes as to speak to a wider audience, but, more importantly, that the attention to detail and particularly to place, to geographical or ecological settings, has been a major advance in historical research, and indeed is crucial particularly to the study of non-European and non-literate peoples. Again such specifics are at the core of this book. Thirdly, to those who criticise technicalities and special terminologies as rendering works incomprehensible except to specialists, the essays respond that one's need to clarify methods and language for each time and society must in logic precede the ability to communicate one's findings to other times and peoples, including one's own. Historians do construct the past no doubt, though we need not worry unduly about the notion that to impose intelligible patterns is so artificial that any pattern is as valid as another: the question is whether an interpretation is built upon the historian's perceptions or in terms appropriate to the time and place he studies; that it does no violence to the past described though it is an object created and different from it; in short not that it was perceived but that it was perceivable contemporaneously. Certainly the result should not then be obscurity for its own sake; it should be more complete communication. And indeed, almost throughout this volume, the authors are searching for appropriate terms, even for new generations of categories.

Finally there is a charge which the essays do seem to me to accept - that there has been too much attention to structure and too little to process in some modern historiography. The societies which emerge in these pages are less definable and more various, and change more subtly, than those conjured up by many more ambitious studies, with their generalizations over space and time. To emphasize exchange and connection is of course to opt for a dynamic rather than a structural view. We are advocating an almost Hindu world image in order to re-think the nature of the countryside, and therefore we are obscuring the borders between things. Thus it is that we have to think ourselves back into Maitland's twilight.

Our purpose is to describe change better, not to deny that it occurred. If 'No man is an Island', and no village either, then (to alter the metaphor) the image we have is of societies as various sets of interlocking gears. Under British rule, as remarked at the outset, communications improved in India in very many senses of the term, with consequences for the number, range and quality of the exchanges between people. We see this in production, marketing, agrarian relations, state action, law, travel, and social, religious and political affairs and organization. The connections are the key. An increase in the number of contacts may reinforce or subvert existing customs: when people are in contact in significantly different ways or for different reasons, and when different people come into contact, then changes or adaptations are inevitable. But the process will not be direct or even; it will be complex and various. Its speed will not be exaggerated: the movement in itself is not new and the pace will differ from place to place. Thus it was, in my view, in India under British rule, and our understanding is not helped by the injudicious application to India of precepts and terms from classical economic theory, derived as they are from European experience and already criticized on these grounds in the nineteenth century. In these regards, I think the papers in this volume present a view which has common features; it should help elucidate the history of India under the British.[14]

*NOTES*

Robb, 'Land and Society: the British transformation in India'

I am grateful to members of the Centre of South Asia's editorial committee for urging me to write this essay, and to all the participants in the 'External Dimension' symposia for ideas from which I have shamelessly cribbed. The paper is however my own responsibility and does not necessarily reflect the views even of those whose contributions also appear in this volume. A version of the paper was read at the Institute of Historical Research, London, in 1982; I am grateful also for comments made on that occasion.

1. F.W. Maitland, 'Township and Borough' in *Selected Historical Essays of F.W. Maitland* chosen and introduced by Helen M. Cam (Cambridge 1957), pp.3-15.
2. 'La Civilisation rurale' in Emmanuel Le Roy Ladurie, *Le Territoire de l'historien* (Gallimard 1973), pp.141-68.
3. I am referring particularly to Clive Dewey's work (see his Cambridge Ph.D. dissertation, 1976).
4. Sir Henry S. Maine, *Village-Communities in the East and West* (London 1871); B.H. Baden-Powell, *The Indian Village Community* (London 1896), pp.1-39.
5. See W.C. Neale, 'Land is to Rule' in R.E. Frykenberg, ed., *Land Control and Social Structure in Indian History* (Madison 1969).
6. Government of India, Revenue and Agriculture Department, Selection of Papers on Agricultural Indebtedness and the Restriction of the Power to Alienate Interests in Land (Calcutta 1898), pp.1-253 and 304-445.
7. George A. Grierson, *Bihar Peasant Life* (1885; reprinted Delhi 1973), p.325.
8. Ratnalekha Ray, *Change in Bengal Agrarian Society* (Delhi 1979). Relying on the evidence of, among others, Sir John Shore, Sirajul Islam agrees that 'subinfeudation' was well advanced in 1790; *The Permanent Settlement in Bengal: A Study of its operation 1790-1819* (Dacca 1979), pp.11-12. See below, page 108.
9. Islam, op.cit., pp.6-8, describes the interests and practices of the eighteenth-century Bengali zamindars in terms which I would sum up as the attributes of a local 'lord'.
10. The same point may be made about Chaudhuri's

figures quoted by Pouchepadass: they relate to prices at revenue sales and are therefore influenced by administrative and other factors, as Pouchepadass points out in discounting the decline in prices later in the century.

11. I have been struck by the similarity between this thought and remarks by A. Piatigorsky in a paper on the phenomenology of Indian religions (see Richard Burghart and Audrey Cantlie, eds., *Indian Religion*, forthcoming).

12. M.N. Srinivas, paper read at the School of Oriental and African Studies, London, 18 May 1982.

13. Gordon S. Wood wrote recently: 'Like some vast protoplasm that divides and subdivides again, history at present seems to be in the process of self-destruction.' 'Star-Spangled History', *New York Review of Books* XXIX, 13 (12 August 1982).

14. We see this, for example, in the similarities in the conclusions between some of the papers. Yang and I note the incomplete contact between British raj and rural populations in Bihar, which Pouchepadass also implies, while Talbot and I both see government as none the less reinforcing some roles and attitudes. The image of the village too - its integration with a wider world and its internal diversity - is shared by essays as diverse as those by Charlesworth, Catanach, Talbot and Ray. For a nineteenth-century precursor of some of these ideas see the opening chapters of B.H. Baden-Powell, *The Land Systems of British India* Vol. I (Oxford 1892). One can trace the links between its view of the villages as neither independent nor republics (pp.170-4) and the pictures in this volume of the fluid, competitive ranks of the peasantry (see below, pp.111, 118-21 and 280-2, and also my article cited in note 6, p.142). It is not to be supposed of course that the papers deny the importance of nineteenth-century or Euro-centric views, as Stein's article shows, or as may be seen in aspects even of Ray's paper: the echoes of Zola, for example, in Banerjee's writing (as on page 297 below, of the ending of *Germinal*). But it is argued that these perceptions and influences are not necessarily or wholly reliable, and other interpretations may be sought: Stein's indigenous traditions or the Bengali realities that show through Banerjee's literary conventions.

# IDIOM AND IDEOLOGY IN EARLY NINETEENTH-CENTURY SOUTH INDIA

*Burton Stein*

Among the several notions that may be entertained about 'external' and 'internal' dimensions of South Asian rural society should be included systematic conceptions, of what such societies ought to be, by its participants: that is, notions about ideology. And where, as in the nineteenth century, European colonial dominance is involved, we should be prepared to consider at least two ideologies, that of the European subjugator and that (or those) of the subjugated. The earlier in the colonial period we seek understanding of rural society, the more likely that there will be two or more ideological frameworks extant, perhaps in conflict, and possibly in some sort of dialectical relationship. The present discussion of the early nineteenth-century onset of extensive colonial dominion over south India attempts to delineate two ideological orders, one indigenous and internal, the other - whatever its claims to the contrary - foreign and external.

It is in the nature of things colonial that we know more about the latter than the former ideology. Natural or not, we do know more about British ideology than we know of south Indian conceptions about rural society, and such Indian conceptions as we *are* invited to know are proffered in early British reports and constructions ostensibly pertaining to rural organization before British rule was established. Among the first possessions of a colonized people to be seized is their history. Thus, however difficult it may be to determine the consequences of early British policies and programmes - intended and unintended - it is far more difficult to determine the history of and the moral reasoning about pre-British agrarian relations apart from British views of them. Moreover, according to British views of south India and elsewhere, previous agrarian relations were seen to have been profoundly altered (for the worse, it is most often assumed) by the hegemonic power of the Mughals, or Marathas, or Mysoreans, or even by Englishmen during the eighteenth century, laying waste to, or at least obscuring, what some Britons thought were stable and even admirable Indian systems of the more remote past.

The Coromandel plain and interior upland which

comprised the Madras Presidency of the early nineteenth century had no significant interlude of Mughal or Maratha dominion. This might have been expected to give a clearer shape to the historical agrarian systems of the southern peninsula of the sub-continent than elsewhere in the East India Company's expanding dominion. Maratha control in the 'Carnatic' and Tanjavur, like that of the Mughal in Golkonda or the successor nizamate regime in Hyderabad and its deputy, nawabship, in Arcot, and the later, brief overlay of Muslim control by the Karnatak state of Haidar Ali and Tipu Sultan, are too easily credited with fundamental changes in the system of the preceding Vijayanagara era. Administrative changes initiated by seventeenth and eighteenth-century military intruders appear actually to have been quite tentative and reversible; administrative nomenclature endured beyond presumed agrarian changes. Still, enough confusion was engendered by these intrusions to baffle early British officials (as well as historians of our own day), and, not to be neglected, these intruders were seen as mere military adventurers whose rapacious exploits provided a justification for British conquests. Early British administrators of the vast new territories under Madras had not the time, the inclination, or the means of discovering what the recent and more distant agrarian pasts and their ideological entailments had been; what these early Company officials chose to know of these pasts was sufficient for their purposes.

Such knowledge is not adequate for our purposes, of course. We should seek to form a correct, or at least better, perception of the internal dimension always implied by assuming an 'external' dimension of rural structures of India at the outset of British rule. To accomplish this depends critically upon a perspective as independent as possible of the understandings of British views of these structures, a commonplace which requires restatement. In every part of British India during the early nineteenth century, a particular view of the internal constitution of rural relations attended the introduction of British policies. Much as we may admire many of these British descriptions of extant rural relations and their presumed reconstructed pasts, we may not accept them as convincing descriptions of either relations or pasts. To be convinced about the internal dimension of rural South Asia, reliance must be placed upon indigenous sources not merely to test the reliability of British accounts and conceptions, but to construct, where possible, a unified conception of Indian rural societies. Not to do so is to remain dependent upon British views which were often uninformed and always interested; we must accordingly seek to understand the idioms and ideology of the Indian rural systems which the British displaced with their power and replaced with their idioms and ideologies.

I mean by 'idiom' a characteristic word, an element particular and 'peculiar' (as the O.E.D. would have it) to a speech community. These are 'key words', the sort that are contained in the indexes of books and counted by content analysts. In the revenue and political parlance of nineteenth and twentieth-century south India, the word 'raiyat' was an idiom; prior to British times an important idiom was *paṅkāḷi* (co-sharer, agnatic kinsman). 'Ideology' is that system of ideas pertaining to politics and society in which idioms are embedded and by which they are encoded, that is, the system from which the idioms acquire the particularity of their meaning. Ideology is argument, or rhetoric, pertaining to what is deemed the appropriate or good in a society or polity; its terms orient actions and give reasoned purpose to them.

## *Internal practice and ideology*

To set the terms of an indigenous agrarian ideology for south India requires delineation of a period the evidence from which can be shown to be relevant and compelling on the matter. That period would seem to be the later - Tuluva and Aravidu - dynasties of the Vijayanagara state, from about 1470 to 1620.[1]

The final 150 years of the Vijayanagara state is the last time during which it might be said that public reasoning about appropriate agrarian relationships in south India was consonant with existing relationships over a very substantial portion of the southern peninsula, or, as it might also be said, that culture and social structure were congruent with respect to landed relation. Before the late fifteenth century, most of Tamil country remained either outside of the ambit of Vijayanagara rule or was treated by the northern (*vadugar*) warriors, consisting of mixed Kannada- and Telugu-speakers, as a dangerous frontier or as a zone of permitted pillage. Only gradually were Tamils and their highly-developed rural institutions brought within the Vijayanagara polity, and then, during the sixteenth century, at the considerable cost of an accelerated decline of these institutions, many of which dated from the Pallava and Chola states of the seventh to thirteenth centuries. The assimilation of Tamils marked the maturity of the Vijayanagara state as well as providing it with the inclusiveness of the 'imperial' entity it represented itself to be.

What then of the nearly two hundred years between this great era of Vijayanagara and the establishment of British dominance around 1800? Can we justify a comparison of ideological formulations - one called 'internal' and the other 'external' - separated by such an interregnum? An affirmative answer is warranted on the ground that while the decline of Vijayanagara during the late sixteenth and seventeenth centuries meant that the congruence between ideology and actual agrarian relations ceased *at the level of empire*, agrarian relations remained intact at local and even at very broad, supralocal levels of south Indian society. Support for this proposition, as well as an explanation of how this occurred is found in the emergence of so-called 'nayaka' kingdoms of the late sixteenth century. These several large 'successor' states confirmed and extended Vijayanagara agrarian arrangements even as they weakened the empire as the powerful enterprise it had been earlier. The Vijayanagara pattern did not languish in these states; rather, as the prevailing model of Hindu polity in the south, that pattern became stronger and more incorporative than ever until the later seventeenth century when an era of violence was unleased in the southern peninsula by Mughals and Marathas which culminated in the wars of the East India Company and the establishment of a new order there as in other places of the sub-continent.

The Vijayanagara pattern was largely ignored or discounted as ancient usage by Sir Thomas Munro and other nineteenth-century officials of the Company; it was nevertheless occasionally used by them in debates over policy. Munro, for instance, made skilful use of purportedly 'Bijanugger' practices of the fourteenth century to provide an historical rationale for his settlement of Kanara ('Canara') in 1800 and especially to support his recommendation to the Madras Board of Revenue for reducing the revenue assessment imposed upon Kanara by Haidar Ali and Tipu Sultan, from whom the tract had been obtained in 1799 by the defeat and death of Tipu. Munro also invoked Vijayanagara praxis to oppose the introduction of the Bengal (zamindari) system in Kanara.[2] These and other appeals to unsubstantiated Vijayanagara practices, excusable in a nineteenth-century publicist like Munro, can hardly be permitted to stand against what has since come to be learned of the Vijayanagara pattern of the fifteenth to seventeenth century.

Several recent works on the Vijayanagara state and society during the fifteenth to seventeenth centuries serve to correct the distorted use of the Vijayanagara past and to contribute to a proper delineation of indigenous ideology. The recency of these works does not commend them so much as their approach, one which seeks to relate political institutions and processes of the time to the social and cultural base of the society, and their treatment of politics and indigenous conceptions of the good as problematic. Accordingly, these works depart from the conventional historiography on Vijayanagara precisely in (with varying degrees of explicitness) challenging older interpretations (or, more accurately, assumptions) about the purported centralized, military polity of Vijayanagara,[3] or a more recent assumption, its 'feudal' polity,[4] and in insisting on viewing agrarian arrangements in the society at various locality, or social base, levels in addition to viewing them in relationship to the 'state' or imperial level. Regardless, however, of the level of analysis, each work further insists on explanations of social processes and cultural relevance; each is concerned with indigenous praxis and theory.

In my *Peasant State and Society in Medieval South India*, which deals with the Chola period primarily, I attempted to indicate the elements of continuity and discontinuity of the Chola state (c.A.D.900-1300) and the Vijayanagara state.[5] Of the works to be noticed here, this essay is most general in focus since the entirety of Vijayanagara history is schematically considered, with an emphasis on Tamil country, and contrasts with the preceding Chola state drawn. With respect to the Vijayanagara political system, the framework of what I called 'the segmentary state' of the Chola period is seen as continuing into the Vijayanagara period with certain significant modifications. These modifications are argued to have had their origin in later Chola times (the twelfth century) when temple-centred urbanization altered older agrarian and trade relations. This, in turn, led to the weakening of certain older rural institutions (for example the locality assembly, *nāḍu*, and the prestigious Brahman assembly, *sabhai*) through which ancient cultivating groups and Brahmans jointly dominated many rural localities. The rise of chiefs and chiefdoms during the late Chola period contributed to, and certainly was advantaged by, this decline of ancient collegial forms; so too some new forms of collegial organization, especially temples, sectarian orders, and supralocal assemblies called *periyanāḍu*. The Vijayanagara state of the fourteenth century was based upon these transformed elements of earlier south Indian polities, but under its rulers, especially those from 1470 on, the structure in which these elements were embedded was further developed and co-ordinated so as to create a substantially altered segmentary state in south India. This state was characterized by greater penetrations of state-level personages into local social systems, on the one hand, and the upward linkage of local chieftains to supralocal levels of the society, on the other hand.

In the Vijayanagara as in the Chola state, thousands of local polities in the southern peninsula of India were bound together *as a state* in their common recognition of a ritual centre, the Vijayanagara kingship. That these kings were often great warriors with large armies was a necessary condition of their ritual primacy; ultimately, theirs was the responsibility of protection of their subjects and of dharma throughout the macro-region of south India. However, force was not the foundation of imperial authority any more than it was the foundation of chiefly authority in the thousands of chiefdoms of which the Vijayanagara state consisted. Royal sovereignty and chiefly rule derived from moral, or dharmic claims; it could scarcely have been otherwise considering the complexity of the polities involved.

Telugu emperors of the second and third Vijayanagara dynasties ruled over a diminishing number of Telugus as Muslim sultanates of the Deccan expanded; there was also a major Kannada-speaking population in Karnataka and a very large Tamil population in the southern parts of the empire. The rule of these Telugu kings extended over different kinds of rural societies as well: over ancient, densely-settled, riverine localities of advanced rice agriculture under prestigious cultivating and Brahman groups in sharply-defined social hierarchies; over more dispersed chiefdoms of mixed wet and dry cultivation where caste hierarchies were more shallow and where religious orthopraxes were diluted by accommodation of lineage and other tutelary cults; and over isolated, essentially, tribal areas of hazardous, dry agriculture and herding in which hierarchical, or vertical, social distinctions, gave way almost completely to horizontal, or spatial, ones of small, scattered polities under petty chiefs. All of this cultural, linguistic, and ecological complexity attained the unity of a state not by overwhelming force - something the Vijayanagara kings never possessed - but only as the ritual hegemony of these kings was given actuality through transactions with a great variety of the chiefs of the macro-region.

K.N. Nilakanta Sastri, in a late formulation on Vijayanagara polity, called the state 'a military confederation of many chieftains co-operating under the leadership of the biggest among them'[6] and 'the nearest approach to a war-state ever made by a Hindu kingdom'.[7] While the latter characterization is accepted by most who have written on Vijayanagara, the former notion has been largely ignored except, possibly, by those whose interpretations are being considered in the present paper. A major conundrum posed by Nilakanta Sastri's confederation idea involves the *amaranāyaṅkāra* system, presumed by him and others to be a central institution of Vijayanagara polity. The term is usually taken to mean the form of land tenure (*amaram*) which supported a military (*nāyaka*) office (*kara*). Whether construed as a centrally-controlled prebend or a form of 'feudal' tenure, as it is sometimes viewed, the amaranayankara system is conventionally perceived as an order of state officials to which is assimilated all chiefly authority and the whole is seen as derived from an imperial grant or delegation. This form of central delegation can be documented in a few cases,[8] but the nayaka title and tenurial form is so ubiquitous as to constitute a generalized title of chiefly authority for the vast majority of local rulers who emerged from the numerous pyramidal polities of which the Vijayanagara state was composed. The standing of chiefs in the Vijayanagara era can be seen to have been progressively transformed from independent bases in thousands of localized agrarian settings to a new ideological base reciprocally linked by ritual claims upon and transactions with the Vijayanagara emperors. Chieftains, or nayakas, of the time are clearly a more powerful and separated stratum of locality leadership; but these chiefs were not, in the main, created by the state. This is best demonstrated in the relationship of chiefs everywhere in the Vijayanagara realm with landed groups and with temples and sects within and beyond the mini-realms of their chiefdoms.

During this period, there was a vast increase in irrigation, especially tank irrigation, and in temples. The two developments are connected. According to the extant historiography of Vijayanagara, there were three major tenurial categories: lands whose income was, in part, under the control of chiefs (*amaram*); lands granted to various eleemosynary holders such as temples (*deva-dāna*) and Brahmans (*saravmāniyam*) for their support; and a small proportion of land some of whose income was deployed to support Vijayanagara fortifications and garrisons. This tripartite division is at once reductionist and arbitrary. All landholding, in effect, involved multiple, often minute entitlements to some part of agrarian production, not to land itself. In the case of eleemosynary tenures, most entitlements originated as gifts (*dāna*), and temples large and small derived a major portion of their support from shares of income from cultivated fields and sometimes whole villages gifted by or with the assent of local chiefs. Temples thus entered into the centre of productive relations by their dispersed entitlements in peasant villages, and village groups and their chiefs simultaneously entered the centre of temple organization as its benefactors.

In many temples, there were established procedures for receiving money gifts to support specified ritual performances by donors, and these funds were deployed in the excavation of tanks and channels. While the temple would receive a part of the new production resulting from these improvements, a major portion was retained by dominant cultivating groups within whose villages the work was undertaken and in which temples already held certain entitlements by previous gifts. To these peasants and their chiefs was provided a sacred security in the best lands of their localities as well as a share of the 'sacred leavings' (*prasādam*) of the gods to whom food offerings were made. Sacred leavings were additionally a currency of sorts for chiefly patronage and for establishing new and wider entitlements. In this way, tank construction on lands on which temples held certain rights through the medium of temple endowments created new resources and new actors in the temple-centred local worlds of south India. Inscriptions from Tirupati and other temples in the dry region of Tamilnadu deal explicitly with such activities in which temples were major transactional arenas and in which agricultural development and resource pooling and redistribution served to bind the mini-realms of chiefs together by ritual means.[9]

This set of connections between temples and irrigation is currently being investigated by Carol A. Breckenridge. A recent preliminary report on her research[10] explores the storage functions of temples in the rural economy of the Vijayanagara period and the nodal place of temple-directed irrigational activities in connecting the peripheral, sparsely-populated dry-farming parts of local societies of south India with their locality centres, often based upon tanks and other forms of irrigated agriculture. Temples stored food and seed, skilled workmen such as tank diggers, and technical knowledge vital for the transformation of dry agricultural regimes to more reliable forms of mixed wet-dry agriculture. Through the varied ritual transactions of temples, resources such as skills and development capital combined with labour to establish ever-wider networks of redistribution and exchange. In the mobilization of resources and labour, temples of a locality were central points in an expanding process of pooling and distribution which, over the course of two centuries, changed the shape of agrarian relations in much of south India. Thus, to her earlier work on the temples in south India as a vital link in vertical relations through honours distributions, Dr Breckenridge has now outlined the elments of horizontal linkage in which temples, again, are shown to have had a critical place.

Carol Breckenridge, as noted, and Arjun Appadurai have made important contributions to the analysis of the ritually-integrative system of the Vijayanagara order, the former in her seminal research on temple organization and its honour-mediated processes and the latter in his analysis of the nexus of relations formed among chiefs and kings, Vaishnava sectarian leaders, and temples in various parts of the Vijayanagara macro-region. In a joint essay of theirs,[11] the distribution of temple honours (*mariyāṭai*) in the context of worship is shown to have been constitutive of the statuses of all involved. Here, shares of consecrated leavings of the gods constituted the authority for the recipient to receive shares (*paṅku*) of resources outside the temple; the ritual context of the temple is not, according to this formulation, a reflection of status, power, and wealth outside, but was the locus for constituting precisely these determinants of relative rank and the entitlements pertaining to them.

In a separate essay on Vijayanagara polity,[12] Appadurai has provided a lucid and persuasive analysis of how temples served as an arena where claims to authority by increasingly powerful chieftains of the age were realized through exchanges with religious leaders. A single system of authoritative relations is seen to combine what in some polities are separated as political and religious hierarchies. Evidence from south Indian Sri Vaishnava temples from the fourteenth to the eighteenth centuries reveal a pattern of ritual and economic transactions involving Telugu warriors and other political leaders, including kings, with powerful Vaishnava sectarian leaders which resulted in the penetration by such political leaders into the most significant of local institutions, temples. Such transactions increased the prestige of sectarian leaders and stimulated considerable competition between two major Vaishnava sect groups, Tengalais and Vadagalais. The transactional process described by Appadurai consists of honours and material resources. Honours were conferred, by temple managers (*sthānattār*) upon kings and chiefs; honours, insignia, regalia (*biruda*) were conferred by kings and chiefs upon sectarian leaders; honours were reciprocally granted by such leaders to kings and chiefs. Material resources (land and money) were granted to temples and to sectarian leaders by political leaders; material resources of sect leaders were conferred upon temples. Noting the asymmetry of transactions between political and sectarian leaders (they exchanged honours, but only material resources went from the former to the latter), Appadurai points to the gain for political leaders of mass constituencies loyal to sect leaders, and he concludes that sectarian leaders played a significant role in the expansion and operation of Vijayanagara political institutions.

The doctoral research of David Ludden on Tinnevelly[13] incorporates many of the elements discussed above, but also opens some novel aspects of the practices comprising the Vijayanagara pattern. In a chapter of his thesis devoted to changes in the agrarian order of Tinnevelly during the Vijayanagara period, Ludden stresses, in addition to ritual transactions, ecological variation and migration in the making of a new agrarian order of the time. To the base of an ancient population of Vellala peasants and Brahmans in the Tambraparni river basin, a set of new peoples attained shares in the agrarian order of the region by the middle of the sixteenth century, thus changing the older Chola-Pandyan order in basic ways. Newcomers to the Tambraparni basin and its hinterland included Telugu warriors and their dependents, Saurashtrian weavers, and Kallar and Maravar peoples long resident in the extensive dry regions south of the river basin. Under a new kingship - that of the Madurai Nayakas from about 1536 onward - an order was created which differed from the ancient Pandyan kingdom which had preceded it in at least one major way: a more clearly defined 'state level' of politics. However, new authority relations, like those of the old, centred on local institutions, especially on temples at the apex of which was the Sundaresvara-Minakshi temple at Madurai. Subordinately connected with this premier temple of the region were new temples at Tinnevelly town (Nellaiyappa temple) in the central portion of the Tambraparni valley and at Tenkasi (the Visvanathisvara temple). Each of these shrines was the locus of its own, local segmental authority; each, however, was also linked to the temple of the Madurai Nayakas. To these three centres of politics and ritual were subsidiarily connected a variety of lesser chieftains many of whom were symbolically joined to the ritual centre at Madurai as dependent soldiery (*pālayak-kārar* or, Anglicized, poligars), each the guardian of a bastion of the Madurai fort of the nayaka-king. Ludden traces a set of 'transactional bonds' connecting these diverse levels in which 'tribute and honor flowed up the segmental pyramid of state relations ... and down the pyramid flowed entitlements to authoritative roles in the system and patronage.'[14] The primacy of temples in all of this sprang from the way that these institutions connected powerful state agents with local, autonomous spheres of society and economy. Under a series of shocks upon the Madurai system beginning with the expansion of the independent Wodiyar state of Mysore from the north, the Marathas from Tanjavur, and the Mughal agent at Arcot who penetrated Madurai territory in the late seventeenth century, the Nayaka's system weakened, and one effect of this was the rise to more substantial chieftaincies of formerly minor military figures (*kāvalkār*). The latter too adopted temples as their redistributive centres leading thus to another increase in these pivotal institutions during the eighteenth century.

The work in progress of Nicholas Dirks completes this inventory of recent and novel interpretations of pre-British, south Indian agrarian practices and theory. In several earlier papers and in his doctoral thesis,[15] Dirks has explored the manner in which ritual transactions, gifting, along with service and kinship relations, established and maintained agrarian relationships, including political ones, in great kingdoms such as the Pallavas and in 'little kingdoms' such as the Pudukkottai in the eighteenth and nineteenth centuries.

Dirks' work is based upon A.M. Hocart's theories of the ritual constitution of political relations. According to the latter's formulations, states such as those of India are incorporative entities, created and maintained by essentially ritual means under kings who are ritualists. Dirks replaces Hocart's anachronistic vedic, sacrificial ritual idiom with prestation, which he convincingly demonstrates to have become the dominant royal incorporative ritual mode in south India in the time of the Pallava kingdom of the eighth century.

In his analysis of the Pudukkottai state, Dirks follows British usage in using the Arabic term *in'am* to gloss a variety of older terms for gifts, and he adduces varied evidence to show how prestations of land as well as insignia and regalia (*pirutu* from the Sanskrit *biruda*) from the Tondaiman Raja of Pudukkottai to persons at various levels of the kingdom, from its military grandees to its village servants, linked all in the realm by ties of 'entitlement, filiation, and power'. Inam titles are seen to have become substantialized as caste names, and entitlements to shares of agrarian production (*paṅku*) and precedent honours (*mariyāṭai*) are seen to define all groups in the realm.

Two other incorporative processes augment that of gift. These are blood ties to the royal family of many powerful chiefly families (*cērvaikkārar*) and the honours exchanges incident upon the entitlement to some service function, for example, military or temple service. This polity of multiple offices held by persons at all levels of the kingdom by virtue of prestation rituals of inams rendered office holders (or inamdars) appropriate and converted the political system of this 'little kingdom' of Pudkkottai into a complex of office (cervaikkarar), collegiate (mirasidars) and kinship (jagirdar) elements. Dirks points to similar arrangements in the neighbouring great kingdom of Madurai where the *kumāravarkkam* ('the family of princes') established by its nayaka kings incorporated the major chiefs of the Madurai realm as an interdining, intermarrying collectivity with each chief holding the additional honour of protecting a bastion of the Madurai fort of the nayaka king.

Temples in Pudukkottai, as elsewhere, linked the Raja to all parts of his realm through his distribution of honours for service or through gifts. Royal endowment to temples (Tondaiman *kaṭṭalai*) and to Brahmans was assimilated to the larger inam system of resources and office entitlement and precedent honours thus contributing to the unified ritual character of the kingdom. Beyond that, the Tondaiman Rajas were donors to great temples throughout the macro-region of south India (for example Tirupati, Ramesvaram, Palni, Madurai) thereby making themselves and their kingdom a part of the larger south Indian world.

The views of pre-modern south Indian society summarized above are neither complete nor are they co-ordinate. These are several conceptions of a society, seen by scholars at various levels and times and understood by them in somewhat different ways. Yet, together, these studies all commence with the assumption that many fundamental aspects of the structure of pre-British society remain problematic, that received historical interpretations require modification, and these were polities about which both praxis and theory must be clarified.

In the matter of theory, of course, there is *our* theory and *theirs*, the understandings of and aspirations for the appropriate society and relationships of an age very different from our own. As to the evidence of how south Indian society in the fifteenth to seventeenth centuries actually worked, there is little difference between the given conventional scholarship and the work discussed above. Thanks to the work of Carol Breckenridge and others, we may henceforward be less inclined to view temples of that time in the way temples are seen today: specialized, governmentally-regulated institutions under professional managers, whose religious function in the past was but one of varied utilitarian tasks among such as others as local credit, land management, education, and markets. We would, on the whole, now see temples as the setting of elaborate ritual activities involving not only the resident deities, but the communities - all of the constituencies of a village, locality, or even great empire - whose joint, often conflictful and always consequential, transactions made, or constituted the communities themselves. The views discussed here would also see kings and chiefs not as immanent, proto-bureaucratic officers, or as transcendent, divine beings, but as political persons whose authority obliged them more to negotiated, ritual, redistributional, and mediational roles than any others.

Theory rather than decisive new evidence give the above works their revisionistic thrust. This is the theory of the modern analyst, of course, not of south Indians of the Vijayanagara era, certainly not in an explicit sense. Indigenous theories of community, realm and kingship in the mature Vijayanagara age have no coherent existence, though all of the fundamental elements of the society of the time discussed above, as in the works of scholarly predecessors, are in generally conformity with prescriptive *dharmasastra* injunctions and *niti* texts of India's medieval age. But, if we lack coherent indigenous theories, we do not lack what must be regarded as equally important, that is, a coherent ideological system which is found in the stylistically elegant preambles of inscriptions, in some poetic forms, in certain forms of state ritual as described in reports of contemporary visitors; it is finally to be found vestigially in reports of the early British period. All of these kinds of contemporary and near-contemporary evidence speak to us of impressive chiefly polities and of elaborate and extensive transactional relationships in which chiefs were central actors and temples were central linking institutions.

The English word 'chief' denotes leadership of a spatially limited and rather primitive sort; its usage most often connotes Amerindian and African political authority. Chief is meant here in the sense that Nilakanta Sastri perhaps meant it in his phrase 'confederation of chieftains' when speaking of the Vijayanagara political system. Though he never explained his meaning, I take his 'chieftain' to be one of a very large number of powerful, local men whose authority might have been derived from such sources as their paramount position in a lineage of locally-dominant cultivators or from an office they might have been granted by a superior authority, a king. The many south Indian terms for 'chief' often imply a royal quality as in the Tamil *arasar* or *arayar*, from the Sanskrit *rājā*, or these terms may simply imply firstness or head, *mudali* or *talaiyār*. What are designated as chiefs here comprehend a broad political domain: at the lowest level, village headmen, and at the highest, a self-styled, but not annointed, *rājā*. All within this domain - whether low or high - shared an appropriate capacity to command and to possess: they have *kṣatra* in their own right, and the execution of this was *kṣatriya*. It is this autonomous authority which Nilakanta Sastri presumably had in mind when using the word 'confederation' with its inherent idea of an association of independent political entities.

The enhanced power and authority of chiefs in the mature Vijayanagara system of the fifteenth to seventeenth centuries distinguishes it from the earlier Chola system. Both political systems were, as I call them, segmentary, in the sense of being composed of numerous, localized pyramidal systems linked ritually to a great dharmic kingship. But, an essential difference in the two polity forms was that the Chola system was at base collegial. Autochthonous local and supralocal assemblies and collective bodies dominated public life; the spokesmen, or chiefs, of such collegial bodies are presented inscriptionally as having little autonomous authority. In the Vijayanagara system, by contrast, chieftainship was more nearly an autonomous level of authority - a 'state level' - with substantial separation from and control over the collegiate forms of the time. Means were developed, moreover, to form relationships with others like themselves and with superordinate kings through the transactional nexus of temples and sects of the age.

The research of Breckenridge, Appadurai, and Ludden referred to above has added much to our knowledge of the transactional nexus of the Vijayanagara age as revealed by temple inscriptions. Dharmic ideology is explicit in the language of inscriptions and implicit in the transactions they describe and sanctify. Groupings of peoples (castes, clans, lineages, local cultic groups and members of bhakti cultic orders) and institutions (villages, temples, mathas) which we might perceive as autonomous were then parts of unified structures defined, indeed constituted, by their interactions with deities, their Brahman and non-Brahman custodians, and with chiefly and royal benefactors as well as great and small sectarian leaders. Their ritually contexted interactions, at whatever level, binding together political, social, and religious hierarchies are precisely the stuff which the conventional historian implies, but does not specify, in speaking of the dharmic character of Vijayanagara.

This transactional system is fittingly further designated as *kṣatriya*, not as that term is usually applied to particular persons and castes, but as the system of transactions among those with *kṣatra*, rightful possession and dominion over material resources (land and money) and honours (the leavings of gods - *prasādam* - and the insignias of worth and standing). Vijayanagara temple inscriptions are expressions of that systemic sense, relating to those endowed with appropriate possession of and control over material and honour resources whose interactions complete what none in themselves could, a morally compelling whole, which is what a realm was.

Another major expression of what is being called the indigenous ideological system of pre-British south India is obtained from literary works of the time, such as *vamsāvaḷi* and *śatakam*.[16] Dirks has demonstrated how the sensitive use of the *vamsāvaḷi* genealogical and panegyric texts can reveal many of the connections of chiefs to others like themselves, to subordinate groups, and to superordinate figures such as the Rajas of Pudukkottai and the Nayaka Kings of Madurai. Such texts, along with inscriptions and judicial records of the British period, delineate the 'co-ordinates of political relations' within such polities as Pudukkottai. These co-ordinates are:

land, kinship, honours, and service. Inams, royal gifts, as seen by Dirks, combine and encompass these elements:

> Each of these co-ordinates was at once a relational trope and a cultural category of entitlement, filiation, and power. As relational tropes they provided the metaphorical language of expression and specification of political relations, and as cultural categories they provided the centrality of kings to social relations within the little kingdom.[17]

In this manner, productive land of the realm, the possession (*kṣatra*) of the Tondaiman Rajas of Pudukkottai was conferred by gift (inam) upon others including warriors and religious personages, and by this ritual act (dana), shares of the Rajas' *kṣatra* were held by many on the basis of either kinship ties to the royal family or service. Dirks estimates that about two-thirds of the land of the kingdom was distributed in this way. Honours through temple transactions established new entitlements (*kāni*) to shares (*paṅku*), reaching downward to the lowest levels of society and uniting all co-sharers in a single, moral system.

The salient characteristic of this moral system was its transactions, and this processual feature was context bound and context sensitive,[18] as well as risky and contingent. Key idioms in the system emphasize these transactional and contingent qualities. The term *kāṇi*, as in the word *kaniyāṭci*, means land and also the right to its enjoyment; its root *kāṇ*, 'to see or mark', signifies that which is seen, marked, or recognized. Kaṇi expresses entitlement by a person or group to some valuable good; this entitlement is public, that is, 'seen or marked' in such contexts as royal durbars and temples. The temple gift was called *kaṭṭalai* (from the Tamil root *kaṭṭu*, to tie or to construct); it signified not only an endowment, but a standard of measure, regularity, and order, a code of conduct for a collectivity such as a caste. Prestation to a god, as to a king, required appropriate standing of the giver. The gift was a claim to such standing by a person or group, and its acceptance by the god through those who worship the god (priests and laity alike) or its acceptance by a king or his agent was not merely a recognition of the claim of the donor to appropriate standing so much as it was constitutive of that appropriateness and to all attendant entitlements. Those sharing in this distinction and its entitlements were called *paṅkāḷi*, co-sharers (Tamil: *paṅku*, share), partners, and also agnatic kinsmen. Kani and panku were and remain terms of corporateness within a moral community and a moral ordering of the material world (land), of social relations (caste), and of ritual relations involving great gods and kings as well as local chiefs and village gods. Relative and absolute place for any of the actors in this moral system - social groups, chiefs, kings, gods, priests - was contingent and hazardous: transactions of a public and ritual nature minutely and continuously defined it.

To the indigenous ideology of inscriptions and *vamsāvaḷi* texts should be added another important ideological medium, a distinctive form of state ritual. Ritual texts and contexts are not the same things even in temples where *āgamas*, technical, ritual texts, govern sacred practices; in the case of royal ritual of the medieval period, in contrast to the ancient period, there are few relevant texts, and one depends upon contemporary description. Such at least is the case of the annual *mahānavamī* (the Great Nine day) festival, a superb example of state ritual, or state theatre, staged in the capital city of Vijayanagara ('City of Victory').

Historians of Vijayanagara have rightly emphasized the central moral quality of its polity; dharmic ideology is seen to have been manifested, primarily, in Vijayanagara's explicit defence of Hindu institutions against the onslaught of Deccani Muslim states, and, secondarily, in the vigorous participation of Vijayanagara rulers and their agents in the support of temples of the realm. This realm (*rājyam*) is easily perceived as a moral community whose essence was annually revitalized in the Mahanavami festival at the capital. According to sixteenth-century descriptions of the festival by Portuguese travellers,[19] the king's arms, horses, and warriors were reconsecrated and ritually restored to their full potency; gifts were exchanged by the monarch with the great men of his empire; animals were sacrificed; the king and his tutelary goddess were worshipped by the assembled great along with their own tutelary deities, priests and dancers. The setting and the actions of this festival are a remarkable realization of A.M. Hocart's conception of a ritually-constituted polity in which the king, as 'ritual principal', incorporates into his own essence the moral qualities of all in his realm. The realm itself is symbolically recreated in the special festival arena of the capital city by placement of the king in the centre of all activities on a raised stone structure (on whose basement ruins one still finds sculpted panels of the events of the festival), surrounded by nine pavilions representing the great subordinates of the kingdom; this representation of the realm is further symbolized in the visual depiction of the kingdom as a body with its nine orifices or gates.[20]

Unlike most temple festivals of the time, the Mahanavami is based upon no specific agamic or technical text; elements of the festival as described appear to be drawn from diverse sources; ancient royal sacrifices such as the *aśvamedha*, or horse sacrifice; from equinoctial nine-day festivals celebrating the legendary perfect prince and avatar, Rama, and the goddess Devi (or Durga); and from the important equinoctial domestic ritual of the 'nine nights', *nava-rātri*. As a royal festival of regeneration, the Mahanavami at Vijayanagara, with its tenth day appendage, *daṣamī*, was perhaps the prototypic royal festival celebrated (under the name of Dasara or Nava-ratri) by the successor nayaka kingdoms of south India, and most lavishly in recent times by the princely house of Mysore. According to modern descriptions of this important state ritual, the basic elements reported from Vijayanagara in the sixteenth century were preserved. Each of the component territorial units of the kingdom is morally defined in relation to the sovereign and his deity; each of these constituent units of the realm as a whole was something of a replica of that realm, complete with its sovereign chiefly centre, its own gods and its own social groups, and the emblems of all are renewed along with their morally-entailed potency in the presence of the anointed king, his followers, and arms. The royal court at Vijayanagara, or at Madurai or Mysore, thus became a temple, and at the same time a world, during the course of the festival. An elaborate set of ritual transactions centred upon the king and his deity served to define all participants as parts of a single sacred universe in the same sense that worship of a village god defined and constituted a lesser world (but no less a world) in its way.

Documents of the early period of British territorial administration in Madras, the late eighteenth century, confirm many of the elements referred to above even as many East India Company officials sought to alter, if not to destroy, the unified structure of meaning in which these elements were embedded. The establishment of British territorial control in south India during the late eighteenth and early nineteenth centuries was coincident with and made possible by the defeat and extirpation of most of the centres of authority of the Vijayanagara age - its chiefdoms and kingdoms. Preserved in the copious appendices of the Fifth Report of 1812[21] are records of this onslaught upon chiefs and 'poligars' throughout the Madras Presidency. Here too are found important statements from about 1800 on the communal character of agrarian relations in the coastal tracts around Madras city which first came under Company administration as well as the first orders to Madras to adopt the Bengal settlement system in its territories. At this time, the raiyatwari conception of Alexander Read and Thomas Munro was little more than a gleam of the eye; few in 1800 would have predicted so robust an offspring as was to emerge as raiyatwari in the course of the decade.

Reports from Lionel Place from the coastal tract called the Jaghire, in the 1790s, describe a communal or corporate land system called *mirāsi* tenure. Place was joined by another able, well-connected Company official, Francis W. Ellis, and together they formulated a set of principles of landholding that they believed had long operated in this part of India and continued in their view to operate still. Their interpretations were backed by rather impressive historical evidence - inscriptions and other authoritative evidence of ancient communal relations - drawn from the most prosperous, irrigated parts of the Madras Presidency upon which the Company depended for its largest revenues. From such evidence and from extant practice reported by Company officials, principles were elucidated based upon two key terms: *kāṇi* and *paṅku*. Possessors of entitlements and shares were construed as holders of immemorial and fixed rights to hereditary land ownership; they were 'proprietors' of lands and villages; and, as fitting, they were always members of high castes, usually Brahmans or Vellalas.

The constructions of Place and Ellis were obviously based upon agrarian relations with which this paper has so far dealt, since they were based, to a limited degree, upon evidence of the Vijayanagara period. However, arrangements of the Vijayanagara period which were contingent and flexible outcomes of the numerous complex interactions discussed above were converted by them into things fixed and absolute; the kani and panku of Place and Ellis were different from those of the earlier period.

## *British Ideology*

In shifting attention to the agrarian idioms and ideology of the early British period in south India, we discover new terms and new discursive contexts. A major formulator of this new discourse was Sir Thomas Munro. His celebrity and dominance as a spokesman and designer of Madras administration should not deafen us to the other powerful voices in Madras in his time - those of Lionel Place, F.W. Ellis, and John Hodgson. However, they and their views were accorded neither the attention nor the authority they deserved in the first quarter of the nineteenth century when Munro's views largely prevailed.

When he died in 1827 after having served in the Madras Presidency for 40 years, Munro was regarded as the founder of a system of Indian administration, which continues still to bear his name, and as among the most able spokesmen on British Indian policy. His writings on public affairs in India began in 1790, earlier than is usually noted, when a letter of his from India was sent by his father in Scotland to the *London Chronicle* (9-11 September) and published on its front page.[22] This letter criticized East India Company policy on relations with Tipu Sultan and the Marathas, and its publication prompted Munro to caution his vicariously ambitious father against other such indiscretions. It was during his tenure as principal collector of the Ceded Districts, from 1800 to 1807, that Munro's stature as publicist became widely noticed, notwithstanding the unprepossessing format of official reports; that recognition culminated in the Fifth Report of the select committee of the House of Commons on Indian affairs of 1812, in which Munro's name, papers, and evidence were given prominence, and his administrative proposals dominated the sections dealing with Madras.[23] Between the Fifth Report and his gubernatorial career (1820-27), Munro's writings gained expanding influence as may be judged from their notice in another major official publication of 1826, on Indian revenue and judicial questions.[24] Finally, as governor of Madras, Munro prepared some 250 policy documents for his council on a variety of subjects,[25] the most important of these being a long valedictory minute on what he believed was to be the eve of his departure from the Madras governorship, 31 December 1824. This last document states his most comprehensive views on British imperialism in India.

Rhetorical analysis of this corpus of official writings presents a daunting and even perverse task not only because Munro's personal correspondence was also copious, but more because here, as in his official writings, his style is blunt, pithy, and plain. As a publicist, or rhetorician, Munro succeeds not by colourful image nor by marshalling authority - both of which expository techniques he disparaged - but rather by terse arguments cast in a technical or expert mode, perfect confidence in his experience, and in a later stage of his career at least, a unified conception of British rule in India. According to canons of classical rhetoric, his form was Atticist,[26] but more simply and relevantly, his style is Scottish in the time of Scotland's intellectual greatness: plain talk, philosophical perceptualism, and attention to history and social forms in human affairs. Munro's confidence must have struck contemporaries as arrogance, but, if so, it was arrogance without conceits - figures of speech rarely embellish his prose. Absent from it, characteristically, were expressions such as those of his protégé William Thackeray; the latter, commenting on a Madras Board of Revenue proposal to treat property in land as divisible among government, renter, and cultivator, observed that this was 'treating mother earth like a Nair lady, and giving her a half-a-dozen husbands to neglect her, while one good man would cherish her with affection.'[27]

Munro's rhetorical success consisted primarily in his masking of artful forms by the artless discourse of the expert. This may be exemplified in his deployment of several technical terms. Because the terms are technical in Munro's usage, they are improbable candidates as metaphorical or rhetorical vehicles. However, the way the terms are used in what is ostensibly 'expert' discourse, reveals that they were actually pillars of an elaborate rhetorical and ultimately ideological structure, informed by judgement and persuasive purpose. The terms are: 'rayet', 'inam', and 'waste'.

These technical terms define the core of agrarian arrangements worked out by Munro in the Ceded Districts between 1800 and 1807 and, subsequently as the 'Munro System' expanded, elsewhere in Madras and Bombay.

'Rayet' (ryot or *raiyat*) designated any person who engaged to cultivate and pay revenue on government land. As Munro explained to the President of the Board of Control in London in 1823, the designation 'rayet' applied to any individual 'whether the public assessment on his land be ten rupees or ten thousand'.[28] 'Inam' was a tenurial category designating land under privileged revenue demand usually satisfied by payment of a quit-rent equivalent to as little as one-tenth of the full revenue demand. In the Ceded Districts during Munro's peiod of supervision, such privileged landholding comprised of 46 per cent of all cultivated lands, and, even in the late nineteenth century, about the same proportion of cultivated lands of Madras and Bombay paid less than full revenue under various inam tenures.[29] Waste was uncultivated, cultivable land; it could refer to lands which had been cultivated within the previous 20 years, but could as well refer to lands not cultivated for even longer periods.

We may examine these terms within the technical operation of Madras land administration, within a rhetorical framework, and finally, briefly, as elements in a unified ideological system.

The raiyatwari revenue system of Munro's design was erected on three terms. The system took its name from the payment of revenue (*vāramvari*) on government land by raiyats directly to government collectors. Inams were construed as payments to various village 'officials' whose functions were essential for the collection of the revenue (village headmen and accountants and their assistants, or 'peons') or whose services were essential to the corporate life of the village, from priests to watchmen. Technically, waste was taken as a measure of the poverty and disorder of the Ceded Districts under its previous, long-time, Muslim rulers. Restoration of order, confidence in government, and a lowered assessment would, according to Munro, lead to extended cultivation of then uncultivated land. Neglected in this notion of waste was the technical fact that much of what was denominated as waste was actually short and long fallows, critical in view of the dry-cultivation regimes and sparse populations of this and most other parts of dry-region Madras.[30] Indeed 'neglected' is too forgiving a term here. The form of agriculture in the Ceded Districts was in many ways like that of the Scotland that Munro, from Glasgow, knew to require short (grass) fallows and longer fallows of seven years.[31] Not only was fallowing in this drought-prone region of India not accommodated in the revenue administration, but the raiyatwar cultivator was compelled to take up waste land as a condition of holding inams and other improved lands, and all cultivators of a village or a taluka were made jointly responsible for revenue shortfalls.

At the level of rhetoric, these terms are shaped by Munro on Burkean lines of historical precedent and morally compelling tradition. Raiyatwar, it was claimed, was *the* indigenous revenue system of India because it was based upon indigenous, historical agrarian relations. The primary unit of society, culture and the economy was the village, and, as Munro wrote in 1806, 'every village, with its twelve ayangadees (village officials), as they are called, is a kind of little republic, with the potail [headman] at the head of it; and India is a mass of such republics'.[32] Thus was launched that classic metaphor which seized a series of great minds from Karl Marx to M.K. Gandhi, and thus, too, was posed a major contradiction in raiyatwar proposals. For, if the village was the basic unit of agrarian organization, Munro's proposal for revenue paid by individual cultivators on specific fields appears misconceived. The paradox is rhetorically dissolved in the following complex way. The village was an autonomous political, economic, and moral universe. At the best of times in the Indian past, it was recognized and supported by kings who made only moderate demands for some part of its production and who did not disturb the age-old allocations of another part of village resources, that is inams, to remunerate village officers and servants. This Indian kings and chiefs could have done as the ultimate 'owners' of the soil. Munro wrote in 1805: 'that there was no landlord but the Sovereign is evident from the form and tenor of all grants of land'.[33] Corporate village membership is transformed by Munro to individual membership by the metaphoric equivalence of the ruler and landlord. This is not original with Munro, but his usage promoted its currency in India; it also altered the idea of 'raiyat', who is changed from being a part of a corporate village body into an equivalent of 'tenant', thereby generating the transcultural metaphor or analogy - Indian sovereign or East India Company to landlord, raiyat to individualized tenant. In this way, both the corporate village and the individual peasant cultivator were preserved as bulwarks against the imposition of the Bengal zamindari settlement while at the same time maintaining the purportedly-direct historical relationship between cultivator 'tenant' and government 'landlord'.

Inams and waste were more difficult to incorporate rhetorically. To Munro's superiors in Madras and in London who queried the great extent of privileged (inam) landholding in the Ceded Districts and the sacrifice of revenue that seemed to entail, Munro argued that ancient custom protected these privileges even if they were not originally granted by great sovereign princes, but by petty village headmen. Resumption of unauthorized inam grants by the Company would be perceived as a violation of custom and resisted. But in addition, inam-holdings by such respectable village men as headmen, accountants, and Brahmans comprised a core of better village lands which were virtually private properties. Here was a foundation for the complete transformation from backward forms of communal landholding to progressive private ones, and 'the raising up of a body of rich and respectable landowners [who] will introduce that just gradation of society essential to the existence and prosperity of every well ordered society'.[34] Waste, a perceived symptom of poverty and overassessment (as well as ignored as a critical fallowing requirement of the fragile agriculture of the Ceded Districts) was rhetoricized by Munro as one of the most significant advantages of raiyatwari over either zamindari or communal tenurial systems. Government possession of waste was a vast potential revenue resource which would gradually be realized, as increased prosperity, population, and private proprietorship in land - all anticipated benefits of British rule - led to extensions of cultivation. Waste was, then, the Company's dividend of progress, a prospective revenue which was, erroneously, alienated under other administrative schemes; waste, it was also argued, was a protected future resource for enterprising Indian farmers seeking to extend their production and their individual wealth.

In considering the transformation of the three terms from the ostensibly technical and expert style to that of rhetoric, it is important to notice that all are non-Indic words whose Indian-language equivalents were rarely used. For the Arabic *ra'īyat*, the Sanskrit *praja*, the Tamil *kuḍi* , or the Kanada *kuḍu* denote cultivator and subject (or citizen), but also connote caste and territorial identities which for Munro bore unacceptable communal meanings.[35] For 'waste' there was the Urdu-derived *taricu* (from the Urdu, *tar*), and the more widely-used, corresponding Tamil word *karambai*.[36] In both, fallow (*ceykār karambu*)[37] is explicitly distinguished from 'immemorial waste' (or *anadi* [*anatti*: worthless][38] *karambu*).[39] Finally, for the Arabic *in'am*, meaning gift from superior to inferior, but reduced in official usage to an hereditary tax-free or tax-reduced land-stipend for some service, there was the ancient Sanskrit word, *mānya*, or its Tamil equivalent, *māṇiyam* ,[40] the root of which (*mān*) means honour or respect,[41] the moral component of which fails to be conveyed by 'inam' as that term was used at the time.

Choosing non-Dravidian words could have been justified by Munro on the grounds that two of them were in the administrative lexicon of the Ceded Districts from previous Muslim rule. However, Munro was never called upon to explain or to defend these terms as were his Madras colleagues on the coast when challenged in their use of the Arabic term *mirāsi* in place of the Tamil, *kaniyāṭci*.[42] Nor was Munro ever pressed to elaborate the countervailing indigenous conception of landholding as a moral entitlement based upon a corporate structure of shareholders, called, among Tamils, *paṅkāḷi*, a term whose semantic reach includes agnatic kinsmen; this unaccountable lapse is the more surprising since Munro had reported the *visabaḍi* form of co-parcenary village in many parts of Cuddapah and elsewhere in the Ceded Districts.[43] Since British rule was thought to be justified by the presumed illegitimacy and excesses of previous Muslim regimes and their Muslim carpet-bagger administrators, it might have been argued by Munro that these terms and the centralized military-fiscal systems to which they pertained were as inappropriate to the land system of the Ceded Districts as some of the excoriated English models being proposed by his British contemporaries. It might also be pointed out that Munro himself was more at ease with Persian than with the Dravidian languages of the people he ruled. However, a more plausible explanation for use of these terms is that they lent themselves best to Munro's rhetorical purposes, for the audience he sought to engage and to persuade was not an Indian one, but an English one in Madras and in London. Both of these audiences conceived that the legitimacy of Company rule stemmed from the conquest of India's Muslim rulers and the appropriation of their sovereignty. Moreover, these terms were well suited to Munro's evolving ideological argument on the nature of British rule in India, an argument which incorporated the rhetorical elements discussed above, only now raised to a high moral level.

Munro's mature ideological position rested on the necessity for a substantial 'native agency', that is, a central place for Indians and Indian institutions in land and judicial administration, and his conception of an enduring British empire in India dedicated to the reconstruction of Indian national character. As most comprehensively argued in his minute of 31 December 1824,[44] Munro recapitulated the supremacy of the raiyatwari system over alternative revenue and administrative systems, especially, in this minute, over mirasi, communal tenure. Behind this apparently needless ingemination was the conversion of an ostensible liability of raiyatwari into a moral advantage. The requirement in raiyatwari administration of a large 'native agency', or reliance upon Indians and Indian institutions, was condemned by Munro's critics on the basis of actual cost and potential 'corruption'. To this Munro answered that the efficient administration and close political control obtained with raiyatwari were indeed costly, but necessary, and that only Indians and certain indigenous institutions could provide these. Munro went beyond this utilitarian response, however. He argued that Indian magistrates and police had already proven superior in the judicial procedure adopted in Madras as a result of his proposals as judicial commissioner from 1814 to 1819. He went even further to say that it was incumbent upon the East India Company to provide high offices to Indians as a condition to its continued rule in India. Only by such a policy of gradually increasing the responsible role of Indians in administration could a durable moral basis for British rule in India be created, and without such a basis, British rule could not and should not last long. Reliance upon Indians, the 'native agency', would promote a reconstruction of Indian 'national' and 'public character', a purpose Munro deemed sufficiently moral to ensure the assent of Indians to British rule of indefinite duration, a permanent empire. At the same time, such high purpose was required for English national character given post-Burkean criticisms of the Indian empire.

In the same way that the policy debate on the proposed imposition of the zamindari settlement of Bengal upon Madras in 1800 shaped Munro's rhetoric and his metaphorical manipulation of the terms examined above between then and 1807, his mature ideology shaped his later rhetoric. Thus, his writings of the period from 1800 to 1807 depict raiyats and holders of inam land (inamdars) as laced, by a web of purportedly civic and egalitarian relations, into a 'great mass of village republics', and this 'great body' of small cultivators should not be delivered into the unsavoury hands of a zamindar, 'who,' Munro said, 'was a kind of contractor' with no other claim to his position than enough money to buy it.[45] By 1814 when Munro returned to India after an extended furlough in England, the target of his rhetoric had changed and with that the metaphorical uses of 'raiyat' and 'inamdar', especially.

The extension of the Bengal system to Madras having been successfully forestalled by Munro's artful reasoning before 1807, he and his friends converted the parliamentary select committee on Indian policies in 1812-13 to belief in his raiyatwar system for Madras. New antagonists after 1814 were proponents of communal *mirāsi* tenure (from the Arabic, *miras*, to inherit) which obtained in some of the most prosperous parts of the Presidency; others, like John Hodgson, pressed for a variation of the zamindari system, long-term renters called *muṭhṭhadār*, often chosen from among village headmen. In response, Munro now speaks of the raiyat and inamdar as distinguished from the 'great mass'; in 1824, he writes:

> One of the greatest disadvantages of our Government in India is its tendency to lower or destroy the higher ranks of society, to bring them all to one level, and by depriving them of their former weight and influence, to render them less useful instruments in the internal administration of the country.[46]

Who are the occupants of these higher 'gradations of society'? They are 'jageerdars and enamdars ... and many principal merchants and rayets'.[47]

Here, we observe, the raiyat and the inamdar have been transformed from one persistent early Munro metaphor, a 'great mass' or 'great body' of smallholding cultivators, citizens, and paid servants of a 'great mass of village republics' into another, a ranked society of individuals. The same system of agrarian relations appears to generate both metaphors: the 'great mass' and the more fashionable 'distinctions of rank'. As Indians were the necessary agents of British imperial control, their aspirations to remuneration, responsibility and dignities must be met; this would preserve and extend social distinctions upon which an ordered society depended. It was in the greatest interest of the British that these aspirations be satisfied and Indian national character fostered, since further decay of Indian public character would injure both British interests and endanger continued British rule over India. Properly pursued, British rule in India was indefinitely long; it would end only when the British voluntarily recognized the fruits of their 'liberal treatment' and withdrew from the sub-continent to leave a reconstructed Indian polity, or 'public character', to assume complete control of a government with which Indians would long have been creatively associated. The shape of that Indian polity was unclear; it had to be developed over a long period of British tutelage.

## *Conclusion*

If it is conceded that ideology - systematic conceptions of what social, or specifically agrarian, relations *ought* to be - can be considered an important dimension of a society and, further, that a focus upon external dimensions entails a consideration of internal ones, then the comparison undertaken above - brief and schematic as it is - may have raised useful and examinable issues. Among these are the following: that where it is possible, as it is in India, to reconstruct the past practices and ideologies of a society subjugated to European colonial rule, such reconstructions are essential in assessing both the degree and kind of change which actually occurred under early colonial rule; that where claims are made by colonial regimes about the justice or appropriateness of their measures on the basis of historical precedence, assessment of such claims must depend on a view of history independent of that appropriated by colonial regimes; and that where, even in the more mature phase of a colonial regime - as in twentieth-century British India - one must explain a mobilization of political forces opposed to certain features of the colonized polity (often lumped together as 'nationalism'), there should be a readiness to consider that some of the means and ends of such opposition may be informed by indigenous elements - including ideological ones - of often ancient vintage.

The brief examination of Munro's rhetorical and ideological usage bears upon some of these points. His later, individualistic raiyatwar rhetoric and ideology were framed with reference not only to communalistic formulations (for example, mirasi) by his British peers in India, but to the existence of transactionally-defined systems of agrarian relations in the south India of his time and to the moral commitment of Indians to these systems. Munro, the ideologue, ignored or denied the existence of such systems as the underpinning of south Indian rural institutions; Munro, the pragmatic rural administrator, employed these transactional systems most adroitly as Frykenberg and Mukherjee were the first to suggest.[48] We see this in several ways. One was the explicit reliance placed by Munro and later raiyatwari administrators on the moral as well as political standing of village headmen and caste leaders in both revenue and judicial matters. Munro certainly grasped the fact that such rural men were able to command the resources necessary to meet revenue obligations because they were central figures in local transactional systems, not merely because they were office holders or in possession of official coercive means. One reason for the failure of the *muṭṭhadari* system of long-term renters that replaced raiyatwar in the Ceded Districts, where Munro served, and elsewhere after Munro's death, was a mistaken conception of the latter sort: revenue defaulting by headmen-renters resulted from the continued high pitch of revenue demand and from the actual limited coercive power of headmen over other dominant landed persons with whom they had long co-operated. The persuasiveness and success of Munro's 1816 judicial reforms which placed magisterial and police functions in the hands of headmen bears on the same point; as long as these men were parts of transactional systems with others like themselves, they could authoritatively adjudicate disputes of all sorts, but deprived of this moral centricity, they could not. In short, had there not been respected 'potails' (headmen) and 'pedda rayets' (leaders of cultivator groups), men capable of exercising morally-compelling village and locality leadership, Munro's system could not have existed in the Ceded Districts nor in other parts of dry-region Madras.[49] As to the older, settled regions of irrigated agriculture (for example, Chingleput, Tanjavur, and parts of Tinnevelly), the 'Munro system' in any of its variant manifestations simply did not exist; here, forms of communal (mirasi) management by Brahmans and Vellalas of agrarian relations were too firmly entrenched for even a seemingly-individualized system of direct relations with government to be feigned. For most of the nineteenth century, in these places, the 'Madras-' or 'Munro-system' was a papered-over chaos with about the same agrarian reality as Potemkin villages.

There were, of course, changes in Madras during the nineteenth century, and agrarian developments were among the most important of these. By the 1840s in many parts of dry-region Madras there were substantial increases in commercial agriculture paced by cotton and groundnuts and, after the middle of the century, impressive market integration as a result of improvements in roads and road transport. But, there is nothing about such development that suggests that the pre-British system of localized transactional relations was irrelevant with respect to these changes or substantially diminished by them. Christopher Baker, in his most recent work on agricultural development in the late nineteenth and twentieth century, suggests the contrary. He has argued that the forms of labour control and capitalization which generated these commercialized agrarian developments were based upon Vijayanagara forms of pooling and command.[50] Whether this view is correct, or whether, in addition, growing market responsiveness by south Indian agriculturists from 1840 to 1890 was a (or the) salient factor, remains to be settled by detailed research. However, changes of even this character may have been fully compatible with older forms of organization which could, in perhaps modified forms, have continued in the newer economic contexts of world capitalism and trade. Both the degree and kind of changes in the late nineteenth-century agrarian order in south India, it is suggested, must be considered in relation to older, pre-British praxis and indigenous theory, not necessarily as opposed to or departing from it.

Similar suggestions can be made about even more recent judicial and political history in Madras where, again, earlier conceptions of a contingent, context-sensitive, transactional system appeared to have continued to be latent in the manifest crises of modernization. Older meanings of appropriate rural relations plagued the formal British court system of Madras until quite recent times. Frustrating Indians and Britons alike, the operation of Madras courts in the nineteenth century and later was vexed by quarrels over entitlements and shares which British judicial institutions could only surreptitiously cognize as paltry property claims since matters of religion, caste, and many issues of personal law were excluded from jurisprudential review.

Finally, we may be seeing the continuity of earlier transactional systems and ideology in the twentieth century political system. Politics of the recent past have been seen, by some at least, to be dominated by 'rural magnates'[51] whose links to city politicians provided the structure of the collaborationist Justice Party of the 1920s in Madras, the organizational base of Congress politicians of the 1930s and, at the same time, the parallel, personal network of M.K. Gandhi, and, finally, for 'syndicate' politicians like Kamaraj Nadar in later decades. While the recent work of David Washbrook and Christopher Baker has cast doubt upon Irschick's earlier, largely unreflective suppositions about ideology in the earlier of these movements, their work has not adequately accounted for the persistent followerships of south Indian 'magnates'. One must agree with Tapan Raychaudhuri's recent comment on the limitations of 'animal politics' (non-ideological, self-interested political action) as a total explanation of modern politics in south India.[52] Older idioms of entitlement, shares, and social recognition (*kāṇi*, *paṅku*, and *kaṭṭalai*), whether expressed as self-rule, self-respect, or anti-Brahmanism, must be considered to have had a vital place. This is not the commanding place of the pre-British era, to be sure, but still a place of expressive privilege for political action.

## *Idiom and Ideology*

The framing conception of this entire discussion is predicated upon the proposition that in examining the external dimension in rural south Asia and assessing its impact, we must be aware of the internal dimension, and that if we are to consider external ideologies, then we must also consider internal ones. Strictly speaking, the external and internal, as opposed and possibly conflicting perspectives, can only be seriously examined for the brief historical time when the exogenous factor is yet new and truly exogenous. That condition existed in Munro's time, but did it continue through Munro's successors? Probably not. A part of the importance that must be attributed to Thomas Munro is that he, like John Malcolm, self-consciously sought to create a distinctive system of administration, one which was purportedly 'Indian', and, explicitly, not one based upon 'European models'.[53] Both men also established 'schools', followers among younger British officials and their Indian subordinates. Whether by deliberate design, as in the cases of the first generation of colonial administrators such as Munro and Malcolm, or not, the principles, institutions, and rationalizations of colonial systems in time became a part of their colonial setting and shaped the actions and udnerstandings of colonizer and colonized alike. The meanings of 'external' and 'internal' are modified to: 'external', given the constraints of the Indian situation; 'internal', given the constraint of foreign rule. This follows the reasoning of the sociologist G. Balandier[54] on the unitary nature of the 'colonial situation', in which, for European and non-European alike, although one is an outsider and the other an insider, there is the fact of a colonial society in which the external and internal have merged, however incompletely, into a single structure. Thus, in south India, as elsewhere in British India, by the late nineteenth century, there is a distinctive Madras Presidency style and structure (administrative tradition, institutional framework, mode of operating, saint-like heroes such as Munro) which differentiates it from other parts of British India and which has incorporated (with whatever distortions) much of the indigenous into its being, while at the same time there has been introduced into south India (again, with distortions) much of the external. Under the conditions of the mature colonial society of the later nineteenth century, we may only with difficulty and prudent hesitation attempt to isolate and attribute significance to earlier, indigenous forms, including ideological ones, that are more readily identified and evaluated in the onset period of colonialism.

Yet, without an attempt to delineate the external and internal dimensions of the early colonial encounter of 1800, we are constrained to accept the external accounts of (descriptions) and accounting for (explanations) the evolution of the colonial society of south Asia and remain, inevitably and eternally, captive of that perspective.

*NOTES*

Stein, 'Idiom and ideology in early nineteenth-century south India'

*Abbreviations*

IOL India Office Library and Records, London
MBOR Madras Board of Revenue

1. This covers the reigns from Narasa Nayaka to the death of Sri Ranga II and is based on no pretended periodization judgement other than those standard in Vijayanagara history; see, K.N. Nilakanta Sastri, *A History of South India* (London 1955), pp.263-90.

2. T.H. Beaglehole, *Thomas Munro and the Development of Administrative Policy in Madras 1792-1818* (Cambridge 1966), pp.45ff; and Walter Kelly Firminger, ed, *The Fifth Report from the Select Committee of the House of Commons on the Affairs of the East India Company, Dated 28 July 1812* (Calcutta 1918; reprint 1969), vol.3, pp. 302-14.

3. The works of K.N. Nilakanta Sastri, T.V. Mahalingam, B.A. Saletore, and N. Venkataramanayya.

4. A. Krishnaswami Pillai, *The Tamil Country Under Vijayanagara* (Annamalai 1964).

5. New Delhi 1980; Chapter 8, pp.366-489.

6. *Sources of Indian History* (Madras 1964), p.79.

7. Sastri, *A History of South India*, p.295.

8. Krishnaswami Pillai, op.cit.

9. B. Stein, 'Economic Functions of a Medieval South Indian Temple', *Journal of Asian Studies* 19, 2 (1960), pp.163-76; and B. Stein, 'Temples in Tamil Country, 1300-1750A.D.', in B. Stein, ed., *South Indian Temples; An Analytical Reconsideration* (New Delhi 1978) - originally published in the *Indian Economic and Social History Review*.

10. In a paper presented to the Association of Asian Studies meeting, Toronto, 13 March 1981, entitled: 'Land as Gift in the Vijayanagara Period'.

11. 'The South Indian Temple, Authority, Honor, and Redistribution', *Contributions to Indian Sociology* (n.s.) 10 (1976).

12. 'Kings, Sects and Temples in South India, 1350-1700 A.D.', in Stein, *South Indian Temples*, pp.47-75.

13. 'Agrarian Structure in South India: Tirunelveli

(Tinnevelly), 800-1900A.D.', Department of History, University of Pennsylvania, 1978. I follow Ludden's use of the toponymic 'Tinnevelly'.

14. Ibid., chapter 4, p.22.

15. 'Political Authority and Structural Change in Early South Indian History', *The Indian Economic and Social History Review* v, 13 (1976); 'Land as Political Relation in the Little Kingdoms of Southern India', presented to the Association of Asian Studies meeting, Toronto, 13 March 1981; and his doctoral thesis on Pudukkottai being submitted to the Department of History, University of Chicago.

16. The *śatakam* is a Tamil verse-form used for the composition of paeans to dominant peasant caste groups during the seventeenth and eighteenth centuries; see B. Stein, 'Circulation and Historical Geography in Tamil Country', *Journal of Asian Studies* v, 37 (November 1977) pp.7-27.

17. Nicholas B. Dirks, 'The Structure and Meaning of Political Relations in a South Indian Little Kingdom', *Humanities Working Paper* 14 (October 1978), California Institute of Technology, p.49.

18. For this phrase and for a great many ideas, I am indebted to Arjun Appadurai's *Worship and Conflict under Colonial Rule*, Cambridge University Press (forthcoming).

19. For an extended discussion of this festival see Stein, *Peasant State and Society*, pp.384 ff; the Portuguese accounts are found in Robert Sewell, *A Forgotten Empire (Vijayanagara)* (London 1900).

20. My thanks to Nicholas Dirks and E. Valentine Daniel for having pointed to the 'nine gates' symbol; also see R.G. Zaehner, *The Bhagavad-Gita* (London 1979), p.208 on *nava-dvārepure* in the *Gita*, pp.5-13.

21. The Fifth Report, vol.3, Appendices, 13-18, pp. 1-210.

22. British Library, Burney Collection, vol.812, p. 294. The entire letter is found in G.R. Gleig, *The Life of Major-General Sir Thomas Munro, Bart., and K.C.B.* (London 1830-31, 3 vols.), vol.1, pp.84 ff.

23. The Fifth Report, vol.3 where Munro's writings occupy 120 of 595 pages.

24. *Selection of Papers from the Records at the East India House relating to Revenue, Police, and Civil and Criminal Justice* (London 1826, 4 vols.).

25. 'Papers of John, 13th Lord Elphinstone; Minutes of Sir Thomas Munro', European Manuscripts, F/87, IOL. The 248 minutes are divided into 164 on military matters, 50 on revenue, 18 on judicial, and 16 on political

matters. A selection of these, with deletions not always clearly indicated, are found in Alexander J. Arbuthnot, ed., *Major-General Sir Thomas Munro, Bart., K.C.B., Governor of Madras, Selections from His Minutes and Other Official Writings* (Madras 1886).

26. See Eugene Garver, 'Ancient Rhetoric and Modern Problems', in Robert L. Brown and Martin Steinman, eds., *Rhetoric 78: Proceedings of Theory of Rhetoric, An Interdisciplinary Conference* (Minneapolis 1979).

27. The Fifth Report, vol.3, pp.589-90; Thackeray's report on Canara, Malabar, and the Ceded Districts, 4 August 1897.

28. Munro to Charles W.W. Wynn, 14 June 1823, IOL, European Manuscripts, Munro Collection, F/151/92.

29. In 1888, 30 million acres of 59 million under raiyatwari in Madras and 21 million acres of 44 million in Bombay were not fully assessed: 'Statistical Abstract relating to British India, 1888', P.P. 1889, v. 82, C. 5852, Table entitled, 'Survey and Assessed Area'.

30. See the various writings of Brian Murton on this matter, e.g., 'Land and Class: Cultural, Social, and Biophysical Integration in Interior Tamilnadu in the Late Eighteenth Century', in Robert E. Frykenberg, ed., *Land Tenure and Peasant in South Asia* (New Delhi 1977).

31. The following works may be consulted: George Robertson, *General View of the Agriculture of the County of Mid-Lothian ... Drawn Up for ... Board of Agriculture* (London 1773); John Naismith, *General View of the Agriculture ... Clydesdale* (Glasgow 1798).

32. Mark Wilks, *Historical Sketches of the South of India in an Attempt to Trace the History of Mysoor ...* (ed. Murray Hammick, Mysore 1930, 2 vols.; originally published 1910), vol.1, p.139 note, Munro's report from Anantapur, 15 May 1806.

33. Munro to MBOR, 25 August 1805, para.3, Madras Board of Revenue Proceedings, P/288/24, IOL.

34. Ibid., para.6.

35. T. Burrow and M.B. Emeneau, *A Dravidian Etymological Dictionary* (Oxford 1961), no.1379, p.114; *Tamil Lexicon, Published under the Authority of the University of Madras* (Madras 1936, 6 vols.), vol.2, p.968.

36. *Tamil Lexicon*, vol.3, p.1766 and vol.2, p.744.

37. Ibid., vol.3, p.1599.

38. Ibid., vol.1, p.187.

39. S. Sundararaja Ivengar, *Land Tenures in the Madras Presidency* (Madras 1921), p.80.

40. D.C. Sircar, *Indian Epigraphical Glossary* (Delhi 1966), p.809.

41. M. Monier-Williams, *A Sanskrit-English Dictionary* (Delhi 1963), p.809.

42. Government of Madras, Selections from the Records of Government, *Papers on Mirasi Rights* (Madras 1862).

43. The Fifth Report, vol.3, p.204: Munro to MBOR, 5 January 1897.

44. There are many incomplete versions of this minute; a full version is most conveniently found in Gleig, op.cit., vol.3, pp.319-90.

45. Ibid., vol.3, p.504: Munro to MBOR. 15 October 1807.

46. Gleig, op.cit., vol.3, p.384: Minute of 31 December 1824.

47. Ibid., vol.3, pp.384-5.

48. 'The Ryotwari System and Social Organization in the Madras Presidency', in R.E. Frykenberg, ed., *Land Control and Social Structure in Indian History* (Madison 1969), p.224; and Frykenberg, 'The Silent Settlement in South India, 1793-1853: An Analysis of the Role of Inams in the Rise of the Indian Imperial System', in Frykenberg, *Land Tenure and Peasant*.

49. Taken from the doctoral dissertation work in progress of Bruce L. Robert on the Bellary district of the Ceded Districts; this work will be submitted to the Department of History, University of Wisconsin. Robert's findings on Bellary confute many of those of David Washbrook in the latter's *The Emergence of Provincial Politics; the Madras Presidency, 1870-1920* (Cambridge 1976), especially on the point of presumed concentration of economic power.

50. I am grateful to Dr Baker for having permitted me to read portions of this latest of his studies which is now forthcoming.

51. Washbrook, op.cit., and Christopher Baker's *The Politics of South India, 1920-1937* (Cambridge 1976), pp. 87ff. Also see the joint work of these two authors, *South India: Political Institutions and Political Change, 1880-1947* (Delhi 1976).

52. 'Indian Nationalism as Animal Politics', *The Historical Journal* 22 (1979), pp.747-63.

53. From Munro's minute, 31 December 1824,in Gleig, op.cit., vol.3, p.320.

54. 'The Colonial Situation: A Theoretical Approach', cited in I. Wallerstein, *Social Change: the Colonial Situation* (New York 1966), pp.34-62.

# A NOTE ON THE TERM 'LAND CONTROL'

*Dharma Kumar*

Peter Robb reminds us that 'our terminology must be general to the extent that we wish to communicate with others and relate our findings to theirs'.[1] But finding a general terminology is easier said than done. Since we are writing in English, we cannot use only Indian terms (and their meaning is often ambiguous even in the original contexts). But there are no agreed terms to describe the holders of the various interests in land. Other specialists will object to the use of common English words like 'landowner' or 'tenant'. The general reader has the awkward habit of demanding an explanation of unfamiliar English words, like 'landholder', or of Indian words like 'raiyat' or 'mirasdar', and trying to define them leads one back into the thorny thicket of Indian land law and administration. There are various escape routes. One is to start with a definition of the Indian or English term and note the exceptions to the definition (there are bound to be exceptions) as one goes along. This sounds simple, but is not - one often finds one has to go back and redefine the term. Another is to put a common English word into quotation marks - as 'landowner' - to indicate that it is not entirely appropriate. A third is to use a variety of terms, hoping that one or other will fit. This is the least illuminating of all methods, but whether it reflects a desire for elegant variation or the hope that one's own uncertainties about definitions will be hidden by a profusion of words, it is commonly used (by the author, for one). Finally, one can adopt a new English word, hoping to avoid the ambiguities and confusions of the old terms; the word 'ownership' has been found particularly misleading by many. New candidates spring up faster than in an Assembly election - 'customary right of physical dominion', 'primary dominion', and 'immediate physical dominion';[2] 'agrarian decision-maker',[3] to name only a few. The most popular candidate in recent years has been 'land control' but before it is finally elected to the position of chief 'organising concept', we should scrutinise its claim carefully.

'Controller' is preferred to 'owner' because the latter is held to suggest the Roman concept of 'dominium' or the modern liberal concept of private ownership, both of which assume a clear dividing line between the public and private domains, whereas this line was blurred in pre-British India. The word 'land-controller', it is argued, thus has the virtue of conveying two ideas: the land-controller has some of the attributes of sovereignty (since one meaning of 'control' is 'rule'), such as the power to tax or to punish, but he is not necessarily the sovereign. The closest analogies, on this view, are African.[4] Stein uses Southall's description of Alur society as a model of the medieval South Indian state; Neale takes the Tiv as a paradigm for all of India.[5] This too is an 'external dimension', and like other external dimensions it can mislead as well as enlighten.

### *African Land Tenures*

Consider the following general characteristics of traditional African systems:

(1) Land was plentiful, so cultivation was extensive.
(2) Land had little exchange value.
(3) But 'control of land was essential to the survival of different groups'. This control was vested in groups (chiefdoms, villages, lineages, etc.) represented by chiefs, elders and or councils.
(4) All members of the group had access to land by virtue of membership of the group.
(5) 'Many rights in land could also be obtained through marriage, migration, friendship and formal transfer' (but apparently not by sale);
(6) The exercise of any right was always limited by obligations and counterbalanced by the rights and privileges of others.
(7) Rights were not always permanent.
(8) Individual and family rights in a particular piece of land could generally only be maintained by 'effective use and appropriation', and the amount of land used by a family was limited by 'technical, economic, and even magical factors'.
(9) On the other hand villages and lineages could maintain claims to the whole of their territory without making full use of all their lands.
(10) The representatives of the land-holding groups defended the 'integrity of the territory', maintained peace, etc., and might have specific rights to taxes, labour, etc. They did not necessarily have the right to allocate land between members and non-members.
(11) Quite often 'different social personalities

exercised rights and claims in the same piece of land; this must not necessarily be interpreted as an hierarchy of tenures or a formal system of successive allocation of land'.

(12) In addition, the movements of groups have led to 'the coexistence of different groups exercising different claims, on the same tract of land'. (Conflicts between the groups did occur, but were 'generally easily settled'.) This co-existence might lead to a variety of new arrangements. 'The autochthonous group might maintain a set of ritual privileges derived from its mythical association with the soil, it might retain the effective control of ownership only on some of its former lands or it might retain almost all its original land rights, the conquerors or newcomers claiming only political control (ruling over men, not over land); or a complex system of overlapping but different land units and rights might be elaborated together with a multiple land-tenure system'.[6]

There are two important points to note in this summary of land control in Africa. Note that rights in land were obtained primarily by membership of a group, such as a lineage, and these rights were given by the land-controller to all members of the group. Amongst the Tiv, for example, a man has permanent rights to 'sufficient' land as a member of his agnatic lineage, but not to any specific piece of land. He is given a farm and has 'precise rights'[7] to the farm while he cultivates it, but once the farm reverts to fallow, his right to that specific piece of land lapses. But he continues to have a right to enough land to support his family. The 'land controller' is the compound head who, according to the Tiv themselves, 'has final and complete control of the size and location of the farms of each man in the compound'.[8]

Secondly, in the African systems of the 'land-control' type, land could not be bought and sold; the Tiv could not even rent land.[9] This is very different from, for instance, medieval South India.

Africanists who use the term 'land controller' generally specify what the powers of and constraints on the land are, whereas Indianists who have borrowed the term have frequently forgotten the obligation to describe the actual system of control.

## *Social Control and Private Ownership*

It is also important to note that 'land controller' is not necessarily a substitute for 'landowner'. Where the legal system permits private individuals to buy and sell land, there can be both land-controllers (that is, those exercising governmental control) and landowners. Take, for example, foreign exchange: Indians who are allowed to keep bank accounts abroad or foreign currency at home are legal owners of foreign exchange, but their rights of transfer, etc. are limited by the powers of the Exchange Controller, as defined by law. If the Exchange Controller's powers are very great one might wish to say that individual rights have little value, or have been attenuated. Indeed, there is always some government or social control over individual rights. But of course the degree of control varies enormously and some assets, such as foreign exchange or land, may be subject to control by a specific agent of government, in specific ways; it is in such cases that one may wish to use the term 'controller'.

Moreover, even if the law forbids the transfer of certain commodities or rights, markets in them may exist; as modern controlled economies show one can have official controllers and de facto 'owners/controllers'. (And markets can also operate when government breaks down, as Lebanon demonstrates.)

Conversely, the law may give the individual full rights of alienation of an asset, but there may be no market in it, because of insufficient supply or lack of demand or of transport or of information. Thus there were sporadic sales of land but no land market in classical Rome.

The term 'land controller' is then particularly useful in two situations. The first arises when certain private property rights, in particular the right of alienation, are not permitted by the legal or social system - the Tiv paradigm. The second is when these private property rights in land exist in law, but in fact someone other than the nominal owner controls the possession, use, sale, etc. of land.

With these general considerations in mind let us examine the use of the term 'land controller' in two cases: Tamil Nadu under the Cholas, and Madras Presidency in the late nineteenth century.

*Tamil Nadu under the Cholas*

Burton Stein[10] has argued that the Chola State was not a centralised bureaucratic state, receiving a regular and large land revenue from its 'territory'; rather the Chola and Pandyan kings performed mainly a ritual function as the 'most important symbol of the sacred moral order', outside a limited core area from which they drew most of their material resources. From the remaining 'Chola' territory they received only small and irregular payments of tribute. Their major source of revenue was raids on the regions of other overlords. South Indian society was marked by territorial segmentation.[11] The Tamil country was divided into micro-regions or *nadus*; these were the basic units of political organization,[12] and economic as well as ethnic territories since 'requirements of the agrarian organisation, given the technology of the age, made for territorially segmented units of production'.[13]

The way nadus were governed differed. In the central area (Daveri basin and Tondaimandalam) the nadus were governed by assemblies;[14] in southern Karnataka and Kongu by chieftains. Stein concentrates on the assemblies: these collected revenue, and also supervised the accounts of temples in endowed villages. The assemblies decided on gifts of land or of the income from land to temples and to Brahmans, the control of trade settlements, and so forth. At a lower level, both peasant and Brahman villages had corporate institutions to manage cultivation and other village affairs: the Brahman *sabha* and the peasant *ur*.

The assemblies consisted not of all cultivators but only of dominant cultivators; Stein does not call them landowners but describes them as follows:

> They alone possessed the valuable land whose income could constitute a gift to the pious and the learned; they alone possessed the means for maintaining the full productivity of these lands dependent as most were upon irrigation works which served the entire locality; and they alone through their control over dependent labourers - both skilled artisans and unskilled field hands who actually carried out field operations - could have assured that once granted, the specified income from villages and lands granted would sustain a flow of income 'in perpetuity'.[15]

The first point to note about Stein's account of Chola society is that 'land control' is exerted at various levels - by the king, nadu assemblies, and village assemblies. Moreover, the nature of the control differed - some 'land controllers' only collected and redistributed taxes or tribute, others took investment decisions, or directed agricultural labour. The king, as we have seen, was hardly important outside the core area. The records do not allow us to say a great deal about the precise nature of the control at the nadu level; somewhat more is known about land control at the village level.

The village assemblies - the ur or the sabha - invested in major irrigation, and allocated water rights; allocated the common village lands to village servants; sold common village land to chiefs or temples, or gifted it to temples.[16] These communal concerns might be managed by committee,[17] or by some other mode of communal decision-taking. But the actual cultivation of the arable was almost always organized by individuals on land they had inherited, or bought or been gifted - exactly as in a system of private ownership. However the allocation of land was made when it was first settled;[18] there is no evidence that village assemblies, or local chiefs, reallocated lands, as in parts of Africa, or as the Russian mir did, to take account of changes in family size. When, for instance, a village assembly (the 'land controllers') wished to donate to a temple land which some individual (or family) owned, they had to buy it from him - who is the 'land controller' here?

The inscriptions record a great variety of transactions in land, entered into by all kinds of parties - Rajas, regional assemblies of peasants or merchants, village assemblies, and individuals, whether Brahman or merchant or peasant. Assemblies and individuals sold land; did rajas do so? The vast majority of transactions recorded in the inscriptions concern donations to temples. But there are exceptions: an inscription of A.D.1238 states that two people had to sell land to meet tax dues.[19] And there is every reason to believe that people bought and sold land for reasons unconnected with temples. People moved, and might want to sell land to do so; others may have bought to expand their farms, or to give to their children.

Some historians say they were not selling land but only rights in land. But this is always so, whether the object in question is land or a knife, though admittedly land gives rise to a much greater complexity of rights and obligations. You can no more have 'absolute ownership' (in the sense of doing what you like with it) of a knife than of land, as you discover when you try to kill someone with it. What particular bundle of rights was alienated depended on the terms of the transaction and on the type of land - lands on which tenants had occupancy rights, 'raiyatwari' land in a dry village involving no communal rights, or a share in a jointly-held village, where the purchaser obtained, in addition to the arable, rights in the common lands, in the village tank, and so on, and perhaps the right to take part in the village assembly and village committees. Even in the so-called joint villages, individual shares and fractions of shares could be bought and sold by the owner,[20] though there might well be restrictions on the purchaser, and relations and other villagers might have pre-emption rights.

Why cannot the sellers of these rights be called land-owners? One reason given is that 'land controller' is better because it conveys more. In particular it conveys that the owner has not only the economic rights of management, income, alientation, etc., but also political powers. But was this true of all land holders, whatever the size of their holding? There is no evidence that land was particularly equally distributed and there must have been some very small plots;[21] women also held land. Were these also part of the land control group? If not, there is a difference between ownership, given by the legal system, and control, partly determined by the actual distribution of wealth, as in all unequal societies, but only partly. Legal rights are not simply a reflection of the distribution of power. The trouble with 'land control' is that it covers in one blanket term the different political, legal, and economic structures, differences made beautifully clear in Geertz's account of pre-colonial Bali where

> control over land and control over people expressed themselves in distinct and uncoordinate institutions .... Differential access to agricultural property was certainly not irrelevant to political power in Bali. But it was not the sum and substance of it either .... There was, in short, no systematic congruence (though there was, here and there, some more or less accidental overlap) between the structure of political authority, the structure of land tenure, and the distribution of land tenancy.[22]

(Comparisons of medieval South India with Bali should be particularly fruitful.)

*Land Control in Madras Presidency*

From the middle of the nineteenth century onwards, the legal and administrative regulations secured, at least on paper, fairly full property rights to the raiyat. The British also instituted a modern government, with an efficient bureaucracy. Why then do historians of nineteenth and twentieth century Madras still find it useful to use the term 'land control'? There seem to be two distinct reasons. First, it is argued that the government took very high rates of land revenue, and evicted for non-payment, so that raiyat's so-called property rights were in fact of little value; officials were in control.

Alternatively (or for a different period), the government was not in fact in such complete control of south Indian society as was once believed. Its writ never penetrated to the village level and in certain areas even above the village level. There were then alternative systems of control. 'Land controllers' had more power than 'officials', not to mention private 'owners'.

As it finally developed, the raiyatwari system gave the raiyat most of the rights of modern liberal land ownership.[23] The Madras Manual of Administration categorically describes the raiyat in the modern raiyatwari system thus: subject to the payment of the land revenue, he 'enjoys an absolute proprietorship over the soil and can deal with or use it in any many he likes'.[24] He had the right to possess; 'physical control' in this case means the right to occupy, to cultivate or not to cultivate; the right to exclude others while no other person had the right to exclude him, apart from his voluntarily giving them a temporary right of possession by leasing out or mortgaging the land. Similarly he had the right to use (except that he could not put the land to non-agricultural uses), to manage and to the income, and the fact that he might voluntarily part with any of these, as, for instance, by appointing a manager, does not affect the issue. He had the right to capital; he could sell and hold his ownership right for an unlimited period. But his right to bequeath the land might be restricted by family law.

The law took little cognisance of any rights other than those of the raiyat (except in Malabar); unlike Bengal no laws recognised the permanent rights of tenants under the raiyat though particular tenants might establish that they had occupancy rights by 'proving a custom, contract or a title, and possibly by other means'.[25] Also forms of communal ownership and management became increasingly rare under the British.[26]

Why then are historians so often reluctant to call the raiyat a landowner? One reason is that the administrative records refer to the raiyat as the 'tenant' of the state. The claims put forward by the British at the outset of their rule that property in land belonged to government by 'ancient usage' to quote Madras Regulation XXXI of 1802, led to the theory or rather fiction that the raiyat was the 'tenant of the State' in raiyatwari areas. This claim was related to their assertion, to quote one case, that 'sovereigns in India have always claimed the right to take the share of the produce in cultivated lands, and fix by executive order the share and commuted money payments'.[27] We still do not know on what basis or at what levels the land tax was fixed earlier. Doubtless there was a great deal of bargaining between taxpayers and tax collectors; the question is whether any principles regarding the legitimate or just or traditional rates were invoked. It is hard to believe that the statements in the law books about the correct rates of land revenue (one-fourth, one-sixth, etc.) were completely irrelevant.

It is true that in the first half of the nineteenth century land revenue rates were extremely high and in the first quarter giving up the land was sometimes forbidden. These two features combined certainly make it difficult to describe the raiyat as a landowner. In any case, land could be thrown up after the middle of the nineteenth century, and moreover from then on the real burden of the land revenue fell. In the twentieth century it was under ten per cent of the gross produce.

A different argument is that the *small* raiyat could exercise few property rights in practice and so his 'ownership' was merely a legal fiction. In the nineteenth century the charge was frequently made that the village headman or moneylender or the rich farmer controlled the small landowners who were thus, to quote and important nineteenth-century report, 'in the worst cases little more than tenants of the lender who prescribes what crops they shall grow and demands what term he pleases'.[28] There is undoubtedly truth in this charge, and indeed it has been made for several parts of India; in the case of the Deccan[29] even more strongly than in Madras. Historians may well be justified in using terms such as boss/dependent or patron/client in certain situations.

But was this always or even generally, the case? How frequently was the small *land owner* prevented from taking decisions, for example, as to what crop to sow on his own land? We may never be able to answer this satisfactorily for the past since in the nature of things the records are not likely to go into the question of extra-legal control.[30] But undoubtedly this is a vitally important issue, as the enormous modern literature on the 'interpenetration of markets' and the control of the creditor over the debtor shows.[31] But it is another question whether 'land control' is an appropriate term for the phenomenon, which from the late nineteenth century onwards at least was increasingly connected with control over sources of credit and of market institutions.

Here again the point is that land ownership and the ownership or control of credit[32] were not necessarily connected. The man who owned the most land was not always the richest nor the one who supplied credit to small landowners, nor were small landowners always indebted to the large landowners. Nor indeed was it necessary to own any land at all in order to invest and to grow, as Attwood's study of sugar cane growers in Maharashtra in the early twentieth century shows:

> Land was simply *not* the scarcest and most expensive factor of production: as mentioned, rents were quite low relative to other costs. Consequently, control of land alone did not mean effective control over the production of sugar cane. The most enterprising cane growers were primarily tenants. The reason they neglected to purchase land as they expanded operations was very simple: *it would have meant tying up their working capital* (which was scarcer and much more expensive). Land was rented from ordinary village cultivators (from those who had more land than they had sons to cultivate it, for example) and also from the few scattered *Rajas*, or princes, in the area. Because control of land alone did not mean control of the production process, these *Rajas* were only able to collect a fixed, monetary rent at a modest rate, just like anybody else.[33]

We still have a great deal to learn about the importance or the irrelevance of legal titles to land, and analyses of court cases should be very useful. There has been no systematic study of court disputes in Madras, or indeed anywhere else in India, as far as I am aware. What sizes of holdings were in dispute? Were the parties members of a family, contesting the partitions of family property, for instance or were they unrelated? Were there cases of defective titles, and if so, how were they settled? How much land was transferred to settle debt, and how useful was legal title in securing credit?

The issue of the control wielded by the large landowner or lender is common to nearly all of India. The alleged inadequacy of governmental control, particularly at the village level, appears to be specific to Madras Presidency; or is it just that historians happen to have studied it here? There were, in the first place, some matters which the government did not attempt to control. On others, particularly issues of land-ownership, there was a conflict between the executive and the courts. And even when the government did attempt to control matters, it was frustrated by an alternative power structure. The rural bosses could deceive, coerce and bribe bureaucrats to achieve ends forbidden by law or government orders.[34]

The use of extra-constitutional authority has thus a long pedigree in South India. Perhaps its most important field was taxation - rural bosses could see that their lands were underassessed and those of others overassessed. The numerous complaints by collectors in the revenue records are witness to this. Here again the question is how important the structure of extra-constitutional authority was and whether 'land control' is the best term for it, especially since the term covers such different types - the old landed gentry, corrupt officials, new farmers who have seized the opportunities thrown up by the extension of markets to grow rich, and to strengthen their position vis-à-vis government.[35]

*Conclusion*

The popularity of the word 'land controller', admittedly, is not a mere matter of fashion; it answers the desire for some word that will avoid the ambiguities of words like landowner or landlord and tenant, drawn, some have said, from alien legal systems, and one might add, not unambiguous even in their 'native' contexts, and in any case quite unsuitable when might mattered much more than legal right. There undoubtedly were, and still are, many such situations and in these 'land controller' may sometimes be a useful term. But sometimes the control of credit or access to administrators or some other factor may be more useful than land; as Attwood has pointed out land is not always the scarce factor even in agriculture.

Why make such a fuss about a word? Because words may convey misleading messages not only to the reader but also to the writer. The historian convinces himself that he has identified the crucial actor - the controller, the decision-maker - and pushes out of mind the complexity of formal legal and customary rights, obligations, and norms[36] that bound the 'land controllers' too in modern and medieval India, the tensions between different systems of rights,[37] and the changing balances of social and economic power.

I am well aware of the enormity of the tasks before us - of the slipperiness of terms like 'law', 'legal system',[38] 'property' and 'ownership';[39] of the peculiar difficulties posed by the classical legal literature of India[40] and the perhaps insuperable problem of determining which laws actually applied in a particular region or period in pre-British India; of the paucity of direct evidence on such matters as the principles on which conflicts were settled and the efficiency of judicial procedures,[41] and the complexity of the different structures of political, economic and social rights,[42] and of the state - but perhaps we would discover more if we asked more precise questions. The modest aim of this note is to uncover some of the questions glossed over by the use of 'land control'.[43]

## *NOTES*

Kumar, 'A note on the term 'land control'

I am indebted for their comments to participants in the seminar on the External Dimension, and in a symposium of the Society for South Indian Studies held in Philadelphia, in March 1980, where an earlier version of this paper was read. In particular I have benefited from the written comments of Dr Nicholas Dirks, Dr Pamela Price and Dr Peter Robb; for instruction over the years in Chola history from Professor Champakalakshmi, Professor Burton Stein and Dr David Ludden; and to Professor Ludo Rocher for discussion on classical Hindu Law, and for permission to refer to his unpublished paper (see n.39).

1. Peter Robb, discussion paper circulated before the symposium, 'External Dimension'. On the need to use English words, also see Max Gluckman, *The Judicial Process amongst the Barotse*...(2nd rev.ed.;Manchester 1973), pp.378-81; Martin E. Gold, *Law and Social Change* (New York 1977), pp.213-14.

2. Eric Stokes, *The Peasant and the Raj* (New Delhi 1978), pp.2, 3 and 7.

3. D.A. Washbrook, *The Emergence of Provincial Politics* (New Delhi 1977), p.84.

4. Cf. Bernard S. Cohn, 'African Models and Indian Histories', in Richard A. Fox, ed., *Realm and Region in Traditional India* (New Delhi 1977). 'Land controllers' are even creeping into European history - for example, Lester K. Little, *Religion, Poverty and the Profit Economy in Medieval Europe* (London 1978), p.20 - but they are fortunately still rare there.

5. Burton Stein, *Peasant State and Society in Medieval South India* (Delhi 1980); W.C. Neale, 'Land is to Rule', in R.E. Frykenburg, ed., *Land Control and Social Structure in Indian History* (Madison 1969), pp.3-17.

6. D. Biebuyck, *African Agrarian Systems* (Oxford 1963).

7. The man makes the farm for his wife, he owns the millet or bean seed, which he eats or pays as tax. The woman, who works on the farm, owns the other crops, such as yams and corn, and must feed her husband and children. The rights of others are also specified. See Paul and Laura Bohannan, *Tiv Economy* (Evanston 1968), p.81.

8. Though in actual practice this may not always be so; ibid., p.42.

9. There is an enormous variety in African land

tenures, and the sale of land is found in several societies, including some described in Biebuyck, op.cit. African systems of shifting cultivation are particularly inappropriate models for India but the analogy has been carried to strange lengths, for example Neale's conclusion that the word 'bigha' could stand for different areas in Bengal: 'A bigha was not an area of land in our sense but a piece of land which satisfied the requirement that the tenure *holder* be able to farm some piece of land whose productivity accorded with his status rights'. (Walter C. Neale, 'Land is to Rule'). But 'bigha' can mean both a fixed unit of area, or a measure normalised for variations in yield; it has in any case no more to do with status than a 'share' in an American joint stock company has. Units of area (or currency) can also be used to stand for percentages. Indians need no more confuse these separate meanings than Englishmen do the various meanings listed by O.E.D. for acre: (1) piece of arable land or field. (2) In the plural, rhetorically, landed estates. (3) A definite measure of land. (And obsolete meanings: (4) Lineal measure, and (5) duel). Will a Chinese social historian, some 1000 years hence, speculate on the English landed warrior's inability to distinguish between fields and fights?

10. Burton Stein, *Peasant State*.

11. Dirks questions this characterisation of the South Indian state; but his criticisms are probably not crucial to the type of issues we discuss; Nicholas Dirks, 'The structure and meaning of political relations in a south Indian little kingdom', *Contributions to Indian Sociology* (July-December 1979), pp.169-206.

12. Stein quotes Subbarayulu's study identifying some 556 nadus in the Chola macro-region by 1300 A.D. containing 2620 villages. Subbarayulu also argues that the 'government' at the level of the Chola king consisted mainly of revenue collection and temple management. The settlements for land revenue were made with the 'chief landholders' of the nadu, and payments were made by each village; Y. Subbarayulu, 'The State in Medieval South India, 600-1350 A.D.', Ph.D. dissertation, Madurai University, 1976. But, unlike Subbarayulu, Stein argues that these nadus came into existence before the Cholas (Stein, *Peasant State*, pp.98-9).

13. Ibid., p.104.

14. Stein points out that the existence of nadus and of nadu assemblies as 'administrative institutions of the Cholas is an inference, since the contemporary records do not refer to them as such (ibid.,p.96).

15. Ibid., p.131.
16. David Ludden, 'Agrarian Organization in a Tinnevelly District: 800 to 1900 A.D.', Ph.D. dissertation, University of Pennsylvania, 1978.
17. One famous Brahman village, Uttaramerur, in the tenth century ran its affairs through five committees: the annual, garden, tank, assessment and gold committees. Francois Gros and R. Nagaswamy, *Uttaramerur* (Pondicherry 1970).
18. There seems to be little discussion of the principles on which newly-settled land was allocated in the literature. One inscription describing the establishment of new villages states, at least in the summary, that the land was divided 'according to Visabadi'; N. Venkataramanayya and M. Somesekhara Sarma, 'Kakatiyas of Warrangal', in G. Yazdani, ed., *Early History of the Deccan*, Parts VII-XI (London 1960), pp.681-2.
19. Y. Subbarayulu, op.cit., p.214. What the buyer did with the land is not known.
20. The operation of these joint villages is very well described by Ludden, op.cit., ch.5. He stresses that individuals could take certain decisions regarding investment and management on their own. On pre-emption, see J.D.M. Derrett, *Essays in Classical and Modern Hindu Law* (Leiden 1976), vol.2, p.388, and P.V. Kane, *History of the Dharmashastra* (reissued Poona 1977), vol.V. Clearly the injunction against selling to people of low caste was not always obeyed since low caste share-holders were found by the eighteenth century, and even earlier, as Ludden shows (op.cit.).
21. A. Appadorai, *Economic Conditions in South India, 1000-1500 A.D.* (Madras 1936), 2 vols., p.232.
22. Clifford Geertz, *Negara* (Princeton 1980), pp.66-7.
23. R.M. Honoré, 'Ownership', in A.M. Guest, ed., *Oxford Essays in Jurisprudence* (London 1961), pp.101-47.
24. Government of Madras, *Manual of Administration of Madras Presidency* (Madras 1885), Vol.1, p.104.
25. S. Sundararaja Iyengar, *Land Tenures in Madras Presidency* (Madras 1916), p.178.
26. Dharma Kumar, *Land and Caste in South India* (Cambridge 1965), pp.15-18.
27. Secretary of State vs. Venkatapati Raju, quoted in S. Sundararaja Iyengar, op.cit., p.170.
28. F.A. Nicholson, *Report regarding the possibilities of introducing Agricultural Banks in the Madras Presidency* (Madras 1895-97, 22 vols.) Vol.1 (reprinted Bombay 1960), p.468.
29. J. Banaji, 'Capitalist Domination and the Small

Peasantry', *Economic and Political Weekly Special Number*, August 1977; Neil Charlesworth, 'Agrarian Society and British Administration in Western India, 1847-1930', Ph.D. dissertation, Cambridge University, 1973.

30. Washbrook makes an interesting indirect inference from Dharam Narain's and McAlpin's figures showing that in Madras cotton growing districts there was a much closer correlation between cotton prices and acreage under cotton than in Bombay or the U.P. He argues that this is a sign of the control of the richer landowners who forced smaller landowners to plant cotton despite their preference for subsistence food crops; Washbrook, op.cit., pp. 73-7. There are a number of statistical questions to be settled before accepting this conclusion (for example, how much of the total land belonged to small raiyats), but there is also the problem that in Bombay the moneylender was accused in even stronger terms of controlling the raiyats. Why were peasants not forced to grow cotton in Bombay?

31. See the writings of Pranab Bardhan, Krishna Bharadwaj, Amit Bhaduri, Ashok Rudra, T.N. Srinivasan, etc. in the *Economic and Political Weekly*, and economic journals.

32. Before 'credit controller' supplants 'land controller', may one suggest that 'creditor' is a useful word, and that 'credit controller', if it be used at all, be reserved for bank and co-operative society officals who lend money they do not own. My fear of the indiscriminate use of the word 'controller' is not an idle one, as Stein's reference to 'individualized wealth controller' in his paper in this volume shows. Is an 'individualized wealth controller' merely a rich man or a man who controls (how?) other people's wealth?

33. Donald W. Attwood, 'Capital and the transformation of agrarian class systems: a comparison of Bengal and Maharashtra, India'; paper read to the Conference on South Asian Political Economy, December 1980. Emphasis in original.

34. R.E. Frykenberg, *Guntur District 1788-1848* (Oxford 1965); C.J. Baker and D.A. Washbrook, *South India: Political Institutions and Political Change* (New Delhi 1975); D.A. Washbrook, *Provincial Politics*.

35. Washbrook, *Provincial Politics*, discusses regional variations and changes over time in the nature and powers of rural bosses. There is an excellent description of the way in which rural bosses operate in Andhra today, using loans, domination of the panchayat, 'coercive buying and selling', and if necessary force, including the physical occupation of land, in Marguerite Robinson, *The Law of*

*the Fishes*, forthcoming.

36. Nicholas Dirks and Pamela Price have both reminded me of the co-existence of different norms that could be used to structure rights or settle disputes before the British; in this connection see Dirks, op.cit., and Pamela Price, 'Resources and Rule in Zamindari South India, 1802-1903', Ph.D. dissertation, University of Wisconsin, 1979. The question is which norm generally prevails; see E. Adamson Hoebel, *The Law of Primitive Man* (Cambridge, Mass. 1967), pp.185-6.

37. Bernard S. Cohn, 'Structural Change in Rural Society', in Frykenberg, ed., *Land Control and Social Structure in Indian History*, brings out some of the features of a transition between two regimes.

38. Max Gluckman, *The Ideas in Barotse Jurisprudence* (New Haven 1972); H.L. Hart, *The Concept of Law* (Oxford 1981); E.A. Hoebel, *The Law of Primitive Man* (Cambridge, Mass., 1967); M.B. Hooker, *Legal Pluralism* (Oxford 1975).

39. W.N. Hohfeld, *Fundamental Legal Conceptions as Applied in Judicial Reasoning and Other Legal Essays* (reprinted, New Haven 1923); Lawrence Becker, *Property Rights* (London 1977).

40. J.D.M. Derrett, *Hindu Law, Past and Present* (Calcutta 1957) and *Essays in Classical and Modern Hindu Law*; P.V. Kane, op.cit.; R. Lingat, *The Classical Law of India*, transl. J.D.M. Derrett (Berkeley 1973); Ludo Rocher, 'Hindu Conceptions of Law', *Hastings Law Journal*, Vol.29, No.6, July 1978.

41. B.S. Cohn, 'From Indian Status to British Contract', *Journal of Economic History*, December 1961, pp. 613-28; V.T. Gure, *The Judicial System of the Marathas* (Poona 1953); Ludo Rocher, 'Father Bouchet's Letter on the Administration of Hindu Law', to appear in Richard Lariviere, ed., *Studies in Hindu Law*.

42. There is a characteristically clear discussion of some of these problems in Max Gluckman, *The Ideas in Barotse Jurisprudence*, pp.86-141.

43. Seminars, like pulpits, tempt one to preach what one does not practise, but I am trying to reform, witness Dharma Kumar, 'Land Ownership in India', Delhi School Working Paper, No.217, March 1980. This paper is now being revised.

# LAND, POWER AND MARKET: THE RISE OF THE LAND MARKET IN GANGETIC INDIA

*Jacques Pouchepadass*

The object of this paper is to illustrate the process of change in rural northern India under British rule in one particular respect: the attitudes and values relative to land. The starting points of this research have been the well-known writings of Sir Henry Maine and Karl Polanyi where the complex processes which are usually lumped together today under the vague term of modernization have been defined respectively as the transition from status to contract, and from non-market society to market society.[1] Such general assumptions naturally call for detailed enquiries. I have sought to use here local archival data collected in North Bihar, in combination with information relating to neighbouring Gangetic regions available in colonial government publications, in order to study the rise of the land market, an important aspect of this transition. The first part of this paper deals with concepts as much as with facts. It is to be taken as a tentative model of the traditional Indian conceptions relating to land and rights in land. I have attempted to show in the second part how the modern conception of land as a saleable commodity has taken root in Bihar, by a slow and imperfect process which has extended over more than a century.

The idea that land is a saleable commodity occurs very early in the classical tradition of India. It appears in the *smṛti* (notably Manu, Yajnavalkya and Vyasa,[2] and has been more than once commented upon in the subsequent literature of codes and treatises up to the end of the classical period. The *vyavahāranirṇaya* (thirteenth century), which quotes various *smṛti* on this point, explicitly labels land as *paṇya*, a commodity that can be bought and sold.[3] But normative texts are nowhere to be taken as a reflection of actual practice, and this is especially true in India. No treatise says whether the sale of land, though a theoretical possibility, is ever practised, and, if it is, whether it occurs only under special circumstances, or belongs to ordinary life. Archaeology alone can help to answer such questions. Various inscriptions of the first centuries A.D. do mention land sales, and even quote land prices.[4] But the sales thus commemorated are alienations with religious purposes, from which no general conclusion can safely be drawn, owing to the risk of misinterpreting symbolic forms as economic fact. Moreover, the *smṛti* themselves place such restrictions on the alienation of land as to alter much of its economic significance. The *mitākṣarā* (eleventh century), speaking on their authority, says that whoever wishes to sell a piece of land must secure the assent of his co-sharers, relatives, neighbours, fellow-villagers, and even of the king. It also recommends that the sale should outwardly appear as a gift, which may imply (according to P.V. Kane) that gifts of land were more common than sales.[5] The unanimous opinion of the eminent British jurists of the nineteenth century who had to probe deep into these matters until the law of alienations was codified by fresh legislation, was as follows: ancient Hindu law does admit the idea that land can be bought and sold, but with such restrictions that in practice sale could occur only exceptionally.[6]

During the centuries of Muslim rule (eleventh to eighteenth centuries), the evidence concerning land sales becomes more straightforward.[7] Qu'ranic law unambiguously recognizes all forms of alienations of land without any restriction.[8] Nevertheless, the sources are not really explicit until the establishment of Mughal rule. It then becomes obvious that what is really sold is not the land as such, but only certain rights to a part of its product. It is the zamindari that changes hands in most cases, that is to say the zamindar's right to a part of the product of the land from which he collects the land revenue in the name of his sovereign. At the village level, this right coexists with a number of other concurrent rights in the product of the same soil. But the zamindar's right alone is apparently freely bought and sold. Clear instances of such sales are available from the time of Akbar onwards. They become numerous under the reign of Aurangzeb.[9] Tenant rights, on the other hand, remain untransferable. And the idea that the land itself could be sold seems utterly non-existent, which is another way to say that the very conception of property as an individual and exclusive right in the soil is unknown.

At the time of the British conquest, even those rights that are apparently recognized as transferable do not seem to be very commonly sold in actual practice. Regulation I of 1793 (the Permanent Settlement) specifies that the estates of the zamindars will be transferable, and adds that they were not so earlier.[10] A quarter of a century later, after patnidars (intermediary tenure-holders) had begun to proliferate between zamindars and raiyats, patni tenures were given legal recognition,[11] and a specific section of the Regulation again declared them transferable (while raiyati tenures remained unsaleable). Such explicit statements in the law cannot but lead to the conclusion, as Justice Field wrote in 1875, that rights in land, during the early period of British rule, were not ordinarily transferable.[12]

Two fairly obvious reasons were usually put forward to account for this fact. The first was that land had little or no market value because there was plenty of arable land available: it was labour, not land, that was scarce (a theoretical assumption, however, that may have been liable to exceptions in the case of the oldest and most fertile agricultural regions and of peri-urban areas). The rural money-lender, around 1790, did not normally lend money to the cultivator on the security of his land, but of his crop, or occasionally other movables.[13] Under circumstances of oppression or famine, a raiyat who was able to give up his land and go out in search of a more considerate master or a less severely stricken area, usually found land and employment elsewhere without difficulty.[14] The instances of sale prices of land rights which have survived from the seventeenth and eighteenth centuries are extraordinarily low. In the seventeenth century, a zamindari would rarely sell for a sum exceeding the land revenue demand of two years, and occasionally for half this amount.[15] In the eighteenth century, prices were still lower. The power and wealth of a local chief then varied more according to the number of his raiyats and the area they could cultivate than to the total area of land he could claim as his domain.[16] This was still true in North Bihar at the beginning of the nineteenth century. The Collector of Saran complained in 1806 that the raiyats of his district were migrating into Gorakhpur, where rents were lower, and was persuaded by the local zamindars to report the fact to the government so that such unfair competition on the part of the Gorakhpur zamindars might be checked by official measures.[17] In a frontier district like Champaran, special rates were offered as late as the end of the nineteenth century to tenants who agreed to settle on waste lands,[18] and then only peasants began to migrate into the malarious northern tracts of the district from the overcrowded regions of Saran, Gorakhpur and Nepal.[19] It goes without saying that land, one century earlier, had practically no value in Champaran.

The other alleged reason for the absence of a significant land market is the heaviness of the land revenue and other taxes and exactions, at least since the Mughal conquest. Mughal sources tend to show that the fiscal demand was usually fixed so as to coincide more or less with the total surplus produce of the peasant. The fraction of the gross product which could be levied as revenue from the village without endangering the cultivator's survival could vary considerably according to soil, climate, social conditions, etc., from place to place. That proportion was a customary figure well known to everyone in each particular region. It could stand anywhere between a third and three-quarters of the gross product. In addition to this usually came miscellaneous dues and levies, either recognized by custom or exceptional and imposed by force.[20] In the princely states of British India, where pre-colonial traditions of government had survived to a large extent, sometimes with enhanced severity, as the princes were guaranteed against any popular upheaval within their territories by the paramount power, the fiscal demand almost always amounted to half the gross product or more. A tax burden of such magnitude may undoubtedly go a long way to explain why the value of land remained consistently insignificant before the colonial period.[21]

Yet purely economic arguments such as these leave part of the question unanswered, because they ignore its ideological aspect. They seem to imply that wherever in India the density of population increases and the fiscal demand grows lighter, land must automatically acquire value even if it had none previously. In other words, it is assumed that quantitative variables at some point may bring about qualitative change, and that land, hitherto not normally considered as saleable, but now becoming scarce and a profitable investment, spontaneously turns into a marketable commodity. The trouble is that by reducing the whole process to a question of supply and demand, one actually presupposes the existence (at least virtual) of the market, while the question may be asked at first whether the very conception of land as a saleable commodity is present in the minds of men. In the princely states at the end of the nineteenth century, for instance, not only did land have little or no price, but in many cases the right to sell land was not recognized. In some of the more important states, such as Mysore and Hyderabad, however, land was occasionally sold, though the right to sell was not officially recognized. And in a few cases, it *was* recognized, a feature which a government report of 1895 interpreted as a consequence of the 'modernization' of certain states.[22] Obviously, the genesis of the land market was still in the preliminary stages at that time in the princely states, and it was a process of ideological change as much as a question of supply and demand.

The idea that any man can as a matter of course gain legitimate control over a piece of land by mere purchase is everywhere a modern idea. In the *smṛti* and specialized Hindu treatises, it is more than once said that land belongs to the man who cleared it.[23] When the officers of the Settlement Department of North Bihar compiled village histories in the course of the first survey and settlement operations (late nineteenth early twentieth centuries), they often heard the local dominant peasants trace their descent back to the founder of their village, to the first settler who originally cleared the land in the jungle, at a date which no one was usually able to specify.[24] It is difficult to extricate historical fact from myth in such cases. But what matters here is that by referring, whether rightly or not, to the man who first brought the land into cultivation as their ancestor, those peasants implicitly sought to establish their legitimate right to occupy that land, in conformity with the accepted norm. The other traditional basis of property in India, according to B.H. Baden-Powell, is conquest.[25] This principle can hardly figure in such explicit formulation in Brahmanical tradition, but the Rajputs, in Tod's time, used to lay stress on the landowning rights they enjoyed as conquerors of the soil.[26] And the lawfulness of ownership by conquest is fully recognized by Islamic law.

Historically speaking, the distinction between conquest and colonization cannot have been hard and fast. They were one and the same thing when conquest meant the occupation of virgin or depopulated land. They were closely related when colonization of marginal lands granted to minor branches of a conquering lineage followed the military conquest itself.[27] Where the conquered land was already inhabited and cultivated, the conqueror had of course no other title to the control of the land than the assertion of superior might. Yet even then, something of the right of the first settler could survive: conquest, at the village level, did not as a rule mean dispossession, but merely subordination of the former dominant groups, who were left in possession of their lands, though with a dependent status.[28] But in any case, priority of settlement could offer no protection against invasion by a stronger party. To hold land, fundamentally, was to wield power.

This being so, it is no wonder that the transfer of land in India during the early decades of British rule should have appeared to European observers as subject to severe customary restrictions. Thomas Fortescue, for instance, speaking of the Jat villages of the Delhi

Territory, where traditions of kin solidarity were strong, wrote in 1820:

> A sharer cannot dispose of his landed property by bequest or gift, nor introduce a stranger without the general acquiescence of the pana or thola, or other division to which he belongs, nor sell it until the sharers thereof in succession up from each superior division have rejected it on the terms proposed, and to themselves meet. In farming, mortgaging, placing in trust, deposit or management and the like, the tacit will of the brotherhood is sufficient; but neither these modes of temporary relinquishment nor the absolute estrangement of it for ever by sale are prevalent.[29]

In other words, the co-sharers as a body had a right of veto on all forms of transfer, whether temporary or permanent. In cases of transfer by sale, they enjoyed in addition a right of pre-emption. All transactions involving land were thus heavily restricted by considerations of power, which stood in the way of the emergence of a free self-regulated land market.

The main cause of land transfer was already indebtedness. But the private sale of land for debt was still far from an established procedure. Land mortgages were common. But the money-lender's only easily realizable security was the debtor's crop and cattle, not his land, which he did not hold as an individual and exclusive proprietor in the modern sense of the word, and thus could hardly sell to outsiders. The mortgage of the land could only serve to strengthen the money-lender's hold on the produce. The *mitākṣarā* law, which was in force in the greater part of the Gangetic plain (outside Bengal), moreover, debarred the head of a family from mortgaging the family land unless under serious obligation and in the interest of the family as a whole. If this condition was not fulfilled, the relatives and descendants of the borrower were not to be held accountable for the latter's debt after his death. Lastly, the prevalent rule of *dāmdupat* prevented a money-lender from claiming as interest an amount larger than the principal. Custom left to itself was thus hardly conducive to the development of private sales for debt.[30]

It must then be explained why the zamindari right stands out as freely alienable as early as Akbar's time, if not earlier. A zamindar collected the land revenue on a well defined territory on behalf of the sovereign.

His remuneration consisted in a grant of revenue-free land, or in a fixed share in the land revenue which his territory yielded. His right co-existed with other rights on the same soil, and was conditional on the punctual delivery of the land revenue he had been appointed to collect. In other words, it was by no means a right of property, it did not challenge the right of occupation of those who lived on the land or tilled it, and when it was sold, it was not the land that changed hands, but only the right to collect the land revenue from it.[31] Many transfers of zamindaris of which a trace has survived in the archives concerned in fact the territories of defaulting or rebellious zamindars, which were confiscated by the sovereign power and granted to other personalities.[32] The low level of the sale prices shows that such sales of zamindaris did not take place within the framework of a market in the strict sense. The amounts quoted rather call to mind the idea of the *salāmī* by which the applicant for an appointment ensured the formal recognition of the authority he approached, and the total of which varied according to the status of this authority and to the standing of the candidate.

When the British arrived in the Gangetic plain, the situation, in short, was the following: land transfers were of rare occurrence, and when they did take place they belonged rather to the political than to the economic sphere, as they involved local transfers of power, and there was no such thing as a price of land based on a prevalent mechanism of supply and demand. In a word, the land market did not exist. The pre-1793 settlements of the East India Company did not alter structurally this state of things. But the Permanent Settlement of 1793, as is well known, marked a new departure. The zamindars were made landlords and vested with full proprietary rights in the Western sense. The amount of the revenue demand was fixed forever. From this the government logically expected a rapid rise in the value of the new estates, as any surplus income accruing from cultivation would now revert entirely to the landlord instead of benefiting the State. As a result, the government felt justified in demanding punctual payment of the land revenue. The estates of defaulting landlords would be at once put to auction (in 1799, however, it was decided that only so much of the estates as was necessary to make up for the sanctioned arrears would be attached). The authors of the Permanent Settlement were quite prepared to see the estates thus slip from the hands of the less enterprising zamindars and pass into those of the more efficient, competitive landlords, who alone could instil a new life into the agricultural economy of Bengal.[33] But the level of the revenue demand was too high for a province that still had to recover from the anarchy of the past decades and the hecatomb of the great famine of 1769-70. A high rate of revenue sales at once set in. It went on during two decades, then swiftly slowed down.[34] In Orissa, as far as can be inferred from the fragmentary statistics available, more than half of the 3,000 local zamindars (whose estates were settled in 1804) were swept away in fifteen years. There is reason to believe that the percentage of dispossessed zamindars was of equal magnitude in the rest of the province between 1793-94 and 1806-07.[35] The percentage, however, was probably lower in Bihar proper. In Champaran, which was almost entirely made up of three vast zamindaris at that time, the number of sales was naturally insignificant. In Tirhut, which comprised about 2000 estates in the early years of the nineteenth century, the figures were as follows during the three worst years:

in 1801 54 estates, or 2.7 per cent;
in 1802 119 estates, or 5.6 per cent;
in 1803 99 estates, or 4.9 per cent.

The total thereafter approximated to ten sales per year (0.5 per cent).[36] The overall average in the district was distinctly lower than the total Bengal average during the said period. These figures relate to public sales. Of private sales at that time nothing is known, though it may be surmised that they were infrequent.

These revenue sales, though numerous at times, were no equivalent to a coherent, open land market. They were forced sales, which means that the supply was not competitive. Free sale had not yet become habitual. The auctions were fairly well attended around Calcutta. But bidders were few in the outlying stations. Francis Buchanan, reporting on the Patna-Gaya area, observed in 1812:

> The assessed land has not yet become a very saleable property. Within these five years, the Collector of Bihar has put up to public auction 72 lots, paying an annual revenue of Rs.33,777, and the whole price has been Rs.53,152, and for no less than 10 of the lots no bidder appeared, and the lands fell into the Company's hands.[37]

In the southern district of Guntur, which had been brought under the zamindari system at the beginning of the nineteenth century, the Collector still noted as late as 1820 that 'no lands of whatever description are usually bought and sold either publicly or by private contract'.[38] Such a case had become exceptional by that date, but the situation described by Buchanan was much more common.

In a fully constituted open market, prices, in theory, are self-regulated, and vary according to supply and demand. All goods of the given category are considered as saleable, and have a theoretical market value which can be determined by expert valuation in relation to the current trend of prices. In the case of land in Company Bengal, prices were either derisively low or non-existent, because land was not generally recognized as a commodity. This can be accounted for in terms of market economy. It may be said that capital kept away from land because trade with Europe or government loans made more profitable investment; that the land revenue still weighed too heavily upon the landlords and that the legal provisions against the defaulters were too dissuasive; that the profitableness of agriculture remained too low, etc.[39] There undoubtedly were potential purchasers of land who reasoned along these lines among the Calcutta entrepreneurs and the Indian officials of the Company (particularly the tahsildars) who were the 'nouveaux riches' of the time. But such people were an insignificant minority. Cultural obstacles to the rise of a land market were just as important as purely economic considerations.

One major reason which dissuaded bidders from attending the public auctions was that it was often difficult for a purchaser to take possession of the land he had bought. In a normal competitive self-regulated market, the tendency of buyer and seller must be as far as possible to set aside personal considerations so as to reach an agreement on business-like terms, both agreeing implicitly on the objective rules of the modern contractual game. While in early nineteenth-century Bengal, land control remained in essence what it had been at all times, that is power over a stretch of land and its inhabitants, legitimized by such considerations as conquest, antiquity of settlement, length of occupation, and so on, the man who purchased land at a public sale after its 'legitimate' owner had been forced to part with it was not unnaturally viewed as an intruder and an usurper, unless he managed to compel recognition by force, which possibly brought everybody back to the more familiar situation of a conflict for power. Cases when defaulting zamindars violently opposed their property being sold by order of the court were numerous after the passing of the Permanent Settlement.[40] In the 24-Parganas as late as the 1830s, the Collector found it most difficult to recover arrears of revenue by putting up shares of estates for auction. No other member of the family of the defaulting co-sharer would dare come forward as a bidder by fear of being outcasted. And a stranger who ventured to do so incurred public reprobation and even physical reprisals for dispossessing the legitimate owner of the land. It happened that a purchaser at auction was eventually forced to give up and return the land to its former owner by private agreement.[41] The buyer of a share was frequently sued by his new co-sharers. Such behaviour was just as prevalent outside the permanently-settled area. In Kanpur district around 1820, a new zamindar rarely dared settle in a village he had recently bought. He would rather employ an agent 'who, backed by the authority of government, is able to realize revenue, and seize upon everything visible and tangible'. 'With the interior domestic economy of the village he (the agent) dare not, however, for his life interfere ... (and) possesses no influence but what the fear of the Darogah inspires'.[42] Auction sales in Shahabad district in Bihar in the 1880s were still dominated by considerations of power: as a rule, one local magnate would make a bid for the land, and all competition would be instantly silenced.[43] Obviously, the land market in such cases worked only in a formal way, in pursuance of legal provisions whose spirit was foreign to the local mind.

More evidence on this point could be adduced if it could be shown conclusively that private sales remained exceptional. The data are unfortunately very scanty on private sales until the last third of the nineteenth century, when land transfers began to be officially registered. We know nevertheless that they were insignificant in number in Midnapur district between 1837 and 1851: the average annual number of private sales was 46, as against 33 public sales.[44] Reference can be made for purposes of comparison to the case of Punjab, where private sales between 1870 and 1874 did not yet exceed the figure of 6,000 per year, while there were 2,006,670 landholders in the province, the average area of land thus transferred amounting to less than one acre per square mile.[45] It must be added that these private sales were only apparently voluntary: most of them were due to the pressure of inextricable indebtedness and to the apprehended action of the courts in decreeing excessive interest.[46] More conclusive evidence can be found in the attitude of the small holders in periods of famine. Land being already saleable under the law, it seems natural that the small zamindars, in times of great stress, should have borrowed on the security of their property, and that many of them should have eventually sold their land. Yet such was not the case in the North-Western Provinces in the 1830s, as Colonel R. Baird Smith wrote in his famous report on the famine of 1860-61:

> The poorer landholders who, in 1860-61, were just able to struggle through the time of greatest need, suffered in 1837-38 as bitterly as did the mere labourers and artizans now. Large numbers of them died of starvation and I find it specially noted that among the 80,000 paupers employed or supported by the magistrate of Agra, a very large proportion was of small proprietors. This was the natural result of their social condition at the time .... Their land was utterly useless unless they could cultivate it; it had no market price, for no man would buy it, or make advances upon it as security, so that their only resource was to become paupers or perish.

In 1860-61, on the other hand, even though the demographic pressure on the soil had grown and grain prices were higher, the number of casualties was lower, and the small holders as a whole fared better through the calamity. The reason for the difference was

> the creation ... of a vast mass of readily convertible and easily transferable agricultural property, as the direct result of the limitation for long terms of the Government demand on the land, and the careful record of individual rights accompanying it, which have been in full and active operation since the existing settlements were made.[47]

Economic factors undoubtedly played their part in this process (the alleviation of the fiscal demand), but side by side with a change of mentality induced by legislation, which tended to turn the land into a commodity, identified and defined as a mere thing, and dissociated from the idea of sovereignty. The report of the Royal Commission on Agriculture in India (1928) later described this evolution as an all-India phenomenon:

> When famine came, it was not the land which was sold;

> the cattle and household goods were disposed of, ornaments were pledged and, when these resources were exhausted, the people deserted their villages and their fields, and wandered in search of food.

Things have changed in a striking fashion, the report goes on to say, particularly since the famine of 1866-67, which was devastating in Bihar. As a result of a whole set of changes, voluntary sales of private property on the open market are becoming common, and small land-holders are now conspicuous by their absence from the famine relief works.[48]

In the course of the nineteenth century, a regular land market did effectively take shape, though in a slow and uneven fashion. Land progressively acquired value, and the trend of land transfers, after the Mutiny, was rising fast everywhere in British India. This evolution proceeded from a complex array of general causes linked with the strengthening of the Pax Britannica, which it would be out of place to review at length here. The first category of factors consisted in the movement of the demographic and agricultural trends: growing pressure of population on the land, extension of the cultivated area and of the acreage under cash crops, long-term rise of the agricultural prices. The second general cause was the development of infrastructures conducive to agri-cultural growth: irrigation and transport networks, and especially railways, which connected isolated rural areas with the wider world, and boosted up the trade in agri-cultural produce. Thirdly, the rise of the land market was fostered by a continous trend of modernizing legis-lation, which placed the people in increasingly secure possession of the land, destroyed the transitional ob-stacles to its commercialization, and systematized the law of mortgages and alienations for debt according to Wes-tern usage. The rules relative to the revenue sale of estates had been gradually mitigated. As early as 1799, payment of the land revenue by monthly instalments had been replaced by annual payment, which eased somewhat the situation of the zamindars, who until then had been running twelve times a year the risk of having their property attached for shortage of cash. Moreover, the same law (Regulation VII) of 1799 had given the zamindars the right to call in the police and distrain the property of their tenants or tenure-holders in case of overdue rents. This summary procedure, being much quicker than law suits, was of great utility to the zamindars in avoiding their estates being put up for auction. Act XII of 1841 further abolished the levy of interest on arrears of revenue, as well as the fines which defaulting landlords incurred. Public sales, by that time, had already become exceptional. The fixed fiscal demand established in 1793 had grown lighter. The purchasers of estates were becoming more confident, and the value of zamindaris was slowly increasing.

Simultaneously, fresh legislation was being passed with a view to clearing the way for a free development of private sales, beginning with sales for debt, which were considered as legitimate from the point of view of the creditors, and as beneficial to the economy at large, land being thus expected to pass into the hands of the more enterprising capitalists. The traditional restrictions limiting land transfers (rule of *dāmdupat*, provisions of the *mitākṣarā* regarding mortgages and the alienation of family property) were nevertheless respected until the middle of the nineteenth century. But the Repeal of Usury Laws (Act XXVIII of 1855) abolished the traditional limitation of interest rates, paving the way for the final release of sales for debt from all restrictions. The juridicial position of creditors was substantially strengthened by the Civil Procedure Code, which came into force in 1859, and by Act XI of the same year. Conflicts of interpretation inevitably ensued, as a result of the contradictions between the new legislation and the *mitākṣarā*, whose provisions were theoretically still in force, on the subject of transfers for debt. Those provisions were ultimately disallowed during the 1870s by orders of the Privy Council and subsequent jurisprudence. The codification of transfers was finalized in the Transfer of Property Act (Act IV of 1882), in which the principle of the sale of land and of four categories of mortgages was unambiguously defined. The procedure of registration, which placed regular transfers beyond dispute, had been instituted earlier by the Indian Registration Act of 1866. During these years of change, the accessibility of modern justice had somewhat improved in the Indian countryside. With all this legal and judicial apparatus, the institutional framework necessary to the development of a regular land market had come into operation, while the value of land was increasing everywhere.

From the second third of the nineteenth century, and especially after the Mutiny, as the volume of land transactions and the trend of land prices conclusively show, a real open market for land began to take shape. Statistics of public sales in nineteenth-century Bengal have been compiled by B.B. Chaudhuri from the correspondence and reports of the provincial Land Revenue Department.[49] I have drawn two graphs on the basis of his figures. They show that the average prices of zamindari land went up in two distinct phases (page 90). One begins in 1805, a year when a zamindari would sell on an average for less than one year's land revenue demand, and culminates in 1814, when the average sale price reached seven times this figure. The average then oscillates until the beginning of the 1850s, only showing a very slow declining trend. Then a new rise begins (c.1850 to c.1870), which raises the average price to approximately ten times the annual land revenue demand. After 1870, the average again decreases slightly, and settles down around six or seven times the annual demand. This latter decline is of course unexpected. It is due to the fact that the nature of the sales, by then, had changed. From then on, land becoming a very valuable asset, hard pressed landlords could resort to the money-lender on a wider scale than before, and avoided sales by all means at their disposal. Estates were sold only when deteriorated by floods or other calamities, or when hopelessly involved, or else in case of acute conflict between co-sharers. In this last instance, it often happened that a powerful co-sharer declared his intention to buy the disputed property, and that no one from the outside dared outbid him, so that the land was undersold. In other cases, the sale prices were also abnormally low, and did not truly reflect the prevalent market rates, of which private sales alone, now much more common than before, could give an accurate idea.[50]

Around 1900, the annual acreage and average price per acre of the proprietary rights privately and publicly sold in the seven districts of North Bihar were as follows: [51]

| *District* | *Area sold as % of total assessed area* | *Sale price per acre (Rs.)* | *Sale price as compared to average annual rent rate* |
|---|---|---|---|
| Champaran | 5.0 | 23-5-1 | |
| Saran | 1.4 | 50-0-0 | 12 times |
| Muzaffarpur | 0.6 | 95-5-2 | + than 20 times |
| Darbhanga | 0.9 | 59-0-0 | 16 times |
| Monghyr | 1.2 | 38-0-0 | |
| Bhagalpur | 1.6 | 32-0-0 | |
| Purnea | 1.6 | 14-8-0 | |

*Graph 1.* Average sale price of zamindari land as multiple of the land revenue demand: annual fluctuation and seven year moving average (1795-96/1826-27)

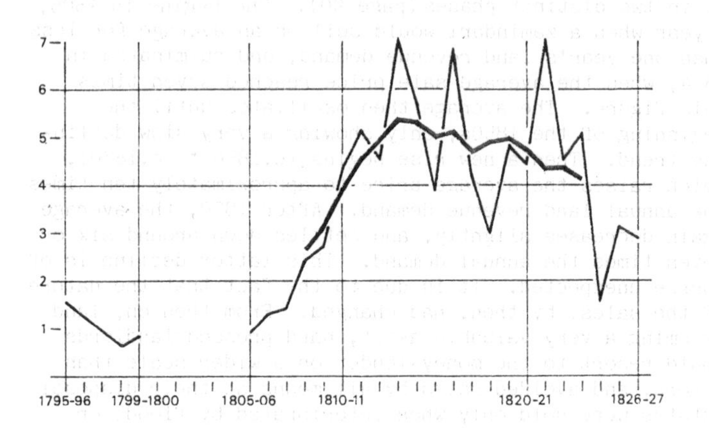


*Graph 2.* Average sale price of zamindari land as multiple of the land revenue demand: quinquennial averages (1848-1894)

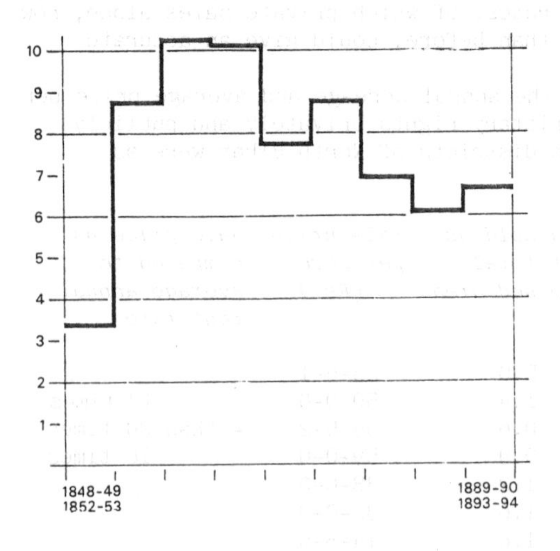

The price figures remained abnormally low in Bhagalpur, Monghyr and Purnea districts on account of exceptional circumstances. In Champaran, the smallness of the average price and the vastness of the area transferred were due to the peculiar conditions that prevailed at tha time in this 'frontier' district. Two simple general observations can nevertheless be made. The relatively homogeneous percentage of the district's assessed area that changed hands annually (1 to 2 per cent in round numbers, leaving aside the Champaran case) shows that the land market had begun to operate with some uniformity all over the region, due allowance being made for normal local variations. The time when land was saleable in some parts and unsaleable in others is past. Secondly, the average value of the land in North Bihar around 1900, as compared to the rate of rent, appears to have been much higher than the Greater Bengal average of the 1850s and 1860s compared to the revenue demand. The difference is even greater than the figures actually show, as the rent rate per acre is considerably higher than the revenue demand per acre, in this permanently-settled area where the latter figure was exceptionally stable.

Twenty years later, in the districts of Champaran and Saran, the figures were as follows:[52]

| *District* | *Area sold as % of total assessed area* | *Sale price per acre (Rs.)* | *Sale price as compared to average annual rent rate* |
|---|---|---|---|
| Champaran | 1.8 | 50-0-0 | 20 to 25 times |
| Saran | 0.8 | 79-9-10 | ? |

The Champaran figures were then drawing close to the regional average, as the population of the district had increased considerably in twenty years. The average value of proprietary rights had doubled. In Saran, it had gone up by 50 per cent.

The land market in North Bihar at the beginning of the twentieth century thus worked by and large in a regular manner. But a gap still existed between the outwardly modern functioning of the market and the signification that the people still attached to the transfers. The sale of land, though a perfectly legal procedure, was not yet commonly viewed as normal. A high percentage of the transfers resulted from mortgage foreclosures or disputes between co-sharers. Purchasers from the outside still found it difficult to take possession of their new lands. Obstruction on the part of the former holders was no longer violent as a rule. But an outsider who bought a share in a joint property usually had a hard time with the other partners. They might either refuse to pay their share of the land revenue when it fell due, which forced the newcomer to pay alone for them all lest the whole estate be put up for sale, or to sue them, and get involved in court proceedings that would drag on for years and cost him a fortune. Another obstacle they might put in his way, a vestigial form of war as it were, consisted in setting the raiyats against him. These difficulties kept the market value of proprietary rights lower than normal.[53] The transferors who mostly sold under compulsion, still considered themselves more legitimate occupiers of the land than the transferees even after the sales had taken place, a state of mind which has been perfectly analysed by Auckland Colvin in his Memorandum of 1872 when dealing with transfers in the North-Western Provinces.[54] In short, tensions of an ideological nature still interfered with the working of the land market instituted by modern colonial legislation, in spite of the demographic and economic trends which stimulated the competition for land.

It must be admitted, moreover, that the level of activity of the market remained very low. Around 1900, except in Champaran district, where the percentage was to fall to the level of the Bihar average twenty years later, not more than 1.6 per cent of the assessed area of any district was ever sold annually. This may mean two different things (which are not mutually exclusive): for one thing, in spite of the facilities given by the law of alienations, the rise of the land market may have been effectively slowed down by the difficulties which the purchasers experienced when taking possession of their lands. Secondly, men of capital may have had other ways, less fraught with risks and trouble, to acquire the control of land, than purchase. One specific feature of this period was the steeply rising trend of mortgages. This form of loan was all the more popular as it was fully sanctioned by traditional usage, and generated profit and influence as effectively as purchase. In a time when the value of land was continuously increasing and when two landholders out of three got into debt,[55] the scope of investment of the money-lender was exceptionally vast. Whether professional or occasional money-lender, he often found it more convenient to let his debtor get hopelessly involved and sink into debt-bondage than foreclose his mortgage and attempt to replace the owner. The indebted owner thus remained in formal possession of the land. If he was a cultivating owner, he went on cultivating it, but his labour and crops now belonged entirely to the money-lender, and the latter was now the real decision-maker on the farm.[56] In this case again, the land market worked in a lopsided fashion, because traditional conceptions ran counter to its normal course.

This discrepancy became even more manifest around 1880 when the question of the transferability of raiyati rights was brought up officially. The public mind, confirmed by traditional law, had it that a tenant who had been cultivating his land uninterruptedly for a long time and who paid his rent had the right to remain on that land, since a man who labours on a piece of land and makes it bear fruit has the first claim on its crops and is entitled to live on it.[57] Nevertheless, tenant rights were subordinate rights and could not be freely disposed of (the term raiyat is an Arabic word which simply means 'subject').[58] John Shore, in his famous minute of 18 June 1789, had made the point that, in his time, a cultivator, by prolonged occupation of a piece of land, acquired a right to its possession, and could not legally be evicted, but that this right did not entitle him to either mortgage or sell the land. Yet one century later, occupancy rights had become in fact alienable. Justice C.D. Field, an indisputable authority in such matters at the time, thus explained how this radical change in accepted usage had come about.[59] In the first place, the estates of the landlords had been declared alienable by law. The intermediary (patni) tenures followed suit some time later. Then came the turn of the tenures of defaulting raiyats, which were declared transferable whenever a zamindar wished to evict and replace a tenant by the procedure of a sale, a convenient device in effect when land was becoming scarce and labour overabundant. From the transferability of raiyati rights on request of the landlords, an easy transition led to the sale of rights by the raiyats themselves with the consent of their landlrods, and then, as the demand for land was growing, to sale without consent. This schematic outline of the evolution of jurisprudence is credible, though the pace of the process must have varied widely from one district to another, and it had not yet completed its course everywhere by the time Field wrote.

According to the Famine Commission of 1880, the transferability of occupancy rights had by then become a fact, and was bound to be sooner or later recognized by the law.[60] The sale of occupancy rights had effectively become common in the districts of the Calcutta region and in Eastern Bengal, both regions which were considered as more advanced than the rest of the province. It was less common in North Bengal, and much less in Bihar. The settlement operations of 1892-99 in Champaran district showed that no such sale had ever occurred in that district before 1880, and that they remained unknown in a great many villages right up to the end of the century.[61] In Bihar as a whole, the area of occupancy rights that was sold at the beginning of the 1880s remained very small (5,752 acres out of a cultivated area of 13.5 million acres in 1883).[62] In fact, as late as the 1870s, occupancy rights themselves were to a large extent unrecognized by the landlords. Such was the case in Muzaffarpur[63] and Champaran districts for instance, where the landlords usually leased out their lands for a maximum of seven years (whereas no tenant could claim a right of occupancy unless he had held the same land continuously for a minimum of twelve years), and were careful to move their tenants about often enough from one plot of land to another within the village area in order to prevent any occupancy rights accruing from prolonged occupation of the same plots by the same tenants. The raiyats everywhere gave in submissively, out of fear, to whatever their landlords decided, and had no idea of the rights they enjoyed under the law.[64]

The question of the transferability of occupancy rights was widely debated, not only in the official spheres, but also in the larger professional associations and in the press (many newspapers acted as mouthpieces for such associations, being financed by them), during the long period when the Bengal Tenancy Bill was being discussed and framed. Full recognition of the principle of transferability was advocated by those who wished to open the land market wider and to clear it from all obstacles. The raiyat, they said, would at last be able to draw the best price from his land if he decided to sell it. He would in any case be made to feel more like a real property owner, and would thus become a more enterprising and energetic cultivator. On the other hand, the principle was opposed by those who feared that the transferability of occupancy rights, once officially recognized, would turn loose the crowd of money-lenders and absentee speculators who were believed to be waiting eagerly for such an opportunity, and would moreover unjustifiably deprive the landlords of part of their traditional authority.[65] It was also pointed out by the opponents of the measure that the land which money-lenders acquired was usually mortgaged land which they bought after foreclosure at wholly inadequate prices, because the sales mostly took place at distant courts, where the real value of the land right in question was not known, and where potential buyers had no desire to compete with the moneyed man who held the mortgage.[66] Eminent zamindars and landholders' associations were officially called upon to give their opinion. They denied at first that free sales of occupancy rights had ever occurred in Bengal. Statistical evidence was then produced to show that they did occur in most districts, though they were not equally frequent everywhere. The zamindars then objected that such sales were conditional on their authorization. A new enquiry was ordered on this point, which showed that wherever transfers of occupancy rights were common, the zamindars' consent was rarely if ever applied for. At best, they levied a fee for the mutation of names in their registers, but often even this was not requested by the purchasers. When the debate was wound up, the authors of the Bill eventually chose to put off action, and leave time for the practice to spread evenly throughout the province, rather than to precipitate matters and to risk running into political trouble with the zamindars. Section 183 of the Bengal Tenancy Act of 1885 thus laid down that the question of the transferability of occupancy rights with or without the landlord's consent was to be left to custom.

This voluntary lacuna in the provisions of the new law meant that the final stage in the liberalization of the land market was not yet reached, though it was drawing close. The relationship between landlord and tenant had been entirely cast in the mould of contractual law, except in one respect, the right of a landlord to choose his own dependents, which was rooted in the traditional conception of the landlord as a power-holder, and which the growing commercialization of occupancy rights was tending to obliterate. The landlords were given a free hand to defend this privilege wherever they could call forth local customary usage as a warrant for their claim. But they soon discovered that this favour was not an unmixed blessing. No one could say what the custom relative to transfers of raiyati holdings was in any particular village, that is to say whether such transfers required the consent of the landlord to be deemed valid. Wherever disputes arose on this point, and there were multitudes of them, the courts had to determine the cases on very doubtful grounds, thus creating questionable precedents. It became a frequent complaint that similar cases were decided by different munsifs in different ways, or even by the same munsif in adjoining villages.

> The existing provision in favour of custom [the Commissioner of Patna observed] was merely an evasion of the difficulty. It was introduced, I believe, as being a convenient compromise between the exponents of the ryots' interest on the one side and the landlord party on the other. The results are so anomalous as to reflect discredit on the law which, as it now stands, leads only to uncertainty and litigation.[67]

Most of the time, however, the courts decided the cases in favour of the landlords who denied their tenants freedom of transfer. But the habit of transfer without consent had already become too deeply ingrained to be stopped by court proceedings. Thanks to the Bengal Tenancy Act, tenant rights were now better defined and more secure than they had ever been, and had become easier still to mortgage and sell. The statistics exhibit a general increase of the transfers of occupancy rights after 1885, a rise which cannot be accounted for only by the stricter application of the rules relative to registration.[68] In Bengal proper, even the under-raiyats, after acquiring occupancy rights in their plots of land, had now begun selling their rights when too much indebted. And the courts now tended to recognize the transferability of these subordinate rights as a fact, though it was ignored by the law. The tendency towards the commercialization of tenant rights was also clear in Bihar, as the following figures show:[69]

| *Districts* | *Number of sales of occupancy rights* | |
|---|---|---|
| | *1883-84* | *1892-93* |
| Patna | 77 | 646 |
| Gaya | 173 | 252 |
| Shahabad | 73 | 28 |
| Muzaffarpur | 988 | 5224 |
| Darbhanga | 356 | 1368 |
| Saran | 39 | 152 |
| Champaran | 261 | 6590 |

The zamindars of Bihar still went on denying, in the name of custom, the lawfulness of these transfers. In Muzaffarpur district during the survey and settlement operations of 1892-9, they admitted such transfers as regular in 257 villages out of 3,737 (6.8 per cent). But it was found that occupancy rights had effectively been transferred in 2,881 villages (77 per cent). The landlords were only half prone to appeal to the courts in such cases, as legal proceedings were expensive and lengthy, and especially hard to bear for the smaller among them, who were by far the majority. They merely refused to effect the mutation of names. But the purchaser of a tenure could very well do without. In this case, the former tenant retained his formal title to the possession of the land, and remained nominally accountable for the rental. The purchaser often kept him on the land as a sharecropper on very harsh terms, and paid out the amount of the rent in his place. Many landlords, in fact, instead of persisting in useless obstruction by refusing the mutation of names, preferred to make money out of what remained of their traditional power, and granted their consent to the buyers on receipt of a substantial salami, or on condition of acceptance of enhanced rents. Moreover, hostile though they were to those transfers when their own authority was at stake, they were prompt to make the most out of the rising market when it was to their interest to do so. Many purchasers of occupancy rights were actually small prosperous zamindars engaged in money-lending, who were busy widening their field of operations by acquiring raiyati rights in their neighbourhood.[70]

The number of sales of occupancy rights continued to go up without break during the early years of the twentieth century. The market attained full regularity during the 1920s. In spite of the persisting insecurity of the purchasers' legal title on the raiyati lands they bought, and of the heaviness of the salamis, the market had become remarkably brisk: 1,125,000 acres of occupancy rights were sold in Bihar and Orissa alone between 1923 and 1928. The average price of the acre was steadily increasing, and reached Rs.192 in Bihar in 1928, a figure reasonably close to the real value of an acre of average arable land. Taking into account the monetary depreciation which had set in before the first World War, the average price of an acre of occupancy right, on the eve of the depression of the 1930s, had gone up by 50 per cent in 25 years.[71]

The transferability of occupancy rights having become

an indisputable fact everywhere, the matter, hitherto left to custom, was again taken up officially, and brought within the scope of modern law. The landlords' customary right of intervention was still acknowledged, but kept from now on within closely defined bounds. Section 26b of the Bengal Tenancy (Amendment) Act of 1928 gave official recognition to the principle of the transferability of occupancy rights, which no landlord thereafter could refuse to admit. The payment of a salami (termed 'landlord's fee') by the purchaser was made compulsory, but the rate of the fee was fixed. The landlord was given a right of pre-emption on any tenure put up for sale on his estate. The tenures of the under-raiyats were also declared transferable, subject to the landlord's consent. Ten years later, in 1938, a new amendment act abolished all restrictions to transfers of both categories of rights, and all rights of intervention of the landlords in the free market of raiyati rights were disallowed.[72]

The legal framework for a free market of raiyati rights was then in operation, as had been the case for proprietary rights since the preceding century. Land, under the law, was now a mere commodity, which could change hands by ordinary contract, no allowance being made any longer for interfering considerations of power. In other words, rights in land being stripped of their traditional political connotations, now belonged exclusively to the world of economic exchange. Legal change, of course, does not transferm mechanically human values and feelings. But it is a fact that the control of land, within the framework of modern legislation, could no more be regarded as synonymous with legitimate sovereignty over the men who peopled that land. This raises some questions as to the kind of 'power' which is left today to the dominant castes, who are still said to hold sway over their villages on account, among other things, of their pre-eminent hold on the land. The rise of the modern bureaucratic state in India under colonial rule has meant that power, that is to say the privilege to use force legitimately, which was previously fragmented along an unstable chain of intermediate and local powerholders, was progressively monopolized by the central governmental structure. The transformation of land into a commodity, and the concomitant disappearance of the idea of sovereignty previously attached to land control, were but an aspect of this transition. The evolution has not yet completed its course, as is shown for instance by the customary judicial prerogatives which the dominant castes still often enjoy at the local level side by side with the official judicial system. But the man who controls the land is now legally bound to use contractual procedures in all his business dealings with his partners and dependents. And the peasants, in the course of the present century, have become increasingly aware of the rights they enjoy under the law. But ample scope is of course left for economic oppression within the bounds of contractual norms, not to speak of open disregard of the law.

## *NOTES*

Pouchepadass, 'Land, power and market: the rise of the land market in Gangetic India'

*Abbreviations*

| | |
|---|---|
| BEC | *Report of the Bihar-and-Orissa Provincial Banking Enquiry Committee, 1929-30* (Patna 1930), 3 vols. |
| DRC | *Report of the Committee on the Riots in Poona and Ahmednagar, 1875 (Deccan Riots Commission Report* (Bombay 1876), 2 vols. |
| Field, 'Note' | C.D. Field, *A digest of the Law of Landlord and Tenant in Bengal* (Calcutta 1879), app.1: 'Note on the Transferability of Ryots' Holdings'. |
| IFC | *Report of the Indian Famine Commission*, 1880, London, 1880-85, 3pts. |
| NLT | India, Revenue and Agriculture Department, Land Revenue, A, October 1895, pro.no.72, Note on Land Transfer and Agricultural Indebtedness in India. |
| RLC | *Report of the Rent Law Commission* (Calcutta 1880). |
| SR | Settlement Report. |

1. Mainly Henry S. Maine, *Ancient Law* (10th ed., London 1905), and *Village Communities in the East and West* (3rd ed., London 1876); and Karl Polanyi, *The Great Transformation* (New York 1911). The present paper owes much to the subsequent research carried out along these lines by Prof. Walter C. Neale in the Indian field, and especially to his essay 'Land is to rule' published in Robert E. Frykenberg, ed., *Land Control and Social Structure in Indian History* (Madison 1969).

2. An anthology of classical texts relative to this question will be found in DRC, II, App.B, pp.65-75.

3. P.V. Kane, *History of Dharmaśāstra*, III (Poona 1946), p.495.

4. Ibid., pp.496-7. See for instance the two inscriptions relative to Bihar quoted in M. Aquique, *Economic History of Mithila (c.600 B.C.-1097 A.D.)* (New Delhi 1974), pp.38-9.

5. P.V. Kane, op.cit., III, p.497.

6. DCR, I, p.92; II, pp.67-77, 89, 256-8.

7. W.H. Moreland, *The Agrarian System of Moslem India* (2nd ed., New Delhi 1968), pp.4, 142.
8. DCR, I, p.92; II, pp.67-77, 89.
9. I. Habib, *The Agrarian System of Mughal India, 1556-1707* (Bombay 1963), pp.154,157-9.
10. Regulation I of 1793, section 8.
11. Regulation VIII of 1819.
12. Field, 'Note'.
13. B.B. Chaudhuri, 'The Process of Depeasantization in Bengal and Bihar, 1885-1947', *Indian Historical Review* II, I (July 1975), p.128.
14. I. Habib, op.cit., p.117, and 'Potentialities of Capitalistic Development in the Economy of Mughal India', *Journal of Economic History*, 1969, pp.37,48. As an example of land desertion in periods of famine (here the Bengal famine of 1769-70), see W.W. Hunter, *Annals of Rural Bengal* (7th ed., London 1897), pp.60-1, 411.
15. I. Habib, *The Agrarian System of Mughal India*, p.151.
16. Sir George Campbell, 'The Tenure of Land in India', in J.W. Probyn, ed., *Systems of Land Tenure in Various Countries* (2nd ed., London 1881), p.226.
17. Letter quoted in R.N. Sinha, *Bihar Tenantry, 1783-1833* (Bombay 1968), p.167.
18. Champaran SR (1900), para.484.
19. *Annual General Administration Report of the Patna Division, 1881-1882*, para.13, and 1882-1883, para. 23.
20. I. Habib, op.cit., pp.190-6.
21. IFC, pt.III, app.3, pp.323,348,417.
22. NLT, pp.8-11.
23. See for instance *Manu*, IX, 44; *Arthaśāstra*,book II, ch.1, 9; etc.
24. Village Notes of thana Dhaka (Cadastral Survey), no.1-15, 42,45, 35c, Champaran Collectorate Records (Motihari), Settlement Department.
25. B.H. Baden-Powell, *The Land Systems of British India* (Oxford 1892), vol.I, p.221.
26. Ibid., pp.222.
27. Compare the studies in ethno-geography published by the geographers of Varanasi on the subject of the colonization of Gangetic India by Rajput clans during the thousand years that preceded the British conquest, and notably among these K.N. Singh, 'The Territorial Basis of Medieval Town and Village Settlement in Eastern U.P., India', *Annals, Association of American Geographers*, 58, 1962; R.L. Singh and R.B. Singh, 'Spatial Diffusion of Rajput Clan Settlements in Part of the Middle Ganga

Valley', in R.L. Singh, ed., *Rural Settlement in Monsoon Asia* (Varanasi 1972); and several contributions in R.L. Singh, K.N. Singh and Rana P.B. Singh, eds., *Geographic Dimensions of Rural Settlements* (Varanasi 1975).

28. Compare R.G. Fox, *Kin, Clan, Raja and Rule. State-Hinterland Relations in Pre-Industrial India* (Berkeley and Los Angeles 1971), pp.88-9.

29. Thomas Fortescue, Civil Commissioner, Delhi, to Holt Mackenzie, Secretary to Government in the Territorial Department, 28 April 1820, in *Punjab Government Records*, vol.1: Records of the Delhi Residency and Agency (Lahore 1911).

30. DRC, I, p.92; II, app.B, p.45; J.H. Morris, Chief Commissioner, note on Proprietary Transfer in the Central Provinces, 30 September 1874, in *Selections from the Records of the Government of India, Home Department*, no. CLV, Land Sale (Calcutta 1879), pp.329-31; NLT, pp.6-7; V.S. Pantulu, *Hindu Law Relating to the Liability for Debt and Alienation for the Same as Laid Down in the Smritis and Interpreted by Earliest English Writers and Decisions of Court from 1807 up to Present Day* (Bellary 1899), pp.24-30 and passim.

31. I. Habib, op.cit., pp.149, 154.

32. A well-documented practice in eighteenth century Bengal: see H.R. Sanyal, 'Social Mobility in Bengal: Its Sources and Constraints', *Indian Historical Review* II, 1 (July 1975). Numerous cases are quoted in W.W. Hunter, *Bengal Ms. Records* (London 1894), vol.I, pp.34-5. Such confiscations remained common in the princely states during the British period.

33. R. Guha, *A Rule of Property for Bengal. An Essay on the Idea of Permanent Settlement* (Paris and The Hague 1963), passim and especially pp.106-8; S.C. Gupta, 'Land Market in the North-Western Provinces (Uttar Pradesh) in the First Half of the Nineteenth Century', *Indian Economic Review* (August 1958), pp.51-7.

34. J.W. Kaye, *The Administration of the East India Company* (London 1853), p.185; B.B. Chaudhuri, 'The Land Market in Eastern India, 1793-1940, part 1: The Movement of Land Prices', *Indian Economic and Social History Review* XII, 1 (January-March 1975), pp.1-5.

35. Ibid., pp.5-6.

36. Muzaffarpur SR (1901), paras.151-72. As for the rate of revenue sales in Bihar generally, see A.P. Macdonnell, Minute, 20 September 1893, Bengal Land Revenue Proceedings, A, Nos.47-61, November 1893.

37. Francis Buchanan, *An Account of the Districts of Bihar and Patna in 1811-1812*, (Patna n.d.), vol.II,

p.569, quoted by B.B. Chaudhuri, 'The Land Market in Eastern India, part 1', p.10. Buchanan made similar observations in other districts of Bihar, *An Account of the District of Shahabad in 1812-1813* (Patna 1934), p. 353, *An Account of the District of Purnea in 1809-1810* (Patna 1928), p.450.

38. *Selections from the Records of the Madras Government, New Series*, No.XI: A Collection of Papers Relating to the Value of Land in the Early Years of the Nineteenth Century (Madras 1916), p.19.

38. B.B. Chaudhuri, 'The Land Market in Eastern India, part 1', pp.11-14.

40. Compare various cases cited ibid., pp.15-16.

41. Collector of 24-Parganas to Commissioner of Alipore Division, 7 February 1834, Bengal, Sudder Board of Revenue Proceedings, A, No.69, 19 September 1834. See also the letter from the Collector of Chittagong to the Officiating Commissioner, Chittagong Division, 14 October 1833, ibid.; and the note by W.W. Bird, dated 8 September 1834, para.6, ibid., no.57.

42. T.C. Robertson, Report, 9 September 1920, quoted by Eric Stokes, *The Peasant and the Raj* (Cambridge 1978), p.74, from the *Selections from the Revenue Records of the North-Western Provinces* (Allahabad 1873).

43. Report of the Land Revenue Administration of the Lower Provinces of Bengal, 1886-1887, para.154, quoted by B.B. Chaudhuri, 'The Land Market in Eastern India, part 1', p.16.

44. H.V. Bayley, *History of Midnapore* (Calcutta 1902), p.91.

45. *Selections from the Records of the Government of Punjab, New Series*, No.XIII: Papers Regarding Alienation of Estates of Insolvent Proprietors to the Money-Lending Class (Lahore 1876), pp.5-6.

46. DCR, I, p.92.

47. Colonel R. Baird-Smith, Report on the Famine of 1860-1861 in the North-Western Provinces of India to the Government of India, Home Department, 14 August 1861, *Parliamentary Papers*, 1862, vol. XL, paras.30 and 58-60. See also S.C. Gupta, op.cit., pp.62-7.

48. Report of the Royal Commission on Agriculture in India (Calcutta 1928), pp.9-10.

49. B.B. Chaudhuri, 'The Land Market in Eastern India, part 1', pp.19.27.

50. BEC, I, p.13; Saran SR (1903), para.543; DCR, I, Memorandum by Auckland Colvin, para.69.

51. Figures compiled from Champaran SR (1901), para. 524 and app.VII; Saran SR (1903), para.543 and app.VIII;

Muzaffarpur SR (1901), para.853-5; Darbhanga SR (1904), para.427-8 and app.VIII; Monghyr SR (1908), para.313, 315 and app.D(VI); Bhagalpur SR (1912), para.232, 234 and app.K; Purnea SR (1908), para.359-60 and app.I(VII).

52. From Champaran SR (Revision) (1922), para.179 and app.V; Saran SR (Revision) (1923), para.100 and app.V.

53. Saran SR (1903), para.543; Darbhanga SR (1904), para.427.

54. Memorandum of the Revision of Land Revenue Settlements in the North-Western Provinces, 1860-1872, s.l, 1872, pp.110-11.

55. According to the Report of the Indian Famine Commission, 1880, part II, p.548.

56. Champaran SR (1901), para.516.

57. RLC, p.111; IFC, p.114. This principle had been explicitly recognized by the early Regulations of the Government of Bengal: see *Papers Relating to the Passing of Act X of 1859* (Calcutta 1883), vol.1, p.28.

58. On the meaning of '*raiyat*', see Neil E.B. Baillie, *The Land Tax of India According to the Moohummudan Law, Translated from the Futawa Alumgeeree* (London 1853), pp. xxv and xxix.

59. Field, 'Note', in which John Shore's minute is quoted. See also *Selections from the Revenue Records of the North-Western Provinces, 1818-1820* (Calcutta 1866), pp.252 ff.

60. IFC, part II, pp.537-8.

61. Compare for example Champaran Collectorate Records (Motihari), Settlement Department, Village Notes of thana Dhaka (Cadastral Survey), nos.21, 24, 25, 29, 37, 49, 135, 210-48, etc.; Village Notes of thana Madhuban (Cadastral Survey), nos.1-20, 22, 24-7, 33, 34, 40, 68, 70, etc. These two thanas are those where the demographic density approximates to that of the most crowded regions of Bihar.

62. *Selections from Papers Relating to the Bengal Tenancy Act, 1885* (Calcutta 1920), pp.355-60.

63. Officiating Collector of Muzaffarpur to Commissioner of Patna, 28 June 1875, Patna Commissioner's Records, General Department, Bihar State Central Record Office (Patna).

64. Memorandum from the Officiating Collector of Champaran, 31 March 1869, to Government of India, Home (Public) Department Proceedings, No.54, 3 July 1869. Compare Monthly Bundles from the Collector of Champaran, Collector of Champaran to Commissioner of Patna, no.631, 27 February 1870, Patna Commissioner's Records.

65. A very clear statement of the arguments of both

parties will be found in Field; 'Note'. A history of the controversy as it developed within the ranks of the administration has been given by D. Rothermund, 'Freedom of Contract and the Problem of Land Alienation in British India', *South Asia* 3 (1973). The anticipations of those who feared that rapid dispossession of the raiyats by the money-lenders were yet only sporadically confirmed at the end of the century: compare Bengal, Land Revenue Proceedings, A, Nos.56-8, August 1898. As for the other regions, some information will be found on this point in V.C. Bhutani, 'Agrarian Indebtedness and Alienation of Land', *Journal of Indian History* XLVII, 1 and 2 (April and August 1969).

66. RLC, para.32.

67. Commissioner of Patna to Board of Revenue, Lower Provinces, 5 March 1896, Patna Commissioner's Records, General Department.

68. Officiating Secretary to Board of Revenue, Lower Provinces to Secretary to Government of Bengal, Revenue Department, 20 June 1894, Government of India, Revenue and Agriculture Department, Land Revenue Proceedings, A, No.72, October 1895.

69. Ibid.

70. Muzaffarpur SR (1901), para.859-66.

71. BEC, I, pp.10, 13-14.

72. Compare historical summary of the legislation in K.M. Mukerji, 'Land Transfers in Birbhum, 1928-1955: Some Implications of the Bengal Tenancy Act, 1885', *Indian Economic and Social History Review* VIII, 3 (September 1971).

# STATE, PEASANT AND MONEY-LENDER IN LATE NINETEENTH-CENTURY BIHAR: SOME COLONIAL INPUTS

*Peter Robb*

The background to this paper is a set of contradictory images. Among external influences on nineteenth-century India, those attributed to the colonial state have assumed major significance; but they have been subject to opposing interpretations. At the two extremes the impression is either of a distant, imperfect and indirect rule, the impact of which was muted, or of a hegemony by whose laws and administration various distortions were introduced. The state is on the one hand a collector of agricultural surplus and used by indigenous groups for their own purposes; it is on the other hand an intervening, even a modernizing agent, altering social and economic relationships, shifting the loci of power, and opening up channels for the exchange of goods and ideas. There seem to be at least two underlying reasons for this debate as for the aspects discussed in my introduction to this volume: the first is the fact that the evidence is largely the product of British administration and often inaccurate, partial or misleading; the second is the failure of modern scholarship to agree on the nature of Indian economies and polities in the eighteenth century.

In the case of Bihar, it is clear that the British government had no reliable information about population, cultivated area, cropping patterns, output, rents and so on, before the present century at the earliest.[1] After the 1870s the Bengal government (under which Bihar then fell) came to believe that it needed statistics for the effective prosecution of its policies; and thus by the 1890s there had been some improvement. This was first because in Indian circumstances data may be assumed to be accurate in proportion to the importance placed upon them (in particular when they involve money, but not when collected merely for record), and secondly because some of the increased activity of the government in this period, in say canal or famine administration, itself generated better than average statistics. In general, however, it may be said that even in this period the collection of information was often unreliable and its processing sometimes inept, that some calculations were so divorced from reality that there was strong and not always unconscious pressure to arrive at 'probable' figures, and that frequently what was being sought was inadequate for present-day purposes. Bengal's predicament was blamed on its administrative tradition, its permanent settlement of the revenue and the want of a village agency. It was also exacerbated by the exigencies of Indian agriculture, at a time when all seasons were 'abnormal', being determined by climatic and other variables. The outcome for the historian must be a reluctance to make definite statements about economic conditions on the basis of statistical evidence. He must be wary also of impressionistic reports: they too were subject to the short-comings and omissions of collection and, more important, were produced within definite though not constant preconceptions and assumptions on the part of the British officials.

I have discussed part of this intellectual baggage in my introduction above: the certainty that the Asiatic way of doing things was different from the European, and that one result of British rule (and in some eyes its justification) was the transformation of aspects of Indian society. There was, in short, a willingness to believe that what could be observed in late nineteenth-century India and particularly any changes there, were in important respects the product of British government. It followed naturally that the eighteenth-century was not only a period in which an old political order had been in decline, but also the culmination of an Asiatic mode of production and of 'pre-modern' social and economic exchange. The recurrent terms used to describe this era are tradition, feudalism (by analogy with the European past), and community, the last defined according to hierarchy, inter-dependence and self-regulation. By explicit contrast nineteenth-century Europe was seen to have evolved (according to several, otherwise contradictory explanations) into a higher form of society, more productive and more integrated but less communal. Supposedly nineteenth-century India was starting out on the same journey. The interpretation depends on a view of the past which has always been open to objections, and it is clear that a major revision of our understanding of the eighteenth century would also revolutionize our ideas about the nineteenth.

The impulse towards such a revision is by no means new. After all it might have been deduced from Baden-Powell's criticism of what he called the unwarranted generalization of Maine's idea of the village community.[2] More recently it was brought to our attention by Dharma Kumar's pioneering work on agricultural labour.[3] Others have mined the ideas of students of Mughal systems, especially Irfan Habib, and have tended to propose earlier starting-points for change in agrarian society. Most notably, it has been suggested that the eighteenth century saw a commercialization of kingship: in northern India a unified merchant class and a service gentry resulted from the activities of the state, and the gentry came, between 1600 and 1800, to capture rural power, to possess and monopolize land rights, and to advance irrigation, roads and commercial agriculture. Monetization resulted from the needs of centralized administration and especially, with the breakdown of the jagirdari system, from the maintenance of armies; it was accompanied by a growth of trade.[4] If this is so, then we might relocate many of the changes associated with British rule: the nineteenth century would become a period not of new directions but of continuities, in economic terms, and British impact would be identified with the decline of the gentry in the north-west, due to administrative recentralization, and with reductions in demand for particular items of trade. By the same token, another recent and provocative work, by Ratnalekha Ray, has challenged most of the suppositions about the impact of the permanent settlement in Bengal. It did not, she claims, displace an ancient aristocracy through its legal innovations; the Mughal zamindar was essentially a creature of politics and not of economic production. It did not establish a market in land for the first time (and nor was the market that arose a free one). It did not, by instituting private property in land, establish for the first time a concentration of economic resources in few hands, to the detriment of self-sufficient peasant communities: there were, it is argued, landless villagers and village landlords before 1793. At issue therefore is not the new relationships created by the British but the impact of the British on the operation of old relationships. The conclusion is that, in spite of the attempt to transform the role of the zamindars, the village land-holding classes generally managed to maintain or improve their position, if necessary by shifting an increased burden on to the poor.[5]

The historian, then, is obliged to cope with unsatisfactory data and to choose between controversial interpretations of the eighteenth century if he is to write convincingly about the nineteenth. In the case of Bihar, with which this essay is concerned, many continuities may be described. Patna and Gaya, for example, were essentially districts of 'hydraulic' civilization, dependent for rice-growing on elaborate, co-operative measures for diverting and storing river flood-waters, through channels and tanks, for which supra-local authority was a pre-requisite. The rental structure, based on various forms of produce-sharing, reflected these realities. In other Bihari districts extensive irrigation was not practised, though in some areas a more limited case for co-operation might be said to have existed in the embankments and the need for reconciling competing interests which they represented. In this region money rents were earlier the rule and rice culture was diluted by popular dependence on poorer grains and various dry crops. Some land was held in huge zamindaris which presumably derived from a looser, military control of underpopulated regions. Other land was held in small segments, which may be taken to reflect the circumstances of long occupation by a dense population in an area of mainly dry agriculture with very localized variations of soil and climate. In detail the contrast between wet and dry pertained throughout the region without being as immediately obvious as in some other parts of India: all irrigated areas had their drier, poorer hinterlands on which money rents were more likely to prevail and in which land control of the zamindari type was either very local or very distant. In general there may be said to be three basic varieties of indigenous power in the countryside in Bihar. There were proprietors whose political control presumably derived from surplus agriculture and irrigation. There were proprietors whose military control or settlement efforts were associated mainly with the military or agricultural 'frontier'. A few of both of these kinds of proprietor were great caste-leaders who lorded over huge areas. Elsewhere (and also within the great estates) was found a third kind of control, where multitudes, mainly of the same few castes, vied with each other over petty holdings: their dominance was a mixture of ritual status and weight of numbers, variable for an individual.[6] British tenurial categories sat uneasily on these realities, embedded as they were in ecology and belief.

In practice, moreover, ownership of land was conditional upon various levels of power and custom, not just in the way Dharma Kumar has reminded us all ownership is conditional, but in the sense that exclusive enjoyment of property was very rarely achieved or perhaps sought. Economic possession of land consists in the ability to cultivate it and enjoy its produce. The latter was certainly not reserved to cultivators in pre-British days, but the non-cultivators' share was always circumscribed by custom and power, and in some cases related to the non-cultivators' contribution. Where produce-sharing was the rule, the harvest was seen as depending in part on the input of the zamindar in providing for irrigation, and in reality was indeed often so dependent. There seem to have been 'agreed rents' in that there were customary proportions which were deemed reasonable in respect of particular types of zamindar or cultivator (rather than of particular soils or crops). Above all there was no collection where the collector's authority did not run, and it may be assumed to have run unevenly: it was restricted partly by the difficulties of administration among dispersed and divided holdings (it was no accident that successful zamindaris were characterized by their support of large numbers of relatives and retainers), and partly by the influence of dominant castes, the Rajputs and Bhumihar Brahmans, who, though prejudiced against actual cultivation, were dispersed throughout different economic roles and might oppose as often as they co-operated with, their powerful caste-fellows seeking control in the locality. There was not everywhere an intermediate level of power such as Ratnalekha Ray has emphasized in Bengal, for many Bihari zamindars were themselves merely controllers in the village (rather than over it). But all zamindars were subject to the need to enforce their will. Their way was not always made easier by the structure of the society. It seems to have consisted at the upper levels of a series of overlays of rights and privileges in which stand revealed rivals who had been ousted by and were perhaps no longer in any sense interchangeable with the present holders of power, but who had not disappeared and who could not be treated as part of an undifferentiated mass of inferiors.

Ownership of land was conditional secondly also because cultivation itself was inhibited: the Bihari cultivator often could not independently determine his inputs, especially of water but also, because of the credit mechanisms and in many cases his lack of individual capital, in terms of seed, technology and labour. This should not be taken as meaning that effective agricultural decisions necessarily lay elsewhere, in the hands of village leaders determining water use, or landlords and money-lenders determining credit. It may be assumed that for the most part dominant personages would have been unable or unwilling to participate in detailed agricultural decisions on the multitude of dispersed holdings within their influence. Their dominance and the interdependence born of divided and interspersed holdings, of a shared labour-force or a shared pool of machinery and cattle, would make for a strong negative control of individual farmers, rather than a definite direction of their activities. In practice, this suggests it would be difficult for the cultivator to show enterprise but he could benefit from effort; it would be difficult for the dominant to encourage improvement in agricultural methods, for example, but easy for them to determine the parameters within which agriculture was carried on. Moreover, such a tendency was certainly reinforced by social norms and preferences; it was a matter of culture as well as of land management. Many refused or failed to change practices (such as high-caste refusal to hold the plough) with which their status was bound up, which were expected of them, and for which they received non-economic rewards.

Nineteenth-century Bihar already represented therefore in many senses a highly-developed society and economy. The division of labour was far advanced as were both internal and external mechanisms for the redistribution of agricultural surplus. This last was a key factor as will be discussed below: within each village, possession of a store of grain between harvests was the primary expression of local power. I believe the chief possessors of this store did not remain constant over time, but the role was none the less a perpetual feature, and essential to the majority of people who kept no such reserves. The system could thus be described as one of redistribution (in return for status) rather than of accumulation, by the elites in possession of land and of the weapons of political power. I suspect that the security of the position of these elites was ultimately enhanced and that the degree of mobility and exchange among themselves may have been reduced under the British. Agricultural productivity was low; freedom from repression was not locally guaranteed, but nor was the ability to repress; and a high degree of collectivity characterized agricultural decision-making at both metaphysical and practical levels.

There was an economy or a series of economies, then, which was both integrated and insulated. It was isolated because production for the market occupied a small proportion of the cultivated area, though of course a larger proportion of the output by value and usually a larger proportion of the effort and capital input of the producers. Market access was restricted by features such as the intervention of the zamindar through produce rents or the activity of the money-lender in buying or acquiring grain at the lowest prices, just after the harvest, or even at a discount on those prices: at prices, that is, which from the producer's point of view reflected relative economic and social power and not market forces. There was too the inhibition of the higher castes against marketing their own crop; there was the practice whereby cash crops were sold to itinerant merchants who sold them to traders who passed them amongst themselves until they reached the handful of dealers who exported goods out of the immediate region. The agriculturist was not involved because his surplus was small, communications were difficult, and trade represented another world to him when it was expressed in money terms. He might store and lend grain and be familiar with the ways of the local *hat* or bazar; he might bargain with the travelling merchant, borrow himself from the mahajan, and in general be a man of substance. But essentially he needed an interpreter and a provider of coin (in the person of the trader or the money-lender), and did not himself venture into the different culture thus represented. On the other hand, at the local level, the integration is also apparent: the itinerant merchant and the bania were not indifferent to local power and status, and the combination of economic functions (rentier, usurer, cultivator) in the hands of single individuals made for interdependence in the villages, just as the absence of a money economy made for a stability of relationships between holders of surplus grain and those with smaller holdings or without land.

These were circumstances which pre-dated British rule; they did not end with its imposition. What then *was* the British role in Bihar? More specifically, for today we are inevitably faced with the issue of poverty, why is Bihar undoubtedly 'backward' in terms of expectations raised by the evolutionary interpretations referred to above? I have chosen, in this essay, to consider some examples of British activity, all measures consciously directed by the British at improving conditions, in comparison with what I take to be the true nature of those conditions. The areas are agricultural productivity, famine and credit. It is a representative but by no means an exhaustive list. In particular I have had to ignore the attempts at social engineering through law, and the building of canals, embankments, roads and railways - the great public works. But I submit that the latter at least were economically less significant in the Bengal Presidency than elsewhere.

The direct attempts to improve agricultural

performance under British rule do not provide a happy story, and what I take to be the underlying reasons for the lack of success are also discouraging. Certainly the predominant tendency among the relatively few British administrators interested in agriculture was towards optimism over productivity. Some might argue with T.W. Holderness that a point would be 'speedily reached ... beyond which increased returns from an acre are not to be expected' and that non-agricultural income must therefore be the salvation of the country.[7] But others in the Government of India took a less Malthusian stance. They believed in the efficacy of agrarian development and in an official role to promote it. Sir John Strachey pointed to the tea industry which he argued would not have started without government help. Sir E.C. Buck, pioneering secretary of the Revenue and Agriculture Department, urged that research had to be undertaken; there could not be instruction at a stage where it implied the mere transfer of European skills.[8] As is well-known, however, such direct intervention as was tried had little impact. The resources of the agricultural departments were small and they could not point to results which would encourage further investment. M. Finucane remarked that his department in Bengal was 'placed, at its creation, on a temporary basis, and ... immediate results were expected in order to justify the continuation of its existence'.[9] Naturally these were precisely the conditions least likely to bring success. Small experimental farms were set up from time to time; in 1892 the government concluded that store could not be set by their results. As I see it, the problem, in general, was first that there was no guarantee of wide applicability for any given method or implement. The British often did talk as if there were known rules: cane should be planted in rows, deep ploughing was best, manure would increase yields and so on. But often these were not demonstrable truths in India, where soils for example, as reported by an investigator in 1890, *tended* to be exceptional.[10] Secondly, improvements had to be appropriate in a wider than merely agricultural sense. Improved ploughs, say, might increase yields and save time,[11] but this might or might not matter: in some areas and soils new ploughs were adopted, but there was often little point in reducing the effort or frequency of ploughing on small-holdings using family labour. With some crops too technological improvements could increase profits - Behea sugar mills at between Rs.80 and Rs.140 came to replace less efficient types, and steam gins for cotton were also a success - but there was no comparable advantage for those dispensing credit and thus determining investment in seeking improvements for, say, a subsistence crop of millets.[12] From a scientific view practicality was not the first point at issue, and cost-effectiveness in the broader sense could not be calculated in an agricultural experiment; most damaging, effort was concentrated on methods, which were what the Indian peasant might have been supposed thoroughly to understand, and broader reforms were beyond the capacity of the experimenter to investigate let alone effect.[13] At various opportunities, therefore, the Bengal government would argue that all the cultivator needed was protection from oppression and free access to the market. But then even if this were so, the government was not in a position to guarantee such needs. It could not even perfect the physical infrastructure, and that alone would not in any case have provided free access in the absence of social and economic reforms - any more than protection itself would generate interest or ability in profit-seeking where these did not already exist.

But I suggest it would be a mistake to conclude on these grounds that Indian productivity did not improve. It was remarked by Finucane, after investigations in the 1890s, that agriculture was not everywhere in that 'stagnant condition ... sometimes supposed'. In Dacca and Burdwan, for example, 'intelligent' cultivators used manure and grew sugarcane on the Mauritius system. In Bihar the 'ignorant' and 'backward' agriculturists did neither. It is worth remarking in this connection that in the 1890s the population of the Patna division of Bihar remained stationary or in some districts distinctly declined, whereas Dacca and Burdwan were among three or four heavily-populated districts which showed increases of between ten and fifteen per cent. (Only 'frontier' regions such as Chittagong and Orissa had greater percentage growth.) Prices too rose in Bihar at a rate below the average for the Bengal Presidency.[14] I do not wish to prejudge any issues, but it is possible at least to speculate that the vigour and enterprise reported in Dacca and Burdwan owed something to necessity or incentive. Or at the least we might point to opportunity and argue that yields might increase without directly-relevant innovation, or technological advance inspired by government - they might, for example, in the *general* impetus generated by a new crop, such as jute, or an investment, such as a canal.

It is fairly certain, moreover, that profitability increased. Here we may see that the government's influence on agricultural production was not confined to its insignificant impact by direct intervention. The rulers encouraged production for the market by the channels they kept open for trade, and by providing circumstances in which prices rose - let us leave for later consideration some of the complex issues raised by these statements - but they may be said to have reduced incentive, particularly in Bengal, by their revenue policies. I wish to take the latter as an example. Permanently-settled areas bore a smaller financial burden than others, and all the indications are that during the nineteenth century the burden became progressively lighter, averaged over the community as a whole, to an even greater degree in these regions than in others. The government took no direct share in the profits from any commercialization of agriculture: in 1899, it was calculated, an acre under sugarcane paid three rupees in much of North India, four in Bombay and Madras, and one in Bengal.[15] Zamindars made political capital out of what they called the attempts to reverse the permanent settlement, but the inroads of new taxation were relatively slight.[16] And the demand was not readily responsive, once resumption proceedings had ended, to expansion of cultivated area. In general what does this imply? It is that the British introduced a stable regulated system in place of a changing ad hoc one, and that its direct demands became less onerous over time. The zamindar was thus provided with easier profits, in so far as government influenced events.

Do we conclude that this influence was also even or socially and politically neutral? I suggest on the contrary that it was symptomatic that Bengal's collections of revenue were notoriously lax: high balances were not due to poor harvests, which influenced them not at all, but to unpunctuality, confusion and inefficiency.[17] Bihari districts consistently featured among those where arrears were largest: for the cesses Shahabad collected less than 80 per cent of the arrears and less than 90 per cent on the current account in each of the six years after 1890, while for the land revenue arrears seem to have built up from the 1880s, in Shahabad apparently because of the great leniency shown over sales for default. In the same period, in Chainpur, the poorest and worst-affected part of the district, those estates which were sold fetched an average of eleven years' purchase in 1880-3 and of 33 years' purchase in 1890-6.[18] This was not an administration, then, which bore heavily on the privileged classes; the very laxness of the administration, however, suggests that it impinged unevenly. Cesses, for example, did not hurt the prosperous who were reputed to use the returns they made at revaluation to overstate their rents (the better to increase them in practice). Revenue administration, if it worked inefficiently, could also be made to work to private advantage, or detriment. Where zamindars were large and dominant they could reap the fullest benefits from the system and its decreasing share of the value of the country's produce. Where they were small or weak, and hard-pressed by dominant but non-zamindari groups, the benefits were less available or apparent, and the advantages were enjoyed by those below them.

Similar points may be made about the court of wards and the administration of government estates. A major purpose of government involvement was political: to preserve great estates, prevent social unrest and ensure 'loyalty'.[19] But, for the zamindars, the result of official intervention by the court of wards, as during a period of minority, was administrative consolidation and financial restraint.[20] Estates were fully surveyed, before this was general in Bihar and Bengal, and new rent rolls were usually prepared, often with substantial benefits to the landlord. There were agricultural experiments which left behind the legacy of money spent on tanks, wells, drainage and irrigation, on roads and tree-planting, all with the avowed purpose of improving the value of the property. In the 1890s 140 estates were controlled by the Government of Bengal, 74 of them under the court of wards; their revenue demand stood at Rs.50 lakhs and their rental income at Rs.90 lakhs.[21] Thus the beneficiaries were large landlords. Who the losers were may be judged from the fact that it was thought necessary in 1895 to expostulate against a tendency of wards management to 'screw every rupee out of the raiyats' for the good of the owner.[22] But though there was one rule for the great estate and another for the small in Bengal, there was still a general government influence. Again we may suspect how this operated by noting that when estates did fall into official hands, administration was very lax. On the one hand the Collector was bound by a complex array of regulations mostly designed to save money; on the other, as even in Gaya district with its produce rents, direct management was by low-paid gomashtas under the ordinary district staff (with the exception of a few occasions when special officers were appointed). Most estates were farmed out: the

Tikari estate, for example, while under the court of wards in the 1880s, consisted of some thousand villages, only 30 of which were held *khas*. Here the government failed to intervene. Below it, on many estates, there were constant disputes between tahsildars and tenants, private battles in which the strongest were the most likely to be able to enlist official aid. The system provided, indeed, for an army of petty functionaries - financed over all by perhaps some ten or twelve per cent of locally-collected revenue - and each of them was potentially an ally or an agent of the locally dominant, but isolated from the bulk of the population by *izzat*, class and function.[23] I suggest that if the profitability of agricultural production did increase in Bihar during the nineteenth century, then the increase is likely to have been unevenly distributed and partly as a result of the actions and more particularly the omissions of the government. The implication is that British rule tended not to even down but to divide up the population.

The extent to which this was true overall, and not just with regard to the gap between the strong and the weak, may be examined in regard to famine and British measures towards it. They are of interest in regard to the fate of those without land. It was said that in Bihar wages had not kept pace with food prices, and that indeed the standard 1½ to 2½ annas a day had altered very little in the twenty years before 1896. This was low by comparison with other regions, but it was a standard, the amount customarily thought appropriate, and not an average of wages actually paid. The latter may have been more responsive to price rises than the former. But more particularly the vast majority of labourers were paid in kind at a level sufficient to provide them with daily food. This is important to the interpretation of famines: bazar prices mattered little to the bulk of the population (cultivators and labourers) so long as there were stocks of food in the villages. When scarcity pushed up prices those on fixed incomes suffered first - many of the artisans, most town-dwellers, widows and other dependents, beggars. Agricultural labourers suffered when the minority of cultivators who kept personal stocks of food and the majority who survived between harvests on credit could no longer afford to employ them; in particular hardship became acute among the landless or the semi-landless when the ground was too hard to plough or there was no crop to transplant or harvest.[24] The famines of the late nineteenth century in Bihar, when they were unusually frequent, were at root scarcities of work (or money in towns and other marginal cases) and not of food.

The official accounts of relief measures bear this out. The practice was to open test works once scarcity was suspected. The results cannot provide a comparative gauge of distress between districts or even famines, as the conditions which determined the numbers in receipt of support varied greatly; but they are a better than average measure for one area or period provided no significant changes of personnel or policy intervened. The death rate too is a fair indicator, though not an uncontroversial one given that the British, largely refusing to report deaths from starvation, attributed so many deaths to cholera and fever and the 'general unhealthiness' of the season. The weekly returns shown in Table 1 suggest rapid reactions to changes in conditions, not a consistent response to a previous harvest failure. The table demonstrates that the numbers on relief and the death-rate were responsive to the rainfall, which was the main determinant of the demand for labour, affecting as it did both the opportunities for the cultivator and the confidence of the money-lender. There is a poor correlation between the numbers on relief and the major food prices, rice being shown because it was the affected area's main crop and marua because it was the main stand-by of the poor. The picture would have been even clearer, in all probability, except that the distribution of the June rainfall in 1892 was uneven, and that month there was an influx of people from an area in which there had been no rain but from which few had previously come to the relief works. In other parts of the district the numbers had fallen very rapidly. So too the rabi (spring) harvest failed in Champaran in 1892 and in June works were opened in the worst-affected area; about 500 attended on two days, but the numbers dwindled as soon as the heavy rain fell. In Gaya at the same time relief works were unsuccessful, regardless of harvest failures, allegedly because of works undertaken privately on the basis of government loans.

The importance of work reflected the region's social composition: the dominant Rajputs and Brahmans almost invariably employed field-workers. It is true that some estimates in 1897 suggested that 90 per cent of those on relief were of the cultivating classes, and 75 per cent were actual cultivators; but another report claimed that the number of cultivators was small. In 1892 those who appeared on relief works in Darbhanga were 'mostly

*Table 1. Relief Works in Muzaffarpur in 1892*

| *Date* | *Relief* (male units) | *Prices* Rice | Marua | *Deaths* Month | Rate | *Rainfall* Parg. | 1892 | Norm. |
|---|---|---|---|---|---|---|---|---|
| 2 April | 2533 | 12.4 | | | | | | |
| 9 | 2967 | | | | | a | 0 | 0.58 |
| 16 | 3444 | 12 | 19.8 | April | 39.95 | b | 1.46 | 1.18 |
| 23 | 4324 | | | | | c | 0 | 1.19 |
| 30 | 3793 | 11.3 | 18 | | | | | |
| 7 May | 4104 | | | | | a | 0.73 | 2.72 |
| 14 | 5759 | 11.3 | 18 | May | 75.34 | b | 1.81 | 2.66 |
| 21 | 7462 | | | | | c | 0.26 | 1.99 |
| 28 | 11120 | | | | | | | |
| 4 June | 12726 | 11.4 | 18 | | | | | |
| 11 | 8426 | | | | | a | 8.39 | 7.53 |
| 18 | 6595 | 11.7 | 18.9 | June | 44.49 | b | 12.46 | 8.03 |
| 25 | 4806 | | | | | c | 4.79 | 6.69 |
| 2 July | 1803 | 12 | 18.4 | | | | | |
| 9 | 286 | | | | | a | 10.44 | 11.81 |
| 16 | 26 | 12.3 | 19 | July | 30.89 | b | 18.16 | 10.59 |
| 23 | 0 | | | | | c | 9.35 | 11.85 |

*Note*: Prices are in seers per rupee. The death-rate is per 1000 inhabitants. The rainfall is monthly and in inches for three parganas (a, b and c), with a 'normal' monthly total.

*Diagram based on Table 1*

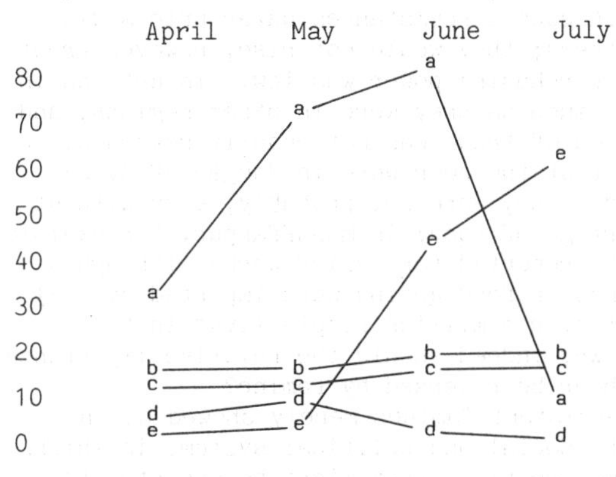


*Note*: The numbers on relief (a) are weekly averages in 100s. Marua (b) and rice (c) are in seers. The deaths (d) are per 100. Rainfall (e) is 5 = one inch (averaging the three parganas).

*Source*: R&A Fam A2 January 1893.

all members of the lower classes', though 'Here and there a few Brahmins may be found'. Given the vague-ness of the term 'cultivator', the assumption seems inescapable that people wholly or partly dependent on selling their labour made up the bulk of the recipients of famine relief, at least for crises of such relatively short duration as those of the 1890s.

Similarly the indications support the corollary to this, the insignificance of price. In Darbhanga the cost of grain changed relatively little over eight months of scarcity in 1892, remaining at 14 to 12 seers per rupee for common rice, though marua hit a peak of 30 per cent above normal. When the highest weekly number on relief exceeded 47,000 in an affected population of 150,000, the official explanation was that wages were set too high and attracted workers from outside the affected area; the suggestion is persuasive given the fact that other districts returned vastly smaller proportions on relief. In Patna town and district prices were at least as high but officials could find no evidence of distress.[25] Again the phenomenon is no doubt explicable in the character of the region. For example, in a tract northwest from Bettiah in Champaran, rather more than half the people were said to have no personal stocks of grain, yet the grain dealers of Bettiah had no agents in the area, and such trade as there was flowed outwards. The most significant exchange, in quantitative terms, in the local economy was therefore the well-to-do providing the poor with the means of survival in return for their labour. In such circumstances bazar prices did not measure distress; they would not rise, however great the need, where purchasing power was low. In Bettiah in 1896 prices were much as they were in other regions, and thus the direction of trade was not readily reversed; yet it was said that the poor were in danger of dying for want of food. They were so, probably, even without an absolute shortage of food: in Muzaffarpur, for example, as many as 14,000 reported for relief works although a net 120,000 maunds of food grains were imported over 3½ months; somewhat over a million people lived in the affected area. Why indeed should the relative importance of price and labour be reversed by famine?

Obviously persistent famines merely showed up the inequities of the social and political system, in which, according to some theories, they might be expected to have generated a crisis. Humanitarian efforts by the British, if at all successful, would therefore have had the indirect but partly deliberate effect of perpetuating inequality. The truth is probably more complicated. It follows, I suggest, from an emphasis on the importance of work, that distress was likely to be seasonal and short-term. Rain would soon provide a demand for labour, and revive the credit which drought had dried up. Unless famine was very widespread labourers would travel to find work; indeed many from Bihar and Benares went every year to the eastern districts of Bengal to help with the harvest (and swelled the relief problems when rains failed there). By the same token a single harvest would not cause distress sufficient to force itself on the attention of the government. In Darbhanga, for example, despite failures at three successive harvests since the bhadoi of 1891, distress appeared for the first time in March 1892: earlier, work had been available in desperate attempts at irrigation. Scarcity, in short, was more of a chronic than a traumatic illness. It had the capacity to enervate but not to transform. The grim consequence, given the augmented death-rate in most years of scarcity, was probably that the effect of a rising birth-rate was reduced and disproportionately so in respect of one section of the population. This is not the same as saying that that section's standard of living was generally depressed; indeed the loss of life would put a limit on the extent to which labour could be underpaid, by reducing the available pool. It may be, indeed, that even with a surplus on average, there was shortage of labour in the best seasons, and for that reason an inhibition of the expansion of labour-intensive agriculture such as sugarcane or winter rice cultivation.[26]

None the less famine relief did channel some resources towards the very poor. Total wages paid over two decades are set out in Table 2. Four pice (one anna) a day was supposedly sufficient to enable a labourer to survive without loss of physique. The government laid down a range of four to six pice a day in rice districts, and three to four elsewhere, as the rate for famine relief work. The higher limit was the sum needed to buy 24 ounces of cleaned rice at a rate of 10 to 12 seers the rupee, or an equivalent amount of a poorer grain, plus four ounces of pulse, one ounce of condiments or vegetables, one ounce of ghee or oil, and half an ounce of salt, the amounts required by the Famine Code.[27] Clearly then the relief provided for survival and little more; on the other hand the payment of famine relief wages may be represented as 16 days' work a month over ten months for the recipients in 1888-9, and nine days over eight months in 1892. (In practice it was rather less

*Table 2 Famine Relief in Bihar, 1873-92*

| | *1873-4* | *1888-9* | *1892* |
|---|---|---|---|
| Affected population | 17764650 | 1049147 | 2531555 |
| Numbers on relief | 2520675 | 45802 | 87715 |
| Relief wages (Rs.) | 1660000 | 476888 | 392322 |
| Wages per worker (Rs.) | 1.5 | 10.41 | 4.47 |
| Period (months) | 9 | 10 | 8 |

*Source*: R&A Fam A2 January 1893

as the payments in Bihar tended to be 50 per cent above the minimum of one anna per day.) To this must be added agricultural and improvement loans which created private employment. Five rupees per bigha were supposed to provide cultivators with the means to buy seed and labour for one harvest: such loans in the three periods shown on the table amounted to Rs.46,000, Rs.291,655 and Rs.142,485. Important though they may have been to individuals at the time, the sums involved are clearly too small and, most important, too irregular to represent a significant input over a longer period, in the way that public works expenditure, or the incomes of army personnel and migrant labour may have done in some parts of India. The payments may thereby be typical of the impact of official expenditure in Bihar: that is, that redistributions of wealth by the state were insignificant and did not disturb the status quo, while the methods of redistribution as of collection tended to reinforce existing power and wealth. Payments, greatest in emergencies, were at best a mild prophylactic against a revolt which structural features already made unlikely. In addition increasing intervention probably did have the effect of beginning to establish in peoples' minds the ultimate responsibility of the state for their condition.

It is to the *operation* of policy, then, that once again we turn to find a fair illustration of the impact of British administration. Famine relief was, it was said, open to abuse: as Sir Alexander Mackenzie conceded in 1897, in Bihar it was loose and lacking in discipline. The Government of India generally thought that Bengal's measures were profligate: relief works were opened more readily there than elsewhere, payments made at a higher rate, and the policy carried out in a 'lordly way', as J. Westland put it. In 1897 Holderness described the expenditure as 'wild profusion'.[28] Consideration of the measures, however, leads to a rather different conclusion. In 1897, when the policy in Bihar was supposed to be at variance not only with contemporary practice elsewhere but with previous Bengali policy, certain features were observed which, on the contrary, seem likely to have been constant. Supervision of the relief works could not be undertaken by experienced officers of the public works department, which was not highly developed in Bengal. The civil officers trying to cope found that their instructions were not always carried out, and that, as in Champaran, those in immediate charge, 'for the most part young men straight from the Bihar School of Engineering', were 'too timid to resist the pressure put upon them to record on the muster roles bodies of people ... coming too late in the day'. In Saran, where the Collector admitted that famine work might have been overdone, the lists of people to receive aid were drawn up by village panches: strikes occurred on these works when attempts were made to enforce a full task.[29] Moreover the works undertaken in Bihar were far more numerous than elsewhere - 40 or 50 to a subdivision in Shahabad and Saran in 1897 - partly because so much of the effort was directed towards tank-construction, as conditions and supplies were unsuitable for road-building. Clearly this increased the difficulties of supervision, and also the attractiveness of the works: it was said that Bihari peasants would not leave their homes and live in relief camps, and in many cases it must have been unnecessary for them to do so. In Muzaffarpur alone disbursements were in the hands of 300 officers scattered over the district; it is hard to see how their reports could have been properly scrutinized. Nor could it be guaranteed that they themselves received accurate reports from the overseers.[30] Finally, the practice in Bengal was to employ able-bodied workers on piece-work at rates that were supposed to give attractive wages with a good workload. The old, many women and the young children were less frequently employed than elsewhere - it was illegal to employ children under ten on the relief works - but, in 1897 at least, such people were often given gratuitous relief in their homes. The tendency too was for the government to take over the relief of the very poor, those normally subsisting on charity, and to do so, it was said, in both badly and lightly affected villages. Up to 55 per cent of those on relief were in these categories in 1897. The suspicion aroused by this policy was that no proper test of need was being applied, and certainly it resulted in some four per cent of the entire population in Bihari districts receiving payments in 1897. It was also apparent, however, that the piece rates in Bihar were set too high for all except professionals: these therefore were presumably among the beneficiaries of the fact that, as the Government of India concluded, 'in similarly distressed areas much more relief has been given in Bengal than in the North-Western Provinces'.[31]

The point here is not that money was necessarily much diverted from the working population: the famine circle officer who absconded from Madhubani with a thousand rupees in 1897 was probably the exception.[32] The point is that famine relief works were able to be manipulated in a number of ways: the ability of the village panch to decide who received relief was obviously a weapon in any battle for political and social dominance; the ability of petty officials to influence which village received a tank as a result of relief work was another; the ability to affect payments within the labour force by intimidating overseers was, at a different level, a third. Such opportunities were multiplied if relief for agricultural labourers, by the policy of gratuitous relief plus the level of task required on famine works, was channelled more through grants to families in separate villages than through camps. Thus it was that famine policy may have been a force for the status quo not just by providing for the survival of some of the poor, but also by reinforcing social, economic and political positions. The beneficiaries of uneven administration must be identified with those already in command of some resources. In short, we expect to find benefits and rewards being made available to the collaborators, agents and intermediaries of the rulers. But equally, once again, the economic impact of British rule, where control was weak, is likely to have been the strengthening of those who were strong, rather than the creation of new positions of power.

What then of credit? Again British interventions provide evidence for the nature of the situation and the way it was changing. We should start from the recognition that credit was essential for agricultural production, because of the seasonal rhythm and the time a crop takes to mature, and of the fluctuation between good and bad years. The government made two forays into the field in our period: the Land Improvement Act (XIX of 1883) and the Agricultural Loans Act (XII of 1884). In theory redistributive, in practice unsuccessful, these advances were unpopular, but not primarily (as might be thought) because the government was ruthless when recovering its money. The terms which were supposed to be offered allowed a first repayment to be delayed for two years, and for the period of the loan to be related to the time by which it was expected to yield a return to the borrower. Collections, moreover, were very imperfect. The Public Demands Recovery Act provided for a certificate procedure, under which a defaulter's property could be bound for the satisfaction of the debt; but collections were moderated according to agricultural conditions and also seem far from unavoidable. Large balances were run up in most districts; in Saran in 1892 execution was stayed for one year even in respect of arrears for which certificates had been issued, while the entire balance of embankment grants was outstanding; in Gaya there were government tenants who had failed to repay loans after nine years.[33] The low interest charged was considered an inducement to allowing the debts to run on. It seems that where government loans chiefly differed from other sources of credit was at the point of supply, not repayment. To appeal to the government involved establishing a new contact in circumstances, in Bengal, where one party to the bargain was neither well-known or eager. The availability of loans was not publicized. Higher district officers were responsible and were not as familiar with the intricacies of the Acts as they might have been. Individual interest mattered more than it otherwise would have done, and even the amounts available depended largely on local initiative: budget allowances, for example, differed from area to area - Patna division was allowed more than twice as much as any other Bengal area in 1895 - but they were strictly in proportion to the estimates. In the Revenue and Agriculture Department they protested at Finance Department cuts in the budget; but in Bengal the budget was regularly underspent, by as little as a third in a high-spending year in Patna division, or by as much as two-thirds in other years. In 1892, during the scarcity in North Bihar, Brahmans and Rajputs were said to be crying out for loans, and yet, to take Darbhanga, an extreme case where the policy was criticized by the government, 85 per cent of applications were refused. For some the reason was insufficient security: unusually, about ten per cent were groups of ten or more people applying on mutual security, and all of these were refused. In other cases would-be borrowers declined because the conditions proposed were unacceptable. No doubt some missed out because their papers were not processed in time. (The

Gaya Collector admitted several such cases while returning part of his grant in 1893.) But in general the reason was probably mainly to be found in the officials' sour reflection that many of the applicants had merely been trying to profit. This may seem an odd position to take about a system intended to protect and improve agriculture and indeed Bengal officials do seem to have been prejudiced on the subject. Opium advances were supposedly applied to general agricultural purposes with connivance of officials; but opium advances were recovered by deductions from payments for the crop. If agricultural and improvement loans were granted for such purposes as buying cattle or implements, it was thought that there was no guarantee, given how troublesome were the collections, that they would not be 'wasted' on marriages or litigation, or 'squandered' on food to save the borrower from work. Even in Gaya where loans were more freely given than elsewhere, chiefly on government estates, the Collector in 1895 was convinced that zamindars applied only when pressed for money and not when they intended to improve their property. Indeed in 1892 the government itself required that the Agricultural Loans Act be restricted more or less to famine relief, and the use of the Improvements Act be encouraged instead. The irony of this decision was that the latter was less well-suited to the needs of petty agriculturists than the former with its simpler procedures.[34]

The first point which might be made about the loans is therefore their comparative lack of impact in Bengal and permanently-settled areas generally. An instructive comparison may be made, for example, with the North-West Provinces where improvement grants totalled nearly Rs.1 lakh in 1887-8, with outstanding balances nearly 4½ times as great, and agricultural loans were running at about Rs.175,000 with a balance of some Rs.120,000. Within these provinces too one might compare temporarily-settled Allahabad division with permanently-settled Benares: in the one new improvement loans totalled Rs. 75,606 and balances over Rs.120,000, while in the other they amounted to Rs.4,500 and Rs.2,000. (About the same time Patna division accounted for Rs.2,400.)[35] These differences indicate the different policies in the various regions but perhaps also their different economic character. It might be argued that the cultivator in Bihar was more unwilling or less able to stand the scrutiny of officials interested in 'genuine' motives for loans and proper security to back them; or that in Bihar both the security and the motives may have conformed poorly with British expectations. Secondly, it may be adduced that one factor determining the distribution of such loans as were granted in Bihar, was the administration by minor officials. In the absence of a record of rights the Bengal authorities were encouraged to complicate their rules; relatively few revenue-payers applied and the investigation of most of the security offered therefore took the officials into that disputed territory, the transferability of tenant rights. Who then was likely to surmount the difficulties and obtain loans? We may disregard agricultural advances after harvest failures in so far as they represented credit for those distressed in proportion to their need; such aid would have no impact for change. It is an open question, however, whether any distribution of aid *was* without distortion, and in general it is obvious that only those with land or independence sought loans: petty zamindars on their own holdings, planters for the lands they controlled, or secure tenants paying money rents, particularly raiyats on government estates. Moreover, villagers were notoriously uneasy about involving officials in their affairs; petty administrators, though they might not relish leaving their offices to journey through the countryside, were nonetheless reputed when they did to take the opportunity for oppression and self-aggrandisement. The readiness with which a loan was sought would therefore depend on tenurial or physical conditions (the government estates in Gaya with their need for irrigation channels were an example of a favourable match between the two); but it would also depend on the disposition of a cultivator to involve an official in his affairs. The tendency of the policy was already to favour those with excellent individual standing, loans on joint security being rare; whether or not the loan was wanted for improvements, it was bound to be best suited to dominant groups and the allies of minor officials. Once again therefore one can imagine a government policy having an unintentional effect which would have been to consolidate the existing distribution of wealth, to provide a means for establishing disputed rights, and so on. Thirdly, however, the infrequency with which this device was used in comparison with, say, partition proceedings - and it would have been infrequent even if all the applications had been successful - implies that credit was not important in Bihar even as an ancillary benefit to be sought from government, except of course in famine years. From this we have deduced already that the features which distinguished official from private provision were a disincentive in themselves. But the reverse may also be true: that the non-official money-lenders were resorted to for positive reasons: because they did not make investigations or pose a threat. Of course ignorance and availability must have played the major part in this preference: so too must the purposes for which loans were required; but from this too we may assume that by and large private credit arrangements met the needs of dominant groups.

This third conclusion was not one often drawn by contemporaries, and we cannot hold to it on negative pleading alone. Let us consider it further through an example of a zamindar in debt, that of Nawab Amir Ali of Patna (Table 3). His property comprised seven estates held

*Table 3* *Unsecured Debts of Amir Ali of Patna*

| *Lender* | *Year* | *Principal* (Rs.) | *Interest* Rate (%) | Total (Rs.) | Per annum (Rs.) | Owing (Rs.) | Months owed |
|---|---|---|---|---|---|---|---|
| A | 1888 | 9844 | 10½ | 3659 | 1033 | 2625 | 30 |
| B | 1889 | 20000 | 9 | 6372 | 1800 | 4572 | 30 |
| C | 1889 | 61075 | 6 | 5969 | 3664 | 2305 | 7 |
| D | 1891 | 1000 | 0 | - | - | - | - |
| E | 1892 | 1000 | 12 | 230 | 120 | 160 | 16 |
| F | 1892 | 3000 | 12 | 545 | 360 | 185 | 6 |
| G | 1893 | 3000 | 12 | 536 | 360 | 176 | 5 |
| H | 1893 | 8000 | 0 | - | - | - | - |
| I | 1893 | 1225 | 6 | 73 | 73 | - | - |
| J | 1893 | 2000 | 15 | 425 | 300 | 125 | 5 |
| K | 1891 | 2000 | 15 | 1250 | 300 | 950 | 38 |
| L | 1893 | 20000 | 12 | 5309 | 2400 | 2909 | 14 |
| M | 1893 | 7000 | 13½ | 2047 | 945 | 1102 | 14 |
| N | 1893 | 8000 | 13½ | 1710 | 1080 | 603 | 7 |
| Totals | | 147144 | | 28128 | 12436 | 15742 | |
| O | 1894 | 7544 | 0-12 | 293 | | | |

*Key to Lenders*: A and B - Biseswar Prasad, Patna; C - M.M. Chaudhuri, Calcutta; D - Bhagwad Prasad, Patna; E - B.K. Mowar, Patna; F and G - Altaf Hussein Khan, Patna; H - Akbar Ali Khan, Patna; I - Mirza Khalil Shiran, Calcutta; J - R.K. Payne, Hooghly; K, L, M and N - B.B. Mullick, Hooghly; O - Others (zerpeshgi leases).

*Source*: R&A Rev A30-1 July 1895 and A1-4 November 1894.

from government and five makarari tenures from Tikari raj. Of these twelve mahals only two were directly managed, yielding an annual income of less than Rs.590. The remainder were leased and produced some Rs.4480. One, already mortgaged, was let to an indigo concern; the nine others were let on usufructuary leases (zerpeshgi) in return for loans which had totalled over Rs.7600 and which were maintained by an annual sacrifice of Rs.1500 in rent. The regular administrative costs of the estate as a whole were over Rs.2600, and the revenue demand was Rs.1340 or 20 per cent of the rental. The table summarises Amir Ali's debts in 1894. The example is perhaps atypical in the extent of debt revealed: Amir Ali had additional sources of income, including government service, and had incurred extra liabilities through his management of the affairs of the former Nawab of Awadh. It is typical, I think, in that the estate was let out rather than directly managed, that extra income was sought in further alienation rather than closer control, that a majority of borrowing was unsecured, and that attempts were made to diversify the sources of credit. It reveals an extraordinary capacity to borrow; it is clear that in extreme cases such as this a man could borrow merely on the strength of hissother borrowing. The hand-to-mouth or rather hand-to-hand existence that is implied is less generally interesting, however, than what the liabilities suggest about those with money to lend. Ali showed great enterprise, with signs of desperation in the partial alienation of his property towards the end, but certainly his finances, as opposed to his standing, would not have borne examination after 1888. At his death his liabilities for interest alone were nearly three times his maximum income from land, quite apart from unknown liabilities in respect of two secured mortgages; no doubt the balances would have been worse without the expedient of the zerpeshgi leases. He achieved all this partly by deepening his debt to existing creditors. It is true that some lent to gain the lease of an estate, or without interest: the latter may have been a technicality on religious grounds (it was a common ploy for Muslims to record a principal larger than the loan) and thus in neither case may Ali have received the full amount for which he admitted liability. Two creditors, M.M. Chaudhuri and Mirza Khalil, were sufficiently commercially-minded to go to law to recover their dues. But the others, representing half the liability, persisted in lending without security in spite of outstanding debts in respect of their own earlier loans.

In the major case no interest had been paid on the first loan since it began. It is difficult to see any economic calculation in such behaviour. It seems as if, after an initial commitment (a mere Rs.2000 for B.B. Mullick, and perhaps mortgages on Ali's estates for Biseswar Prasad), men felt themselves bound to continue advancing money with what must soon have been very little expectation of recovering interest or perhaps even the principal.

The impression given by this one example may be reinforced by others. In one estate in Shahabad the poorest villages had been unable to obtain credit locally; they were financed instead by travelling banias who were said to return each year in the hope of recovering their investment only to be forced into lending out more. So too in a report on a private agricultural bank set up by a sugar planter, L.H. Mylne, the pre-existing system was described as being one in which the general rate of interest worked out at not less than 30 per cent, but in which the mahajans were usually of the cultivating classes and seldom had better security for their loans than a day-book kept in a very irregular fashion. Only a man 'with a very poor record or reputation' would fail to obtain temporary credit without security, and the mahajan, though seemingly a 'veritable Shylock', was usually 'a fair-dealing man' and 'very frequently', indeed, 'much of a fool, who would melt into rupees when an over-whelmed debtor from whom he could not possibly recover all his dues, cringes before him and invokes his aid as "Sahuji".' With such a man, one suspects, economic status would become important mainly when social status was low. The experience of running an agricultural bank also gave an insight into several of the features usually considered objectionable about the way money-lenders operated. For example, they were known to collect their dues at the harvest, usually at a discount on market prices, which effectively raised the cost to the borrower. After a few years Mylne too found himself on the threshing floor, for otherwise, he explained, his borrowers would conceal a good deal of the produce which should have been sold to meet their commitments. (Being present had another advantage too, for future transactions: it enabled Mylne to observe exactly the margin against which the tenant could borrow.) Mylne's key problem as an agricultural banker seemed to be that the debtors simply did not take the repayment of debts very seriously, which is equally a comment on the bania's mode of operation to which they had previously been accustomed. Mylne attempted to secure the release of some tenants from existing debts by allowing the alienation of parts of holdings on usufructuary mortgages, in the hope that the cultivator would then be induced to save to recover possession of his land. Mylne had found that, when instalments were due, the debtor usually defaulted, incurring what 'might be called penal rates of interest' on the balance, and such accumulations of debt were seldom paid off. We must assume therefore that some proportion of them would have been lost to the money-lender. And what of the blame placed on banias who did acquire land? Mylne's borrowers would say to his tahsildars: 'why ... be anxious, is not my land worth' so many rupees? It was in such a way, Mylne speculated, that lazy and reckless men ended up as serfs paying high rents or as mere share-croppers on what had been their own lands. Yet he himself found that the tendency among the great majority was for the debit balances to increase, even though his bank was trying to 'save' the tenants from themselves and refusing loans which they were unlikely to be able to repay. Thus the rapacity of the bania seems not to have been essential to the process of alienation.[36]

Some of the arguments about money-lenders have been discussed above, in my introductory essay. In the money-lender's popular image, his iniquities fuelled indignation because he was presented as a rapacious parasite: the poor cultivator forced by famine to borrow in order to survive would, as one pamphlet put it, receive Rs.15, execute a bond for Rs.20 and admit liability for interest at 63 per cent.[37] From then on his fate was sealed, though in detail it was not clear why prosperous regions tended to be the most indebted or how the debts of the poor grew year by year when on the one hand credit was supposed to dry up in hard times and on the other they were so rapidly enmeshed and the bania was greedy for their land. Secondly, the money-lender was objectionable because his present operations were thought to be very much a creation of the nineteenth century (though again there was no detailed explanation of how credit had been organized in earlier times). Thirdly, according to a strong current in British official thinking the bania stood in the part later to be played by the 'disloyal agitator': he subverted the existing order; he was an interloper against whom the cultivators needed protection; and his hold had been strengthened by British legal innovations (in this case laws on property and contract). The tribes of Thakurs, Jats and others who had settled on the land in north India were said still to owe allegiance to chieftains who had become their landlords, and to abhor the intrusion of the bania (as of Muslim purchasers of land). Such changes would be a 'fertile source of disturbance' and of far greater evils in future: prediction was attractive in these spheres as it avoided the inconvenience of evidence.[38] But the money-lender was not a single category: there were specialists, there were traders who gave out advances, there were zamindars and raiyats who lent to their fellows. If the British were critical of activities which led to the accumulation of land other than for direct cultivation, this was a moral rather than an economic judgment: it led them to a confusing impasse between a welcome for self-maximizing individualism and fears of anarchy due to social change. In discussing the impact of the Bengal Tenancy Act, which was supposed to have increased the alienation of smaller holdings, the Commissioner of Patna Division concluded that there were those, often of low caste, who purchased land because they wished to extend their cultivation, and the regions where such men were found (Saran and parts of Muzaffarpur) were 'advanced'; and that there were also people who acquired land only to sublet it and who were thus 'landgrabbers pure and simple', and the regions where they predominated (such as Champaran) were 'behind the times'. The Commissioner proposed legislation to permit transfer only to a 'bona fide cultivator, or at least a tenant of the same class as the transferor' - the very aim which was to be attempted in the Punjab Alienation of Land Act in 1900.[39] But in economic terms it is misleading to equate borrowing with land alienation, and impossible to distinguish between alienation to outsiders and neighbours, seeing that each may lead to subletting or to a concentration of resources. It is not clear after all that the visiting bania-trader is in practice more of an outsider to the bulk of his clients than the dominant cultivator-money-lender is to his. Thus the money-lender might have been seen as an agent for redistribution from the slothful to the thrifty, or for the creation of more efficient units of production; or he might have been presented as a useful insurance for the cultivator, and anxious not to become involved in agriculture. In the latter case, the problem would be not that he forced change by bringing harsh realities home to the cultivator, but that he tended to protect him from the consequences of his behaviour and even at the worst to allow him to survive in situ, producing in the old way.

Some money-lenders certainly grabbed land and made it more productive; others grabbed it to rack-rent and thus reduced total spending power and thwarted development. But it is possible too, and supported by the indications that money-lenders did not operate strictly on their bond or lend solely on the basis of commercial judgments, that money-lenders were economic depressors not because of an extension in their influence but because of its socially-conservative features. In that case, if the British were in error, it was in trying to curb the operation of a commercial instinct that was but imperfectly at work. Thus we come to the same point in this as the earlier examples, in regard to change and continuity in nineteenth-century Bihar and the role in both of the British government: that it is possible that the British did not so much bring about radical changes across in a wide spectrum, as intensify some trends, and exaggerate or ossify social characteristics.

I shall conclude this essay by turning to some general aspects of production, considered in relation to the ways the evidence may be used. Three features may be agreed about the nineteenth century: that prices rose considerably, that population rose to some extent, and that cultivation was expanded to an unknown degree. We cannot analyse these increases systematically: the figures for prices, for example, are not strictly comparable,[40] and they are not complete, in the sense that no weighted index of them can be produced, allowing for the volume of trade in different years and seasons, and the different roles played by the same crop in different places.[41] More important, we cannot assume for Bihar as we might for Britain that price rises themselves had a decisive or general impact on production. Whatever advance the money economy was making it was a process far from complete in nineteenth-century Bihar. We have a problem of diagnosis which reflects a substantive difficulty. In particular, methodologically-speaking, the problem presented by non-standard and regional measures early in British rule did not simply go away as the century progressed. Just as what a zamindar meant by a bigha could still not be relied upon in 1900, so too - but more seriously - the purchasing-power of the rupee and its significance as an economic indicator fluctuated from place to place; and it did so in largely unknowable ways, with harvests, communications, rents, opportunities for labour and so on. A rent of two rupees an acre in Darbhanga, equivalent to perhaps 36 seers of rice, is not more or less the same as a rent of two rupees in Shahabad, where it represents 28 seers. (And though the British used a standard, otherwise the seer itself was a measure which still meant different things in different places.) In this society economic measures were, in short, not objective. By the same token, rents did not relate constantly to output or costs and thus to the quality of the land; they were influenced by caste, tenure and custom, and moreover, even when recorded in rupees, they were very often paid in kind or in services and in amounts which varied according to circumstances. It is not a simple question, then, to ask who could or should have benefited from changes in agricultural production. It is implied, however, that opportunities were not evenly distributed. Again we suspect that change in Bihar was not broadly-based, but subject to peculiar and local distortions.

On prices, it is impossible to distinguish consistently between district headquarters and elsewhere. We cannot even be sure that bad harvests affected prices similarly in different districts. The returns for 1889-92, the last year being one of scarcity, suggest that there was often as much or more variation between areas in the same season as between seasons in the one area (Table 4). With such figures, how could we generalize about the impact of price rises? They illustrate the dangers of using a monetary measure to interpret a largely non-monetized economy. With further data, however, they might enable us to identify possible beneficiaries of price rises, as of the British expansion of government: they remind us that some areas, groups and people were strategically placed. If we interpret the table, we see that Bhabua's prices were high, presumably because it was poor and economically isolated; similarly they did not vary greatly because relatively few of its people were potential consumers. Elsewhere in Shahabad prices were moderate because of the canals which increased rice production and reduced the scarcity of 1892. In Saran, on the other hand, prices were high and stable: if accurately reported, they reveal a relatively rich district's dependence on rice imports. Elsewhere in 'poorer' districts, prices were generally lower but also more volatile - the Champaran returns were doubtless affected by food imports from Nepal in 1892, and would otherwise have varied more considerably. To all this complexity, evidence of a poorly integrated market in rice, we must add the large seasonal variations and the social and other distortions of prices paid to producers. Obviously, though, even on these

*Table 4* *Lowland Rice Prices*

| | 1889 | 1890 | 1891 | 1892 | Maximum Variation |
|---|---|---|---|---|---|
| *Patna* | 89 | 108 | 104 | 88 | 20 |
| Barh | 78 | 110 | 104 | 77 | 33 |
| Bihar | 94 | 117 | 109 | 87 | 30 |
| Dinapur | 74 | 100 | 97 | 77 | 26 |
| *Gaya* | 94 | 104 | 91 | 70 | 34 |
| Nawada | 104 | 124 | 115 | 88 | 36 |
| Jahanabad | 94 | 110 | 107 | 77 | 33 |
| Aurangabad | 102 | 112 | 103 | 80 | 32 |
| *Arrah (Shahabad)* | 95 | 103 | 99 | 78 | 25 |
| Buxar | 91 | 100 | 92 | 80 | 20 |
| Sasaram | 96 | 100 | 98 | 76 | 24 |
| Bhabua | 85 | 88 | 86 | 71 | 17 |
| *Muzaffarpur* | 87 | 101 | 96 | 82 | 19 |
| Sitamarhi | 85 | 117 | 106 | 84 | 33 |
| Hajipur | 90 | 105 | 96 | 80 | 25 |
| *Darbhanga* | 95 | 119 | 104 | 88 | 31 |
| Madhubani | 93 | 124 | 107 | 98 | 31 |
| Samastipur | 89 | 109 | 101 | 82 | 27 |
| *Motihari (Champaran)* | 84 | 106 | 100 | 91 | 22 |
| Bettiah | 100 | 122 | 104 | 107 | 22 |
| *Chapra (Saran)* | 77 | 79 | 77 | 67 | 10 |
| Siwan | 85 | 102 | 100 | 85 | 17 |
| Gopalganj | 83 | 98 | 91 | 90 | 15 |

*Note*: 100 = 15 seers per rupee.
*Source*: R&A Agric B17 June 1891, Rev B19 July 1890, B16 May 1892 and B16 November 1893.

figures, the people who had most opportunities were those who could store grain over time, or move it over space; and the areas in which the enterprise of increasing rice production would be least risky and most profitable would be those supplying such markets as Patna and Muzaffarpur towns, or Shahabad and Saran districts.

The significance of the fact that prices may have risen by two or three hundred per cent in the nineteenth century is thus specific rather than general and the degree to which the range of fluctuations between areas, seasons and years narrowed in the same period is open to debate. Similarly, Bihar's population seems to have risen during the nineteenth century before levelling off in 1880s (the rises of this century are another matter) and the temptation is to suppose that this led to 'involution' or 'poverty-sharing': the pauperization and equal misery of the vast majority in which it is so easy to believe from today's vantage point. The other indications of expansions of cultivation and modified land use could thus be merely desperate and unsuccessful ploys in crowded and land-hungry districts. And yet it is not certain that population pressure forced the changes, as we can see if we examine them more closely. Marginal lands and those liable to flooding were settled, but many of them - in north Bihar for example - under the aegis of European and Indian planters. Forests contracted, and there was increased competition over their resources, changes apparently tempered by government controls but perhaps more accurately, induced by them. Late in the century too there was an increase in the building of embankments, in which the rulers again played an ambiguous role, but in which the most evident protagonists were planters seeking to increase their profits and cultivators to protect their livelihoods. Most important, however, a significant expansion of agricultural production may have occurred in the least obvious area: the increase in cultivation in under-utilized villages in heavily-populated areas, chiefly by non-resident cultivators. Some of these villages were dry, and the change marked the extension of irrigation. More of them, in the Bihar of the nineteenth century, were relatively under-populated, having larger-than-average holdings, with high-caste raiyats perhaps who were ready to sub-let to industrious or needy neighbours. But most of the under-utilized villages, I would guess, were those gradually subjected to more intensive land-use, encouraged by the British revenue and legal systems and by economic opportunities. An inquiry into the system of fallowing in north Bihar, for example, produced from the more experienced observers, agreement that it was no longer much practised in the 1880s. Few raiyats, it was said, were trying to do anything but get as many crops as possible during the year, though they were paying more attention than previously to irrigation and manuring.[42] Was this because they were now pressed so closely to the soil that increased efforts were necessary for survival? Many observers thought, on the contrary, that it was precisely because no such crisis had as yet been reached that

Bihari cultivators were unreceptive of the improvements in methods which some eager officials showed them. We need to understand this change better. It seems likely that there had never been a fallow system in the sense of a deliberate and regular avoidance of cropping in one season in order to reap a better harvest in the next; the vagaries of the climate would have made this unwise. (An exception would be where the return was guaranteed or partly received in advance, and indeed some indigo and opium lands *were* left fallow.) But certain villages and perhaps originally all villages had had areas of land which were used for grazing or gathering and only periodically for cultivation; they had provided fallowing informally to the extent that cultivation shifted from year to year, which it seems to have done quite apart from any voluntary rotation - often enough, for example, when holdings were transferred or as a result of flood or drought. The tendency during the nineteenth century, I believe, was for more and more of such land to be brought regularly under the plough. Resident cultivators who were not in a position or who were not permitted to increase their holdings therefore found themselves under pressure both on their own lands and in respect of areas which had once been, in effect, common to the village. Evidence of this may be found in the many complaints at the inroads made by outsiders (meaning people, often of lower caste, from other villages) who would pay competitive rents; and in the many disputes between proprietors and cultivators over liabilities, rights and measurements. (I do not mean to re-open our earlier debate about whether landownership in India was wholly an innovation of British laws; I mean merely to suggest that quarrels were indicative of changes in marginal land-use as well as, no doubt, in the extent to which legal title was seen to be valuable and able to be translated into physical possession.) In short, I believe that the exploitation of Champaran, so clearly marked by its increase in population but also clearly an effect of entrepreneurial efforts, was repeated on a more intimate scale within districts whose population was more stable.

Having said this, we must still remember that the increase in cultivated area cannot be precisely measured and our difficulties are multiplied if we include (as we must) consideration of any increase in double-cropping.[43] We cannot be at all certain also on productivity per acre. It was assumed not to have increased greatly, but the assumptions were based on impressions, inappropriately and inconsistently presented, by untrained and probably uninterested observers,[44] or on rare and unrepresentative sampling and experiment,[45] producing figures which were (as described in 1898) 'practically valueless'.[46] The important point is that if we can assume that population pressure did not generate the changes we can observe, then we must also assume that the changes were for someone's benefit. The obvious candidates, at least in the medium term, are those in possession of the land in question: that is, existing groups in the society, such as landlords who could enforce their will and dominant cultivators elsewhere. Changes in land-use may be related to power, or so I am suggesting, as much as to necessity, and therefore do not represent political or social upheavals. The pressure of population was not more central than the pressure of profit.

But it may also be agreed, perhaps, that there was no fixity of practice in Bihar. A curiosity of the records, for example, is the confusion between observers about which harvest was the more significant in any one region, a confusion that seems to go beyond the obvious disparities in judgments on the different bases of value, purpose or acreage. About Muzaffarpur it was stated in 1896 that the bhadoi involved the largest acreage and the aghani was almost as important. In 1899 the rabi was shown, by survey, to be far more significant by this measure, in comparison with the bhadoi, though it too was rivalled by the aghani. If we look at subdivisional and pargana figures we find variations too, rabi acreage exceeding bhadoi by a ratio of 2:1 in some areas and less than 5:4 in others. The certainty is that there were very local variations in the pattern, but also that the importance of different harvests varied from year to year. The determining factor was, indeed, the climatic character of the season: more consistent influences - for example, the price of particular products - were by no means automatic incentives to production (and of course if the revenue demand had ever fulfilled such a role it was declining in significance as the century wore on). A consequence of the degree of flexibility induced by the climate, moreover, was undoubtedly an ability to react to other stimuli - official or economic - within existing values and customs, and without any change in expectations comparable with the apparent changes in production or opportunity. Perhaps the most interesting feature of the expansion of cultivation, for example, if my explanations are correct, is the extent to which it did *not* represent effort of a different kind on the part of the primary beneficiaries: they did not have to seek out new crops, techniques or markets; they merely had to let out the land which was within their control.

This analysis directs our attention to the continuing features of Bihari society and its physical environment, and not to the incidents and errors of British rule, when we seek to understand the region's present economic, social and political 'backwardness'. Nonetheless the long period of British rule is part of the environment. I have suggested it did not introduce quick or fundamental changes. It influenced some particular *roles* (say, zamindar, peasant, bania), but it perhaps did not transform their respective *spheres of operation*. It confirmed the substantial zamindar, the surplus cultivator and the 'conservative' money-lender, more or less regardless of any effort on their part or changes in their attitudes or behaviour.[47] Bihar may have been different, in this respect, from some other parts of India. If the British, in Bihar, before the twentieth century, encouraged the existing social disposition rather than changed it, and if they made the benefits for advantaged sections easier to obtain, as I believe, then they retarded or reduced the likelihood of fundamental change, either in attitudes or methods.

I make the chronological proviso deliberately. It seems quite possible to argue that the growth of state power and political organization and the changes in economic circumstances led ultimately to a weakening of the position of some formerly-powerful groups during the twentieth century; in short, that the upheavals in late twentieth-century Bihar may be traced to changes beginning in the 1880s and 1890s. My present argument does not preclude such an analysis; but it suggests that the tendency of British rule in Bihar was to delay the onset of such changes and not to advance them, because of the laxity of administration under the permanent settlement, the nature of Bihari society and economy and the partial and incomplete character of the exchanges between the rulers and the ruled. Perhaps the most important point to emerge from this discussion - important because it bears upon the difference between 'backward' Bihar-Benares and the 'progressive' Doab or Punjab - is the relevance of what the British government did *not* do in the permanently-settled areas. Did the British offer less of a challenge and fewer opportunities in Bihar in comparison with temporarily-settled regions, because of the Bihar administration's comparative weakness, distance, inappropriateness or partiality? If so, we must turn on their head in one sense the ideas associated in the nineteenth century with the work of Maine: to deny not only a necessary evolution common to all societies, but also the moral and functional superiority of gradual, society-wide change over rapid, sector-induced development. Moreover, if I am right, then the Bihar effect appears to be another example of 'differential impact', first described by Eric Stokes and now being amplified in detailed studies.[48]

*NOTES*

Robb, 'State, peasant and money-lender in late nineteenth-century Bihar: some Colonial inputs'

*Abbreviations*:

| | |
|---|---|
| AgH | Agriculture and Horticulture Branch |
| Agric | Agriculture Branch |
| Fam | Famine Branch |
| Gen | General Branch |
| PCR | Records of the Commissioner of Patna (Bihar State Archives, Patna) |
| R&A | Proceedings of the Revenue and Agriculture Department, Government of India (National Archives, New Delhi) |
| Stats | Statistics Branch |

PCR citations include basta, collection/file number, and date, when found. R&A citations give Branch, series (A, B or C), proceeding number, month and year, and refer to the proceedings proper and/or to papers kept with them.

1. There was no reliable information, for example, on which to base the Son canal scheme, and in Saran district in 1873-4 famine relief was conducted in the belief that 50 per cent of the area was under winter rice (the crop that had failed) wereas an inquiry in 1875 concluded that the true proportion was 28 per cent; and that people depended on rice (large quantities were imported from Burma) whereas the majority ate mainly millets (available from the North West Provinces). By the 1890s however it was thought that progress had been made in the records, reducing errors, misapprehension, want of uniformity and faulty returns. See Home R&A AgH A 167-76 October 1879; R&A Fam B 5-6 July 1898. On the collection of information see Clive Dewey, '*Patwari* and *Chaukidar*' in A.G. Hopkins and Dewey, *The Imperial Impact* (London 1978).

2. B.H. Baden-Powell, *The Indian Village Community* (London 1896), pp.3 ff.

3. Dharma Kumar, *Land and Caste in Southern India* (Cambridge 1965).

4. C.A. Bayly, 'Gentry, Merchants and Agrarian Society in Northern India in the early nineteenth

century', unpublished paper given at the symposium on the external dimension in rural South Asia, 12 December 1981.

5. Ratnalekha Ray, *Change in Bengal Agrarian Society* (New Delhi 1979).

6. See Peter Robb, 'Hierarchy and Resources: Peasant Stratification in late nineteenth century Bihar', *Modern Asian Studies* 13, 1 (1979).

7. R&A Fam C 6 April 1901.

8. Home R&A AgH A 167-76 October 1879; R&A Agric A 26 February 1895.

9. R&A Agric A 7-11 May 1891.

10. J.A. Voelcker; R&A Agric A 9 July 1890. This did not stop the Dumraon experimental farm from being justified by its 'representative' character, and the failure of an earlier farm at Arrah from being attributed to its worse-than-average soils; PCR 341 10/63-9 1884-5. Experiments showed, moreover, that sugarcane in trenches did well at Dumraon and Burdwan but not at Sibpur; deep ploughing was profitable at Dumraon one year but not the next; manure in very large quantities suited good varieties of cane but actually seemed detrimental to poor varieties; only best quality saltpetre (90 per cent nitrate) paid for cereals, and ground bones and phosphates did not; R&A Agric C 13-15 March 1900 and A 9 December 1892.

11. One experiment gave, from a 9-inch furrow with an iron plough, more than three times the output of that from a 3-inch ploughing with a wooden implement.

12. This is more important than what has sometimes been implied, that the departments and farms endlessly developed inappropriate remedies: some ploughs were too heavy or expensive or unmanageable, but others selling for as little as two rupees were introduced in significant numbers in some areas; the best known was the 'Kaiser' distributed from Kanpur; R&A Agric A 3 January, A 17 April 1892, and B 8-9 January 1896. On the other hand cultivators might well ask if a higher yield of sucrose would be rewarded by a higher price, if different and often increased labour demands suited the procurement practices or family arrangements, or if the return from extra outlay compensated for the risk of increased debt.

13. The reforms included changes in marketing, social relations, tenancy and so on, in order that the best option could be chosen rather than the least damaging. Above all there was competition for scarce resources: in 1909 in Shahabad the government itself

tried to control the exploitation of timber and other forest products by declaring the Rohtas plateau a protected area, and alternative schemes for fuel such as a plan of 1881 to plant trees had no effect; what then was the point of proving the efficacy of cattle dung in huge quantities, as in one experiment?; R&A Forests A 30-1 June 1909; PCR 334 10/15 1881-2.

14. R&A Agric A 7-11 May 1891; *Census of India* I, Pt 1 (Calcutta 1903), pp.47-50.

15. R&A Rev B 54-66 June 1899.

16. Patna district paid Rs.356,000 in road cess, revised to Rs.462,000 in 1893-4.

17. The point is administrative rather than on the permanent settlement itself - indeed in Bengal a far higher proportion of temporarily-settled (non-raiyatwari) or government estates than of permanently-settled estates were in arrears (though the former categories included settled estates whose proprietors had failed to meet demands). But Bengal's record was far worse than that of any other province overall, though its revenue demand was lighter.

18. See R&A Rev A 88-92 June 1890, B 12 June 1891, A 29-31 June 1897, B 10-11 June 1899, A 27-8 October 1908; PCR 363 12/22 1895-6. There were some special reasons in other districts; in Patna for example instalments were collected by mistake according to the Christian calendar instead of the fasli year with the result that receipts were late and temporary deficits were repeatedly recorded in the returns.

19. The saga of the Hathwa heir illustrates the last aspect. The estate, one of the largest in Bihar, had come under the court of the wards in 1896. In 1909 local officials expressed alarm that the Maharani and her then diwan, Devendranath Dutt, were exercising an unhealthy influence over the young heir, bringing him up 'to regard all officials ... with the deepest distrust and animosity, and inspiring him with feelings of hostility' towards the government itself. As a result Dutt was summarily dismissed, with a pension in view of his previously distinguished service, and the Maharani was divested of control over her son who was removed to Mayo College in Ajmere under the guardianship of an English officer. This was not much to the taste of the Government of India, members of which knew the Maharani personally, but they objected to its clumsiness not the motives behind it; indeed they worried, as they modified some of the measures, about the political consequences of alienating a family so important

in Bihar and so long 'noted for its loyalty'; R&A Rev A 3-8 September 1910. See also, on Buxar, PCR 339 14/28 1883-4 and 341 14/28 1884-5.

20. For example the extent to which relatives could draw on the estate was limited: the *sradh* of a Hathwa grandson was allowed Rs.1000 when his father's ritual had allegedly cost nine times as much; R&A Rev B 29-30 January 1903.

21. R&A Rev A 29-31 June 1897.

22. There was also criticism of failure to heed orders calling for liberal expenditure on improvements. See PCR 345-6 10/110 1887-8; R&A Rev B 47 October 1894, B 5 November 1895 and A 11-12 May 1900. Court of wards procedure was not much liked in Bengal, and the Government of India itself, at least while under the influence of Denzil Ibbetson, did not consider there were very strong political reasons for protecting most Bengali zamindars from themselves. The law was not often applied merely because proprietors were in financial difficulties (though this was permissible if requested and in the public interest). Bengal intervened when the owner was in some way 'disqualified' (in the terms of the Act) and at one time opposed an amendment to allow action without consent for indebtedness; R&A Rev A 1-4 November 1894 and A 4-24 May 1897. By contrast when the Maharani of Dumraon, considered politically objectionable, refused to adopt an heir the Bengal government was prepared to push through a law to allow it to take over management of the estate; the Government of India demurred, arguing that the Maharani could not be called incompetent (she had a life-interest and the question on which Bengal wanted to legislate was on whether she was a proprietor under the Act); R&A Rev A 26-30 April 1897, A 21-3 June 1898 and B 16 September 1905.

23. The establishment was quite large: 23 estates in Gaya provided employment for 123 patwaris, clerks, gomashtas and so on, whose wages accounted for some 13 per cent of the rental, and in Patna in 1895-6 the gross demand from government estates was over Rs.227,000 of which some Rs.35,000 was spent locally on collection and other costs; PCR 345-6 10/103 and 110 1887/8, 352 10/20 1890-1, and 363 12/6 1895-6; R&A Rev B 52-3 April 1894.

24. These considerations render meaningless the official claim that the cultivating classes enjoyed substantially increased income under the British but that the average was depressed by the plight of the

labouring population; J.B. Fuller, 7 February 1902, R&A Fam A 22-4 February 1902. See R&A Fam B 19-28 December 1896 and A 104-8 January 1897.

25. R&A Fam A 12 June 1892. A petition for relief was received from Patna; R&A Fam B 52 March 1892.

26. For the foregoing see R&A Fam A 6 January 1892, A 20-1 May 1892, A 12 June 1892, A 35-6 July 1892, A 1-2 November 1892, A 2 January 1893, A 71-81 and 101 January 1897 and C 16-20 May 1897.

27. R&A Fam A 26 March 1892, A 1-2 November 1892 and A 2-15 September 1893.

28. R&A Fam A 101 January 1897, A 71 April 1897, A 17-18 June 1897 and A 26-7 November 1897.

29. R&A Fam A 101 January 1897, A 101 July 1897 and A 27 October 1897.

30. R&A Fam A 39-41 and 88-9 February 1897, A 80-3 June 1897 and A 114-17 August 1897.

31. R&A Fam A 26-9 April 1897, A 122-4 June 1897, A 121-6 July 1897, A 101 July 1897, A 114-17 August 1897 and A 27 October 1897.

32. R&A Fam B 3-4 July 1893 and B 1 February 1899.

33. In Champaran in 1891 Rs.20,000 were outstanding from 1888; Rs.43,000 were due and by 1892 Rs.67,000. In Muzaffarpur Rs.9000 were paid of Rs.40,000 due in 1890; in Darbhanga Rs.12,000 of Rs.29,000. Saran's total was Rs.60,000. See below, note 34.

34. Patna division spent Rs.6500 of 17,500 allowed for loans in 1894, Rs.33,850 (31,000 for floods in North Bihar) of Rs.57,000 allowed for advances. In 1893 it spent Rs.111,500 of 142,000; Shahabad approved 180 of 260 applications. On loans see R&A Rev B 44 and 52 October 1890, B 16 November 1891, B 61-2 March 1893, A 54-5 September 1893, A 8 October 1895; Fam A 20-1 May 1892, A 12 June 1892 and A 2 January 1893; *Pioneer* 31 March 1890 and 14 December 1892; PCR 353 35/1 1890-1, 354 12/7 and 355 22/6 1891-2, 357 12/9 1892-3, 359 23/2 and 57 1894-5, 361 23/2 1894-5 and 363 12/6 1895-6.

35. R&A Rev B 38 October 1890.

36. R&A Rev B 52-3 June 1895.

37. 'The Growth of Debt among Cultivators of Oudh etc' (Lucknow: Church Mission Congregational Press 1891), R&A Rev B 26-7 May 1891.

38. R&A Rev A 43-6 September 1894.

39. PCR 358 12/9 1893-4. For the view of the money-lender as an interloper and subversive see for example Denzil Ibbetson's remarks, R&A Rev A 72-3 October 1895; see also A 1-8 May 1891. It is possible of course to see alternatives to the orthodoxy. In the Central

Provinces it was thought bania castes were extremely numerous, becoming more wealthy, and punctuating their progress upwards with extravagant celebrations; often they had ousted the 'old cultivating mulguzars'. Yet, as proprietors, they profited not through rents but by squeezing their tenants for interest payments. The conclusion may be that banias tended not to become managers of land as opposed to controllers of it. It is noteworthy that in 1891 20 per cent of the land in the Central Provinces was supposed to have changed hands since settlement, one half of that to money-lenders, and that proprietors held 'the lands still left to them only at the discretion of their creditors'. This, supposed to illustrate the severity of the problem, might also be interpreted as showing the reluctance of the bania actually to take possession of property mortgaged to him. Secondly, as was also observed, foreshadowing Malcolm Darling, indebtedness was greatest among agriculturists who occupied good soils on low rents and revenue assessments: money-lenders therefore were not necessarily to the fore where poverty was greatest. This might be interpreted as proving merely that the bania was aiming to gain control of the best land, the temptation being greatest where the revenue demand was lowest: thus Ibbetson claimed the money-lender was often conducting the illegitimate business of trying to obtain land, and at the same time observed how a canal plus a railway could ruin larger owners on a tract of land by increasing its value and their credit-rating and encouraging idleness and extravagance. But the former does not necessarily follow from the latter: credit would be better in more fertile lands because of the greater income and security provided, even for a mortgage which was expected to be redeemed. Finally one of the richest money-lenders in the Provinces claimed to be owed Rs.4 lakhs by cultivators and to expect to recover only 1½. Once again then it seems that not all of the banias' operations maximized their commercial advantage; R&A Rev A 9-14 May 1891, A 20 May 1893 and A 5-6 September 1894.

40. Only in the 1890s were soundings extended so as to include marts other than central ones, but they still represented prices 'prevailing' on the last day of the reviewed period (not at other times); for some commodities rates were given quarterly, for others twice a year and for others again annually; yearly rates were based on returns in the year in question but from different numbers of returns for each commodity. Some

averages were calculated over different seasons without regard to the fact that the wholesale trade occurred very largely in one season; comparisons between areas were based on the same products, whereas of course these played different roles in different places. In Darbhanga transactions in the rice trade in the 1890s were conducted in non-standard seers and local pice, and officials had therefore to translate from one measure to another. Worse still, as the producers' price was the one in which government was interested, all figures were subject to deduction of a 'usual' but unspecified margin between wholesale and retail prices, a deduction that was intended to vary from time to time and place to place after 'careful' inquiry. See R&A Stats A 2-3 March 1892, A 1-2 June 1893, and Fam A 12 June 1892.

41. See returns of wheat, rice and maize prices in four seasons and various districts; R&A Fam B 3 October 1905.

42. PCR 334 12/4 1880-1.

43. The Muzaffarpur survey in the 1890s revealed an 'increase' of 7½ per cent in net cropped area, in comparison with previous but unreliable estimates. Until 1896-7 moreover returns included areas where crops had failed and others had been sown subsequently; and in general area is a blunt indicator especially when it is difficult to record acreage under different crops (in Bihar mixed cropping was the rule except for rice).

44. The relative outturn at each harvest was recorded in annas, an inherently subjective measure which was shown in 1906 to have led to estimates 20 per cent too low on average (since 1892): 16 annas was supposed to mean an average crop but was generally taken by the police sub-inspectors and kanungos who reported to mean a bumper one. (On the other hand 4 annas clearly meant a poor harvest by any standard.) Elementary errors were also made: an average outturn for rice in Patna, Shahabad and Gaya in 1896-7 was calculated by adding the first-class yield to the average, and for wheat by adding the maximum, minimum and mean; while the provincial average was arrived at by dividing the sum of the district averages by the number of districts!

45. It was unsound to extrapolate from small numbers of crop-cutting experiments; and indeed in 1896-7 the Bengal director of land records decided that the results of three years' experiments were so indefinite and unreliable that he merely returned the figures for the previous quinquennium after slight modifications.

46. R&A Fam A 5-6 July 1898. For the above account

(and notes) see R&A Agric A 20-1 February 1908, A 5 February 1899, Fam A 5-6 July 1898 and B 22 August 1899, and Gen A 3 February 1899; PCR 341 10/63-9 1884-5.

47. This interpretation may be almost endlessly applied. There were reports, for example, that the South Bihari irrigation systems were working less well than previously, at the end of the nineteenth century. This could mean that the British had undermined the order under which the systems had flourished, or that changing climatic, economic or demographic conditions had found the old systems wanting. Certainly British administration, though more highly developed than that of the past, was probably also less well equipped to assist local irrigation and, with the permanent settlement, less motivated to do so. But equally it could mean - and so I would argue - that any decline reflected decisions by zamindars and is adequately explained by the inference that the successful had less need to guarantee output to secure a sufficiency of income, while the impoverished could not be certain of retaining the profits of their investment.

48. See Eric Stokes, 'The first century of British colonial rule in India: social revolution or social stagnation?' in *The Peasant and the Raj* (Cambridge 1978) and, for example, Ian Stone, 'Canal Irrigation and Agrarian Change under Colonial Rule: A study of the U.P. Doab, India, 1830-1930' (Cambridge Ph.D. 1980).

# BETWEEN BRITISH RAJ AND SARAN RAIYAT: THE DEVELOPMENT OF LOCAL CONTROL INSTITUTIONS IN THE NINETEENTH AND EARLY TWENTIETH CENTURIES

*Anand A. Yang*

Historical writings on the British raj abound with discussions of the imperial structures of rule. In contrast, the processes and mechanisms by which government extended down to the grass-roots level and impinged upon the 'little world' of Indian raiyats (peasants) have received relatively little attention. A number of recent regional and local studies, however, have taken the first steps in reconstructing the undergirdings of Pax Britannica by showing that 'the British had ... native organisations strong enough to deliver large armies, taxes and authorities into their hands, yet weak enough to be cajoled into doing so, rather than unite and resist the invaders'.[1]

This essay investigates this relationship of 'consultation and control' by highlighting the British attempts to penetrate to the sub-district levels by linking the kanungo (registrar), the patwari (village accountant), and the chaukidar (village watchman) to its ruling machinery. These three institutions were to serve as the state's direct channels to the larger society of peasants. Development of such a local infrastructure would have endowed government with a system of primary control institutions, thus reducing the necessity of relying primarily upon local allies or connections. '[L]ike any colonial regime,' the British raj too 'was perpetually pulled in opposite directions by the need to leave the ruled-over society alone and equally pressing need to deal with it in an effective way.'[2]

This analysis of the workings of the kanungos, patwaris, and chaukidars is based on the experience of the north Bihar district of Saran in the nineteenth and early twentieth centuries. Although the concern here is not to examine comprehensively the entire apparatus of the ruling machinery, the focus on these three institutions will provide a framework for scrutinizing the nature and effects of official control in a specific economic and social setting.[3]

*The Context of Official Control*

Events during the Mutiny/Rebellion in Saran show that British control in 1857 rested on several flimsy supports, two of the principal ones of which were powerful local allies and the administrative machinery. Precisely these two props were utilized by the Deputy Magistrate of Sewan in eluding rebels approaching from the neighbouring district of Champaran. In his flight he was helped not only by landholders, but also by petty 'native' police officers.[4]

Such bulwarks further ensured, even in the absence of British officials, that 'the general tone of the people was for peace and order'. Other than 'two or three cases of Riot and boat plundering', as the District Magistrate reported on his return, not 'one single offence [was] committed ... which can be said to have arisen out of the disturbed state of the district'.[5]

That such supports were vital to the stability and maintenance of British rule is also explained by the conditions which led to rebellion. As Eric Stokes concludes from his district-level analyses of 1857, 'the critical factor in rural reactions was the presence or absence of a thriving magnate element heavily committed by interest to British rule'.[6] Thus the year 1857 was relatively quiescent in Saran because landholders 'as a body behaved well since the commencement of the disturbance'.[7]

Furthermore, for most loyal landholders, co-operation with the government in 1857 was a continuation of a long-standing relationship. Its roots were established during the initial penetration by British rule into the local society of Saran which induced relatively few changes in the indigenous controlling structure of the district, especially in superior rights in the land. And although the Rajput maliks (proprietors) who had lost all their estates did 'kick up a row', the only local outburst in 1857, it was 'not so much to fight Government as against the men who have bought up their estate'.[8]

In the absence of British officials in late July and August 1857, order was also maintained by the junior civil servants. In addition to the police, 'Cazee' (Judge) Ramzan Ally took charge in Chapra; and in Sewan, Syed Hossein Ally, sheristadar (registrar) of the Sub-Deputy Opium Agent and Mohammad Wajid, the 'Moonsiff' (Civil Judge).[9]

Despite these fragile local bulwarks, however, the

viability of British rule in Saran was never seriously threatened in the nineteenth and early twentieth centuries, because, ultimately, the regime's power rested on its superior military force and its coercive capabilities, which were always sufficient to contain and defeat any local challenges. And during periods of crises, the British were quick to impress local populations with their decisive edge. Consquently, when they returned to Saran in 1857, they came with a military force. Although hostilities in the district had been of a limited nature, the presence of a few companies of European and Sikh soldiers was considered necessary to provide 'the most beneficial effect on the district'.[10] In the wake of the 'cow riots' of 1893-4, similar considerations prompted the Saran Magistrate to request that the regiment marching through the district's southern edge also pass through the centre. According to this official, such a display of force was 'conducive to the maintenance of order'.[11] An unequivocal expression of this fundamental source of state control is also evident in the words of the Commissioner of Patna:

> The government of the Empire is not Bengali nor Hindustani, nor composite, but British. The Empire is held together solely by British supremacy, and a declaration of equality between the British and the natives would be nonsense. The Army furnishes the clearest and simplest illustration. The Army in India is the backbone of the Government.[12]

In their self-perceptions though, the British were more likely to emphasize the blessings ushered in by their rule than the institutional bases of control, or their military prowess. Implicit in such self-congratulations was the notion that control stemmed naturally and inevitably from the prosperity and law and order which the Raj had brought to its subjects. The following remarks of a Bihar administrator are a good example:

> To the vast mass of the people have been secured equal and just laws, personal freedom, independence and liberty, such as they never knew before; trade and commerce have developed and expanded .... The reign of might has given place to the reign of law. But where can the list end? Turn where one will the conditions of life in India have undergone a change that only those who know the country can take fully

into account.[13]

In the late nineteenth century, such beliefs were also expressed in the idea that government was a guardian of the peasants against the landed elite. Indeed, the heroic magistrate toiling against innumerable odds to bring the local oppressive zamindar to justice is a standard image in the recollections of the British officers.[14]

In such presentations there are few references to the actual structure and functioning of the system of government control. Where details exist, they generally follow the administrative manuals. No doubt, these accounts were intended as charters legitimizing the Raj, and were not explanations of how the British ruled. After all, big kingdoms as well as little kingdoms operate in a political order maintained and legitimized through a set of ground rules based on 'rituals, traditions, myths and histories'.[15]

For Saran's administrators the ideal was that of 'Revelganj', a town in the district named after a former colelctor. He is eulogized in the marble inscription which was put on his tomb in 1883 at the suggestion of the Lieutenant-Governor of Bengal:

> In this grave lies Henry Revel, Collector of Customs under the East Indian Company from whom the town of Revelganj derives its name .... [I]n 1788, and during a long residence close to the spot he succeeded in gaining the esteem and affection of the surrounding people, who raised the tomb over his remains, and whose descendants still cherish his memory with religious veneration.[16]

Apparently his tomb was the object of 'posthumous honours' by the populace who regarded him as a 'defied hero'.[17]

But the Revelganj model was an ideal that could not be emulated easily. Sir Alexander Muddiman, who was in Saran at the turn of the nineteenth century, observed in his diary: 'I doubt if the tomb of future collectors will be utilized in this way.'[18] Indeed, the records of administrators in the late nineteenth and early twentieth centuries suggest that considerable ambivalence underlay the rulers' sense of self-confidence. One Saran Magistrate expressed it in the following words:

> It is generally the fashion to describe the feelings

> of the people as good and loyal; I believe myself that it would be much more correct to describe it as simply acquiescent. I do not think there is any actual discontent with our rule ... but I cannot say that anything like the active feeling of loyalty exists in the minds of either Hindoos or Mohammedans .... [A]t best we are an alien and, worse than that, an unbending and unsympathetic race, and the race we are called upon to rule is essentially a feeling and impulsive one. The consequence is, that as we never thaw to them, they never open to us; and we must all ... feel that as we come to the land strangers, so we leave it, and that scarcely any of us penetrate beyond the outward shell of native feeling.[19]

Although these remarks are couched in cultural terms, they accurately characterize the limited British interactions with Indian society. Government institutions simply did not extend into local society. Nor was its machinery especially geared to economic or social problem-solving, although its coercive forces could be mobilized to crush any rebellion in the farthest corners of the mofussil.

Such drawbacks of the state's ruling institutions were evident in its handling of the 1866 famine. In a far more revealing and subtle way than the events of 1857, this crisis in 1866 showed the limitations of British rule. As in the other districts of Bihar, Saran's administrators were slow in recognizing the advent of famine conditions. Consequently, their ameliorative measures were inadequate. Although there was a series of poor harvests from the autumn of 1864 onwards, government did not take action until October 1865, when the Collector organized a meeting of 'native gentlemen' to purchase cheap grain from other districts to sell at cost. In November, the Collector reported the failure of two-thirds of the rice crop, but still pinned his hopes on the rabi (spring) harvest. Only after a hailstorm had destroyed a large part of the district's crops in February 1866 did local officials recognize the severity of the situation. Then as relief works and centres opened up, they finally perceived 'the depth and distress and misery into which the wretched inhabitants ... were plunged, or of the extent of relief which would have to be afforded them'.[20] As the subsequent inquiry report noted, when people went to obtain food at the relief centres, finally opened up in June

1866, they were 'already in a moribund state, to whom the first meal gave the death blow'.[21] Nor was relief afforded on a scale commensurate with the needs of the people. According to one indigo planter, there were not enough Europeans and trustworthy natives to establish additional centres.[22]

Nor surprisingly, the famine inquiry report was highly critical of the lack of official links to local society, particularly the tenuous links to the central government. The report urged that the police be made entirely subordinate to the district officer and the number of channels between the provincial government and the district officer be reduced. Otherwise, the Bengal district officer was in a weaker position than his counterparts in other provinces because he enjoyed less 'influence, knowledge, and executive power'. Yet, in keeping with the British image of the 'Oriental people', the magistrate and collector needed to have in his hands 'all live Executive authority of the Government'.[23]

District officers were also said to lack 'external symbols ... [and] the Magistrates, who among an alien people maintain no unnecessary private establishments, appear abroad as plain, unpretending men who go to their offices like clerks'. Nor were these officers familiar with local conditions because they were transferred so frequently. This report also recommended the development of a subdivisional system by creating an executive establishment at the sub-district level. At its head would be a subdivisional officer serving as the link between the 'European and native systems of Administration'.[24]

Nevertheless, the lack of penetrating institutions at the local level persisted throughout the nineteenth and early twentieth centuries as government efforts to fill this gap were defined inevitably by its larger imperial aims. In Anil Seal's words:

> The British wanted to pull resources out of India, not to put their own into India. Therefore, the administrative and military system had to pay for itself with Indian revenues. At the top, this called for a skilled bureaucracy capable of handling large issues bearing upon the economy and the army. But at lower levels this control had to be looser .... In the localities the main tasks were to secure the cheap and regular collection of revenue to see to it that the districts remained quiet.[25]

Such considerations were crucial in determining government's relationship to local society. In Saran in the late nineteenth and early twentieth centuries there were never more than five or six official Europeans stationed in the district; including indigo planters, the total number of Europeans was only about 100, less than one per cent of the district's population. Therefore, the main-springs of control were government's relations with its allies.[26]

Certainly, there were inherent tensions in this relationship. On the one hand, government needed powerful allies, and on the other, it had to contain them from threatening the authority of the State. Since its local connections were landed magnates with their own networks of power and influence, it was in the State's best interests to see that the power of its allies remained localized and within the framework of the Raj, and that their impositions on the rural society were restricted so as not to cause any major peasant outbreaks. But in the period under study, there were no serious challenges to state authority and power, not even in 1857.

Furthermore, unlike the Mughals, the British did not have to contend with secondary or regional powers, for, in establishing their rule, they had effectively removed these two levels.[27] Not until the development of the nationalist movement in the twentieth century were there any real challenges at the supra-local level. Coupled with the perennial need for money, the absence of opposition meant that government did not have to watch over its allies too closely. Moreover, as the permanent settlement in Bengal and Bihar had stabilized the important question of revenue, only a minimal system of official control was sufficient to ensure its flow. Thus government's ties to local landholders and its attempts to expand its administrative machinery were directly related, each shaping the character of the other.

### *Kanungos and Patwaris*

In 1924 Saran had only two kanungos. Moulvi Wali Muhammad worked the Chapra subdivision, while Shital Prasad was in charge of both Siwan and Gopalganj subdivisions. The former had read up to the preliminary standard of the Calcutta University and knew surveying. The latter had reached the level of the B.A. examination, passed the kanungo's examination and received surveying training.[28] Shital Prasad's duties consisted of: (1) collection of rent from tenants of government estates (7 villages); (2) survey and settlement of petty government estates in diaras (alluvium); (3) measurement of government lands covered by government buildings; (4) crop cutting under section 40 of the Bengal Tenancy Act; (5) miscellaneous enquiries; (6) pauper suit enquiry; (7) probate enquiry; (8) takavi (government loans) distribution enquiry; (9) takavi collection; (10) deep stream verification; (11) enquiry into the solvency of sureties; (12) enquiry regarding alluvion and diluvion of government estate; (13) inspection and replacement of boundary marks; (14) demarcation of lands; (15) similar work in Gopalganj subdivision.[29] The kanungo, as part of the government's administrative machinery, was particularly useful because he did not impose in its finances. According to the Collector of Saran who argued for the retention of this post, 'for each kanungo dispensed with a sub deputy collector would have to be appointed ... and the ultimate result would be the introduction of a higher paid officer to do the work that is at present being done by the kanungo'.[30]

On the other hand, government found little cause to appreciate the patwari. A 1914 report explains why: (1) that the patwari is in fact the servant of the zamindar and under his control; (2) that his papers, even when their production can be enforced, are of little or no value and are not required at all since the preparation of a record-of-rights; and (3) that his continued presence in the villages as a quasi-government servant is harmful as in many cases he instigates litigation and foments disputes.[31] Despite various regulations, government's control over the patwaris was tenuous. Figures collected under the provisions of Regulation XII of 1817, by which landlords had to refer their appointment, dismissal, and remunerations to the collector, show that they were rarely complied with in Saran. In the five years between 1908-9 and 1912-13, there were only 91 cases of appointment, 53 of dismissal, and 39 regarding remuneration. Production of patwaris' accounts during the same period was even less, numbering only 24.[32]

Moreover, noticeably absent in these twentieth-century descriptions is any reference to a working relationship between the kanungo and the patwari. Apparently the character of this system was transformed under British rule, although the change was already under way at the outset of the Raj.[33] In the Mughal administrative system at the pargana level, the kanungo was the state's 'permanent repository of information concerning the revenue receipts, area statistics, local revenue rates, and practices and customs.' He was also considered to be a 'friend of the peasants'. His subordinate at the village level was the patwari who was an accountant on behalf of the peasants. He was an employee of the village, and every village had one.[34] The effectiveness of this system stemmed from the inherent tensions between the kanungo who was the government's agent and the patwari who spoke for the village. As part of the Mughal administrative machinery at the pargana level, the former also represented the deepest extension of the state into local society.[35]

In the initial years of British rule, the kanungo-patwari system was closer to its Mughal predecessors than its twentieth-century counterpart. According to an official account:

> Kanungos in the earliest days of British administration appear to have been a quasi-hereditary village agency, analogous to the patwaris, though in a superior position. They were organised and remunerated by Government in the first instance to hold the balance between landlord and tenant, and while securing the position of the latter, to ensure that Government received its fair share of the profits of the land by collecting and registering all the information necessary for the purpose. In course of time the latter function in a large measure superseded the former, and in the middle of the nineteenth century these officers were mainly statistical accountants, the scope of their duties being fixed rather by tradition than by statute or executive order.[36]

Indeed, writing in 1787, W.A. Brooke, the revenue chief of Patna, stated that there were 'canoongoes in every pargana in Bihar whose forefathers originally received their appointments from the [Mughal] King and had sanads granted to them at the time'.[37] Another report noted that 'their office is not only for life, but hereditary to families'. Invariably, these early descriptions also highlighted the importance of this officer's information for 'any accounts from the mofussil'.[38]

In a similar vein, the Fifth Report of 1812 described the kanungo as the 'confidential agent of Government' who acted as a check over village officers. In such a system, as his subordinate at the village level, the patwari's 'business was to see that cultivators were not subjected to exaction or oppression, to register their payments of rent and record their rights'.[39] None of these early records suggest that the kanungo or the patwari was involved with revenue or rent collection.

Even in the initial period of British rule, however, the kanungo-patwari system was in a state of disrepair. Following Warren Hastings' unsuccessful attempt to revive the system in 1783, the office of kanungo was abolished in 1793. And once the permanent settlement was established, government considered collection of agricultural statistics and other such tasks of the kanungo as no longer necessary. However, patwaris were retained in the expectation that their knowledge would be useful in landlord-tenant suits, and in cases of the partition of estates. But without his customary supervisory officer to regulate him, the patwari increasingly became part of the control structure of the zamindar in the nineteenth century. As a result, his 'public and impartial village record-of-rights was turned into "a private and hostile record under the control of the zamindars"'.[40]

## *Patwaris*

In 1815 the Court of Directors failed to convince the authorities to make the patwari a government-paid servant. The Government of India argued against the proposal because it claimed that this would make the village accountant even more capable of oppressing the peasantry and defrauding government. By intriguing with the raiyat, he would seriously injure public revenue by bringing ruin on the zamindar. It also objected on the grounds that a cess would have to be imposed to pay the patwari, which would be a violation of the permanent settlement. But as a later official report admitted, 'the cumulative power of patwaris backed by Government would have been so great that even a well-organized opposition could not have long withstood it'.[41]

Rather than incorporate patwaris into its administrative system, government decided instead to re-establish kanungos to supervise them. While Regulation

II of 1816 legislated the latter back into existence, Regulation XII of 1817 endowed government with additional supervisory controls over the former. Section 16 of this regulation described the duties of a patwari as:

> To keep registers and accounts of his village or circle according as the revenue authorities might appoint; to deliver every half year to the canoongoe a complete copy of such registers and accounts of his village or circle according to custom ... to deliver every half year to the canoongoe a complete copy of such registers and accoutns, showing distinctively the produce of the khureef [autumn] and rubbee [spring] harvests; to perform other customary duties and services.[42]

Such a system, however, was untenable. In the absence of a well-developed infrastructure, government found even nominal supervision of the patwari difficult because he was paid by, and therefore largely responsible, to the zamindar. Yet the legislation of 1817 re-defined him as a 'joint agent of the landlords and their Tenants acting under the control of the public officers for the benefit of all parties concerned'.[43] But faced by attempts to apply these regulations, for instance, in estates in pargana Nanpur, Muzaffarpur district, the patwaris absconded rather than provide information.[44]

Other instances similarly reveal the lack of any governmental presence at the local level. An 1825 report of the Collector of Muzaffarpur showed that the district's patwaris generally disregarded the rule about filing half-yearly papers with the kanungo's office. And when government peons were sent to summon patwaris, they were turned out of the villages. On another occasion, a village accountant explained his inability to provide papers because his malik would not release them.[45]

Complaints about the patwari and the kanungo were quite frequent. An 1827 report of the Board of Revenue described the former as completely under the sway of the landholder, whom it referred to as the patwari's 'taskmaster'. Authentic information was therefore virtually inaccessible to government under the existing system on 'land tenure, the produce of the soil, and the portion of it which, as representing tax on land rent, is available to zamindars'. This report also found kanungos wanting because their office served little judicial purpose, and their information was misleading. Consequently, they were abolished for the second time while patwaris were retained primarily in Bihar.[46]

Although government lacked supervision over the patwari, it could and did legislate to exercise greater control. Regulation IX of 1833 required patwaris to file duplicates of their papers in collectors' offices. But local enquiries in 1837 showed that such a procedure was not followed in most of the districts of Bihar and Bengal. The incomplete state of their registers was noted again in 1863 by the Commissioner of Patna but no remedial action was taken.[47]

Clearly, there were few government links with the patwari. In Saran it was not even possible to determine who the recognized accountant of each village was. Few patwaris' cases had been instituted in the district, therefore suggesting that zamindars appointed and dismissed them without reference to district authorities. In the words of one Saran Collector, patwaris 'though nominally public servants ... [were] really the private servants of zemindars'.[48]

This administrator also observed that patwaris generally received from two to four rupees per month exclusive of perquisites. In addition, well-to-do patwaris were said to lend money and grain on interest, but did not keep shops. In Saran they were of 'respectable' caste, primarily Kayasth, as the following table indicates, and their office was hereditary.[49]

*Table 1* *Caste Composition of Saran's Patwaris, 1884*

| *Subdivision* | *Thana* | *No. of villages* | *No. of patwaris* | *Kayasth* | *Other* |
|---|---|---|---|---|---|
| Chapra | Chapra | 207 | 156 | 97 | 3 |
| Gopalganj | Gopalganj | 100 | 118 | 97 | 3 |
| Siwan | Siwan | 140 | 145 | 98 | 2 |

*Note*: Identification of Kayasths was based on last names of patwaris. Where this was not possible, the patwari was included with the category of 'Other' castes.
The Chapra entry includes generally at least one patwari to a village, but in many cases one patwari worked in two or more villages, or there was more than one patwari per village.

*Source*: Chowkidari Papers, English Translated Lists,

in Saran Collectorate, Faujdari Bastas, English Correspondence, 1884.

Figures compiled during the 1893 recruitment of patwaris for official surveys and record-writing show that the office continued to be largely hereditary. These statistics mention that government trained 19 patwaris and 44 warises, or heirs of patwaris, from pargana Sipa and 45 accountants and 91 heirs from pargana Kuari.[50]

The following summary by the Commissioner of Patna rounds out the description of the nature and functions of the patwari in Saran and other districts of the division:

> Usually there is one putwaree in one village, but sometimes there are many more, each shareholder having one patwaree for his share .... It is his duty to keep the biggits, the khusra [field-book] of measurements, and all the various village accounts. He grants receipts for rent collected by the gomastahs [landholder's agent]. As a general rule, the putwaree does not collect the rents, but does so occasionally, especially in villages where there are no gomastahs, and the putwaree is considered sufficiently trustworthy. Putwarees are generally of the Kaiet caste; but sometimes a Koormi or even a Mahomedan putwaree is to be met with. Their office is not absolutely hereditary, but in practice it has generally become so; the zemindar finding it convenient to put in the place of a deceased putwaree his son or some close relation who has undergone a course of apprenticeship under his predecessor, and has thus acquired a knowledge of the estate and its tenants.[51]

A subsequent report in 1880 further elaborates on the subordinate nature of the patwari's ties to the local landholder. His duties were described as:'(a) collecting rents; (b) giving receipts for rent; (c) giving pottahs; (d) attendance at the civil court on behalf of the zemindars in rent and similar suits; (e) attendance in butwara [partition] proceedings; (f) attendance on behalf of the zemindar in settlement proceedings; (g) the performance of all correspondence and accounts for the zemindar whenever required; (h) to be present at the *danabundi* or *batai* [produce-rent divisions] in villages where the system is in force; (i) to settle new lands for the maliks; (j) acting as the zemindar's representative in all minor matters between him and the revenue authorities.'[52]

Nevertheless, as the sole repository of village accounts, the patwari was also a potential threat to the landholder. The increasing subdivision of landholdings meant that there were often several estates within the boundaries of a village instead of an entire village forming an estate or part of one. In such instances if there was only one patwari in a village, his accounts became the focus of much jockeying between the different co-parceners. Often shareholders appointed their own accountants.[53] That his information could be a double-edged sword for the landholder was observed by a Collector of Saran during his cold weather inspection in 1883. In his words, 'patwaris are as a rule simply the tehsildars [rent collectors] of the proprietors and in cases of disputes between the landlord and his tenants if not partisans of the former are sure to be the partisans of the latter'.[54]

No wonder official attempts to revive the patwari were opposed by the district's landholders. It was not to their advantage to have further encroachments of the state or for the anomalous status of the patwari to be defined better. In the words of the manager of the Hathwa estate, the district's largest landholding:

> It is a well-known fact that the patwaris of Bihar are a set of low-paid, unscrupulous men, with a statutory position which enables them to fill their own pockets at the sacrifice of the interests of the raiyats and zamindars alike, particularly in the case of villages owned jointly by several proprietors, where no individual landlord can exercise any effectual control over them, the result being that they become the *de facto* proprietors of the villages.[55]

Such fears were unfounded though, because government attempts to reorganize the kanungo-patwari system failed consistently. Since they neither paid sufficient attention to local conditions nor implemented legislation effectively, the results were always incomplete. Not surprisingly, the official review of the numerous reorganization efforts of the 1870s concluded that the 'accounts filed by the patwaris are worth absolutely nothing, and consequently do more harm than good, and may be the means of misleading the authorities'.[56]

Government's various experiments, especially its

appointment of kanungos at the subdivision level, also led to the final rupture of the vital kanungo-patwari relationship. Hereafter, the former would have only revenue and statistical functions without any supervisory responsibility over the patwari. Attempts to 'revive' the patwari also failed to produce any tangible results. Until the Lieutenant-Governor pointed it out, even the initial 'Draft of Rules for the Appointment of Putwaris' was framed in terms of patwaris to estates. But at his urging, these rules were revised to attach them to villages or circle of villages.[57]

Furthermore, as local officials quickly discovered, their intentions to reorganize the accountant as a village officer clashed with an already prevailing system. District after district in Bihar reported that patwaris were linked to estates and not to villages. And where a village was held by several shareholders, every one had his own accountant. Patwaris also adapted to partitions in an estate by farming out new estates to their family members.[58]

Even efforts to gain nominal control over the patwari met with little success, and elaborately framed rules remained largely unenforceable. If landholders at all registered their accountants with district authorities, their returns showed nominations made by estates and not by villages. When A.P. MacDonnell took charge of Saran in 1879, the patwari rules of registration had been in effect four years. But as he noticed only in 1,605 of the district's 5,231 villages had patwaris been legally appointed.[59] More important, the official drive in the 1870s to have duplicate accounts filed at the collector's office yielded few returns. Papers were not turned in for a single village in Saran. Nor was such abysmal failure difficult to explain:

> It seems thus far to have been assumed that the putwaree system in Behar had retained a vitality which called for nothing more than some measure of reform and re-organization in order to make the village accounts a source of valuable information, to the revenue authorities, and to restore the putwarees to the status which the Regulation of 1817 intended them to hold ... [whereas] the system had not so much to be reformed as to be reconstituted.[60]

The 1870s attempt represented government's last sustained and systematic effort to link up with the village accountant. Thereafter, concern over the patwari arose periodically, but only as a question of repealing the patwari regulations. In 1895 the Government of India opposed the Lieutenant-Governor of Bengal's suggestion for repeal. Although the central government conceded that he was not 'all that could be wished', it argued for his retention on the grounds that he was the sole link between the 'state and the cultivator'. A 1914 proposal for repeal because because the Bengal Patwaris Regulation XII of 1817 was 'a dead letter in most districts' stirred less response. Government simply put off the repeal issue by saying that the time was 'inopportune'.[61]

Officially, therefore, the patwari remained identified as a government link on the statute books. But as these repeated efforts to incorporate him into an administrative apparatus constructed at the sub-district level reveals, the locus of power here resided in the networks emanating from the zamindar's estate. Indeed the estate was the crucial arena which provided the framework for the organization of local control systems.[62]

### *Chaukidars*

In their extension down to the sub-district levels, the British also attempted to tie the chaukidars, or village watchmen, to their control-and-communications infrastructure. In his testimony before the Indian Statutory Commission in 1928, the Inspector-General of Police for Bihar and Orissa enthusiastically referred to them as the 'reporting agency for all the departments of the Government. In other words, they are the pillars of the Constitution; they are the foundations on which everything is laid'. They were also said to perform such police tasks as 'protecting approaches to a village to catch burglars or dacoits, thing that you have not got sufficient police to do'.[63]

Chaukidars had played a similar role under the Mughals. They had, however, no official ties to the state as they were considered servants of the village community who maintained them by a share of the crops or by rights to some village lands.[64]

As in the case of the patwari, the British sought to co-opt the chaukidar as a source of information. Unlike the former, however, the latter's information had little intrinsic social or economic value. The government held him responsible for communicating information on crime along with the 'village headman ... owner or occupier of land, and the agent of any such owner or occupier, and every officer employed in the collection of revenue or rent of land on the part of Government ...'.[65]

As these menial duties suggest, chaukidars were of low social status; in Saran, often Dusadhs or Ahirs (see below, Table 2). The lowly position was also reflected in their petty wages. Of Saran's 6,203 chaukidars in 1875, 5,576 were paid in cash at an annual average of Rs.9/8/3, while the remaining 627 held rent-free holdings of an average area of two to five bighas (a bigha equals five-eighths of an acre). This income was supplemented by perquisites linking the chaukidar to the landholder and the village community. He received presents from the village on festivals such as Diwali, Holi, and Dashara, and also on other important occasions such as births and marriages. If there was a bazaar or *hat* (periodic market) in the village, he was allowed to collect a small levy on the articles sold. For night duty the landholder provided him a blanket or some clothing. Some made additional sums for assisting the malik in collecting rents. According to one Saran magistrate, all this added up to as much as Rs.20 to Rs.30 per year.[66]

*Table 2 Caste Composition of Saran's Chaukidars, 1884*

| | *No. of villages* | *No. of chaukidars* | *Dusadhs* | *Ahirs* | *Chamars* | *Other* |
|---|---|---|---|---|---|---|
| Chapra | 156 | 244 | 148 | 50 | 4 | 42 |
| | | | *61* | *20* | *2* | *17* |
| Gopalganj | 100 | 126 | 67 | 38 | 2 | 19 |
| | | | *53* | *30* | *2* | *15* |
| Sewan | 140 | 180 | 133 | 25 | 5 | 17 |
| | | | *73* | *14* | *3* | *10* |
| Total | 396 | 550 | 348 | 113 | 11 | 78 |
| | | | *63* | *21* | *2* | *14* |

*Note*: Caste identifications are based on last names. 'Other' indicates Muslim, Kayasth, Kurmi, Bhar, Gond, Musahar, and those whose caste could not be determined. Figures in italics are percentages.
*Source*: Chowkidari Papers, English Translated Lists, in Saran Collectorate, Faujdari Bastas, English Correspondence, 1884.

The chaukidar, however, was a crucial figure in

rural administration. This importance grew as government's links to the local level became increasingly more tenuous in the nineteenth century. Not only were chaukidars a major source of information, but with the police so thinly stretched across the district, they were also in effect, 'the real police of the country'.[67] For instance, Saran's 408 policemen in 1872 meant one policeman to every 6.5 square miles and one to every 5,058 persons. On the other hand, the 6,067 chaukidars in 1872 extended to every .44 square miles and there was one to every 340 of the population. Moreover, the police figures are misleading because at least one-fifth of the entire force was generally on guard duty over prisons and treasuries, and more than one-fifth on town, municipal or harbour duty.[68]

Although the importance of incorporating the chaukidar into the official system was widely recognized, few administrators were able to recruit his services. The touring Assistant Magistrate of Sewan spoke for several generations of local officers when he commented on the chaukidars of Siswan village, 'here as elsewhere all simply useless'.[69] But, as in the case of the patwari, there was considerable agreement that the tie to the chaukidar had to be maintained, regardless of the imperfections.

Government's intentions to strengthen its links to the village watchman were written into the Bengal Act VI of 1870, or the Village Chaukidari Act. This Act aimed at correcting what was considered to be the primary reason for the inefficiency of the system: the irregularity of his pay. By creating chaukidari panchayats, or councils of three to five villages, to control the appointment, dismissal, and maintenance of village watchmen, this Act sought to recast him as a servant of the village community rather than of the malik.[70]

Such reforms generated the same problems that the efforts to reorganize the patwari did. Structural changes were to be designed at a level of local society which lay beyond the reach of the government machinery. For the village watchman to function as a government connection, he had to be extricated from his close ties to the local control structure, whether emanating from the estate or the village. And as in the case of the kanungo and the patwari, official attempts to co-opt the chaukidari system revealed the limited penetration of the British raj into local society.

That implementation of the chaukidari legislation

required considerable commitment and effort on government's part was clear from the outset. The initial application of this legislation in 30 select villages in Patna district hinted at a wide range of problems. Where the 'panch' members were Bhumihar Brahman or Rajput, they assessed themselves and their friends lightly, 'and the poorer and more dependent classes with undue severity in order to make up the deficiency; that distraint has been frequently resorted to, and partiality is shown not only in the assessment but even in the collection'. Moreover, raiyats were charged twice because they not only paid the levy imposed by the chaukidari panches, but also the customary chaukidari cess to the zamindar, which, in many cases, had become consolidated with the rent.[71]

Despite the apparent shortcomings of the Patna experiment, government pressed for extension of the Act to additional districts in Bihar. When Saran's turn came in 1875, the Magistrate raised several objections, expressing particularly strong doubts about the effectiveness of the panches; and arguing, 'apart from the difficulties of appointing a punchayet, that it would be sanguine to expect that they will take much interest in the work for which they get no remuneration'; he doubted 'the expediency of placing in the hands of an irresponsible committee the power of assessing their fellow villagers'; and thought

> that in most villages, even if the Act is introduced and the punchayet is appointed, things will remain much as they are at present, and the malik or zemindar will be held responsible for the regular payment of the chowkeedar, and collect the chowkeedari cess as heretofore from the villages.[72]

He also argued for postponement in the introduction of the Act because the district officers were 'fully engrossed by the collection of famine advances, by the introduction of the salt rules, and the emigration scheme, road cess'.[73]

In overruling the objections of the Bihar district officers, the Lieutenant-Governor acknowledged the difficulty of finding 'intelligent and literate men to form Panchayets', but believed that it could be overcome by recruiting the head raiyats in every village. Nor was he concerned about the chaukidari cess paid by raiyats to zamindars since the permanent settlement, because as he explained 'after this lapse of time it is impossible to say whether this cess, like other cesses, is not part of the rent'.[74]

Although Act VI of 1870 was extended to Saran in July 1875, its provisions were not fully applied until the 1890s. Much to the dissatisfaction of one Commissioner of Patna, an 1877 report showed that chaukidari panchayats had been appointed in only 1,501 of the district's 4,646 villages.[75] But by 1894 there were 3,205 villages with panchayats and 3,641 chaukidars under Act VI of 1870, only 543 and 562 respectively still outside the official provisions.[76] The biggest gains were made in the early 1890s, partly as a reaction to the anti-kine killing riots of 1893-4, which the British in Bihar found especially disturbing.[77] In its wake special provisions were introduced to Patna division, whereby in villages under the Chaukidar Act, the district officer was entitled to appoint headmen from chaukidari panchayats, either the principal or collecting member. These headmen were to be concerned with such activities as: '(a) Circulation of letters or notices or signals ... (b) The visits of itinerant lecturers or preachers (c) The collection of funds for any common purpose ... (d) The meeting of sabhas or other similar associations (e) The possession of unlicensed arms (f) The passage through or assemblage in the village of a body of persons.'[78]

Whereas government found the chaukidari connection useful in matters relating to the security of the state, it continued to encounter all the problems it had hoped to solve with the passing of the 1870 Act. In the words of the Magistrate of Saran, the provisions of this Act were 'distasteful to panchayets, ryots, chaukidars alike'.[79] Successive district officers noted that villagers were reluctant to serve on panches. As one Saran jeth raiyat (head raiyat) complained of his continuing misfortunes, 'my crop was bad, my house was robbed, and now I am made a punch'.[80]

The 1883 Chaukidari Committee investigating the workings of the 1870 Act stated that if service on panchayats was voluntary, there would be no panchayats in a great majority of the villages. Its reports also cited several reasons why the office was considered 'as a calamity and not an honour': (1) appointment was practically compulsory and lengthy; (2) it was unremunerative and therefore not inviting for the well-to-do villager; (3) it was undignified because it involved visits to rate payers of lower social standing; (4) it created antagonism among fellow-villagers, especially towards the collecting member; (5) it rendered the panch's property subject to government confiscation in case of arrears. (6) In general, supervision by local officers and police was disliked, and (7) voluntary regularity of payment was alien to indigenous customs and practices.[81]

Although many of these were cogent arguments, they were not pieced together to gain the larger picture. For Saran the evidence suggests that village-level controllers were generally nominated as panches anyway. And where they were not, such an appointment in itself was not likely to confer power or influence. According to one Saran Magistrate, panchayats had been inefficient until he reorganized them by recruiting influential raiyats. In another report, this same officer explained that village chiefs were 'the class of men from among whom panchayets are usually selected'.[82] For such men selection was not likely to create any enthusiasm, since it involved working toward a framework which, in effect, would diminish their hold over the chaukidar. Not surprisingly then, this Committee encountered many fictitious panchayats which were formed only when accounts were to be submitted.[83]

In 1892 government turned over the power of appointing chaukidars, determining their number, and fixing their salaries to the district magistrate, leaving only the right of nominating to the panchayats. Nothing, however, was done to ensure the effectiveness of the latter institution.[84]

Even the long-standing concern with ensuring the systematic and timely remuneration of village watchmen produced few results. A.P. MacDonnell, who made the application of the Chaukidari Act his major task during his tour as magistrate in 1879, reported that throughout Saran he 'found that the pay of the chaukidars was in arrears for periods varying from six months to two years'.[85] The report of the 1883 Chaukidari Committee arrived at similar conclusions. Where there was any regularity in remuneration, it was due to executive action. Particularly in Saran there had been a 60 per cent recourse to issue of warrants to realize the demands to pay them.[86]

Furthermore, notwithstanding the official efforts to oversee the workings of the village watchmen, they remained bound to the local control system. As one Commissioner of Patna noted they were 'so entirely the creatures of the village authorities that they often accept whatever wages the latter choose to pay and acknowledge payment in full for their wages'.[87]

In the 1890s government renewed its efforts to establish a strong chaukidari connection. Its new approach was to recruit higher caste village watchmen. The logic behind this was that villagers would take a more active role if these officers were of higher social standing. In the past administrators had frequently complained that chaukidars were of criminal tribes and often implicated in the crimes committed in their neighbourhood.[88]

Most chaukidars, however, continued to be drawn from the Dusadh caste. As an 1893 report explained, it was 'difficult to induce men of good caste to accept owing to past traditions'.[89] Subsequent accounts described scattered successes in the districts of Bihar: 16 Rajputs recruited in Saran, one Rajput in Champaran, one Bhumihar Brahman and one Rajput in Muzaffarpur; 50, 16 and 21 men of higher caste in Gaya, Shahabad and Darbhanga respectively. Saran's enlistment drive was especially successful. Of the 653 higher caste men recruited in 1895, 210 were in that district. But these figures were achieved only after the Magistrate issued an order that no vacancy was to be filled in the future except by high caste men. And since chaukidari panchayats failed to nominate 'qualified' candidates, the police had to shoulder the burden. Occasionally there was cause for optimism, such as registered in the offical report for 1895, which declared that 'the traditional objections of Rajputs and others were overcome, until in the end even *Army Pensioners* have come forward and some several disciplined old soldiers wearing medals may be seen in chaukidar's uniform at the weekly muster parades'.[90] These were men on whom government pinned its hopes for a 'strong and serviceable village Police system ... which will go far to break up the old chaukidari thieving organ and be a valuable intelligence and preventive medium'.[91]

Yet this approach too failed to strengthen official links with the chaukidars. Moreover, there was opposition to such a recruitment strategy at the highest reaches of government:

> In Bengal ... it may undoubtedly be well to secure the services of the more respectable castes and classes. But the menial clases, as village servants, are more amenable to orders and ordinarily maintain better watch and ward than the higher castes. Even members of the criminal classes ought not to be

> rejected if they are induced to settle down to an honest life .... [92]

As in the case of patwaris, government was unable to make chaukidars directly subordinate to itself. Nevertheless, its efforts came much closer to the mark than with the former, as they were tied in with its local administration, namely, the police, Its greater success also stemmed from the fact that chaukidars were primarily menial servants and not crucial links who had to be detached from existing networks of power and control. Yet, in spite of repeated reform attempts in the nineteenth and early twentieth centuries, chaukidars served, at best, two masters, as they were never completely wrested away from the networks of estate and village controls.[93]

*Conclusion*

This study of the kanungos, patwaris, and chaukidars in Saran in the nineteenth and early twentieth centuries reveals a British raj with fragile extensions into local society. No doubt, these connections were flimsy because of its system of rule which relied heavily upon local allies. In addition, they were restricted because of the state's imperial considerations. And since it enjoyed a monopoly of coercive powers, it could afford to virtually abdicate its power in local society.

Its repeated, but half-hearted, attempts to establish links to the sub-district levels by reorganizing the kanungos, patwaris, and chaukidars therefore failed consistently. Especially by the late nineteenth century it was too late to arrest the tendency of local control institutions to be organized by estate and village systems of control. Thus the efforts to revitalize the kanungo-patwari connections were blocked by an already existing system of informal control emanating from landholders' estates, while the experiments with chaukidars faced not only the networks of estates but also that of village society. Government's inability to incorporate these officials into its own administrative apparatus was proof that the framework for the organization of local control systems lay beyond its circle of power. Indeed, linkages between British raj and Saran raiyat were defined by the networks of estate and village systems of control in the nineteenth and early twentieth centuries.

*NOTES*

Yang, 'Between British raj and Saran raiyat: the development of local control institutions in the nineteenth and early twentieth centuries'

*Abbreviations*

| | |
|---|---|
| b. | basta or bundle(s) |
| B&O | Bihar and Orissa (government of; proceedings of) |
| BOR | Board of Revenue, Bengal |
| BRO | Bihar State Central Record Office, Patna |
| Coll | Collector or Collectorate |
| DM | Deputy Magistrate |
| GOB | Government of Bengal (Proceedings of) |
| IOL | India Office Library and Records, London |
| LR | Letters received, or sent |
| M | Magistrate |
| Muz.SR | Muzaffarpur Settlement Report (see note 40) |
| PC | Commissioner of Patna Division |
| PCR | PC's Records (BRO) |
| Rev | Revenue (Department of; Proceedings of) |
| SM | Magistrate of Saran District |

All proceedings and consultations were seen at the IOL. Letter books and bastas (district and commissioner's records) were located at the BRO.

1. Ronald Robinson, 'European Imperialism and Indigenous Reactions in British West Africa, 1880-1914', in H.L. Wesseling, ed., *Expansion and Reaction* (Leiden 1978), p.142. Some examples of this approach are C.A. Bayly, *The Local Roots of Indian Politics: Allahabad, 1880-1920* (Oxford 1975); Robert Eric Frykenberg, *Guntur District, 1788-1848: A History of Local Influence and Central Authority in South India* (Oxford 1965); Thomas R. Metcalf, *Land, Landlords, and the British Raj: Northern India in the Nineteenth Century* (Berkeley 1979); Chittabrata Palit, *Tensions in Bengal Rural Society: Landlords, Planters and Colonial Rule, 1830-1860* (Calcutta 1975); F.C.R. Robinson, 'Consultation and Control: the United Provinces' Government and its Allies, 1860-1906', *Modern Asian Studies* 5 (October 1971), pp. 313-36.

2. J.C. Heesterman, 'Was there an Indian Reaction? Western Expansion in Indian Perspective', in Wesseling,

op.cit., p.52.

3. For a detailed discussion of official and non-official systems of local control, see my forthcoming 'The Limits of Control: Agrarian Relations in an Indian district, Saran, 1857-1920'. Also Clive Dewey, '*Patwari* and *Chaukidar*: Subordinate Officials and Reliability of India's Agricultural Statistics', in Dewey and A.G. Hopkins, eds., *The Imperial Impact: Studies in the Economic History of Africa and India* (London 1978), pp.280-314, for a fascinating discussion of the limitations of the records generated by these village officials.

4. DM (Lynch) to SM (W.F. McDonnell), no.2, 9 September 1857, S.Coll, LR 1854-9 (from Sewan DM), BRO.

5. M (W.F. McDonnell) to PC, no.37, 18 February 1858, LR March 1857 to March 1858 (SM to PC).

6. 'Traditional Elites in the Great Rebellion of 1857: Some Aspects of Rural Revolt in the Upper and Central Doab', *The Peasant and the Raj: Studies in Agrarian Society and Peasant Rebellion in Colonial India* (Cambridge 1978), p.188.

7. M (W.F. McDonnell) to PC, LR March 1857 to March 1858 (SM to PC).

8. M (McDonnell) to PC (W. Tayler), demi-official, 13 August 1857, PCR General b.105 (Monthly bs. from 1854, from SM).

9. See M to PC, no.314, 9 October 1857 and no.307, 7 October 1857, LR March 1857 to March 1858 (SM to PC); DM (Lynch) to M (McDonnell), no.61, 2 February 1858, LR 1854 to 1859 (from Sewan DM). The district was divided into subdivisions in 1848: Chapra and Sewan. A third, Gopalganj, was created in 1875.

10. DM to M, no.531, 12 February 1858, LR 1854 to 1859 (from Sewan DM).

11. He also requested the regiment to take the same course during the next trooping season. See 'General Administration Report of the Patna Division for 1894-95', GOB General (Miscellaneous) September to December 1895, November, p.943. See also my 'Sacred Symbol and Sacred Space in Rural India: Community Mobilization in the "Anti-Cow Killing" Riot of 1893', *Comparative Studies in Society and History* XXV (October 1980), pp.576-96.

12. Remarks made during the 1882-3 furore over the amendment of the Code of Criminal Procedure to provide Indian jurisdiction over European subjects. See PC to GOB, 6 May 1883, GOB Judicial 1884, July, p.143.

13. J. Reginald Hand, *Early English Administration of Bihar, 1781-1785* (Calcutta 1894), p.82.

14. For instance, see Sir Alexander Muddiman,

*Memoirs* (for private circulation only) (Allahabad 1930), pp.24-5. Muddiman was Assistant Magistrate in Saran in 1899-1900 and Acting Magistrate in 1901. Also John Beames, *Memoirs of a Bengal Civilian* (London 1961), p. 180.

15. Bernard S. Cohn, 'Political Systems in Eighteenth Century India: The Banaras Region', *Journal of the American Oriental Society* LXXXII (July-September 1962), p.313. Also his 'Rituals of Authority in a Colonial Society: The Imperial Assemblage at Delhi in 1877', paper presented at a Conference on Intermediate Political Linkages in South Asia, University of California, Berkeley, 16-18 March 1978.

16. Cited in L.S.S. O'Malley, *Bihar and Orissa District Gazetteers: Saran* (rev. ed. by A.P. Middleton, Patna 1930), p.150.

17. See 'Reports on Hindu Religion', Saran District, District Reports received by the Superintendent of Census Operations for Bengal, 1901-2, Risley Collection Mss. Eur. E. 295/7, IOL.

18. Muddiman, op.cit., p.50.

19. Cited in Annual General Report of the Patna Division for 1871-2, GOB General (Miscellaneous) 1872, October, p.43.

20. Secretary, Relief Committee (G.J.S. Hodgkinson) to PC (J.R. Dalrymple), no.32, 9 July 1866 and Coll. (F.M. Halliday) to F.R. Cockerell, no.290, 29 December 1866, Miscellaneous File Book of Letters re Late Scarcity, 1866, BRO. Also see Coll (J. J. Grey) to PC (Dalrymple), no.163, 14 November 1865, LR from 16 August 1865 (to PC).

21. Parliamentary Papers (Commons) 1867, vol.170, 'Papers relating to the Famine in Behar including Mr. F.R. Cockerell's Report', p.16.

22. N. MacDonald, Sereepur Factory, to PC (F.M. Halliday), 12 February 1867, Miscellaneous File Book of Letters re Late Scarcity, 1866.

23. GOB, *Famine, Bengal and Orissa, 1866* vol.III, *Further Report on the Famine in Bengal and Orissa in 1866* (Calcutta 1867), pp.1, 8. From the Government of India down to the police in the district the official chain extended through the Government of Bengal, and the Board of Revenue, to the commissioner of the division and the collector of the district.

24. Ibid., pp.8, 11, 15.

25. 'Imperialism and Nationalism in India', *Modern Asian Studies* 7 (July 1973), pp.327-8.

26. Between 1871 and 1921 the district's population

ranged from 2 to 2.3 million. For additional details, see my 'The Limits of Control'.

27. For such an analysis, see Bernard S. Cohn, 'The Initial British Impact in India: A Case Study for the Benares Region', *Journal of Asian Studies* XIX (August 1960), p.430.

28. 'Statement showing the existing strength of kanungos in the Tirhut Division - individual qualifications and their distribution', with PC to BOR, 12 June 1924, B&O Rev 1924, October, p.46.

29. The other Saran kanungo performed essentially the same tasks. See ibid.

30. Coll (P. Meerza) to PC, n.d., B&O Rev 1924, October, p.49.

31. 'Note on Patwaris in Bihar', BOR to B&O Rev., 20 June 1914, Annexure A, B&O Rev January to March 1915, January, p.39 (hereafter cited as Note on Patwaris, 1914).

32. Similar returns came in from other districts of Bihar, see Annexure B, loc.cit., p.40.

33. See B.K. Sinha, 'The Office of the Qanungo in Bihar - Its Abolition and Restoration following the Permanent Settlement', *Bengal Past and Present* LXXXVI (January to June 1961), p.11, for an interpretation which asserts that British actions were solely responsible for the change.

34. Irfan Habib, *The Agrarian System of Mughal India, 1556-1707* (London 1963), pp.125, 289-90; P. Saran, *The Provincial Government of the Mughals, 1526-1658* (Bombay 1972), pp.274-5; Noman Ahmad Siddiqi, *Land Revenue Administration under the Mughals (1700-1750)* (Bombay 1970), pp.19-20.

35. Ishtiaq Husain Quereshi, *The Administration of the Mughal Empire* (Karachi 1966), p.231, points out that 'the parganah was the hub of rural administration under Muslim rulers .... It was as important as the district under the British'.

36. 'Kanungo Establishment in Bihar and Orissa', with J.R. Dain (Rev) to Secretary BOR, 5 April 1924, B&O Rev 1924, October, p.3. For a similar description, see Hand, op.cit., p.53.

37. Cited in K.P. Mitra, 'The Office of the Qanungo in Bihar', *Indian History Records Proceedings* XXI (1941), p.18. Also see J.D. Patterson, Registrar of the Kanungo's Office, 'Report on the Office of Kanungo', 18 May 1787, in R.B. Ramsbotham, *Studies in the Land Revenue History of Bengal, 1769-1787* (Bombay 1926), pp.162-97.

38. Controlling Council of Revenue at Patna to

Warren Hastings, Governor General, 31 August 1775, Patna Factory Records, 2 January to 28 December 1775, IOL, and letter from Council of Revenue, 17 October 1774, cited in Ramsbotham, op.cit., p.148.

39. Cited in Note on Patwaris, 1914, p.39.

40. Muz.SR - C.J. Stephenson-Moore, *Final Report on the Survey and Settlement Operations in the Muzaffarpur District, 1892 to 1899* (Patna 1922)- p.73, and F. Hawkins, Coll of Sircar Sarun to BOR (Wm. Cowper &c.) 13 September 1793, Bengal Revenue Consultations 18-25 September 1795, 18 September, no.49. See also Girish Mishra, *Agrarian Problems of Permanent Settlement: A Case Study of Champaran* (New Delhi 1978), pp.135-42,and Metcalf, op.cit., pp.299-305, for similar findings.

41. Muz.SR, p.73. There is also evidence suggesting that kanungos still existed and could therefore have been revived easily. In Muzaffarpur many ex-kanungos and their heirs continued to draw on their nankars, or lands assigned for their subsistence.

42. 'A Regulation for the better administration of the Office of Putwaree in the Province of Behar, passed by the Governor General in Council', A.D. 1817 Regulation, Bengal Board of Commissioners at Behar and Benares, 17 May to 9 June 1817, 21 May, no.270D and enclosures, IOL. See also GOB Rev to BOR Land Rev. no.2525, 20 September 1873, GOB Rev July 1873-5, September 1873, p.25.

43. Ibid.

44. Muz.SR, p.74.

45. Ibid., p.76.

46. Note on Patwaris, 1914, pp.36-7; Muz.SR, p.77.

47. Note on Patwaris, 1914, p.37.

48. Cited in GOB, *Bengal Government Selections, Papers regarding the Village and Rural Indigenous Agency Employed in Taking the Bengal Census of 1872* (Calcutta 1873), pp.57-8.

49. Ibid. See also Dewey, op.cit., p.282, where he describes patwaris as belonging 'to the highest reaches of village society. They were members of rich peasant families, or the families of successful moneylenders and traders. Their caste status was comparatively high; and their control of the land revenue records ... gave them power over their fellow-villagers .... Above all, they were literate and numerate.'

50. 'Note by W.C. Macpherson, Officiating Director of Dept. of Land Records ... 20 July 1893', GOB Rev September to December 1893, November, p.1134.

51. GOB, Selections, p.56 (see above, note 48).

52. Officiating PC (J. Ware Edgar) to BOR, no. 1113B, 7 September 1880, Bengal Rev 1880, December, p.48.

53. See 'Patwari System in Behar', especially BOR to GOB Rev, no.712A, 21 October 1880, GOB Rev (Establishments) 1880, December, p.41.

54. Coll (C.C. Quinn) to PC, no.127G, 30 April 1883, PCR b.338, 1883-4.

55. Babu Bipin Behari Bose, Manager, Hatwa raj, to PC, no.105, 17 October 1893, GOB Rev January to April 1894, February, p.187.

56. Under-Secretary GOB (C.W. Bolton) to BOR Land Rev, no.3355-1762 L.R., 15 December 1880, GOB Rev 1880, December, p.53.

57. Kanungos originally existed at the pargana level. See GOB Rev to BOR Land Rev, no.2525, 20 September 1873, GOB Rev July 1873-5, September 1873, p.26. Also BOR to GOB Rev, no.712A, 21 October 1880, GOB Rev 1880, December, p.41.

58. PC (F.M. Halliday) to BOR, no.248R, 4 May 1880, GOB Rev 1880, December, p.49.

59. Ibid. According to MacDonnell he registered nearly as many more in a four-month period as there were when he joined the district.

60. Ibid., p.50. The difference in number of villages noted here and in other estimates is because of the varying concept of 'village' by different officers, and under different regulations.

61. BOR to GOB Rev, no.712A, 21 October 1880, GOB Rev 1880, December, p.40. In Madras the role of the karnam, or patwari, diminished while the position of headman rose in significance under British rule. For this interesting contrast, see Christopher Baker, 'Madras Headmen', in K.N. C audhuri and Clive J. Dewey, eds., *Economy and Society: Essays in Indian Economic and Social History* (Delhi 1979), pp.26-52.

62. For additional discussion, see my 'The Limits of Control'. 'Estate' in this essay refers to all the holdings of a family; large landholdings were generally made up of several mahals (the collectorate fiscal unit) or 'estates'.

63. Evidence of W. Swain, Patna, 14 December 1928, *Indian Statutory Commission*, vol.XV, *Extracts from Official Oral Evidence* (London 1930), p.295.

64. Jadunath Sarkar, *Mughal Administration* (5th ed., Calcutta 1963), p.13; D.J. McNeile, *Report on the Village Watch of the Lower Provinces of Bengal* (Calcutta 1866), pp.5-6.

65. See 'Obligations of landholders and others in regard to crime', Rules drafted by Colonel Skinner, District Superintendent of Police, Saran, with no.569, 5 July 1883, GOB Judicial (Police) 1883, August, no.4.

66. Officiating M (G.E. Porter) to PC, no.505G, 15 April 1875, GOB Police 1875, May, p.142. According to Dewey, op.cit., p.282, chaukidars 'were members of economically depressed families and socially-despised castes. Often they became *chaukidars* because they were too physically infirm to work as labourers, and lacked the capital to set themselves up as tenants. They were illiterate and quasi-numerate'.

67. Comments of SM, cited in 'Annual General Report, Patna Division, 1872-73', GOB General (Miscellaneous) 1873, November, p.909. See also Sewan DM (J.F. Lynch) to SM (W.F. McDonnell), no.54, 15 September 1856, Saran Coll, LR from 1854 to 1859 (from Sewan DM).

68. W.W. Hunter, *A Statistical Account of Bengal*, vol.XI, *Districts of Patna and Saran* (London 1877), pp. 344-5; 'Strengths, Cost and Distribution of Police Force, District Saran', in GOB, *Twenty Years' Statistics 1883-84, 1903-1904*, vol. B, *Police* (Calcutta 1905?), p. 162. See also my 'The Agrarian Origins of Crime: A Study of Riots in Saran District, India, 1866-1920', *Journal of Social History* XIII (Winter 1979), p.290.

69. 'Tour Diary of Assistant Magistrate of Sewan from November 1866 to March 1867', PCR b.107, LR 1863-7 (from SM). For a similar comment, see PC (T.R. Davidson) to GOB, no.31, 10 June 1837, GOB, *Committee on Improvement of Mofussil Police, Bengal, 1838* (n.d.).

70. 'Working of the Village Chowkeedaree Act in Patna District', GOB Judicial April to July 1872, June, pp.6-19.

71. Officiating PC (S.C. Bayley) to GOB, 26 April 1872, GOB Judicial, April to Juen 1872, June, p.7.

72. Officiating M (G.E. Porter) to PC, no.505G, 15 April 1875, GOB Police 1875, May, p.143.

73. To which Sir Richard Temple, the Lieutenant-Governor, commented marginally, 'Say I do *not* admit this. It looks as if Mr. Porter fears the work which I am sure, cannot be the case.' Ibid.

74. PC (Bayley) to GOB Judicial, 10 May 1875, 168J, and 'Marginal Remarks by the Lieutenant-Governor', GOB Police 1875, July,p.10.

75. Of the 4,646 villages, 205 of them were said to be 'non-existent' and the rest supposedly too small for panches because they had less than 60 houses. See PC (E.W. Molony) to GOB, 17 July 1877, no.243J, GOB

Judicial (Police) 1876-7, August 1877, p.21.

76. Officiating PC (H. Luttman Johnson) to GOB, 17 October 1894, no.60G, GOB Judicial October to December 1894, December, no.70.

77. In 1892 there were 2,684 chaukidars under Act VI, 3,967 in 1893, and 4,509 in 1894. See 'Village Police', in GOB statistics, p.159 (see above, note 68).

78. Officiating PC (Johnson) to GOB, 2 November 1894, no.637G, and Notification no.4988J, 18 December 1894, GOB Judicial October to December 1894, December, nos.72-4.

79. Cited in PC (E.W. Molony) to GOB, 17 July 1877, no.243J, GOB Judicial (Police) 1876-7, August 1877, p. 21.

80. Cited in 'Annual General Report, Patna Division, 1879-1880', GOB General (Miscellaneous) 1880, August, p.103.

81. The usual procedure was for the police to submit a list of five or more suitable men whom the magistrate accepted with little scrutiny. See 'Report by ... Committee appointed to enquire into the workings of Act VI of 1870 to Government of Bengal', 27 April 1883, PCR b.289.

82. 'Criminal Administration Report for Patna Division, 1879', PCR General b.281, 1880; 'Annual General Report, Patna Division, 1879-1880', GOB General (Miscellaneous) 1880, August, 103.

83. See above, note 81.

84. Workings of the new Chaukidari Act, I (Bengal Code) of 1892, Report from Officiating PC (H. Luttman-Johnson), GOB Judicial (Police) January to April 1895, April, pp.165-9.

85. Cited in Criminal Administration Report (see above, note 82).

86. See above, note 81.

87. 'Police Administration Report, Patna Division, 1884', PC (F.M. Halliday) to GOB, 6 April 1885, PCR General b.291, 1885. See also David Arnold, 'Crime and Crime Control in Madras, 1858-1948', in Yang, ed, *Crime and Criminality in British India*, forthcoming, for a similar description of the *talaiyari* (watchman) in South India.

88. GOB to Government of India, 9 January 1890, GOB Judicial January to April 1890, January, p.11. Also Sir Edmund C. Cox, *Police and Crime in India* (London 1911), p.47.

89. GOB to PC, 3 May 1893, no.32J-D, PCR General b. 308, 1893.

90. 'Police Administration Report for 1895, Patna Division', PCR General b.313, 1896.

91. Ibid.

92. 'Report of the Indian Police Commission and Resolution of the Government of India', Parliamentary Papers (Commons), vol.57, 1905, Cmnd.2478 (London 1905), p.33.

93. Thus they provided an easy target for the civil disobedience movement of the 1930s. Popular sentiment against them was widespread in Bihar because of their links to government and to rural elites. For details on the anti-chaukidari campaign, see Stephen Henningham, 'The Contribution of "Limited Violence" to the Bihar Civil Disobedience Movement', *South Asia* II (March and September 1979), pp.60-77.

# THE ORIGINS OF FRAGMENTATION OF LANDHOLDINGS IN BRITISH INDIA: A COMPARATIVE EXAMINATION

*Neil Charlesworth*

At the heart of a vigorous peasant economy is often a central contradiction: a continuous problem of land organization. Malcolm Darling noted it when he remarked of the Punjab: 'the more fertile the land the more it is split up, as fertility and population go together'.[1] In short, favourable conditions tend to create high demand for farms, the source of valuable agricultural produce, and growing numbers, both typically reflected in pressure on the land. The consequences are potentially momentous. A resultant more intensive cultivation can bring striking short-term gains for productivity,[2] but the long-term implication is normally, at least, the restoration of equilibrium in per capita performance and often the 'locking' of society into a complex tenurial pattern, prohibitive of innovation and development.

Such a process seemed to occur, with spectacular virulence, in British India. During the late nineteenth and early twentieth centuries the size of units of ownership and cultivation on the land apparently plummeted and the Royal Commission on Agriculture in India of 1928 devoted a whole chapter to 'the subdivision and fragmentation of holdings' as a major problem.[3] In a well-known study in 1917 of Pimpla Soudagar, a village in western India (a region we shall be using as a case study), Harold Mann commented that

> in the last sixty or seventy years the character of the land holdings has altogether changed. In the pre-British days ... the holdings were usually of a fair size, most frequently more than nine or ten acres .... Now the number of holdings is more than doubled, and eighty-one per cent of these holdings are under ten acres in size.[4]

The problem seemed equally grave elsewhere in India. Making direct comparison with Mann's village, R.L. Bhalla's report on the Punjab village of Bairampur in 1922 remarked that 'in Bairampur the evil out-Herods Herod':[5] here the smallest unit of cultivation was as tiny as 0.01 acres compared with 0.05 acres in Mann's case study.[6] Across the massive Bengal Presidency pressure on land had also become acute. By 1940 31.1 million acres of land in the possession of peasant tenants was apparently split between as many as 16.4 million tenancies.[7]

Even so, of course, this was far from an exclusively Indian or even Asian phenomenon. Darling pointed to eastern France, parts of Italy and Spain and especially Sardinia as contemporary victims of 'the evils of small holdings'.[8] One great historical paradigm is the impact of the expansionary booms of the thirteenth and sixteenth centuries in western Europe, which apparently produced substantial change in land organization. In sixteenth-century Languedoc, for example, Le Roy Ladurie speaks of the economic and social developments of the age as a 'driving force that dispersed the village lands in an irresistible wave of divided successions'.[9] In Tudor England, Joan Thirsk writes, 'the size of holdings was falling alarmingly and complaints to this effect were explicit'.[10]

Here, then, is some fundamental tendency within peasant economies, but the interlinked processes involved are undoubtedly complex. The phenomenon which British officialdom in India called 'subdivision' - the tendency for individual units of ownership or 'holdings' to grow in number and diminish in size - would seem to follow from a rise in agrarian population or a sectoral shift of employment towards peasant agriculture. 'Fragmentation', however - the further, increasing division of holdings into a number of small, scattered units or 'plots' - raises questions of a different ilk. There was no logically deducible reason why numbers of units of cultivation within holdings should proliferate; why the 156 holdings in Pimpla Soudagar should be divided into 718 separate plots[11] or why, in one village of the central Punjab, '584 owners cultivate 16,000 fields, whose mean size is only one-seventh of an acre'.[12] Indeed fragmentation, with plots 'as scattered as autumn leaves',[13] imposed obvious technical constraints on agriculture, which might appear particularly burdensome under conditions of subdivision. Thus one official, writing of a western Indian village with plots only 22 feet wide, commented that 'such a division makes effective tillage and irrigation impossible'.[14] In the Punjab 'land is wasted in innumerable boundaries ...; rotations cannot be varied, nor can valuable crops be properly supervised'.[15] Fragmentation in the Central Provinces 'complicates each simple agricultural operation. For instance, the carrying of manure to each separate field absorbs valuable time and entails an incalculable amount of labour which would be saved if the holding were compact'.[16]

Yet, again, this precise and seemingly inconvenient coincidence of subdivision and fragmentation is closely paralleled in other peasant societies, even those which were to achieve relatively high levels of economic development. The subdivision of cultivation units, which was proceeding apace in thirteenth and sixteenth-century western Europe, may well have been accompanied by progressive fragmentation, for Thirsk notes of her Tudor protests about subdivision that 'implicit in these complaints was also an increase in the number of parcels'.[17] More fundamental, fragmentation in India is mirrored by one central feature of the western medieval economy: the 'scattering' of strips within the open-field system. 'Scattering', since it seems to involve the same technical constraints as Indian fragmentation, is perhaps the most perplexing aspect of open-field agriculture. From the studies of Seebohm and Vinogradoff onwards the problem has received widespread attention from medievalists and in the modern literature a prominent and fiercely-fought debate over the origins of the phenomenon has developed.[18] Whilst most such medieval studies are still determinedly self-centred, Joan Thirsk perceptively commented in one contribution to the discussion that 'we may ... learn something from the study of peasant cultivation in present-day Asia, Africa and South America, where examples abound of intermingled strips'.[19] In turn, the medieval western experience might cast important light on the modern problem of land organization in South Asia. In what follows, then, we shall explore the origins of subdivision and fragmentation in early twentieth-century India, where applicable with the direct help of the western medieval paradigm.

The organization of landholding in a peasant society represents, of course, a complicated, necessarily pragmatic response to a range of economic, social and cultural influences. Charles Wilson has emphasized the limited freedom to manoeuvre of the medieval British peasant: '*once set*, the pattern of open field farming was capable of even *modification*, let alone total reorganisation, only with the greatest difficulty'.[20] Yet the special importance of the Indian phenomenon is that we can see changes occurring and, further, can closely trace the historical evolution of subdivision and fragmentation. In western India the early twentieth-century process was apparently especially dramatic. Between 1904-05 and 1916-17 alone, the total number of officially-recorded cultivation-holdings in the Bombay Presidency rose from under 1.5 million to over two million: the number of holdings under five acres in size more than doubled.[21] The statistics for 1924-25 presented to the Royal Commission on Agriculture revealed that 48 per cent of Bombay holdings were by then smaller than five acres and a further 40 per cent between five and 25 acres in size.[22] In all-India terms this might not seem especially alarming but in many parts of western India, especially on the relatively arid Deccan plateau, comparatively large units had been traditionally required to support a peasant family. These statistics, then, provide a sharp contrast with earlier estimates: as late as 1892-3 the average size of holdings had been recorded at just over 30 acres in the Southern Division.[23] Pimpla Soudagar closely followed the pattern, for whilst five acres and under was the norm by the time of Mann's investigations, the average-sized proprietary holding had stood at fourteen acres in the mid-nineteenth century.[24]

Fragmentation, also, was intensifying by the early twentieth century. In Pimpla Soudagar, as we have seen, the average holding contained perhaps four or five distinct plots[25] and Mann's second case study, the village of Jategaon Budruk further east in the Deccan, confirmed the trend, for here 146 landholders cultivated 561 plots.[26] Fragmentation, too, was not confined to larger holdings or regions of relatively extensive land availability. In the Konkan, the coastal belt to the south of Bombay city, a region of denser settlement, more intensive cultivation and smaller holdings than the Deccan plateau, proportionately similar degrees of fragmentation were evident. Thus in Ratnagiri District here 'the intricate parcelling of the land' was such that 32 typical villages investigated in 1917-19 'were found to contain 88,000 subdivisions'.[27] Here the process reached its logical culmination with, by the 1920s, 'cases ... where a single cocoanut tree is a hissa (plot) and is moreover jointly owned by several persons'.[28] But western India was no special victim of these developments. In Bairampur, situated in the submontane region of the Punjab, fragmentation, as we noted previously, was probably more intense and certainly had eaten into land organization earlier: the number of plots in the village had more than doubled between 1851-2 and

1884-5.[29] And, to take another sharply contrasting locality, in Dacca District of east Bengal by 1917 'the average size of the cultivated field ... is less than half an acre, each eagricultural worker possessing six fields'.[30]

How can we explain this phenomenon, particularly the superficially 'irrational' tendency for even small holdings to become split into scattered plots? The simple answer, offered by most officials, was the impact of 'the laws of inheritance customary among Hindus and Muhammadans'.[31] Since holdings, on the death of their peasant holder, were usually divided equally between sons, land would apparently become sharply subdivided in conditions of expanding population. Fragmentation, however, would also result, because custom typically demanded further division of the holding, granting an even share of good and bad land to each son. This explanation of changes in land organization - partible inheritance in conditions of population growth - not only seems the obvious answer for the modern Third World but is even, now, a powerful recognised interpretation of scattering in the medieval open-fields. In an important revisionist article, Joan Thirsk challenged the widespread assumption of some early emergence of the phenomenon and declared the twelth and early thirteenth centuries as 'possibly the crucial ones' in the development of the open-field system.[32] In that period increasing numbers, linked even in England to the likely prevalence of partible inheritance, ensured that the peasantry was 'compelled to cultivate its land more intensively':[33] hence scattering 'became a highly desirable arrangement, since it gave each individual a proportion of land under each crop in the rotation'.[34]

This type of explanation, of course, has always had wide currency for continental Europe, where the extent of partible inheritance is a much less controvertible issue: Le Roy Ladurie's Languedoc is the classic victim of population pressure linked to egalitarian inheritance procedure.[35] Yet in this analysis the consequences of the process are clear and devastating. In a neo-Malthusian account like Le Roy Ladurie's, the system contained its own self-righting mechanism, the pauperization of the sixteenth century inexorably leading to the 'crisis of the seventeenth century' as the Malthusian scissors shut. Here, however, a sharp contrast with the Indian case emerges. In the subcontinent, famine and mortality crisis became notably less, not more, frequent during the first third of the twentieth century.[36] Whatever the reasons - perhaps increasingly effective official intervention to ameliorate subsistence crises[37] - the Malthusian trap has not been closed in India, at least not with medieval violence. Subdivision and fragmentation, then, did not inevitably create self-righting economic crisis, but instead continued to evolve spontaneously.

As a result, our Indian case would appear to require a sharper interpretative cutting-edge. This, perhaps, might be provided by Geertz's well-known model of 'agricultural involution', developed to describe the situation in modern Java. In Geertz's Java rapidly increasing population was soaked up on the land, producing features similar to those in India: 'tenure systems grew more intricate; tenancy relationships more complicated; cooperative labour arrangements more complex - all in an effort to provide everyone with some niche, however small, in the overall system'.[38] For students of modern Asian peasantries, Geertz's work seemed a valuable extension of the western neo-Malthusian accounts, because he recognized that involution, in per capita-output terms, did not necessarily represent immediate sharp deterioration. Involution, in fact, by creating more intensive cultivation of the land, was the mechanism, economically as well as socially, whereby growing numbers could be accommodated on the proceeds of agriculture. At the same time, since there was no possibility here of an agricultural surplus being made available to other sectors of the economy or for any new dynamic thrust developing within agriculture, the process was 'ultimately self-defeating' in developmental terms.[39] This would appear to describe the Indian situation in the early twentieth century: intensifying subdivision and fragmentation, the absence of any constructive developmental role by agriculture and yet the successful assimilation of these features amidst the absence of any serious subsistence crisis.

Yet, at root, Geertz too is a neo-Malthusian. The engine of involution in Java was a sharp, sustained increase in population averaging two per cent per annum between 1830 and 1900.[40] The crucial nature of the demographic dynamic is highlighted by Geertz's emphasis, in his comparison between Java and Japan, on 'the critical four decades of the mid nineteenth century - 1830-1870' when the only significant contrast between the two is in population trends.[41] If, therefore, we can demonstrate a close correlation between subdivision and fragmentation in India and the rate of population growth, then, remembering the universality of partible inheritance in the subcontinent, the problem would appear to be solved.

Here, however, the fundamental difficulty emerges. India, contrary to many assumptions, did not enter into the realms of rapid aggregate population growth rates until the 1920s: throughout the nineteenth century and down to the Census of 1921 her overall levels of population increase were below international averages.[42] Nevertheless, subdivision and fragmentation were accounted desperate problems in many provinces before 1920. The local cases highlight the lack of strict correlation. In Bairampur, for example, we have noted a ferocious fragmentation process from the middle of the nineteenth century and yet this was within a district, Hoshiarpur, where pressure on the land was consistently eased by recruitment to the army and emigration.[43] Even more striking is the case of western India. Despite the statistics revealing massive subdivision and fragmentation in train between 1900 and 1920, the total population of the Bombay Presidency rose by just 4.1 per cent between the Censuses of 1901 and 1921.[44] Another crucial factor would be, of course, the extent of availability of new land: during the nineteenth century the amount of land in cultivation had undoubtedly expanded considerably throughout British India.[45] In fact, over the Bombay Presidency the process was firmly continuing in the early twentieth century and the average gross cultivated area increased by 13.8 per cent between the period 1902-07 and the era 1919-24.[46] If anything, then, aggregate per capita land availability was rising in the Bombay Presidency down to 1920 (though a sharp reversal was possibly to follow), but Bombay officials were wringing their hands about the evils of progressive subdivision and fragmentation well before 1920. Only in Bengal, where population/land ratios *were* manifestly worsening before the First World War,[47] was there direct historical correlation between rapid population growth and extending subdivision and fragmentation.

At this point we must define our problem more precisely. The argument is not to deny that population pressure and inheritance practice can be and have been important, perhaps the most important, agencies of changes in land organization. Even in the case of Bombay Presidency, slow overall population growth was partly the outcome of occasional high mortality crisis, the impact of periodic scarcity and, in particular, of the great influenza epidemic of 1918-19. As a result, at times in many localities pressure of numbers did undoubtedly build up temporarily, driving down size of holdings and plots. Again, amidst a strictly egalitarian inheritance procedure, fragmentation might develop even in conditions of static overall population levels: deviation in individual family size would still obviously occur and hence always lead to the breaking up of some holdings. Yet against this has to be set the constant potential for consolidation set in train by migration, bachelorhood and the absence of male heirs in other families, influences which exist to some extent even when population is growing rapidly. In general, the swift extension of subdivision and fragmentation, certainly in western India, clearly antedated any serious deterioration in per capita land availability and, further, the former phenomenon seems entirely out of proportion to the latter throughout. Other forces, then, must also have been at work.

In addition, there are serious conceptual problems over ascribing subdivision and fragmentation solely to population pressure linked to inheritance procedure. As an explanation it offers either too little or too much. Now clearly, if population were growing consistently rapidly with holdings ruthlessly broken up on strictly egalitarian principles, the whole process would prove exponential and the units of cultivation would be driven downwards in size extremely quickly. This could undoubtedly happen. Thirsk cites a lordship in Radnorshire, Wales, subject to partible inheritance, where 'it was not unusual ... for a small tenement to be divided into thirty, forty and sometimes more parcels in three or four generations'.[48] If this was what was happening in India the land should have become intensely broken up with increasing devastation, particularly as population started to increase at faster than international averages after 1921. In fact, as we shall see, whilst subdivision and fragmentation was typically extending markedly in the first two decades of the twentieth century, the process was not universal, did not operate in an exponential fashion, and, crucially, might even subsequently be reversed by consolidation processes in some places. The same objection, then, stands for India which Dahlman has recently voiced against the Thirsk explanation of scattering in the medieval open-fields: if partible inheritance was the entire cause of the phenomenon, why, especially in conditions of population growth, was there not universal, ever-intensifying scattering?[49] At the other extreme, however, it is perfectly easy to construct models where partible inheritance does not lead to fragmentation, if sufficient attention is given to families which produced no male heirs. In this way, Dhairyabala Pandit earlier noted our problem by showing that demographic pressures linked to inheritance procedure could not have caused subdivision and fragmentation in particular south Gujarat villages: migration, bachelorhood and lack of male heirs kept the numbers to be allocated land relatively constant.[50] Bruce Campbell, too, has recently made exactly the same point for a case as contrasting as the Norfolk township of Martham in the thirteenth and fourteenth centuries: here scattering seemed so out of proportion to population growth that 'if the parcellation of land was the outcome of partible inheritance alone it must therefore have been a much more protracted process ... than has often been appreciated. For it to have produced the profound fragmentation of land which existed in Martham in 1292 would have taken several centuries'.[51] But in India, as we have seen, changes were proceeding more rapidly than that.

Here, however, another observation about the Indian situation is relevant. Can we distinguish between the evolution of the two phenomena of subdivision and fragmentation? The detailed village case studies, by Mann, and by Bhalla on Bairampur, clearly indicate that, to some extent, the forces operated in tandem. Nevertheless when examining the general statistics on land, such as those quoted earlier for the Bombay Presidency, one wonders about the nature of the differentiation. Where fragmentation is defined, that would appear likely to be reasonably accurate, but it is clearly conceivable that what was actually 'fragmentation' might occasionally be delineated as 'subdivision'. Most peasants' total landholdings were becoming split into a much larger number of small, geographically-separated plots. Sometimes, even, plots would be held in different villages: in these villages' revenue records especially, such allotments of land held by an outsider might easily be described as 'holdings' when manifestly they were actually 'plots'. In general the likelihood is strong that 'plots' were intermittently recorded as 'holdings': tracing common ownership among the plots would be a tedious and complex business unpalatable to many village officials.[52] The simple point, then, is that the general revenue records probably exaggerate the extent of subdivision and understate that of fragmentation; to what degree is impossible to estimate. This hypothesis, too, correlates with our demographic evidence. Subdivision presumably *must* be the outcome overwhelmingly of population pressure, unless a strong sectoral movement of employment towards agriculture is occurring. If the dynamic of the process was rather less strong than the revenue records of the early twentieth century indicate, that might help to explain the discrepancy of slow aggregate population growth down to 1921. Equally, however, this would highlight the problem of fragmentation, which, as we have already noted, seems inexplicable entirely in terms of demographic patterns.

It is arguably, then, fragmentation which presents the most important and intellectually-challenging problem of land organization in British India. This, of course, directly parallels the phenomenon of scattering in the medieval West, that 'pivotal' characteristic of the open-field system.[53] So can the debates about the origins of scattering help our analysis? Unfortunately many of the traditional explanations of scattering - the demands of particular ploughing operations, the pattern of colonization of land, the existence of a communal, shareholding concept of land tenure[54] - whilst they may have firm echoes within the Indian situation, are essentially undynamic. McCloskey has underscored this inadequacy in explaining the medieval phenomenon: 'one or another deus ex machina .... is lowered into action to scatter the plots, but when it has been lifted back into the rafters, the question arises why its effects persist'.[55] How much more pertinent is this reservation in examining the progress of fragmentation in early twentieth-century India. Yet the same lack of correlation with the Third-World experience afflicts some of the most ingenious modern explanations of scattering. Dahlman's recent study in particular, whilst cogently demolishing many long-established theories, advocates a solution which rests on the communal ownership of grazing land in the medieval system: scattering was to achieve 'the creation of an incentive for the farmer to participate in the collective decisionmaking and control necessary to regulate the use of the large grazing areas in both the commons and in the arable fields .[56] One might, however, question whether this can really be the correct solution to a phenomenon which is so closely paralleled in societies lacking widespread communal organization of grazing and even a large livestock farming sector. In general, the focus of the medieval debate might be effectively sharpened if its participants could remember Thirsk's stricutre on the relevance of the Third World comparison.

The most common economic interpretation of scattering, recently reasserted by McCloskey,[57] is risk-aversion. Peasants, it is alleged, preferred scattered strips and plots because, even if there were productivity losses, this offered greater stability of income: clearly annual fluctuations of production should more satisfactorily balance out over a number of far-flung plots, possibly growing different crops and with divergent cultivation methods. Risk-aversion, too, might be especially important in India where agriculture was so dependent on highly variable and uncertain climatic conditions. For India, a dynamic element could be built into the explanation if it were argued that risk-aversion was becoming markedly more important by the early twentieth century. In this vein, some would certainly claim that buoyant conditions in Indian agriculture were abruptly ended with the famines and poor seasons of the late 1890s[58] and the untreated agricultural statistics do imply some sharp turning-point in per capita performance during the early twentieth century.[59]

This type of explanation, then, seems to take us closer to the heart of the phenomenon, but, as an all-pervasive model, the risk-aversion thesis is open to the objections powerfully raised by Fenoaltea[60] and Dahlman.[61] Why should peasants be so committed to this peculiarly intricate method of risk-aversion when many others are open to and in fact used by them? Simple storage is the most obvious response,[62] but there are numerous aspects of the peasant economy and society which possess important insurance potential, notably relationships between cultivators and landed elites.[63] In India the most important risk-aversion strategy has always been borrowing: the vast, extensive agrarian credit and debt network in part existed as a form of sophisticated social security against crop failure. When such alternative risk-aversion mechanisms existed, it is hard to see why so dramatic a land-orientated strategy as fragmentation should be so widely required.

Fenoaltea's own explanation for scattering is strikingly original: the phenomenon - and also the question of allocation of land by the manorial lord between demesne farming and renting out[64] - is the product of transaction costs. In the case of scattering, the problem is labour market transaction costs.[65] Monocultural production on a homogeneous, integrated holding would incur costs of employing and supervising labour at the demanding times of the agricultural calendar. Scattering, however, with the diversified methods and products of cultivation it offers, spreads the labour load more evenly. In sum, scattering, Fenoaltea argues, was 'designed to maximize productivity by optimizing self-employment'.[66] This interpretation in turn might be married with Chayanov's well-known explanation of peasant responses:[67] Chayanov would agree that it is more important for the peasant to use family labour effort effectively than to adopt the solution which would seem to offer short-term profit maximization. Again, for our Indian case, a dynamic element could feature in the model if it could be shown that labour market costs were rising, progressively increasing the desirability of optimal maximization of self-employment. We enter here, of course, realms of very limited knowledge. However, it is interesting to note in this context Michelle McAlpin's argument that, for cotton producers at least, labour costs might have been starting to rise significantly by around 1900.[68] Comment about high labour cost as the persistent complaint of rich peasant entrepreneurs is certainly legion in the same Bombay official records of the early twentieth century which highlight the sharp deterioration in size of units of land.

Fenoaltea's interpretation, in sum, appears to advance explanation significantly, because, like Geertz, he stresses that fragmentation did not necessarily involve productivity loss. Strong elements of the truth of this highly complex phenomenon undoubtedly reside here, and with the analysis based on population pressure linked to inheritance procedure and McCloskey's risk-aversion thesis. Nevertheless, one retains the feeling that other crucial influences remain unidentified, even for the medieval West. The ease with which all the monocausal interpetations so far advanced can be challenged suggests this, for writers like McCloskey and particularly Dahlman are far more persuasive in undermining established arguments than in proving their own. However, if these reservations exist in interpreting the medieval phenomenon, how much more powerful are they for India where we have to explain a strongly progressive historical force. None of the analyses of medieval scattering appear to be sufficiently dynamic to account for the case of early twentieth-century India.

However, the debate has brought advance. The great virtue of the recent contributions by economists has been that they assume some degree of economic motivation behind scattering, rejecting any semblance of what Dahlman calls 'the dumb peasant model'.[69] This has particular importance for the Indian case, because it is clear that fragmentation in many areas was fiercely supported and clung to by the peasantry. By 1920 officialdom was moving tentatively towards action to ameliorate the situation and legislation to promote consolidation of holdings was introduced in the Central Proinces in 1928, in the Punjab in 1936 and in the United Provinces in 1939.[70] In some provinces, too, the Co-operative Departments' activity promoted consolidation. These efforts, however, had varying impact. They had much their greatest success in the Punjab, but in the United Provinces the consolidation schemes were 'very unpopular by 1947'.[71] In the Bombay Presidency legislation was eventually introduced in 1947,[72] but this was the final chapter of a long and wearisome story. A first bill to encourage the formation of 'economic holdings', subject to inheritance by primogeniture, had been introduced into the Bombay Legislative Council by Keatinge, the Director of Agricutlure, as early as 1917.[73] Within a year, however, it was withdrawn because of widespread official objections.[74] This pessimism of Bombay officialdom concerning the possibility of effecting voluntary consolidation - widely shared, for example, within the Co-operative Department, the dynamic instrument of change in the Punjab[75] - seemed to be based on realistic assessment of local experience. In 1925, F.G.H. Anderson spent some time attempting to encourage the voluntary reduction of fragmentation in one Deccan village, Kamthadi in the Purandhar taluk of Poona District. His efforts enjoyed no success whatsoever: the peasants 'would not think even when they already hold 20 or 30 fields in different parts of the village of surrendering say one of their shares in the superior land soil in exchange for an area of the inferior even on payment of the panchayat-assessed value of the difference'.[76]

The Kamthadi case underscores a vital point about fragmentation. It was not entirely imposed on the peasantry by the tyranny of social convention: to a large extent the cultivators deliberately chose it. This in turn suggests a point which has been implicit in much of our argument. If fragmentation was not entirely the product of inheritance practice, then the alternative mechanism seems to have been the market: peasants presumably bought or leased into small fragments. In fact the most superficial glance at the village reports confirms that this was so. In distinguishing between fragmentation of cultivation and the splitting-up of ownership rights, Mann's study of Pimpla Soudagar suggested that the latter was here 'settling itself by two processes': 'the abandonment of village life ... by an increasing number of people' and 'the subletting of a large amount of the land by its holders'.[77] The subletting process, however, was the very engine of fragmentation of cultivation. The cultivator who wished to obtain more land 'can only get it by renting from a holder, and the holders who are most likely to lend are precisely those who possess only a small fragment .... To get large enough cultivation he has hence to take many such small patches'.[78] Similarly Bruce Campbell points to the impact of the land market on the organization of fields in his medieval Norfolk case. His powerful emphasis on the scope and influence of the market holds with at least equal force for early twentieth-century India: 'its potential lay in its ability to sustain a much higher volume of turnover ... than could ever result from inheritance custom, and to enable tenants to make deliberate changes in the size and layout of their holdings'.[79]

This last point raises another aspect of the hard core of economic motivation which appears to lie behind fragmentation. The layout of even the most broken-up fields does not appear to be entirely chance. As in the medieval West, the most common form of fragmentation was a division into strips, presumably permitting the operation of ploughing within small-scale units: where plots were squares this often signalled, as in parts of the Konkan, an intensive garden crop agriculture which had dispensed with the plough.[80] Again, there appears to exist in many localities an optimism size of plot, to which a large number conform. Keatings remarked how the largest holdings were typically divided into the greatest number of plots: in three Deccan villages he examined, holdings over 50 acres in size averaged nearly six plots each whereas those of under five acres were typically split into only one or the plots.[81] In this locality then - and this was within the dry famine-belt zone of the east Deccan where relatively large amounts of land were required to support a family - plots normally seem to have been between about three and ten acres in size. The implication is that there was not fragmentation beyond that which permitted a certain scale of technical efficiency in local agriculture.

To summarize, then, what we have concluded so far: fragmentation in early twentieth-century India seems to be, at least partly, a market-orientated response showing symptoms of precise economic motivation. The same remains a possible aspect of 'scattering' in the medieval West, especially following recent emphasis on the prevalence of a buoyant peasant land market in the England of the thirteenth century, the hey-day of the open-field system.[82]

But what was the main economic force behind market-promoted fragmentation? One important clue lies in the provincial and regional differences within India in the extent of fragmentation and, later, of consolidation. Fragmentation was certainly not confined to the poorer and more backward areas of India. Darling commented, of the problem in the submontane tract which included Bairampur, that 'nowhere is it worse than in the more thickly-populated parts of this area',[83] and yet this was a region of 'unusually bountiful' nature, which 'in its richness recalls the plain of Lombardy'.[84] Within the Bombay Presidency, Keatinge named the Konkan, the west Deccan and parts of Gujarat as the areas where 'the land has become subdivided to an excessive extent and fragmented in a manner which is generally recognised to be intolerable'.[85] In the east Deccan, he suggested, the problem was much less severe. This impression is confirmed by the more limited extent of fragmentation - even remembering that larger land units were required here for a given output - in Keatinge's three east Deccan villages mentioned earlier and in Jategaon Budruk, the second and more easterly of Mann's two village case studies. In the latter too, significantly, fragmentation of cultivation was less intense than the division of ownership rights, unlike the situation in Pimpla Soudagar.[86] Hence within western India fragmentation was apparently least threatening in the area of least secure agriculture, the famine-belt east Deccan.[87] In contrast, the problem evoked most comment on the lands of the west Deccan served by canal irrigation. Here Keatinge counted 30 plots in one typical holding.[88] For some officials 'the curse of excessive subdivision' threatened to undermine the whole value of the canals if water was to 'be sent down a long channel merely in order that a particular minute patch at the end of that channel may be watered',[89] and special legislation for the irrigated tracts was canvassed in 1918.[90]

Should we then conclude that fragmentation went particularly with a more prosperous, progressive agriculture? This would certainly be, in India, a more reasonable hypothesis than the opposite that it was the outcome of poverty and backwardness. Nevertheless it still does not fit the facts, particularly at all-India level. The most agriculturally dynamic province of British India was unquestionably the Punjab: rather more than a third of the total cultivated area here - nearly twelve million acres of land - was irrigated by canal schemes by 1940.[91] Here, however, whilst fragmentation reared its head early, the problem was most smoothly combatted. By 1940 the Punjab Co-operative Department had consolidated over a million acres of land and a further 52,000 acres had been reconstituted by the Revenue Department.[92] By the time of the Second World War, fragmentation was a much more severe and pressing problem in a notably more agriculturally-backward province like Bengal.

However, it still may be possible to suggest some common features, uniting the regions where fragmentation was most severe and most persistent. We need at this stage to consider again what fragmentation was offering to the cultivator. Its great virtue presumably is diversity: there is a larger opportunity than in a consolidated holding to utilize different techniques and grow different crops. Many explanations of medieval scattering - the risk-aversion thesis and the whole logic of partible inheritance - rest on this facet. Were there, then, particular local conditions which highlighted the need for and advantages of diversity? Two possible answers come to mind. Firstly, ecological factors might shape the situation. The holding of a number of different plots would become very much more useful, even necessary, if land conditions varied so much that certain important crops could only be grown on part of the village lands. Secondly, diversity might be a special advantage if conditions for commercial agricultural production were favourable: the cultivation of a wider range of marketable crops would be facilitated and, further, peasants might find it more convenient to produce for the market from certain plots and meet family consumption needs from others.

The existence, then, of a dualistic type of agriculture in conditions of favourable commercial incentive would seem to make fragmentation especially valuable.

Can we demonstrate that these factors were significant in particular regions of India? The case might be initially tested in the Deccan, where there seems real contrast between lessened severity in the east and an intensive degree and persistence of the fragmentation problem in the west. The west was certainly more commercialized: its more reliable climatic conditions permitted the cultivation of a wider range of crops and in the canal tracts sugarcane was extensively grown. Even in a dry-crop village like Pimpla Soudagar, for example, whilst the millet foodgrain, jowar, covered nearly half the cultivated area, important crops of wheat and vegetables for the Poona market were grown.[93] Thirty miles further east, however, in the unreliable rainfall and 'poor, shallow and hungry' soils of Jategaon Budruk, agriculture almost entirely depended on the millets, pulses and some wheat.[94] Yet commercial production in the west Deccan was won, in most villages, from particular, ecologically-suitable lands. In a vitally important passage, Mann described the region around Pimpla Soudagar as 'a country of the most contradictory character. Whenever a hollow existed, it has been filled with the washings from the decay of the higher lands, giving a rich valley; the higher lands themselves have been washed bare until a hard layer of rock has been reached'. As a result,

> the transition from the bare rocky uplands to the smiling valleys with deep soil is sharper than almost anywhere. A few yards will separate sometimes a piece of bare rock giving at the most a very thin grass herbage, and a rich deep black soil capable of growing the biggest and finest crops of sugarcane. We have passed along a road where there was rock on one side, and a crop of sugarcane giving a yield of thirty to forty tons per acre on the other.[95]

This was closely echoed by Anderson's description of Kamthadi village: here parts of the village lands constituted 'a high plateau, almost a mountain side, where only scanty grass will grow and rocks emerge abundantly', but elsewhere within the village were soils 'deep, rich and well watered both by wells and by pats'.[96]

This, perhaps, reveals the real roots of fragmentation.

The diversity of conditions within west Deccan villages necessitated the acquisition of a range of scattered plots if different types of production were to be practised, and, unlike in the east, the favoured soils could develop a genuinely more progressive commercial agriculture, providing a direct incentive to obtain some small stake in them. The phenomenon of agricultural dualism was most dramatic on the canal tracts, where the provision of reliable water supply enabled an intensive cash-crop agriculture to be carved out from the most arid conditions. Not surprisingly, the canal lands were the most fragmented: the incentive to acquire a tiny plot here was substantial. This explanation, it should be noted, not only accounts for fragmentation created by market processes but also, arguably, underlies any part of the process set in train by inheritance procedure. Proponents of the argument that inheritance practice caused fragmentation as well as subdivision still have to explain why it was so important to heirs to have an equal share of different types of land. Anderson was genuinely perplexed to understand why in Kamthadi 'each of the brothers insists on having every superior or inferior patch exactly equally divided amongst them'.[97] Variation in soil conditions and the advantages of diversity of production form the most likely explanation.

Is, however, this agricultural dualism thesis applicable in any other parts of India? One important case comes from the Chhattisgarh region of Central India, comprising the three districts of Bilaspur, Raipur and Drug. Here intense fragmentation of landholdings was long-standing and, indeed, had been deliberately stimulated and institutionalized by special custom:

> in ancient times when the feeling of equality was strong, everyone insisted on getting a piece of every kind of land in the village and the result was what is known as *lakhabhata*, the periodical redistribution of village land to insure that all cultivators had a share in all the different qualities of soil.[98]

The formal practice of lakhabhata, 'deeply engrained on the country' at the time of the British takeover,[99] had lapsed, British officials claimed, during the nineteenth century, but it left a legacy of 'holdings consisting of infinitesimal areas scattered over the surface of several square miles'.[100] The problem here was so severe that it prompted one of the first attempts at ameliorative legislation. In 1928 the Central Provinces

Consolidation of Holdings Act was introduced specifically to apply to the Chhattisgarh districts.[101]

Superficially this was a special case, where fragmentation rested on social structure and custom. Most reports attributed it to a simple egalitarianism of the village communities, 'practically communes in which everybody had an equal right to a share in the land'.[102] If this, however, was the sole influence, it is hard to explain why fragmentation remained intense nearly a century after formal lakhabhata had supposedly become uncommon. Fragmentation, too, imposed particular technical constraints on rice-growing Chhattisgarh, since, for reasons of time, it often necessitated simple broadcast sowing and prevented careful transplantation of the crop.[103] Yet peasant cultivators typically clung to their fragmented plots with the same stubbon determination as in parts of the west Deccan. Anderson's experiences in Kamthadi were mirrored by the efforts of a Central Provinces settlement officer, H.E. Hemingway, in 1906. As part of settlement operations in Raipur District he attempted a full land consolidation in two villages: 'in the first I actually redistributed some 200 acres, and the tenants had to admit that the distribution was perfectly fair; ... yet they would have nothing to do with it. "Everybody had lost" was the way they had put it'.[104]

Explaining what these cultivators had lost requires closer examination of the local economy. Chhattisgarh, to the east of Nagpur and close to the Orissa borders, is a great plainland, watered by the Mahanadi and Seonath rivers. With the prevalence of rice cultivation, its appearance in the 1930s was of 'a rolling expanse of paddy densely populated and closely cultivated'.[105] Population pressure, then, was undoubtedly one influence on land organization for by the twentieth century this was 'one of the most thickly inhabited tracts of the province'[106] and little cultivable land remained waste. However, demographic forces, again, seem not to be the sole agent, for why, then, had fragmentation developed and been institutionalized so early? The clue may lie in local geological conditions which were highly 'Deccani' in type. One settlement officer described the Chhattisgarh landscape as a

> succession of gently undulating slops from ridge to *nala* (streamlet) and from *nala* to ridge. The ridges consist in the main of red lateritic soil locally named *bhata*, while in the valleys is found black

> soil capable of growing the finest crops without the aid of irrigation. Betwixt and between lie *matasi*, the yellow soil, and *dorsa*, the combination of the yellow and the black. Thus there are, so to speak, four contours to each slope. Some freaks of nature are of course met with, and not infrequently I have found a stretch of *matasi* rice land below a ridge clothed with *dorsa* or a *bhata* ridge grade rapidly into *kanhar* without any intervening soil.[107]

The same report further detailed the implications of this for diversity of cultivation. The bhata ridges were 'on the margin of cultivation', typically used for poor grazing and, even if cultivated, capable of yielding 'only one crop in three years'; matasi was an excellent rice soil but 'only of use for the *kharif*, and ... quite valueless for *rabi* crops'; the black soil (kanhar), in contrast 'will yield a second crop of really good quality. Embanked *kanhar* has been known to yield a second crop of wheat'.[108] Here, then, was quite exceptional variation in soil conditions, often over very short distances, and it suggests a direct explanation for the origins of lakhbhata. Under such circumstances, fragmentation offered substantial advantages because it was the only way of guaranteeing most cultivators a share of the better soil. Furthermore, since with such intensity of soil diversity expansions in cultivation would bring in good or poor new land in a variable and unpredictable manner, the right of continual redistribution was in the majority's interest. Here was a classic example where the diversity fragmentation offered clearly outweighed the technical inefficiencies it imposed.

At this stage, however, any commercial agencies were a slight influence. Lakhabhata in its origins was clearly concerned with security and reliability of production, for even in the mid-nineteenth century Chhattisgarh was a remote region with small-scale, isolated markets. This situation was transformed, between the 1860s and the 1880s, by the advent of important rail routes, criss-crossing the region: in particular, Bilaspur became a major junction of the Bengal-Nagpur trunk line and of the subsidiary Katni-Umaria route. The outcome was a marked expansion in cultivation of commercial crops for export, especially wheat. In Raipur District, for example, the area growing wheat increased from 141,000 to 229,000 acres between the revenue settlements of the 1860s, and those of the late 1880s, the latter representing nearly eleven per cent of the net cropped area.[109] Similarly, in Bilaspur District wheat production extended over more than ten per cent of the land in cultivation by 1890.[110] On our interpretation, these developments - undoubtedly exacerbated in the Chhattisgarh case by substantial population growth - would have significantly increased the advantages of fragmentation by stimulating diversity of cultivation and raising the opportunities available to holders of good land. This, perhaps, helps to explain the devoted commitment to the legacy of lakhabhata which Hemingway encountered. By then, new impulses towards McCloskeyite risk-aversion may also have entered the equation. Chhatisgarh was severely affected by the climatic disasters of the late 1890s and in Bilaspur District the famine of 1897 alone claimed a death rate of over ten per cent.[111] Again, a system which offered the individual peasant differing soil conditions and cultivation patterns would seem to improve chances of survival amidst such a cataclysm.

Yet not all economic and social change worked to maintain and stimulate fragmentation. It became apparent by the 1920s and 1930s that energetic, co-ordinated official action, whilst still suffering numerous local rebuffs, could - in some areas of India - reverse the process and successfully consolidate holdings. This proved true of Chhattisgarh, for the Consolidation of Holdings Act 1928 enjoyed some impressive results. In Drug District, for example, the lands of 129 villages had been consolidated by the end of 1931 and the settlement officer could then proclaim that 'a stage has now been reached when it is no longer necessary to preach to the people the advantages of consolidation'.[112] Although the now resolute official intervention was obviously in part the cause, peasant attitudes here did seem to be changing. Why should this occur? If our thesis about the influence of commercialization holds any validity, one possible explanation follows. In Chhattisgarh by the 1920s the legacy of the devastating famines of the late 1890s, follows by uneven climatic conditions in the early twentieth century, had struck - as Harnetty has argued for Central India as a whole[113] - a powerful blow at commercial agriculture. Wheat cultivation and export contracted severely, as peasant cultivators retreated to the traditional foodgrains. By the late 1920s wheat's share of the net cropped area had declined to seven per cent in Bilaspur District[114] and only 2.4 per cent in Raipur District.[115] Rice, the leading food crop, had enhanced its position and now covered around three-quarters of these districts' lands. Consquently, diversity both of cropping patterns and, probably, of agricultural methods was lessening markedly: in such circumstances the trend was for the value of fragmentation to be reduced.

However, this could hardly have been the universal, dominant influence behind consolidation processes, for these enjoyed their most spectacular successes in the most commercially-buoyant province of India, the Punjab. The Punjab Co-operative Department began its organized, local attempts to reconsolidate lands in 1921 and by the late 1930s was regularly consolidating over 100,000 acres per year.[116] Again, some of the reason for the success lay with well-directed official zeal and commitment. Most of the work was accomplished, on the co-operative principle, by 'Consolidation of Holdings Societies' but they were supported by increasing numbers of trained supervisory staff. Even so, there were noticeable regional variations in the results of their activities. Much the greatest consolidation achievements came in the Jullundur Division of central Punjab and within this in the three districts of Hoshiarpur, Jullundur and Ludhiana. They boasted over half the total membership of the Consolidation of Holdings Societies in 1938.[117] This, of course, was the classic region of intense fragmentation, highlighted in Darling's writings on the problem,[118] but it was also, by the early twentieth century, the site of marked technical improvement in agriculture. Here the proverbially 'enterprising' Jat cultivators, drawing also on family funds remitted from the canal colonies and abroad, continually sought to innovate and adapt to maximize production. In Jullundur, Darling commented in 1925, 'between the last two settlements the number of wells, already large, increased by 42 per cent'.[119]

This case, despite the apparent contrast with Chhattisgarh, might still illustrate conditions which fit our general thesis. It could be argued that the very technical development of Jullundur Division's agriculture permitted the conspicuous success of consolidation here. In Bairampur, even at the time of Bhalla's report of 1922, considerable agricultural dualism was evident: the lucrative crops of sugarcane and cotton occupied about 30 per cent of the cultivated area, whilst the majority of the land remained under wheat, maize and fodder crops.[120] However, large-scale well construction of the type in Jullundur, involving substantial extension of irrigated agriculture, may later have crucially moderated dualism, creating a shift towards a new homogeneity at higher levels of economic performance. Consequently, the need for fragmentation would lessen. In this way, uniformity of production at higher technical efficiency would tend to provide some positive incentive for consolidation, as the Bengal Land Revenue Commission of 1940 noted on a visit to the Punjab. Commenting on the absence of any thrust towards consolidation in Bengal, the Commission's report remarked of the Punjab that 'the greatest advantage of consolidation in a province where the crops depend entirely on irrigation is that the peasant proprietor whose plots are consolidated is in a position to sink a well which he could not do if his plots were scattered all over the village'.[121] In total, the Punjab Government claimed, the consolidation operations of the 1920s and 1930s generated the construction of nearly 4,000 new wells.[122]

The linkage between successful consolidation and technical improvement also emerges in Chhattisgarh. The main official response to the exigencies of famine was the construction, during the 1920s, of several large new irrigation schemes in the region. For example, in Drug District, where consolidation in the wake of the 1928 Act proved so effective, 'the face of the district has been changed by the completion in 1923 of the Tandula irrigation system' which was capable 'of irrigating no less than 29 per cent of the total rice area of the district'.[123]

Our investigation, then, does indicate that the degree of agricultural dualism, shaped also by existing commercial conditions, can promote fragmentation or permit successful pursuit of consolidation. We might now attempt to correlate this with the historical pattern of India's economic development, if it is accepted that this must be a rough-cast exercise, subject to intense regional and local variation. In many regions, however, fragmentation seemed to develop rapidly during the first quarter of the twentieth century and, further, to resist attempts at amelioration, whereas during the late 1920s and 1930s officially promoted consolidation schemes did enjoy some successes. The first period, arguably, marks some sort of culmination in the type and process of agricultural commercialization promoted by British rule in India.[124] Cultivation of most commercial crops extended considerably, particularly cotton: India was the main source of raw material for the great export-led expansion of the Japanese cotton industry in the 1910s.[125] Nevertheless, we cannot assume that the period was one of easy prosperity in peasant agriculture. It was marked by a sharp, widespread inflation, which threatened those whose income was insecure. The general rise in prices, however, seems to have been most marked in the export crops, where inflation was fuelled by the rapid growth of international demand, and consquently their value was especially enhanced. Thus in Pimpla Soudagar Mann estimated that crops of vegetables could yield a value of between Rs.25 and Rs.30 per acre and sugarcane as much as Rs.100 whilst the foodgrains only provided, in market terms, between Rs.10 and Rs.15.[126] Under these circumstances the incentive to acquire the smallest stake in production of the most lucrative crops was at a premium, both for any profit-maximizing rich peasant and for the poor peasant whose predominant concern was security. This was why, in a village like Kamthadi by the 1920s, it was the best quality land which became 'tremendously cut up', the consquence of 'the ambition of everybody in the village to own about a guntha of irrigable land'.[127] Anderson's visit to Kamthadi in 1925, however, marked the culmination of the expansionary era. During the late 1920s prices of most crops started to slump and settled at new lows amidst the depression of the early 1930s. In these circumstances some of the special utility of fragmentation was gone. Consolidation in some regions could become a realistic option and especially where technical improvement, usually in the form of enhanced irrigation provision, was working to level up divergences of performance.

It is argued, then, that one vital root cause of fragmentation in early twentieth-century India was agricultural dualism, diversity of conditions within villages. In turn, its rapid development rested most on market responses by the peasantry to a particular stage and particular circumstances within the process of agricultural commercialization. Whether these developments have any firm echoes elsewhere is too complex an issue to examine here, but at least some lowest common denominator of correlation with the medieval West might exist. In this vein, Dahlman emphasizes in considering the English open-field system, that 'England is a country of very varied soil patterns and qualities'.[128] Equally, the twelfth and thirteenth centuries in the West - the period identified by Thirsk as so significant in the evolution of the open-field system - seem to have provided the type of expansionist commercial conditions, with active land markets, evident in early twentieth-century India. And, remembering that in many parts of the West, notably in England, consolidation was to win on a far greater scale than yet in India, it may be quite possible that some of the roots of the decline of the open-field system lie in technical improvement, moderating dualism.

Yet, finally, important social parameters shaped fragmentation in India and marked a sharp contrast with the eventual evolution of equivalent influences in the West. The Indian process depended to a significant extent on the nature of land markets. Clearly if a widespread aristocratic, landlord or even yeoman elite had been able decisively to inhibit, control or distort the land market, then the bulk of the peasantry would have been denied the vital quality of widespread access to different types of land, upon which fragmentation depended. Landlord power, where it existed, was typically exerted towards consolidation, seen as the 'rational' policy even where elites had no direct economic interest in the nature of land organization. Chhattisgarh exemplifies these themes. Effective consolidation here, before the introduction of the 1928 Act, was usually the outcome of assertive malguzars, the local landed elite, 'getting much of the best land into their own hands under the pretence of encouraging *chakbandi* (as consolidation of holdings is called)'.[129] Most peasant cultivators, however, were apparently capable of identifying and preventing such operations. Even where the malguzars were the formal landowners, consolidation drives were 'not very successful as the tenants suspected and in some cases rightly that this was merely a ruse to deprive them of their best land'.[130]

How, though, were the mass of the Indian peasantry in most parts of the subcontinent able to resist such pressures and preserve their access to the land? Recent work by Robert Brenner may be of use here.[131] In criticising neo-Malthusian explanations of change in western agrarian societies, Brenner reasserts the importance of social structure. Particularly apposite are his views on France for this was clearly the major western country where the mass of the peasantry established their claims over the land most successfully over the longest time-period. The French state, Brenner argues, was a major influence by developing as 'a "class-like" phenomenon, that is [as] an *independent* extractor of the surplus, in particular on the basis of its arbitrary power to tax the land'.[132] The state emerged as 'a competitor with the lords'[133] for the surplus of peasant production, and hence had a powerful interest in weakening the authority and control of landed elites over the peasantry: thus 'in France strong peasant property and the absolutist state developed in mutual dependence upon one another'.[134]

Whatever the validity of these views for France, one might suggest that the British raj in India shared many of the characteristics of Brenner's French state. Indeed the imperial state's quest to extract taxation revenue from the land was even more important in view of the raj's necessarily self-financing nature within the wider context of empire. Brenner's suggestions may, also, perhaps cast light on the drive towards peasant proprietorship in Indian government policy during the first half of the nineteenth century and on post-1858 tenancy and indebtedness legislation. These policies, of course, had a marked impact on some of the regions which were to experience severe fragmentation: in the west Deccan not only overlord pretensions but also the wider administrative activities of the old Maratha district revenue officials were sharply cut down to size.[135] Yet throughout India by 1900 any surviving feudal aristocracy had received short shrift. The appearance of authority might persist, as with the Awadh talukdars, but typically at the price of lack of direct control over events on the ground.[136] What British rule did succour was a mass of petty peasant privilege; in the west Deccan, for example, a bewildering volume of small-scale rights to inam (revenue-free) land. In these ways, arguably, the state had sustained the conditions permitting the widespread access to land which underpinned fragmentation.

This whole line of argument might seem to cut across a widespread current orthodoxy on the existence of social stratification in Indian agrarian society in the late nineteenth century.[137] But such stratification was a matter of differentiation within peasant groups who retained close social and cultural affinities. In addition, stratification processes may have been crucially moderated during the early twentieth century, as the extending commercialization process distributed income more widely through mechanisms such as increasing labour wages.[138] If so, the optimum social conditions for fragmentation to occur were created.

In the end, it was this social structure which was decisive in the inevitable long-term contrast between the evolution of land organization in India and in most western countries. In Britain, in particular, when the nature of economic, social and technical conditions changed, land consolidation would occur predominantly under the aegis of gentry and yeomen elites and eventually assume the shape of enclosure. In India even the process of consolidation would develop, as in the Punjab, under the firm control of an independent peasantry.

*NOTES*

Charlesworth, 'The origins of fragmentation of land-holdings in British India: a comparative examination'

I would like to thank, for advice on reading, Clive Dewey, Dharma Kumar, Bob Milward, Alistair Orr and, before his untimely death in February 1981, Eric Stokes.

*Abbreviations*

| | |
|---|---|
| BLRP | Bombay Land Revenue Proceedings (with vol.no.) |
| SR | Survey or Settlement Report |

1. Malcolm Darling, *The Punjab Peasant in Prosperity and Debt*, ed. Clive J. Dewey (New Delhi 1977), p. 28.
2. Of course the current orthodoxy among development economists argues for an inverse relationship between farm size and land productivity in most contemporary peasant economies. See, for example, K.B. Griffin, *The Political Economy of Agrarian Change* (London 1974). But these opinions may be challenged. For an argument that the inverse relationship depends on particular levels of technology see Ajit Kumar Ghose, 'Farm Size and Land Productivity in Indian Agriculture: A Reappraisal', *Journal of Development Studies* 16,1 (October 1979), pp.27-49.
3. Parliamentary Papers, 1928, Cmd. 3132, Report of the Royal Commission on Agriculture in India, Ch.5.
4. Harold H. Mann, *Land and Labour in a Deccan Village: No.1* (London and Bombay 1917), p.46.
5. Ram Lall Bhalla, *Report on an Economic Survey of Bairampur in the Horshiarpur District* (Lahore 1922) p.34.
6. Ibid.
7. Government of Bengal, *Report of the Bengal Land Revenue Commission* (Alipore, Bengal 1940), Vol.1, para. 169.
8. Darling, op.cit.,p.29.
9. Emmanuel Le Roy Ladurie, *The Peasants of Languedoc*, trans. John Day (Chicago 1974), p.93.
10. Joan Thirsk, 'The Origin of the Common Fields', *Past and Present* 33 (April 1966), p.145.
11. Mann, op.cit., No.1, p.47.
12. Darling, op.cit., p.42.
13. Ibid.

14. G. Keatinge, *Agricultural Progress in Western India* (London 1921), p.221.
15. Darling, op.cit., p.29.
16. L.S. Carey, *Report on the Land Revenue Settlement of the Raipur District of the Central Provinces, 1885-89* (Bombay 1891), para.51.
17. Thirsk, 'The Origin of the Common Fields', p.145.
18. The modern debate was, perhaps, inaugurated by Joan Thirsk with her article, 'The Common Fields', *Past and Present* 29 (December 1964), pp.3-25. This called forth a response from J.Z. Titow, 'Medieval England and the Open-Field System', ibid. 32 (December 1965), pp. 86-102 and a reply by Thirsk, 'The Origin of the Common Fields', ibid.33 (April 1966), pp.142-7. Recently, several economists have focused on the special problem of scattering. Stefano Fenoaltea has produced two studies: 'Authority, Efficiency, and Agricultural Organization in Medieval England and Beyond: A Hypothesis', *Journal of Economic History* 35, 4 (December 1975), pp. 693-718, and 'Risk, Transaction Costs, and the Organization of Medieval Agriculture', *Explorations in Economic History* 13, (1976), pp.129-51. D.N. McCloskey, too, has made two notable contributions: 'The Persistence of English Common Fields' in W.N. Parker and E.L. Jones, eds., *European Peasants and Their Markets* (Princeton 1975), Ch.2, and 'English Open Fields as Behaviour Towards Risk', in P. Uselding, ed., *Research in Economic History: An Annual Compilation* Vol.1 (1976). McCloskey's arguments generated a debate with Charles Wilson in the *Journal of European Economic History* 8 (1979), pp.193-207. These articles have now been succeeded by two important general surveys: Robert A. Dodgshon, *The Origin of British Field Systems: An Interpretation* (London 1980) and Carl J. Dahlman, *The Open Field System and Beyond* (Cambridge 1980). See, also, the articles in Trevor Rowley, ed., *The Origins of Open-Field Agriculture* (London 1981).
19. Thirsk, 'The Origin of the Common Fields', p.143.
20. Wilson, op.cit., p.198.
21. BLRP 11330, February 1923, A, p.65, Note by Deputy Secretary, Bombay Revenue Department, on 'Proposals to check excessive subdivision and fragmentation of holdings', Attached Table.
22. *Royal Commission on Agriculture in India* (London 1928), Vol.2, Part 1, paras.3504-7, Evidence of Harold H. Mann.
23. Annual Jamabandi Reports for the Central and

Southern Divisions of the Bombay Presidency, 1982-3, Appendix No.9.

24. Mann, op.cit., pp.45-6.

25. Ibid., p.47.

26. Harold H. Mann and N.V. Kanitkar, *Land and Labour in a Deccan Village. No.2* (London, Bombay, Calcutta and Madras 1921), p.44.

27. BLRP 11193, March 1922, A, p.293, Report by the Settlement Commissioner, No.S.V. 322, 30 August 1920, para.1.

28. BLRP 11330, February 1923, A, p.65, Note on 'Proposals to check excessive subdivision and fragmentation of holdings', para.17.

29. Bairumpur SR, p.33.

30. F.D. Ascoli, *Final Report on the Survey and Settlement Operations in the District of Dacca, 1910-17* (Calcutta 1917), para.109.

31. Report of the Royal Commission on Agriculture in India, para.119.

32. Thirsk, 'The Common Fields', p.23.

33. Ibid., p.24.

34. Ibid., p.9.

35. See Le Roy Ladurie, op.cit.

36. B.M. Bhatia, *Famines in India. A Study in Some Aspects of the Economic History of India, 1860-1945* (London 1967).

37. Michelle B. McAlpin, 'Death, Famine and Risk: The Changing Impact of Crop Failures in Western India, 1870-1920', *Journal of Economic History* 39, 1 (March 1979), pp.143-57.

38. Clifford Geertz, *Agricultural Involution. The Process of Ecological Change in Indonesia* (Berkeley 1968), p.82.

39. Ibid., p.80.

40. Ibid., p.69.

41. Ibid., p.137.

42. For the details, see Kingsley Davis, *The Population of India and Pakistan* (Princeton 1951); Ajit Das Gupta, 'Study of the Historical Demography of India' in D.V. Glass and Roger Revelle, eds., *Population and Social Change* (London 1972), pp.419-35; M.D. Morris, 'The Population of All-India, 1800-1951', *Indian Economic and Social History Review* 11, 2-3 (June-September 1974), pp.309-13.

43. Darling, op.cit., p.26.

44. Neil Charlesworth, 'Trends in the Agricultural Performance of an Indian Province: the Bombay Presidency, 1900-1920' in K.N. Chaudhuri and Clive Dewey, eds.,

*Economy and Society. Essays in Indian Economic and Social History* (New Delhi 1979), p.134.

45. B.H. Farmer, *Agricultural Colonization in India since Independence* (London 1974), Ch.1.

46. Charlesworth, op.cit., p.135.

47. Rajat Ray, 'The Crisis of Bengal Agriculture, 1870-1927: The Dynamics of Immobility', *Indian Economic and Social History Review* 10, 3 (September 1973), pp. 244-79.

48. Thirsk, 'The Common Fields', p.13.

49. Dahlman, op.cit., p.34.

50. Dhairyabala Pandit, 'The Myths around Subdivision and Fragmentation of Holdings: A Few Case Histories', *Indian Economic and Social History Review* 6, 2 (June 1969), pp.151-63.

51. Bruce M.S. Campbell, 'Population Change and the Genesis of Commonfields on a Norfolk Manor', *Economic History Review* 2nd Series, 33, 2 (May 1980), p.185.

52. A significant factor here is that full land surveys, involving detailed measurement and description of the land and its organization for revenue purposes, had not occurred very recently in many parts of the subcontinent. In the Bombay Presidency, for example, fresh surveys were entirely abandoned in the early years of the twentieth century and detailed information depended on modifications of existing records.

53. Dahlman, op.cit., p.30.

54. These explanations and their backgrounds are well reviewed in Robert A. Dodgshon, 'The Landholding Foundations of the Open-Field System', *Past and Present* 67 (May 1975), pp.3-29.

55. McCloskey, 'The Persistence of English Common Fields', p.95.

56. Dahlman, op.cit., p.125.

57. McCloskey, 'English Open Fields as Behaviour Towards Risk'.

58. See Eric Stokes, 'The Return of the Peasant to South Asian History' in *The Peasant and the Raj* (Cambridge 1978), p.276.

59. George Blyn, *Agricultural Trends in India, 1891-1947: Output, Availability and Productivity* (Philadelphia 1966).

60. Fenoaltea, 'Risk, Transaction Costs, and the Organization of Medieval Agriculture', pp.130-4.

61. Dahlman, op.cit., pp.61-2.

62. In medieval Europe the demesne granary 'was reported to as a matter of course'. Fenoaltea, 'Risk, Transaction Costs, and the Organization of Medieval

Agriculture', p.133.

63. Even in a feudal system, as in medieval Europe, 'serfdom was not a one-way street: both parties, the lord and his serf, accepted mutual obligations when the oath of fealty was given and accepted ... a lord who could not collect rent from a villein in a bad year could not just evict him - he had responsibility towards his tenant and villein'. Dahlman, op.cit., p.62.

64. Fenoaltea, 'Authority, Efficiency and Agricultural Organization in Medieval England and Beyond, pp.693-718.

65. Stefano Fenoaltea, 'Risk, Transaction Costs, and the Organization of Medieval Agriculture', pp.141-9.

66. Ibid., p.130.

67. See Daniel Thorner, Basile Kerblay and R.E.F. Smith, eds., *A.V. Chayanov on the Theory of Peasant Economy* (Homewood, Illinois 1966).

68. Michelle B. McAlpin, 'The Effects of Expansion of Markets on Rural Income Distribution in Nineteenth Century India', *Explorations in Economic History* 12 (1975), pp.289-302.

69. Dahlman, op.cit., p.38.

70. S.K. Agarwal, *Economics of Land Consolidation in India* (New Delhi 1971).

71. Ibid., p.11.

72. Ibid., p.8.

73. BLRP 10333, June 1918.

74. BLRP 10558, November 1919.

75. See I.J. Catanach, *Rural Credit in Western India. Rural Credit and the Cooperative Movement in the Bombay Presidency, 1875-1930* (Berkeley and Los Angeles 1970), p.174.

76. BLRP 11473, Juen 1925, A, p.441, Report by F.G. H. Anderson, Settlement Commissioner, No.S.V.465, 6 April 1925, para.5.

77. Mann, op.cit., p.49.

78. Ibid., p.53.

79. Campbell, 'Population Change and the Genesis of Commonfields on a Norfolk Manor', p.186.

80. Some very illustrative detail and mapping is given in Keatinge, *Agricultural Progress in Western India*,pp.217-21.

81. G. Keatinge, *Rural Economy in the Bombay Deccan* (London 1912), p.40.

82. This is evident from M.M. Postan, 'The Charters of the Villeins' in *Essays on Medieval Agriculture and General Problems of the Medieval Economy* (Cambridge 1973) Ch.8. Alan Macfarlane, *The Origins of English*

*Individualism* (Oxford 1978), esp. ch.4, adduces much evidence on the existence of an active peasant land market in medieval England, though he perversely regards this as a feature which prevents its characterization as a 'peasant society': in fact, exchange of land and resources through some type of market is of the essence of all but the most primitive peasant society.

83. Darling, op.cit., p.28.

84. Ibid., p.24.

85, Keatinge, *Agricultural Progress in Western India*, p.70.

86. Mann and Kanitkar, op.cit., p.47.

87. This, of course, throws further grave doubts on the validity of the risk-aversion thesis, at any rate in the Indian context. If this had been the dominant motive-force, one would surely have expected most pronounced fragmentation in the regions especially susceptible to famine.

88. Keatinge, *Agricultural Progress in Western India*, p.220.

89. BLRP 10142, April 1917, Report by the Commissioner, Central Division, No.V 1264, 5 September 1916, para.2.

90. BLRP 10333, June 1918.

91. Report of the Bengal Land Revenue Commission (1940) Vol.2, Appendix 7, p.36.

92. Ibid., p.47.

93. Mann, op.cit., p.53.

94. Mann and Kanitkar, op.cit., p.69.

95. Mann, op.cit. p.8.

96. BLRP 11473, June 1925, A, p.441, Report by F.G.H. Anderson, No. S.V.465, 6 April 1925, para.8.

97. Ibid., para.5.

98. P.S. Rau, *Final Report on the Resettlement of Drug District of the Central Provinces* (Nagpur 1933), para.54.

99. Carey, Raipur SR, para.66.

100. Ibid., para.51.

101. Agarwal, op.cit., p.9.

102. A.E. Nelson, ed., *Central Provinces District Gazetteer: Raipur District. Vol.A* (Bombay 1909), p.143.

103. Carey, Raipur SR, para.51.

104. H.E. Hemingway, *Final Report on the Land Revenue Settlement of the Raipur District of the Central Provinces* (Nagpur 1912), para.52.

105. Chhotelal Verma, *Final Report on the Resettlement of the Khalsa of the Bilaspur District of the Central Provinces, 1927-32* (Nagpur 1932), para.2.

106. Ibid., para.65.
107. Carey, Raipur SR, para.9.
108. Ibid.
109. Ibid., para.47.
110. Parshotam Das, *Report on the Land Revenue Settlement of Bilaspur District of the Central Provinces, 1886-90* (Nagpur 1892), para.11.
111. See J.E. Hance, *Final Report on the Land Revenue Settlement of Bilaspur District of the Central Provinces* (Nagpur 1914), ch.5.
112. Rau, Drug SR, para.54.
113. See Peter Harnetty, 'Crop Trends in the Central Provinces of India, 1861-1921', *Modern Asian Studies* 11, 3 (July 1977), pp.341-77.
114. Verma, Bilaspur SR, para.22.
115. C.D. Deshmukh, *Final Report on the Revision of the Land Revenue Settlement of the Raipur District of the Central Provinces, 1926-31* (Nagpur 1932), para. 48. The impression of precipitate decline from the earlier level of 11 per cent is somewhat misleading since buy the late 1920s Drug District had been constituted and had 'robbed' Raipur of some of the most important wheat-growing areas of the old Raipur District. Nevertheless, the statistics for Raipur and Drug leave no room for doubt that wheat cultivation had retreated considerably.
116. See, for example, Report on the Working of Cooperative Societies in the Punjab, 1937-38 (Lahore 1939), para.35.
117. Ibid., Statement B.
118. See Darling, op.cit. chs.3 and 4.
119. Ibid., p.43.
120. Bhalla, Bairampur SR, pp.62-3.
121. Report of the Bengal Land Revenue Commission, Vol.1, para.157.
122. Report on the Working of Cooperative Societies in the Punjab, 1937-38, para.35.
123. *Papers on the Resettlement of Drug District of the Central Provinces* (Nagpur 1933), Resolution No. 357-16-4, 16 May 1933, para.2.
124. For detail on the expansion of commercial agriculture in western India in the period, see my 'Trends in the Agricultural Performance of an Indian Province'.
125. See S.J. Koh, *Stages of Industrial Development in Asia* (Philadelphia 1966), pp.140-5.
126. Mann, op.cit., p.53.
127. BLRP 11473, June 1925, A, p.441, Report by

F.G.H. Anderson, No.S.V.465, 6 April 1925, para.8.

128. Dahlman, op.cit., p.106.

129. Hemingway, Raipur SR, para.52.

130. Rau, Drug SR, para.54.

131. Robert Brenner, 'Agrarian Class Structure and Economic Development in Preindustrial Europe', *Past and Present* 70 (February 1976), pp.30-75.

132. Ibid., p.69.

133. Ibid.

134. Ibid., p.71.

135. On these issues, see my 'Agrarian Society and British Administration in Western India, 1847-1920' (Cambridge Ph.D. 1974), ch.1.

136. P.J. Musgrave, 'Landlords and Lords of the Land: Estate Management and Social Control in Uttar Pradesh, 1860-1920', *Modern Asian Studies* 6, 3 (July 1972), pp.257-75.

137. This literature is well reviewed in Stokes, op.cit.

138. I have canvassed this argument in my 'The Russian Stratification Debate and India', *Modern Asian Studies* 13, 1 (February 1979), pp.61-95.

# PLAGUE AND THE INDIAN VILLAGE, 1896-1914

*I.J. Catanach*

Rural civilization, Emmanuel Le Roy Ladurie tells us, 'should be regarded first and foremost from the view-point of demography'. [1] This paper is about epidemics - specifically, epidemic plague in the late nineteenth and early twentieth centuries - and epidemics, especially in rural areas, can be seen primarily in demographic terms. But we do not intend to do so here. For one thing, in India before about 1920 - or arguably in India before independence[2] - endemic disease (especially malaria), and the sum of many merely local outbreaks of disease, were probably, as in late medieval and early modern Europe,[3] more important demographically than were epidemics. Furthermore (and Le Roy Ladurie would understand this point), epidemics are of interest at least as much for the light they throw on what may loosely be called 'structures' and on *mentalités* (the 'consciousness of a society' to use Rajat Ray's term),[4] as they are of interest for the history of the population.

Epidemics have a dramatic quality to them. An epidemic, by definition, has to spread, often to spread rapidly, over a comparatively wide area. Communication, 'connexion', is involved. People frequently try to flee from an epidemic: movement is involved again. An epidemic strikes with little or no warning. For this reason it often gives rise to fears, which are transmitted from one locality to another: again the element of 'connexion' (the major theme of this symposium) is apparent. And fears generated by an epidemic often lead to a search for culprits, human or suprahuman. Social tensions may be displayed[5] - but so too, as in Russia in the cholera epidemics of the 1830s,[6] may some basic social cohesion, and some basic social adaptability, reveal themselves. There may be attempts to pacify, rather than to resist, the institution or the 'outside' force thought to be causing the visitation. An epidemic, then, can provide us with a sudden, vivid picture of the real nature of a society; a variety of underlying relationships can be brought sharply into focus.[7] This would seem to be particularly the case when the disease is comparatively new, and therefore all the more alarming, as with plague in India in 1896 and the following years.

2

Plague, which for a time came to be thought of as yet another disease which it was all too easy for India to give to the rest of the world, appears in fact to have come to India from outside, although there are those who argue that it had long been endemic in the Garhwal area and had periodically spread to other parts of India. Certainly there is little reason to doubt that in 1896 it came to India by steamship from Hong Kong.

In India, as in other parts of the world in other eras, plague was to quite a considerable extent an urban disease. It was in cities - Bombay itself, Pune, Kanpur - that some of the most notable plague-related disturbances occurred in the early days of the epidemic. To begin with, the authorities in India were confident that the disease could be confined to the cities.[8] But by the middle of 1898 plague had spread over much of rural Bombay; by the turn of the century it was making its appearance in the rural areas of the United Provinces, Bihar and the Punjab. In the Punjab, indeed, plague was primarily a rural affair.[9] There is not a great deal in common between these 'plague provinces'; this paper tends to concentrate on the Punjab. But it may be noted here that the Indian 'village' in all these areas was no mere creation of the imagination of the revenue official or the census enumerator (as it sometimes tended to be in the south and east of India); Sir Herbert Risley was guilty of only a mild over-simplification when he asserted in 1905 that 'wherever rural tracts have suffered from plague it will be found that the villages are large and compact and are frequently surrounded by a wall. This is the case in Punjab, in parts of the United Provinces and in [the] Deccan where I have seen Marhatta [sic] villages with a wall 15 feet high and gates which were regularly guarded.'[10]

By what means was plague spread from the city of Bombay to rural India? We now know that plague - or, to put it more correctly, the bubonic plague of the most recent pandemic[11] - is not normally spread by direct human contact; an intermediary, a 'vector' has to be involved. It is true that, since dead rats have often seemed to precede plague (indeed, Muslim tradition associates plague with dead rats), some suspicion, quite early in the epidemic, fastened on rats. But they were thought to be only a secondary factor. As a report of 1898 put it: 'when human *vahans* or carriers were guarded against, Plague rode in on a sick rat'.[12] It was only in the first decade of this century (and in spite of some discouragement from an investigatory Commission made up in part of medical luminaries of the day)[13] that attention was directed not simply to the rat population but more especially to the state of the fleas on those rats - the state of the fleas which could bite human beings and thus communicate the disease.[14] While plague-smitten fleas doubtless sometimes travelled from Bombay to district towns and beyond in bundles of clothing, or even on the person, it seems likely that the fleas, and their murine 'hosts', were often transported amidst grain, and other bulk merchandise.[15] The dissemination of plague through the movement of merchandise would not have been possible without the railway; Gandhi was not altogether wrong when, with plague in mind, he described the railway as a 'distributing agent for the evil one'.[16] In mofussil towns plague had a habit of breaking out in grain merchants' houses - and above their grain stores were often sleeping quarters, used temporarily by customers from the rural areas. Kanpur was probably the leading centre from which plague spread in northern India; as one report put it, a considerable portion of that city could be described as 'one large granary'.[17] It has to be recorded here that in 1897 official 'scientific' theory in India was that plague could not easily be carried in merchandise.[18] This theory was, of course, honestly enough arrived at; it was merely based on incomplete observation. But it was a convenient theory for the authorities to have at a time when widespread famine required the movement of large stocks of grain within India; it was a convenient theory, too, at a time when European tea and jute exporters in India were nervous about world reception of produce from plague-ridden India,[19] and the Secretary of State in London was telling the Viceroy that he was 'more concerned about plague than famine' because a 'market once lost, or even partially deserted, is not easily regained'.[20]

The rat flea, then - or rather a particular type of rat flea, *Xenopsylla cheopis* - travelling more often than not in merchandise, brought plague to the railway towns of northern and western India. (The absence of Xenopsylla cheopis on rats in coastal Madras does much to explain the absence of plague in that area.)[21] From railway towns the spread of plague can sometimes be traced along cart roads and the like.[22] But the pattern of outbreaks of plague in the rural areas was irregular: plague had a mysterious habit of circumnavigating a village, or even a part of a village, in one season, only to spring up in that village or part of a village a year or two later. The very arbitrariness with which plague struck was, of course, one reason for the fears that it often inspired. The fact that plague-stricken rats rarely moved from village to village was noticed quite early. But it was only in the 1960s that the role in the spread of plague (in rural northern India) of field rodents, gerbils, came to be fully appreciated. The warrens of these rodents link the villages in a pattern that certainly does not follow straight lines on the map - or roads or footways. It is in these warrens, rather than amongst rats, that plague is preserved over the hot summer months - unless the system of warrens is then destroyed by monsoon floods.[23] At the beginning of a new season the gerbils re-infect village rats. It is *Tatera indica*, the Indian gerbil, which provides the vital 'connexion' in rural India so far as plague is concerned. Professor Frykenberg once wrote of the Madras Presidency being, metaphorically, 'tied to the earth by countless tiny threads and ... made captive to Lilliputian systems of power'.[24] In a quite literal sense, rural northern India was at times of plague tied to the earth - tied to the meanderings of a small, rather playful creature over and beneath the fields. In a way that Le Roy Ladurie and the *Annales* school would certainly appreciate, man was by no means master of his fate.

Yet, given the dominant official view in the 1890s of the way in which plague spread, it is not surprising that a primary concern of the authorities was the movement of men - from city to village, and from village to village. If the movement of men were controlled, it was thought, plague would be controlled. The surviving records reflect this belief - to the benefit, it must be said, of the historian. It is true that even in the later years of British rule most Indians did not travel very far from their birthplace at any time in their lives.[25] But we may still agree with Morris David Morris that Indians have probably long been 'as mobile as, for example, the populations of Western Europe at equivalent stages of economic development'.[26] By the time plague broke out there were, as Gyan Pandey points out, 'long trails of migration' from India's rural areas to its growing industrial cities and elsewhere.[27] Certainly the plague records cast a great deal of light on the city of Bombay's links with its rural hinterland. These links had been strengthened by the coming of the railway;[28] the number of passengers carried annually on India's railway system, it is worth remembering, more than tripled between 1882 and 1902.[29] As plague mortality increased in Bombay in the early months of 1897, and as officials dithered over restrictions to be placed on rail passengers, 'special' after 'special' pulled out of Bombay railway stations. Still great throngs of people were left trying to obtain tickets and places on the trains.[30] Women and children tended to go first, but men soon followed. The districts for which they were bound were (if we may judge from tables of those stopped at Pune railway station on suspicion of being infected with plague) mainly Pune and Satara - the two leaders amongst Deccan districts contributing migrants to Bombay.[31] The virtually complete dependence of the city of Bombay on its hinterland for its sweepers became apparent in the efforts which officials made to stop the railways from selling tickets to such persons.[32] Without its 'sanitary staff', it was claimed, 'in a fortnight the City would have to be abandoned'[33] - 'dependency theory' in reverse, it might be said. Steamers operating on the Konkan coast, and local craft, carried their share of the traffic from Bombay, too; the British owners of the steamer service took the opportunity to double the fares they charged.[34] And there were reports from beyond the borders of the Presidency - from Allahabad [35] and from Gyan Pandey's Azamgarh[36] in the North-Western Provinces, for example - of refugees from Bombay returning home, and, of course, ostensibly bringing plague with them. It may be that (as Morris David Morris has asserted) many migrants to the cities had not normally returned to their villages as frequently as some of those connected with Bombay's mills claimed.[37] Nevertheless, especially in the early days of plague, links with home villages, if they had been temporarily somewhat forgotten, were speedily revived: 'look brother,' was the cry, 'if die we must, let us die at home.'[38] By February 1897, Bombay's October 1896 population of approximately 846,000 had been, it was estimated, reduced to about 450,000.[39] Many cotton mills had been brought to a standstill. There was an exodus of considerable proportions again in January 1898.

Pune had its hinterland, too. The ill-fated W.C. Rand (in charge of plague operations in Pune until his murder in June 1897) poured scorn on those well-to-do members of the city's municipal government who chose to leave for quite distant places where they had relatives, or land, or both.[40] Many of Pune's student population left for other parts of Maharashtra, too. For eight years Fergusson College lost many of its students as soon as plague descended for the season;[41] as Ellen McDonald has shown,[42] that College, even though it was heavily dominated by Brahmans, at about this time drew fifteen per cent of its students from villages and another seventeen per cent from taluka towns. Pune is itself 'a city grown out of many villages';[43] large numbers of its more ordinary inhabitants had connections with surrounding villages, to which (unless they were very poor, or had jobs that kept them in the city) they tended to flee at times of plague. In September 1899 it was found that only 52,000 of Pune's population of 133,000 remained in the city.[44] There is a similar report of the Bombay Karnatak town of Dharwar 'pouring thousands of refugees into the surrounding villages'.[45] Here, in Western India, anyway, there was no sharp distinction, so far as movement of people was concerned, between the 'town' and the 'countryside'; the phrase 'rural-urban continuum' is the one which comes most easily to mind.

Some of the most vivid and analytically-useful descriptions of the movements of village people at times of plague came from the Punjab. There, Muslims tended to stay put. Traditional Muslim teaching was (with some exceptions) that it was impious to flee God's justice - and indeed ultimately his mercy - as shown forth in epidemics.[46] The 'small local mullas', as N.J. Maynard called them, tended not to know about the 'exceptions', or to ignore *fatwas* about the 'exceptions' which British officials diligently obtained from some of the more learned.[47] There can be little doubt that, in the case of Punjabi Muslim villagers, ideology, of a sort, triumphed so far as their attitude to plague was concerned. Non-Muslim Punjabi villagers, on the other hand, tended at first to flee to nearby villages when plague broke out. Often they had 'friends' - the result of caste and marriage links - in these villages. For a time marriages and caste meetings affecting several villages were severely discouraged.[48] The authorities in a couple of tahsils tried compiling lists of the inhabitants of each village 'with notes of the localities in which their marriage connections' resided.[49] Such lists would surely be of interest to the modern anthropologist, if they could be found; the anthropologist would certainly find something of value in the reports of two Indian Medical Service officers, C.H. James ad Edmund Wilkinson, on the early impact of plague in Jullundur and Hoshiarpur districts.[50] These reports contain detailed histories of the comings and goings of individuals, before and during the plague, in over seventy Punjab villages. From them we obtain a picture of a rural Punjab which is very much on the move. Brahmans go on pilgrimage to Hardawar; merchants move from village to village; *hakims*, *baids*, leechwomen and 'eye-doctors' (Rawals) travel constantly in search of custom; members of so-called 'criminal tribes' continue their wanderings; in spite of prohibitions a *kazi* goes to infected villages to read prayers and to see to the bathing of the dead; men visit a *pir*; a Sikh carpenter runs away; the clothes of the dead are sometimes given to or taken by others from outside the village (we are now able to see the significance of this fact in the spread of plague).

What we are dealing with here, of course, are the 'extensions' of the Indian village, which Morris Opler examined in a key paper of the 1950s.[51] A companion piece to Opler's was Rudra Dutt Singh's article on the 'unity' of the Indian village.[52] Some of this 'unity' is to be found in the way in which plague-free villages in the Punjab often rebuffed visitors from plague-ridden villages, especially if the visitors were not related to influential people in the former. It was not merely officials who had 'contagionist' ideas. In many villages in Ludhiana in 1901-02 there was a 'regular state of seige, and not even a Kanungo or tahsil chaprasi could obtain admission'.[53] In Ambala district it was a 'common thing to find roads diverted so as not to pass directly through a village'.[54] Yet it would be a mistake to overemphasize village 'unity' in the face of plague, in the Punjab and, certainly, elsewhere. When, in 1902, an attempt was being made to inaugurate a scheme of mass inoculation against plague in the Punjab

> a lambardar would report that a hundred or so in a village were ready [for inoculation] and a day would be fixed [for the visit of the medical team]; the evening before the opposite faction would circulate an enormous lie ... which would completely put the applicants off and destroy any chances of inoculation in the village.[55]

And in the very different social circumstances of Patna district, in Bihar, 'complete strangers and beggars' were sometimes shut out of villages at times of plague, but 'no chaukidar could interfere with the Rajput or Babhan zamindar', whether he came from an infected area or not.[56]

One further aspect of 'connexion' in rural India needs to be mentioned at this point. Even in the early years of this century a great many agriculturists relied on migratory labour for a number of operations, especially harvesting. For example, in the Punjab, hillmen descended annually to the Hoshiarpur and Jullundar districts;[57] labourers from the 'old' districts of central Punjab migrated annually to temporary work in the new canal colonies. With the coming of plague such labourers, naturally enough, increasingly avoided affected districts. The canal colonists, who had 'constant postal and personal intercourse'[58] with the districts where they had their original homes, frequently fled to those home districts when plague broke out in the colonies; crops were sometimes left unharvested.[59] The villages of the canal colonies were, of course, artificial and very recent creations. But it can be said that in the 'old' districts of the Punjab, and in most of the rest of northern and western India, the coming of plague demonstrated that the 'average' village in the late nineteenth and early twentieth centuries was rarely particularly isolated. The coming of plague also demonstrated that (in spite of the assumptions of contemporary advocates of 'local self government' and of co-operative societies), at the level of ordinary social intercourse, the 'average' village was not always especially harmonious.

3

Government measures against plague in the rural areas, and the response to them, are, again, best documented in the Punjab. There, from the beginning, Punjab 'paternalism' lost no time in asserting itself; there, and elsewhere, measures taken to try to control plague must undoubtedly be seen as part of that 'irruption of government into the regions and localities' which Dr. Seal rightly sees as marking the later years of the nineteenth century in India.[60] At first, officials in the Punjab attempted to isolate completely, by means of police cordons, the few villages in which plague had broken out. Several thousand policemen were employed in this work until the sheer extent of plague made the cordoning of all affected villages impossible.[61] H.J. Maynard, who was to rise to higher things but who was then a Junior Secretary to the Punjab Government, was responsible for formulating much of the province's early plague policy. Later in his Indian career Maynard was capable of criticizing that policy with rare frankness. 'There should have been', he wrote, 'no chaprasis or constables, hustling and plundering headmen, village proprietors and kamins alike'.[62] But the damage was done; as early as April 1898 there was a riot at the market town of Garnshankar, in Hoshiarpur district,[63] and the rumour began to circulate that the government was poisoning the wells.[64] The rumour was heard again in 1901 and, as we shall see, in 1907. Similar well-poisoning rumours had been present in Broach district in Gujarat as early as January 1897,[65] and were to be found in Bihar in 1899-1900.[66]

In 1902 Sir Charles Rivaz, the Lieutenant-Governor of the Punjab, determined upon a new plague policy, and announced it with rather a flourish: it was to be the mass inoculation with Haffkine's vaccine which we mentioned earlier.[67] Various new rumours, about the nature of inoculation, were soon abroad. Maynard summed them up in his colourful - perhaps over-colourful - style:

> The needle was a yard long; you died immediately after the operation; you survived the operation just six months and then collapsed; men lost their virility and women became sterile; the Deputy Commissioner himself underwent the operation and expired half an hour afterwards in great agony ....[68]

One is reminded of the *médecin empoisonneur* - the doctor who was really a poisoner - in the mythologies of France in the sixteenth century and of Russia, Hungary and France in the cholera epidemic of 1831-32.[69] (In India, after the plague epidemic, the notion of the *médecin empoisonneur* seems next to have reappeared during the population control campaigns of Mrs. Gandhi's state of emergency.) Rumours during the plague epidemic about doctor-poisoners were suddenly given some substance when, on 30 October 1902, at a place called Malkowal in Gujarat district in the Punjab, nineteen of those inoculated contracted tetanus and died. There is some doubt as to whether all or any of those who died at Malkowal had been pressed against their will to undergo inoculation,[70] but at the Government of India level W.S. Marris could note that it was 'an open secret that inoculation measures in the Punjab were far from being entirely voluntary'.[71]

1907 was, of course, a year of troubles in the Punjab, especially in the canal colonies: boll worm in the cotton crop of 1906 had been followed by locusts, hailstones, rust in the wheat crop of early 1907, and a fearfully hot wind before the coming of the monsoon.[72] On top of all this came plague: at least 675,000 - almost three per cent of the province's population - died from plague in the Punjab in 1906-07.[73] 1907 saw political activity, with Lajpat Rai deported from the Punjab and then brought back on the orders of the Government of India.[74] It is certainly possible to see plague as a contributory factor in the political unease in the Punjab at this time: John Morley, Secretary of State for India, was one who was very willing to do so.[75] In April 1907 Ajit Singh - wrongly thought to be a close associate of Lajpat Rai[76] - was reported to have told a mass meeting in Rawalpindi, 'Plague is working havoc among you, and it is better to die the more honourable death of the martyr for your country'.[77] Rumours about government poisoning of wells and tanks appear to have spread very rapidly at this time; villagers were said to have put guards over their old wells, and to have sunk new, temporary wells.[78] There was apparently a new rumour at this time, too: in Rawalpindi and Attock districts it was said amongst Muslims that their children were to be circumcised by government officials, and killed in the process.[79]

The well-poisoning rumours bear much resemblence to rumours which circulated about Europe at the time of the Black Death; then it was the Jews who were said to be responsible for the well-poisoning.[80] Such rumours have been said to be 'divers': they may seem to surface, disappear, and then surface again, often in a different era and a different civilization.[81] But such a sociological observation does not really help the historian very much. Given the special concerns of this symposium, what needs to be explained is exactly who originated these rumours and, especially, how they were passed on from village to village. Here we are in rather difficult territory. Indian newspapers undoubtedly sometimes spread rumour amidst townspeople by printing stories ostensibly heard in the bazar; to save themselves from prosecution they would, of course, promptly deny that there was any truth in the allegations. But it has to be admitted that, especially in the Punjab, there is a question as to the extent to which newspapers circulated in the rural areas at this time, the extent to which, in fact, there was a 'rural-urban continuum' so far as newspapers were concerned. Professor Barrier does not give us a great deal of specific guidance in this matter, although he points to a considerable increase in the first years of this century in the number of newspapers published in the Punjab,[82] and to a considerable increase in rural politicization around 1907-08.[83] Banias and *baids* were reported by the British-owned *Civil and Military Gazette* of Lahore in 1898 to be circulating well-poisoning rumours[84] - presumably as they moved about the villages, and as men came to them in the bazars. Banias were blamed again in 1901 for spreading 'false rumours', which led to a riot, in the village of Shahzada, in Sialkot district.[85] But banias, before and after the Punjab Alienation of Land Act of 1900, tended to be the *bêtes noirs* of the British in the Punjab, and they may have been unjustly blamed. Baids and *hakims* had cause to be opposed to the British at this time: since 1889 they had been discountenanced by the Punjab government[86] (though there were soon to be some efforts made to draw hakims into the official struggle against the plague).[87] In 1907 it was often 'Aryas' (members of the reformist/revivalist Arya Samaj) who were blamed for the circulation of rumours.[88] It is perhaps significant that the well-poisoning rumours seem to have been at their height in the rural areas surrounding Rawalpindi not long after the reported speechmaking of Ajit Singh in the city. But such allegations from the British do not take us very far. There does not appear to be any mention in the records of so-called 'snowball letters' being passed from village to village,[89] nor are runners mentioned,[90] though there is little doubt that in 1907 rumour moved with considerable speed in the rural Punjab. One reasonably hard piece of evidence is possibly to be found in the conviction in May 1907, at Hasan Abdal in Attock district, of one Swami Gusain Dyal, or Gosain Swami Dyal, for fostering rumours that government was spreading plague by 'causing pills to be thrown into wells and streams'.[91] A tahsil chaprasi who was reported to be a disciple of the Swami was convicted of actually throwing pills made of flour into the streams. But, of course, by May 1907 Sir Denzil Ibbetson and his officials, especially those in the Rawalpindi area, were determined to prove large-scale conspiracy, come what may.[92] The Swami's previous brief appearance in the records was as a man of 'religion';[93] he may have been a convenient scapegoat in 1907.

It is possible, indeed, that (like some of the official informers of the period) we may exaggerate the degree of social and political tension which plague created, or even simply exacerbated. The millworkers of Bombay departed rapidly in 1896-97, and again in 1898. but they were back at work again within a few months (or at least many of them were - there was a suggestion that sometimes their places were taken by new hands);[94] they returned more rapidly in 1898. A perusal of sources other than the *Tribune* gives an impression that the Malkowal incident did not have quite the serious psychological effect in the Punjab that some officials feared and some Indian politicians looked for.[95] In many an Indian village, furthermore, the tendency to flee from plague could be reasonably easily turned to useful purposes. In Bombay, and in Punjab if the season was warm enough, many villagers soon did not need a great deal of encouragement from officialdom to 'evacuate' a stricken village and to set up a new temporary village, housed in huts made of gunny-bags and the like, at some distance from the old village. In fact, to some extent such villagers, especially in Bombay, were simply following precedents established in earlier epidemics.[96] The Indian villager, it is worth saying yet again, is not lacking in basic adaptability.[97]

In 1897, after the Rand murder in Pune and various other troubles, some of them connected with plague, and after the Calcutta newspaper, the *Englishman*, had shouted that India was on the verge of another Mutiny, Elgin, the Viceroy, asked his provincial governors what they thought was the real situation. The reply of Anthony MacDonnell, Lieutenant-Governor of the North-Western Provinces, is worth quoting, if only for the fact that the India Office resurrected the file and sent it off to Minto, Viceroy in 1907, when he was hard pressed in the Punjab. Plague and famine were at work, said MacDonnell; 'in fact a heavier burden has been laid on the country than it has known during the century'. But 'in these circumstances', he concluded, 'it is a surprising thing that "disorder and unrest" [have] been so little observable'.[98] One further opinion may be quoted, that of Clifford Gill, who had considerable experience of plague as a medical officer in the Punjab in the earlier years of this century. He believed that epidemics could not often be said to be 'the proximate or remote cause of civil strife'.[99]

Yet as one considers plague in India it is not always possible to agree with Gill. MacDonnell, indeed, in his plague policy in the North-Western Provinces (especially in the cities) showed himself to be peculiarly sensitive to the possibility of 'disorder and unrest'. He refused, for example, to prohibit the pilgrimage to Hardawar, and disagreed with the Government of India prohibition of the Muslim *haj* in the first year of the plague. 'In India,' he told Elgin, 'you *cannot foresee* what will come of interfering with religious observances'.[100] Eric Stokes insisted, with the activities of organizations such as the Arya Samaj in mind, that beneath the surface in India in the last years of the nineteenth century, 'the tinder of mass politics was drying slowly in the sun'.[101]

On occasions, certainly, one has the feeling that there was tinder about in the rural areas of northern and western India at the time of plague. But the tinder may not always be easily recognisable as that of 'mass politics'. For the tension which plague undoubtedly often induced worked itself out at least as much in 'non-political' ways as it did in, for example, well-poisoning stories which had a distinctly anti-British tone to them. It is important to remember that village India sees life in suprahuman as well as in human terms. 'When an outbreak [of plague] is apprehended', Maynard tells us,

> there are signs of religious revival. A Granthi is installed under a canopy or in the village rest-house to recite the Scriptures; 'Havan' is freely practised; public prayers are offered in the village mosque; hard work is done on the excavation of the tank; the poor of the neighbourhood are collected and fed. The lower deities or demons are also not forgotten; fakirs are summoned and highly fed for the performance of their charms; the village site is surrounded with a circle of stakes, with demons' heads roughly carved on top to serve as supernatural guardians.[102]

(It may be indeed that at this somewhat special ritual level rather more 'unity' was shown in the village at times of plague than was displayed in other ways.) Even today, large numbers of people seem to be involved, when epidemic threatens, in rituals by which villages attempt to induce the disease to pass them by. For example, a woman, often of low caste, may be taken to be 'possessed' with the disease, placed in a cart and carried with much ceremony to the borders of the village. Alan Beals has described memories of such an incident which occurred during a plague epidemic in a Mysore village.[103] In rural Bombay, during the plague epidemic with which we are concerned, strenuous efforts were made, at the ritual level, to 'pass on' the disease from one village to another. 'Offerings' of goats, cooked food and liquor were carried from village to village 'over a distance', it was claimed, 'of 50 or 100 miles until the course terminates in a jungle or forest, where the offerings find their resting place'.[104] One is reminded of the mysterious *chapatis*, probably connected with a prevailing cholera epidemic, which circulated from village to village prior to the Revolt of 1857.[105]

But it seems that to begin with Indian villagers had a number of problems in connection with ritual behaviour towards plague. The first was a problem of perception, or perhaps description. Plague was, as we have seen, something new for virtually all the Indian villagers it attacked in the late 1890s. By 1919, Norman White, Sanitary Commissioner with the Government of India, could say that plague could be readily identified as such by the average villager.[106] But this was not always the case in its early days. (Indeed at this stage at least one European doctor in India made some rather spectacular misdiagnoses.)[107] Plague was seen in the village as a type of 'fever' - and yet it presented new and strange aspects. The confusion about the nature of plague is perhaps reflected in the number of different words in each Indian language by which plague appears to have been eventually described;[108] significantly, *pleg*, the Indianized form of the English word, was sometimes adopted. Now a goddess of disease is generally considered in rural India to be both the cause and (if properly pacified) the preventer and curer of that disease.[109] It is quite possible for a disease goddess - Sitala, for example - to have 'command' over a number of diseases.[110] But it is surely significant that Indian villages found it necessary to 'create' a plague godling where there had been none before. She became the plague mother, the Bombai Ki Mayan, and joined Sitala in Deva's temple.[111] Only when that had been done, it can be argued, could plague be thought of as possessing an appropriate suprahuman dimension; only then was it no longer quite as alarming as it had been. Thus, by the time Clifford Gill was in charge of plague operations in the Punjab, from 1909 until 1911, he could indeed find that the almost annual advent of the disease was 'marked by extreme humility and patience'.[112] This attitude was, one suspects, very much akin to that famine 'mentality' which Arthur Geddes discerned in the Deccan east of Pune some years later.[113] Clifford Gill could even assert (with regard to epidemics in general) that 'the most virulent pestilence in short lived and [the] ill-effects disappear with astonishing rapidity and with them all memory of the epidemic'.[114]

Gill exaggerated, even so far as plague in the years from about 1909 was concerned. But it can certainly be said that, at the level of government, plague fairly rapidly ceased to be a fearful novelty, although mortality from plague was to remain high for another decade. As early as 1907 the Private Secretary to the Viceroy could say that plague 'has been so long with us, over ten years now, that the authorities have got accustomed to it and, quite unconsciously, no doubt, have come to look on it very much as they regard malaria'.[115] In a sense, in fact, in the governmental as well as in the popular mind, plague was ceasing to be an 'epidemic'.

## 4

Because of the quite considerable psychological resilience of the Indian peasant, the problem of the results of plague in rural India is mainly one for the historical demographer - and in this paper, it will be remembered, we largely eschew demography. In general, it may be said that even if the demographic effects of plague did not disappear with 'extraordinarily rapidity' (to use Clifford Gill's phrase), they worked themselves out in less than a generation. For various reasons, mainly biological,[116] plague in India did not have many lasting demographic effects. Given the emphasis of this paper on 'connexion', only one aspect of this question deserves our attention here.

The most frequently heard complaint in the rural areas of the Punjab and of Bombay in the years of plague and immediately after the shortage of agricultural labour. Plague was universally blamed for this situation by potential employers of labour. 'It has always been represented to me', wrote F.W. Kennaway, the author of a Punjab assessment report of 1908, 'that the chief damage to any village has been caused by mortality amongst chamars'.[117] C.H. Atkins, Deputy Commissioner of Ferozepore, prophesied in the same year that 'the position of the *kamins* seems likely to undergo a great revolution in the course of the next few years as they are placed in a position of great independence by the demand for labour and by high wages'.[118] The province's Season and Crop Report for 1909-10 claimed that 'village menials who had been accustomed to work at customary rates from time immemorial have emancipated themselves and demand competition wages. A striking feature of the present time is the great mobility of labour, labourers moving freely to places where they can obtain the most remunerative employment'.[119] It is tempting to see these changes as largely the result of the coming of plague; it is tempting, indeed, to see some sort of 'emancipation' of agricultural labour occurring in the Punjab at this time which was of a variety not altogether different from the emancipation of rural labour that is sometimes supposed to have occurred in Europe after the Black Death.[120] But it would be unhistorical to yield to these temptations. As Kennaway noted in 1908, there is not a great deal of evidence that village menials suffered from plague to a greater extent than did other classes.[121] Furthermore, as we have seen, labour was becoming more mobile in the Punjab, and much of the rest of India, before the arrival of plague. Labour was short in the Punjab because the Punjab, especially the canal colonies area, was developing economically. A secondary reason was that, again especially in the canal colonies, many 'agriculturists', so-called, were increasingly unwilling to undertake labour themselves.[122] A somewhat similar comment could be made about contemporaneous complaints of a shortage of rural labour in Gujarat.[123] In much of the rest of the Bombay Presidency there was undoubtedly a shortage of rural labour reported about the time of the 1911 Census,[124] but there were other reasons besides plague for this state of affairs, notably the continuing attractions of the city of Bombay, and the labour requirements of large irrigation works in the rural areas.

## 5

In the period in which plague was though of as an 'epidemic' it certainly provided the historian with a good deal of insight into the nature of 'connexion', both physical and mental, in rural India. The Indian village which has emerged from our study has been one that was still largely at the mercy of uncontrollable 'environmental' forces. But it was a village which was by no means a 'village republic', as Charles Metcalfe had defined it seventy or so years earlier.[125] It was not isolated - it had its links with the cities as well as with nearby villages and railway towns - and it was not particularly united in everyday matters. Especially by means of rumour it could blame its ills on the 'government', but it frequently did not see matters in terms that are easily recognisable as 'political'. It still felt it necessary to interpret such an event as a plague epidemic partly in terms of the rituals of folk religion; plague had to be fitted into the so-called 'traditional' scheme of things. In time, in its own way, the Indian village learnt how to cope with plague, as it had learnt how to cope with other epidemics, and with famine. That, perhaps, is what Clifford Gill was really driving at.

## *NOTES*

Catanach, 'Plague and the Indian Village, 1896-1914'

*Abbreviations*

| | |
|---|---|
| IOL | India Office Library and Records, London |
| MSA | Maharashtra State Archives, Bombay |
| NAI | National Archives of India, New Delhi |
| P.P. | Parliamentary Papers, Great Britain |
| Prog(s) | Proceedings |

This paper has benefited greatly from discussion at the December 1980 London seminar, and at an Oxford seminar convened by Dr. Tapan Raychaudhuri and Dr. Gopal Krishna in February 1981. Dr. Richard Burghart, of SOAS, has assisted in the development of my anthropological awareness.

1. Emmanuel Le Roy Ladurie, *The Territory of the Historian* (trans. Ben and Sian Reynolds; Hassocks, Sussex 1979), p.89.
2. See Morris David Morris, 'Trends and Tendencies in Indian Economic History', *Indian Economic and Social History Review* V, 4 (1968), pp.366-7, no.106.
3. See M.W. Flinn, 'The Stablisation of Mortality in Pre-industrial Europe', *Journal of European Economic History* III (1974), p.290; R.S. Schofield, 'Crisis Mortality', *Local Population Studies* No.9 (1972); Robert Gottfried, 'Epidemic Disease in Fifteenth Century England', *Journal of Economic History* XXXVI, 1 (1976), p.269.
4. See Rajat K. Ray in this volume, below.
5. See, for example, René Baehrel, 'La haine de classe en temps d'épidémie', *Annales: Economies, Sociétés, Civilisations* VII, 2 (1952); Baehrel, 'Epidémie et terreur: Historie et sociologie', *Annales historique de la Révolution française*, XXII (1951).
6. Roderick E. McGrew, *Russia and the Cholera 1823-32* (Madison 1965); cf. Elisabeth Carpentier, *Une ville devant la Peste. Orvieto et la Peste noire de 1348* (Paris 1962).
7. See, for example, Louis Chevalier, ed., *Le choléra: la première épidémie du xix^e siècle* (La Roche-sur-Yon 1958); Asa Briggs, 'Cholera and Society in the Nineteenth Century', *Past and Present* 19 (April 1961);

R.J. Morris, *Cholera 1832: The Social Response to an Epidemic* (London 1976).

8. Lord Elgin (Viceroy) to Lord George Hamilton (Secretary of State), 13 January 1897, Hamilton Collection, MSS. Eur. D. 509/4, IOL.

9. F. Norman White, 'Twenty Years of Plague in India with special reference to the Outbreak of 1917-18', *Indian Journal of Medical Research* V (1918-19), p.198.

10. Risley, Note, 8 November 1905, with India Home Sanitary (Plague) A Progs, February 1906, Nos.327-47, NAI.

11. For theories about the ways in which plague may have spread in earlier pandemics - for example by the agency of the human flea - see Jean-Noel Biraben, 'Current Medical and Epidemiological Views on Plague', in *Plague Reconsidered: A New Look at its origins and effects in 16th and 17th Century England* (A *Local Population Studies* Supplement) (Matlock, Derbyshire 1977), pp.25-36. This is a translation from a chapter from Biraben's *Les hommes et la Peste* ... (Paris 1975).

12. Report of the Bombay Plague Committee ... for the period extending from the 1st July 1877 to the 30th April 1898, under the Chairmanship of Sir James MacNabb Campbell, K.C.I.E. (Government of Bombay, 1898), p.58. *Vahan* is a reference to the mount on which the Hindu disease goddess Sitala (see above p.229) is supposed to ride.

13. Report of the Indian Plague Commission, pp.75-7. P.P.1902 (Cd.810) lxxii.

14. Such an understanding emerged from the work of P.L.S. Simond in Paris, J. Ashburton Thompson in Sydney, Australia, Glen Liston in India, and from the important studies of the 'Commission' set up in India by the Plague Advisory Committee. This Committee had been brought into being by the Secretary of State for India, the Royal Society and the Lister Institute of Preventive Medicine. The reports of the 'Commission' were published as supplements to the *Journal of Hygiene* in the first two decades of this century; some are republished as *Reports on Plague Investigations in India* (Cambridge 1914).

15. See F. Norman White, Report on Plague in Rawalpindi City, August 1917, India Education Sanitary B Progs, August 1917, No.23; also India Education Sanitary A Progs, April 1918, Nos.21-22, NAI.

16. M.K. Gandhi, *Hind Swaraj* (1909), *Collected Works of Mahatma Gandhi*, Vol.X, p.27.

17. T.H. Gloster et al, 'Epidemiological Observations

in the United Provinces of Agra and Oudh 1911-12', *Journal of Hygiene*, Plague Supplement V (Supplement to Vol.XV April 1917), p.826.

18. E.H. Hankin, Chemical Examiner and Bacteriologist, North-Western Provinces, to Bombay Government, enclosed A.M.T. Jackson, Under Secretary Revenue Bombay, to India Home No.1600 of 26 February 1897, India Home Sanitary Progs March 1897, Nos.202-3; see also Progs Nos.204-9, Vol.5188, IOL.

19. See the telegrams dating from the early months of 1897 in Papers Relating to the outbreak of Bubonic Plague in India, pp.3-15, P.P.1897 (C.8386) lxiii, and in Further Papers Relating to the Outbreak of Plague in India, pp.3-11, P.P.1897 (C.8511), especially p.6: Telegram from Viceroy to Secretary of State, 2 April 1897.

20. Hamilton to Elgin, 21 January 1897, Elgin Collection, MSS. Eur.F.84/15, IOL.

21. L. Fabian Hirst, *The Conquest of Plague: a Study of the Evolution of Epidemiology* (Oxford 1953), pp.357-8.

22. See W. Wesley Clemesha, Report on Plague in Patna District during the Cold Weather of 1899-1900: part of Enclosure No.18 with Revenue Sanitary Letter from India No.19 of 25 October 1900, L /E/3/114 IOL; also M. Greenwood Jnr., 'Statistical Investigation of Plague in Punjab. Second Report: On the connection between Proximity to Railways and Frequency of Epidemics', *Journal of Hygiene* XI (December 1911) (Plague Supplement No.1).

23. M. Baltazard and M. Bahmanyar, 'Recherches sur la Peste en Inde', *Bulletin of the World Health Organization*, XXIII, 2-3 (1960).

24. Robert E. Frykenberg, 'Traditional Processes of Power in South India: An Historical Analysis of Local Influence', *Indian Economic and Social History Review* I, 2 (1963), p.134.

25. Gail Omvedt, 'Migration in Colonial India: the Articulation of Feudalism and Capitalism in the Colonial State', *Journal of Peasant Studies* VII, 20 (1980), pp. 187-8.

26. Morris David Morris, *The Emergence of an Industrial Labour Force in India. The Case of the Bombay Cotton Mills, 1854-1947* (Berkeley 1965), p.42.

27. Gyan Pandey - in his paper for the symposium - on the 'External Dimension'; see Peter Robb, ed., *Rural South Asia: Linkages, Change and Development* (London 1983).

28. Compare Anand A. Yang, 'Peasants on the Move: A Study of Internal Migration in India', *Journal of*

*Interdisciplinary History* X, 1 (1979), p.53.

29. 1882: 59 millions; 1902: 197 millions. Nalinaksha Sanyal, *Development of Indian Railways* (Calcutta 1930), p.199.

30. P.C.H. Snow, *Report on the Outbreak of Bubonic Plague in Bombay, 1896-97* (Government of Bombay 1897), p.20.

31. Statement of Plague Cases discovered by the Municipal Medical Men at the Poona Railway Stations; Statement of Suspected and True Plague Cases found by Southern Maratha Railway Medical Men at the Poona Railway Station, *Supplement to the Account* [by M.E. Couchman] *of Plague Administration in the Bombay Presidency from September 1896 till May 1897* (Government of Bombay 1897), pp.62-5, 67-8.

32. Snow, op.cit., p.8.

33. Ibid., p.7.

34. Bombay Port Health Officer No.269 of 9 February 1899, enclosed Memo from Plague Commissioner No.345 - P.C. of 17 February 1899, Bombay Plague Progs, No.1696 P., 8 March 1899, Vol.5779, IOL.

35. H.W. Stevenson, Report on the Outbreak of Plague at Mau Aima, District Allahabad ... 20 May 1900, p.1., with Revenue Sanitary Letter from India No.16 of 23 August 1900, L/E/3/114, IOL.

36. Antony MacDonnell, Lieutenant-Governor, North-Western Provinces, to Elgin, 4 February 1897, MSS.Eur. F 84/70, IOL.

37. Morris, op.cit., p.98.

38. *Times of India, Overland Weekly Edition*, 22 January 1898, p.82.

39. *Report of the Indian Plague Commission*, p.10.

40. Draft of Report to Government by the late Mr. Rand ... Chairman, Poona Plague Committee, in *Supplement to the Account of Plague Administration in the Bombay Presidency, 1896-97*, pp.4-13.

41. *The History of the Deccan Education Society compiled and in part written by P.M. Limaye* (Poona 1935), p.178.

42. Ellen E. McDonald [Gumperz], with the assistance of Hannah S. Branstetter, 'Social Background of the Educated Elite in late Nineteenth Century Maharashtra', in Ellen E. McDonald and Craig M. Stark, *English Education, Nationalist Politics and Elite Groups in Maharashtra 1885-1915* (University of California, Berkeley, Center for South and Southeast Asian Studies 1969), p.19.

43. Damodar Dharmanand Kosambi, *An Introduction to the Study of Indian History* (Bombay 1956), p.38.

44. A.F. Woodburn, Acting Chief Secretary Bombay, to India Home, No.7332 - P. of 21 October 1899, Bombay Plague Progs, Vol.5780, IOL.

45. J. McNeill, Acting Collector, Dharwar, to Commissioner, Southern Division, No.RP/218 of 2 February 1900 enclosed Bombay Government General Department Resolution No.4620 - P of 27 July 1900, Bombay Plague Progs, Vol.5971, IOL.

46. See Michael W. Dols, *The Black Death in the Middle East* (Princeton 1977); also Dols, 'Plague in Early Islamic History', *Journal of the American Oriental Society* XCIV, 3 (1974).

47. Maynard, Commissioner, Multan, to Government No.755 at 13 August 1907, Punjab Home (Medical and Sanitary) A Progs, November 1907, No.31, Vol.7552, IOL.

48. Maynard, Deputy Commissioner, Ambala, quoted E. Wilkinson, *Report on Plague in the Punjab from October 1st, 1901, to September 30th, 1902*(Government of Punjab 1904), p.24.

49. Maynard, Junior Secretary, Punjab Home (Plague), to all Commissioners and Superintendents in the Punjab ... No.554 Home (Medical and Sanitary) of 4 April 1898: Enclosure No.78 with Revenue Sanitary Letter from India No.11 of 12 May 1898, L/E/3/109, IOL.

50. C.H. James, *Report on the Outbreak of Plague in the Jullundur and Hoshiarpur Districts of the Punjab, 1897-98*(Government of Punjab 1899); James, *Report on the Outbreak of Plague in the Jullundur and Hoshiarpur Districts of the Punjab during 1898-1899* (Government of Punjab 1902); C.H. James and E. Wilkinson, *Report on the Outbreak of Plague in the Jullundur and Hoshiarpur Districts of the Punjab during 1899-1900* (Government of Punjab 1901) (Microfilm from National Documentation Centre, Pakistan, Pos.5548, IOL). See also the evidence of James and Wilkinson, *Indian Plague Commission, Minutes of Evidence*, Vol.II, pp.77-118, and Maps in Appendix XXXIII (1-6). P.P.1900 (Cd.140) xxxi.

51. Morris E. Opler, 'The Extensions of an Indian Village', *Journal of Asian Studies* XVI, 1 (1956).

52. Rudra Dutt Singh, 'The Unity of an Indian Village', ibid.

53. J.G. Silcock, Deputy Commissioner, Ludhiana, quoted Wilkinson, *Report on Plague in the Punjab, 1901-1902*, p.54.

54. Maynard, quoted ibid., p.24.

55. S. Browning Smith, District Plague Medical Officer, Amritsar, quoted E. Wilkinson, *Report on Plague and Inoculation in the Punjab from October 1st*

*1902 to September 30th 1903* (Government of Punjab), p. 60.

56. Clemesha, op.cit.

57. Report of the Season and Crops of the Punjab for the Year 1903-4 (Government of Punjab 1904), p.3.

58. Muhammad Shafi, 'The Punjab Colonies. A Memorandum. Confidential', 27 June 1907, Morley Collection, MSS.Eur.D.573/12, f.39[a], IOL.

59. See note 57 above.

60. Anil Seal, 'Imperialism and Nationalism in India', in John Gallagher, Gordon Johnson and Anil Seal, eds., *Locality, Province and Nation: Essays on Indian Politics 1870-1940* (Cambridge 1973), p.9.

61. Punjab Government Resolution No.359B - L.P. of 4 March 1901, quoted *The History of Plague in the Punjab, with a Memo. of the Measures adopted for dealing with it and Instructions regarding the Measures to be adopted in 1902-03* (Government of Punjab 1902) [hereafter Punjab Plague Manual 1902], p.3.

62. Maynard, Commissioner, Multan Division, to Government No.755 of 13 August 1907, Punjab Home (Medical and Sanitary) Progs, November 1907, No.31, Vol.7552, IOL.

63. Punjab Plague Manual 1902, p.4. See also *Civil and Military Gazette* (Lahore), 1 May 1898; according to this report 'the townsmen of Garhshankar merely headed a combination of malcontents from neighbouring villages'.

64. *Civil and Military Gazette*, 23 April 1898.

65. *Bombay Gazette*, 21 January 1897.

66. Clemesha, op.cit.

67. Punjab Government to Government of India No.567 S.-P. of 30 June 1902, quoted Punjab Plague Manual 1902, pp.35-38.

68. Maynard, Deputy Commissioner, Ambala, quoted Wilkinson, Report on Plague in the Punjab 1901-1902, p.28.

69. Baehrel, 'Epidemie et terreur', pp.120-1; Baehrel, 'La haine de classe', p.359.

70. Even the *Tribune* was not sure on this point: see its issues of 18, 20, 22 November and 2 December 1902.

71. W.S. Marris, Note, 9 August 1903, with Home Sanitary (Plague) Deposit Progs, October 1903, Nos.2-4, NAI.

72. Report on the Season and Crops of the Punjab for the Year 1906-07 (Government of Punjab 1907), p.2; Annual Report of the Chenab, Jhang, Chunian and Jhelum Colonies for the year ending 30th September 1907:

Report of the Chenab Colony: II, Lyallpur District, pp.10-11.

73. White, 'Twenty Years of Plague ...', p.194.

74. See N. Gerald Barrier, 'The Punjab Disturbances of 1907: the response of the British Government in India to agrarian unrest', *Modern Asian Studies* I, 4 (1967); Barrier, 'Punjab Politics and the Disturbances of 1907' (Unpublished Ph.D. dissertation, Duke University 1966).

75. Secretary of State for India, Speech on East India Revenue Accounts, 6 June 1907. Great Britain Parliamentary Debates, 4th series, clxxv, 876.

76. Barrier, 'The Punjab Disturbances', p.369.

77. See Maclagan, Chief Secretary, Punjab, to Sir H. Risley, Home Secretary, India, No.695 of 3 May 1907, India [Home] Political Confidential Progs, August 1907, No.149, Vol.7590, IOL.

78. Daily Reports on the Political Situation in the Punjab, 16 and 17 May 1907, with Home Political B Progs, July 1907, Nos.57 and 59, NAI.

79. Daily Report, Punjab, 29 May 1907, loc.cit., No.101.

80. Philip Ziegler, *The Black Death* (Pelican edn., 1970), p.99. The similarity has been noted before; see C.A. Gill, 'Epidemics', *Encyclopaedia of the Social Sciences*, Vol.V, p.571.

81. David White, 'The power of rumour', *New Society*, 17 October 1974, p.137.

82. N. Gerald Barrier and Paul Wallace, *The Punjab Press, 1880-1905*, Asian Studies Centre, Michigan State University,Occasional Papers, South Asia series No.14 (Research Series on the Punjab No.2), 1970, Tables 5 and 6, pp.164-5.

83. Barrier, 'Punjab Politics', pp.207,317,320.

84. *Civil and Military Gazette*, 23 April 1898.

85. Punjab Plague Manual 1902, p.7.

86. John C. Hume Jr., 'Rival Traditions: Western Medicine and *Yūnān-i-tibb* in the Punjab, 1849-1899', *Bulletin of the History of Medicine* LI, 2 (Summer 1977), p.230.

87. For example, J. Frizelle, Officiating Deputy Commissioner, Lahore, Unofficial No.4P of 27 July 1906, Punjab Home (Medical and Sanitary) Progs, August 1906, No.55, Vol.7279,IOL. R. Sykes, Deputy Commissioner, Sialkot, to R.E. Younghusband, Commissioner, Lahore, No.232 of 30 July 1907, favourably endorsed by Younghusband in his No.393 of 26 August 1907, Punjab Home (Medical and Sanitary) Progs, November 1907, Nos.39 and 41, Vol.7552, IOL.

88. For example, note on Ajit Singh, with E. Maclagan, Chief Secretary, Punjab, to India Home, 3 May 1901, India [Home] Political Confidential Progs, August 1907, No.149, Vol.7590, IOL.

89. Found in various agrarian disturbances in Bihar. See Anand A. Yang, 'The Origins of Crime: a Study of Riots in Saran District, India, 1886-1920', *Journal of Social History* XIII, 2 (Winter 1979), p.297, and Peter Robb, 'Officials and non-Officials as Leaders in Popular Agitation: Shahabad 1917 and Other "Conspiracies"', in B.N. Pandey, ed., *Leadership in South Asia* (New Delhi 1977), p.191.

90. Found in the Deccan Riots of 1875. See I.J. Catanach, 'Agrarian Disturbances in Nineteenth Century India', *Indian Economic and Social History Review* III, 1 (1966), p.72.

91. Maclagan, Chief Secretary, Punjab, to H. Risley, Home Secretary, India, D/O No.377 - S.B. of 15 May 1907, and enclosures, with Home Political B Progs, July 1907, No.54, NAI. See also *Civil and Military Gazette*, 23 April 1907.

92. Barrier, 'The Punjab Disturbances', p.369.

93. See Barrier and Wallace, op.cit., p.60.

94. *Bombay Gazette*, 1 May 1897.

95. See Wilkins, Report on Plague and Inoculation in the Punjab, 1902-03, pp.46,60.

96. J.K. Condon, *The Bombay Plague, being a History of the Progress of Plague in the Bombay Presidency from September 1896 to June 1899* (Government of Bombay 1900), p.14.

97. Compare in the economic field, Dharm Narain, *The Impact of Price Movements on Areas under Selected Crops in India 1900-1939* (Cambridge 1965), though see the review article on this book by Michael Lipton, 'Should Reasonable Farmers Respond to Price Changes?', *Modern Asian Studies* I, 1 (1967).

98. MacDonnell to Elgin, 16 July 1897, bound with F.A. Hirtzel, 'Note to Sir Charles [Egerton] 10/7/07', J & P 1896A in L/PJ/6/456,IOL.

99. Gill, op.cit.

100. MacDonnell to Elgin, 16 February 1897, MSS. Eur.F.84/70, f.141, IOL. See also MacDonnell to Elgin, 14 March 1897, ibid., ff.230-1).

101. Eric Stokes, 'Traditional resistance movements and Afro-Asian nationalism: the context of the 1857 Mutiny Rebellion', *The Peasant and the Raj* (Cambridge 1979), p.128.

102. Maynard, quoted Wilkinson, Report on Plague

in the Punjab, 1901-1902, p.23.

103. Alan Beals, 'Strategies of Resort to Curers in South India', in Charle Leslie, ed., *Asian Medical Systems: A Comparative Study* (Berkeley 1976), pp.195-6. See also Bruce Elliot Tapper, 'Widows and goddesses: female roles in deity symbolism in a south Indian village', *Contributions to Indian Sociology* (N.S.) XII, 1 (1979), and (for an earlier description of what appears to be essentially the same ritual) R.H. Kennedy, *Notes on the Epidemic Cholera* (Calcutta 1827), pp.ix-x. Compare also Alan Macfarlane, *Witchcraft in Tudor and Stuart England* (London 1970), p.197.

104. *Bombay Gazette*, 6 April 1897.

105. Pratul Chandra Gupta, *Nana Sahib and the Rising at Cawnpore* (Oxford 1963), p.36.

106. Norman White, op.cit., p.191.

107. Very early in the epidemic Dr. W.J. Simpson, Health Officer, Calcutta, diagnosed as plague what was in fact a case of syphilis. He announced his diagnosis to the *Englishman* and panic ensued. See Notes on the Cases reported as Plague in Calcutta, *Papers Relating to the Outbreak of Bubonic Plague in India up to March 1897*, pp.41-2. Simpson went on to become something of an authority on plague, and (from England) a leading critic of Government of India plague policy.

108. *Pleg*, significantly perhaps, was often used in Bengali. In the Hindi-speaking areas *pleg* was sometimes used; *mari* and *mahamari* occurred more frequently. *Mari*, especially, refers to other diseases besides plague. *Gola rog*, sometimes used to describe plague, is more specific than either *mari* or *mahamari*. (I owe some of this information to Dr. Stuart McGregor.) In the Punjab *waba* and *ta'un* were commonly used. These are Arabic-derived words; *ta'un*, at least since the Black Death, has had a fairly specific reference in Arabic to plague (see Dols, *The Black Death in the Middle East*, Appx.II), and the use of the word in the Punjab indicates mental links with the 'great tradition' of Muslim thought about plague.

109. Beals, op.cit., pp.186-8; Tapper, op.cit., p.11.

110. L.S.S. O'Malley, *Bengal District Gazetteers*, VIII, *Patna* (Government of Bengal 1907), p.64; B.G. Bang, 'Current Concepts of the Smallpox Goddess Sitala in Parts of West Bengal', *Man in India* LIII, 1 (1973), especially p.72; V.V. Ramana Rao, 'Indian Goddesses of Epidemic Diseases', *Bulletin of the Institute of History of Medicine* (Hyderabad) 1, 1 and 2 (1971), p.47.

111. L.S.S. O'Malley, *Census of India 1911, V,*

*Bengal, Bihar, Orissa and Sikkim, pt.i, Report* (Government of Bengal 1913), p.228; William Crooke, *Religion and Folklore of Northern India* (revised for the press by R.E. Enthoven; London 1926), p.118.

112. Gill, op.cit.

113. Arthur Geddes, 'The Social and Psychological Significance of Variability in Population Change, with examples from India, 1871-1941', *Human Relations* I, 2 (1947), especially p.187.

114. Gill, op.cit.

115. Note by 'J.R.D.S.' [Dunlop Smith] to Viceroy (with Note on Plague by Sanitary Commissioner) 18 June 1907, enclosed Minto to Morley, 27 June 1907, MSS.Eur. D.573/12, f.25, IOL.

116. In spite of the occurrence of more than ten million deaths from plague in twenty years, the variety of plague which came to India in 1896 does not seem to have been so virulent as the late classical or the medieval strains. See the explanation of the work of the French biologist R. Devignat in John Norris, 'East or West? The Geographic Origin of the Black Death', *Bulletin of the History of Medicine*, Ll, 1 (1977), p.21.

117. F.W. Kennaway, Assessment Report on the Thanesar Tahsil of the Karnal District, 1908, Punjab Revenue and Agriculture (Revenue) A Progs, June 1909, No.8, Vol.8120, IOL.

118. Quoted in Report on the Season and Crops for the Year 1907-08 (Government of Punjab 1908), p.8.

119. Report on the Season and Crops of the Punjab for the Year 1909-10, pp.8-9.

120. See Ziegler, op.cit., chapter 15, for the debate on the economic effects of the Black Death.

121. Thanesar Assessment Report, 1908. The fall in numbers of 'Chamars' in the Punjab recorded in the 1911 census, as compared with that of 1901, was in part the result of conversions to Sikhism. See Pandit Harikishan Kaul, *Census of India 1911, XIV, Punjab, pt.i, Report*, p.100.

122. See Annual Report of the Colonization Officer, Chenab Colony, p.9, in Annual Report for the Chenab, Jhelum and Chunian Colonies for the year ending 30th September 1904 (Government of Punjab 1905).

123. Season and Crop Report of the Bombay Presidency 1913-1914 (Government of Bombay 1914), p.7; also A.L.M. Wood, Collector, Kaira, quoted Land Revenue Administration Report Part II, of the Bombay Presidency ... for the year 1905-06 (Government of Bombay 1906), p.5.

124. P.J. Mead and G. Laird MacGregor, *Census of India, 1911, VII, Bombay pt.i, Report*, p.325; compare G.S. Curtis, Commissioner, Central Division, quoted Land Revenue Administration Report, Part II, of the Bombay Presidency, 1911-12 (Government of Bombay 1912), p.28.

125. Minute by Sir Charles Metcalfe, 7 November 1830, No.84, Appendix to the Report of the Select Committee (1832); frequently cited, for example (critically), in B.H. Baden-Powell, *The Land Systems of British India* (Oxford 1892), pp.170-4.

# MUSLIM POLITICAL MOBILIZATION IN RURAL PUNJAB 1937-46

*Ian Talbot*

During the years 1937-46 politics in the Punjab were dominated by the struggle for power between the Muslim League and the Unionist Party. The landlord Unionist Party had crushed the urban Muslim League in the 1937 elections in which it had won just two of the 86 Muslim seats. The League almost immediately afterwards set about recovering from this severe setback by extending its influence into the countryside. As late as April 1944 it had made little headway. However in the crucial 1946 provincial elections it swept to a dramatic victory, capturing 75 of the Muslim seats.

This spectacular improvement in its fortunes which had momentous implications for the future of the subcontinent has recently been attributed by Shahid Burki to the successful coalition between the middle class dominated Muslim League and the lower stratum of the rural population. He portrays the League as providing the necessary leadership and resources to enable the rural poor to defeat the landlords who remained, 'opposed or at best lukewarm to the Pakistan movement'.[1] This explanation immediately raises the questions, precisely how did the League bypass the traditional holders of power in the localities? And how can this interpretation be reconciled with the fact that the majority of its candidates in the Punjab in 1946 were landlords who had only very recently transferred their allegiance from the Unionist Party? Despite its inadequacies it does however open up a number of questions which are of importance to a discussion of the external dimension in rural South Asian politics.

How important to successful rural political mobilization is a party's ability to bring resources and leadership from the world beyond the locality to the support of its local political struggles? Is it possible to talk in terms of an outside party mobilizing a passive rural society? To what extent can the role that is played by traditional social networks within the locality be ignored in the business of winning support for political parties? Finally, in what circumstances can external influences succeed in fracturing the local political system?

This paper attempts to answer these questions by

examining in detail the Muslim League's efforts to win support in the Punjab countryside during the years 1937-46. We shall first however turn to the political developments which had occurred in the province during the period of dyarchy which preceded this.

Before the Montagu–Chelmsford reforms were introduced in 1919, the Punjab had lagged behind other provinces in its constitutional development. The reforms extended the franchise and transferred control of certain 'nation-building' subjects of administration such as local self-government and education to Ministers who were responsible to the Legislative Council. Until its creation political activity in the Punjab had been localized. Only occasionally, usually in the face of a common enemy, had the numerous rural political factions acted in a wider political framework than that of the locality. In the West Punjab the local factions were led by large landlords and by the rural religious elite, the Sufi pirs who had been drawn into politics despite the original opposition of such Sufi orders as the Chishtis to all political entanglements. Many of the pirs and the *sajjada nashins* (head ulama) of the shrines were closely connected by marriage to the leading landlord families and were themselves large landowners. In the East Punjab where there were fewer large estates[2] leaders of the dominant kinship groups rather than the landlords or pirs usually headed the local factions. Even after the creation of the Legislative Council, factionalism underpinned the Punjab's political activity. The ruling Unionist party functioned more as a grand coalition of the leading factions than as a modern political party. The landlords and pirs acted as brokers between the village communities and the provincial political system. At election times they mobilized their tenants and disciples to vote for the Unionist Party in return for the promise of access to government patronage. The Unionist Party thus did not need to develop any machinery for fighting elections. It merely stood by and watched whilst the local faction leaders fought it out amongst themselves. The successful candidates were those who wielded the greatest personal influence in the villages. The Unionist Party automatically recognized the victor in each constituency as its official candidate. In most of the constituencies of the Legislative Council and later of the Provincial Assembly, candidate selection was far more important than the actual electioneering itself. The British had drawn the boundaries in such a way that nearly all the rural seats were under the control of the leading local landlord families. The Congress and the Muslim League made little headway in the province despite their establishment of branch organizations and parliamentary boards to contest the elections as they were unable to field candidates who possessed a firm social base in the countryside.

The Muslim landlords' power in the agriculture structure of the West Punjab rested on their ability to control such scarce resources as fertile land, water, labour and credit. It was further reinforced by the fact that there was no strong village community to stand between the landlord and his individual tenants and that most landlords continued to live in their home districts despite the attractions of urban life. A landlord who lived on his estate was not only able to exercise his economic influence more closely but also to emphasize his social dominance through the adjudication of *biraderi* disputes[3] and the working of the *jajmani* relationship.[4] Punjabi landlords maintained close links with their estates in part because the region was unsettled, but in the main because social status was derived from the ownership of land.[5] Land was the major source of an individual's *izzat* (prestige).

Even though the Muslim landlords of the West Punjab lived on their estates, the existence of a strong village community could still have diffused their power. The 'villages' which were recorded in the British land revenue records for such areas of the West Punjab as Jhang and Shahpur were however merely administrative creations made for the sake of convenience and simplicity. The population of these areas continued to live as they had always done, scattered around wells and did not form a homogeneous proprietary body.[6] Thus no communal barrier existed to protect the tenant from his landlord's power. The landlord was indeed the 'lord of the land'. The head of the Kot Gheba estate in the north western Attock district even kept his own retinue of mounted followers all dressed in scarlet tunics, whom he had instructed in the use of 'lance and sword'.[7] He was complete lord and master of his land, 'his tenants feared him, admired him and even liked him, whilst they certainly always obeyed him'.[8] Throughout this part of the province, 'the cardinal principle of the strong owner [was] that the tenant is a serf, without rights or priviliges, but when this has once been admitted the tenant is not badly treated'.[9] The threat of eviction always hung over the tenants and ensured their loyalty to their landlord's faction.

British rule reinforced the economic importance of the large landlords and pirs. They were better able to take advantage of the commercialization of agriculture than were the smaller owner cultivators and the tenants.[10] The development of irrigation in the south west Punjab consolidated the power of such large tribal *maliks* as the Tiwanas and Daultanas and converted them into a powerful landowning class. The peasants' reliance on their landlord patrons for credit and employment increased because of the agricultural revolution brought by the British. They needed credit more than ever before to pay the regular British land revenue taxes which were levied in cash rather than kind. Rising prices for essential commodities and foodstuffs and fluctuations in the value of cash crop production also increased the demand for credit relief. Loss of access to uncleared land and common pasturage together with rapid population growth led to increased fragmentation of holdings and meant that the peasants needed extra sources of employment to survive. By 1939 it was estimated that 90 per cent of all landowners possessed uneconomic holdings and would thus need to turn to the landlords for employment.

The peasants' growing economic dependence on their landlord patrons increased their local political power. Moreover, the landlord's improved economic position enabled them if it was necessary to buy votes and bribe local election officials on a wider scale than before. British rule also increased the landlords' and pirs' importance as brokers between the villages and the wider world. In the Mughal and Sikh period they had acted as intermediaries between the peasants and the central authorities collecting for example the peasants' land revenue assessments and paying it for them and protecting them from external attacks. But the rural elite's ability to influence the British government which soon became a major source of credit, employment and business activity within the province added importance to their role as brokers. The British institutionalized it in the local government post of *zaildar*. He was in charge of a number of villages which were grouped together in an administrative unit known as a *zail*. The zaildar was held directly responsible for ensuring that the district authority's orders were carried out in the area under his jurisdiction and was empowered to supervise the work of the village officials within the zail. Only the leading landlords were chosen for this position of responsibility and there was eager competition for the post. This was not because it was lucrative - zaildars were only paid around Rs.300 a year in the 1930s - but because it enhanced the incumbent's already considerable power. Villagers looked to the zaildar for patronage and intercession on their behalf with the district authorities. He was the government as far as many of them were concerned, granting them access to the benefits of the world beyond the mud walls of their village.

British rule also provided the landlords and pirs with opportunities to operate on a wider economic and political scale than before. Their power became less localized as from the 1880s onward they acquired land and property outside their home districts mainly in the Canal Colonies but also in some of the towns. Province-wide marriage contacts developed between landowning families as a common landlord interest began to emerge.[11] These assumed considerable political importance as they aided the development of the Punjab Unionist Party.

British policy had been geared to encouraging a loyalist landlord interest in politics from the 1840s. Patronage in the form of grants of land in the Canal Colonies, appointments such as that of zaildar in the machinery of local government and honorary ranks and titles were liberally distributed to the landlords and pirs in order to gain their support. In such areas of the Punjab as Rohtak where few large landlords existed, the British attempted to create a landowning class. They linked the interests of the Muslim landlords of the West Punjab with those of the Sikh landlords of the central tract and the Muslim and Hindu peasant proprietors of the eastern regions by the 1901 Alienation of Land Act. This measure halted the expropriation of the Punjab's farmers by the urban Hindu money-lenders, a process which had increasingly accompanied the commercialization of the province's agriculture. For the purpose of the Act, the population was divided into non-agriculturalist and agriculturalist tribes. The former were forbidden to permanently acquire land in the countryside. The British went a stage further in encouraging the creation of an intercommunal agricultural class interest in 1919, when they granted agriculturalists a preferential right of recruitment to government service.[12] The 1919 Montagu-Chelmsford reforms completed the institutionalization of the division between the province's rural and urban communities. Separate electorates were created for the towns and the countryside; only members of the statutory agricultural tribes were allowed to stand as candidates for the rural seats. The towns were allocated just four of the 34 Muslim elected seats in the Legislative Council.[13] The British in this way created the framework in which an intercommunal landlord party could successfully operate. The difficult task had still remained of organizing the independent rural members into a political party. This was achieved in 1923 when the Punjab Unionist Party was created largely as a result of the efforts of Chhoutu Ram and Mian Fazl-i-Husain. Its victory in the 1937 provincial elections was thus the logical conclusion of over 80 years of British policy in the Punjab.

Most of the province's leading landlords and pirs were successfully returned as Unionist candidates. In the eastern districts however the ties of economic dependency between a tenant and his landlord were less important in deciding voting than kinship loyalty. The kinship group (biraderi) was the most important unit in the Muslim social structure. Its membership hinged entirely on the tracing of descent through the paternal line. Children always belonged to their father's biraderi and most marriages took place within it. The ideal marriage was that of a cross cousin type - marriage to a father's brother's daughter. Indeed an individual's status was judged on his ability to give his daughters in marriage only to members of his own biraderi. Control of marriage was a major factor in maintaining biraderi cohesion and as a result marriage transactions were strictly regulated by a kinship group's ruling council (*panchayat*). It took on a wide range of welfare and 'professional' functions and operated amongst kinship groups which continued to pursue traditional occupations on similar lines to the medieval guilds in Europe.[14] There was a tendency for the specialization of 'council' functions. One panchayat for example operated as the kinship group's spokesman with government and ensured political solidarity, whilst another usually composed of older members concerned itself with adjudication in such 'internal' matters as inheritance disputes. Whether they were elected or hereditary, the panchayats wielded considerable coercive powers. The threat to expel a household from a biraderi could be likened in some respects in its severity to that of excommunication from the medieval church. It would leave the household defenceless in an often hostile world and would make future marriage transactions which were so important difficult or indeed impossible. Defiance and violation of a kinship group's norms was therefore a rare occurrence.

Not all kinship groups of course achieved an ideal degree of cohesion and solidarity. The strongest biraderis within the Punjab always existed amongst the peasant proprietors. In the constant struggle to maintain their economic independence they needed the strength which kinship solidarity brought. Their biraderi organization was as a result tightly disciplined and took the form of successive tiers of 'ruling councils' which linked village 'councils' with regional and even provincial confederations of panchayats. Amongst the landlords however personal and political rivalries often precluded kinship solidarity. The households of their kinsmen tended to be dispersed which weakened their power. Biraderi solidarity was not so important to the large landlords as it was to the peasant proprietors. Their leadership of rural society rested not on the strength of their kinship ties but on their economic power. Within the groups of tenants, landless labourers and village menials, ties of economic dependency remained stronger than their loyalty to their fellow biraderi members. Landlords had taken over the role of the panchayat in settling disputes amongst them.

When the British devolved power to popularly elected bodies from the 1880s onwards the kinship group became an important channel for mobilizing political support. Its panchayat traded its votes in return for patronage. Political solidarity was encouraged when its members saw the benefits which accrued from this exchange system. Improvements in communications made greater group solidarity possible. The leading biraderis established a network of organizations throughout the province and during the 1920s and 1930s established their own 'tribal' newspapers, the leading example of which was the *Jat Gazette*. These newspapers helped reinforce biraderi solidarity and ensured that they spoke with one voice in politics.

Amongst the voters of the East Punjab and the Canal Colony districts in which strong groups of peasant proprietors existed, the kinship group played a vital role in vote gathering in the 1937 provincial elections. The Unionist Party was careful to select as its candidates in these areas the council leaders of the dominant kinship groups. The Muslim League and the Congress were unable to match it in this policy as they commanded little support amongst the rural population.[15] Within the Lyallpur Canal Colony constituency for example the largest number of voters were members of the Arain biraderi. The Unionist Party therefore supported Mian Nurullah who was President of the provincial Arain Council as its candidate. His ability to call on the kinship network for political support enabled him to comfortably win the seat. In a similar way the Unionist Party supported the Secretary of the Punjab Rajput Council for the Tarn Taran constituency in which the Rajput biraderi was strong. In the eastern Rohtak district of the province, the Unionist Party swept the board in both the rural Muslim and Hindu seats because it had captured the support of the leading Jat biraderi.

Even more effective than the kinship group in mobilizing support for the Unionists were the Sufi religious networks based on the shrines and the relationship between a pir and his disciple (the piri-mureedi relationship). The pirs' popular religious influence sprang from the belief that they had inherited charisma (*baraka*) from their ancestors, the Sufi saints who from the eleventh century onwards had played a major role in the Punjab's conversion to Islam. The shrines (*dargahs*) at which the pirs were centred were of far greater importance to the peasants' religious life than the austere mosque. During the course of a year, multitudes of people visited them to seek spiritual blessing. A great trade in amulets was carried on. Over the years shrines became associated with particular miraculous powers. A shrine in the Shahpur district for example was famous for curing toothache! One in Hissar was renowned for its power of exorcism, whilst yet another in the same district was resorted to by sufferers from dog bites. Shrines became major centres of economic importance both as employers and as consumers of local produce. Many of the larger ones provided outdoor relief for their neighbouring areas by opening dispensaries for the sick, and soup kitchens (*langar-khanas*). Food was also distributed during a shrine's *Urs* celebrations which were held on the anniversary of its saint's death when his soul was believed to have entered into a union with God.

As the shrine's wealth increased, the outlook of their pirs and sajjada-nashines (custodians) became similar to that of other landowners. They tended to support the political status quo whether it was Muslim, Sikh or later British. This was encouraged by the large amounts of land which governments from the time of the Delhi Sultanate down to the British granted them in order to ensure their loyalty. The requirement for becoming a shrine's sajjada nashin shifted from spiritual merit to political loyalty to the central authority.[16] Control of the shrines enabled the state to deepen the roots of its authority in the countryside. For their part the pirs benefited from the government patronage which came their way in the form of honours and land and they had their considerable local authority enhanced by their collaboration with government.

The British restored land to those shrines which had suffered during the Sikh interregnum. In true Mughal fashion they associated pirs with their role by conferring Provincial and Divisional darbar seats on such of their leading representatives as the Diwan of Pakpattan and the sajjada nashin of the influential shrine at Multan of Sheikh Baha'ud-Din Zakariya, while lesser pirs were granted such honours as zaildarships and honorary magistracies.

Over the centuries the leading shrines acquired large amounts of land as the state's land grants were in addition to the considerable waqf endowments which they received from individuals. The descendants of Baba Farid, the Punjab's leading Sufi saint, possessed by the twentieth century a tenth of all the land in the Pakpattan tahsil in which the shrine was situated, some 43,000 acres in all.[17] Part of this land had in fact come to them as state gifts during the period of Sikh rule.[18] The Shah Jiwana Bukhari Syed estate in Jhang was nearly 10,000 acres in extent,[19] whilst the pirs of Jahanian Shah owned nearly 7,000 acres[20]

Hand in hand with the transformation of the Punjab's pirs into important landowners went a change in the piri-mureedi relationship which was to have important political consequences. An aspirant disciple (*murid*) of a pir took an oath of obedience to him (*bayat*). He thus entered into the piri-mureedi relationship. The pir thereafter acted as his disciple's spiritual guide and mediated between him and God. At the same time he was also the agent for bringing about his material desires through the exercise of his baraka. The disciple in return was expected to be absolutely obedient to his pir. The relationship between a pir and his disciple was likened to that between the Prophet and his companions.[21] It was formalized and ongoing[22] and created a focus of loyalty which was capable of transcending although it could also reinforce biraderi ties. During Sufism's early period the immense political potential of the piri-mureedi relationship was unfulfilled because it was not sufficiently widespread. The first Sufis in the Punjab initiated only a small number of disciples who thereafter lived with them at their 'hospices' (*khanqahs*) and studied and undertook spiritual disciplines at their direction. But by the twentieth century this had changed. Shrines had proliferated and the piri-mureedi relationship had lost its original elitism. Almost every Muslim in the Punjab had by this time given bayat to a pir. Indeed to be without a pir was a cause for reproach. Pirs possessed large numbers of disciples. Pir Fazl Shah of Jalalpur in the Jhelum district alone claimed to have 200,000 murids. Despite its expansion the piri-mureedi relationship retained its discipline and cohesion as its underpinning remained the absolute obedience enjoined upon a disciple to his pir. The improved communications brought by the British increased the pir's contact with their disciples. They could visit them more easily during their customary tours and could even dispense their political 'advice' through the columns of the local newspapers. Because they could command support from members of rival kinship groups and because their networks of disciples spread over the length and breadth of the Punjab, pirs played a crucial role in vote-gathering when the franchise was extended and politics became provincialized.

The importance which the Unionists attached to their co-operation during the 1937 elections comes out clearly in the following words of Mohammad Bashir, the Unionist Party organizer for the Gurdaspur district. 'Villagers, you know, follow these "Pirs" blindly .... Take care of the "Pirs". Ask them only to keep silent on the matter of the elections. We don't require their help but [that] they should not oppose us.'[23] In fact a number of pirs played a leading role in the elections as candidates and propagandists for the Unionist Party. The pirs of Shergarh and Shah Jiwana were influential in mobilizing support for the Unionists in the Canal Colony districts. The Unionist Party successfully approached 14 of the leading pirs of the Punjab and its surrounding areas to issue an election appeal on its behalf.[24]

The only response which the Muslim League could make to this was to issue an appeal to the Punjabi Muslims exhorting them in the name of Islam to vote for the candidates of the Muslim League Parliamentary Board.[25] The fact that it was published in Urdu, the language of the educated townsmen rather than Punjabi revealed the limited extent of the Muslim League's appeal to the rural population. The composition of the Muslim League's touring propaganda committee further highlighted the difficulties under which it laboured in attempting to mobilize rural support. There was only one landlord amongst its fifteen members, no less than seven of whom were lawyers or urban politicians from Lahore.[26] The League's influence in the countryside was so weak that it encountered great difficulty in finding candidates who were willing to oppose the Unionists. A derisory eight candidates finally fought under its banner.

The Unionist Party's victory in the 1937 elections created a major problem for the Muslim League. It had to undermine the Unionists' entrenched position if Jinnah's claim that it was the sole representative of Indian Muslims was not to sound embarrassingly hollow and his bargaining position in all-India politics be seriously weakened. Almost immediately after the elections the League therefore attempted to make up some of its lost ground by launching a massive rural propaganda campaign. Workers were sent to the villages to establish primary League branches and its membership fee was reduced to only four annas to make it possible for the villagers to join. The Punjab League hoped at this time to enrol as many as 20,000 new primary members in the Lahore district alone.[27] A number of the League's provincial leaders toured the countryside in order to whip up support for this campaign.[28]

Here then is a classic example of an outside political organization coming in to mobilize into action a passive rural population. Even before this campaign was called off by the pact between Sikander, the Unionist Premier, and Jinnah in October 1937,[29] it was apparent that the League's efforts were meeting with little success. The villagers remained steadfastly loyal to the Unionist Party. The League's leaders blamed this on the peasants' fear of the bureaucracy. The police certainly made it obvious that they were watching closely all the League's activities. But the resilience of the local political system to its incursions at this time had far deeper roots than this. They lay in the mass of the rural population's loyalty and obedience to the local political elite, the landlords, pirs and biraderi leaders.

After the Lahore resolution was passed in 1940 it became imperative for the Muslim League to destroy the

Unionist Party's influence in the Punjab which formed the heartland of a future Pakistan state. This was a difficult task as following the Jinnah-Sikander pact its provincial organization was firmly under Unionist control. It therefore had to rely on the efforts of the Punjab Muslim Students Federation and on urban politicians and religious leaders to popularize its demands for Pakistan in the countryside. It increasingly adopted religious slogans in an effort to appeal directly to the villagers over the heads of the rural elite.

Even before the Pakistan resolution was passed, the Muslim League had resolved to use festivals 'to promote political unity and social solidarity amongst the Muslims of India'.[30] Mosques, because of their importance as centres of Muslim life, were similarly used to spread League propaganda. A grandiose proposal was once placed before the All-India Muslim League Working Committee to use 5,000 mosques in the Pakistan areas as League missionary sub-centres.[31] Propagandists were advised when they visited a village to join in the prayers at the local mosque and gain its imam's permission to hold a meeting there. Muslim League meetings were held regularly in mosques especially after the Friday prayers. Students who played an important part in League propaganda work not only in the Punjab but throughout India had been especially trained to appeal to the voters along religious lines.[32] Students from the Punjab Muslim Students Federation were advised to follow the Prophet's example in all things during their visits to the villages. They were to join in the prayers at the mosque or lead them like 'Holy Warriors'. Their speeches were to be filled with emotional appeal and always to commence with a text from the Qur'an, invoking God's protection and praising His Wisdom.[33] Because of its importance in north Indian society, poetry, particularly that of Iqbal, was to be declaimed at such meetings.[34]

When the Jinnah-Sikander pact finally collapsed in April 1944, the Muslim League stepped up its plans to saturate the villages with propaganda. Its provincial leaders continued however to ignore the need for winning over the rural elite's support. 'It is now becoming clear', wrote its General Secretary, Mian Mumtaz Daultana, himself a landlord, in July 1944, 'that in view of the determined government opposition our basic strength must come not from the landlords or the Zaildar-Lambardar class but from the masses of the Muslim people.'[35] During June and July 1944 large Muslim League conferences were held at Montgomery, Lyallpur, Sheikhupura, Sargodha, Jhang, Sialkot and Rawalpindi.[36] For the first time ever primary League branches were established in such rural areas as Sargodha, and Mianwali. In July alone it was reported that 7,000 members had been enrolled in these two areas.[37] Throughout most of the province, however, the Muslim League's propaganda campaign made little impact on the mass of the rural population.

> League attempts to penetrate the village, [the Governor noted in July 1944,] have been mainly confined to somewhat disjointed tours by peripatetic members of the Muslim Students Federation, the distribution of propaganda pamphlets and approaches to village officials. These moves in spite of the Islamic appeal behind them have so far had little effect on the Muslim masses who are concerned with tribal and economic considerations [rather] than with party politics and do not appear to have affected the communal situation adversely.[38]

The Unionists continued to win district board and provincial assembly by-elections throughout 1944. In August for example they defeated the Muslim League in the Sialkot district board elections;[39] they also retained the Hoshiarpur and Kangra and Jhajjar Legislative Assembly seats. The Unionists' influence in the Dera Ghazi Khan district remained so great that the Muslim League was unable to field a rival candidate to Sardar Ghaus Mazari in the by-election which took place in its southern constituency in April 1945.[40] In many of the western districts of the Punjab it was faced with the same problem of having to resolve local factional rivalries which had impeded Mian Fazl-i-Husain's efforts to establish a popular base for the Unionist Party there a decade earlier. In the Gujjar Khan and Rawalpindi districts, factional rivalry was so acute that parallel Muslim Leagues competed against each other.[41] As late as May 1945 the Muslim League could still only boast a membership of 1½ lakhs in the Punjab.[42] Why had the League's campaign achieved so little success? The answer mainly lies in the fact that the League's appeals were being made through the wrong channels.

The Aligarh students who played an increasingly important part in the Muslim League's propaganda work had difficulty because they were outsiders in winning the rural population's confiedence. They even had problems in some cases in making themselves understood because of the villagers' ignorance of Urdu. The urban politicians who formed the League's mainstay at this time had little authority and respect amongst the provinces'farmers. The League's efforts to use Islam as a mass mobilizer thus made little impact because its religious appeals were mediated by outsiders who lacked personal influence in the villages and because they were based on sources of Muslim authority, the Qur'an, the alim and the mosque which were 'external' to the illiterate 'pir-ridden' villagers.

It increasingly became clear to the League's leaders that a differnet approach would have to be adopted if the Punjab was to be won over to support the Pakistan scheme. Although it contradicted the two nation theory an appeal would have to be made to the 'tribal' loyalties of the Punjabi Muslims. The support of the traditional brokers of political power, the landlords and pirs, was needed. In addition, an appeal would have to be made to the villagers' economic interests if they were to risk opposing the dominant Unionist Party. The League did not immediately adopt all these new strategies. It was not until late in 1944 that it switched its attention from organizing local branches to winning over elite support. But it did make a start early that year in appealing to the rural population by exploiting the growing wartime discontent.

Whereas earlier in the war the countryside had escaped the worst effects of economic dislocation, by 1944 it suffered as much as the towns from these. Until 1944 high prices for wheat and other agricultural produce had compensated the province's farmers for inflation and shortage of consumer goods. But that autumn a substantial and sustained fall in agricultural prices set in.[43] Grain prices staged a recovery in the first few months of 1945, but as the year progressed the farmers became increasingly reluctant to market their goods. Political insecurity, the unfavourable prospects for the 1946 rabi crop and the enticement of the black market all contributed to this. By December 1945, wheat, maize and gram had virtually disappeared from the open market.[44] Many of the province's towns even in the Canal Colony areas began to experience a wheat famine. The large landlords of the west Punjab still brought at least part of their grain to market but virtually none came from the peasant proprietors of the east Punjab. The Unionist

Government was forced to requisition grain from the villages there. This aroused such great opposition that as a result disturbances broke out in the Ludhiana, Hoshiarpur and Ferozepore districts right in the middle of the 1946 elections.[45]

Despite these favourable circumstances, it is unlikely that the Muslim League would have adopted on a large scale the policy of exploiting wartime discontent if it had not been for the large number of communists who were entering its ranks at this time.[46] They were already skilled in this type of propaganda having used it successfully in the villages of the central Punjab during the winter months of 1943.[47] The Punjab Muslim League attempted to crystallize rural opposition to the rationing and requisitioning of grain supplies which had been forced on the reluctant Unionist Party by the Central Food Department.[48] It also expressed the growing dissatisfaction with the Unionist Party's failure to control inflation and to curb the profiteering activities of the Hindu and Sikh business class. It benefited immensely from the large wartime civil supply contracts from the army and the government. This was unpopular not only with the small Muslim business class but with the large landlords who had previously been the main recipients of any lucrative government patronage. Most important of all, however, the Muslim League linked the solution of the rural population's wartime economic and social problems with the successful establishment of a Pakistan state. Members of the Punjab Muslim Students Federation were directed when they visited a village, to 'Find out its social problems and difficulties to tell them [the villagers] that the main cause of their problems was the Unionists [and] give them the solution - Pakistan'.[49] Muslim League propagandists took medical supplies which had become difficult to obtain during the war with them to the villages.[50] They also distributed cloth there and endeavoured to obtain increased ration allowances for the peasants.[51] This policy was in marked contrast to the Unionists, who appeared increasingly out of touch with the needs of the rural population.

The strategy of exploiting wartime discontent became even more popular from the summer of 1945 onwards, when large numbers of demobilized soldiers returned to the province only to face massive unemployment.[52] The Muslim League won great support in the major recruit-areas of Rawalpindi and Jhelum by providing work for the ex-servicemen in its organization and by showing concern for their problems. It hammered home the message that although the Unionists had given vast amounts of patronage to the 'recruit hunters' during the war, they were now offering to the returning soldiers, 'a meagre bonus of Rs.5 per head [and] 50,000 acres of land for a million soldiers in the Punjab'.[53] Despite its late development in these traditionally 'loyalist' areas, the Muslim League captured all six of the rural seats in the Rawalpindi and Jhelum districts in the 1945 elections. It also swept the board in the peasant proprietor areas of the east Punjab which had suffered badly from wartime dislocation. Although there were other factors at work in the League's success in these areas, notably the influence exerted in the Muslim League's favour by Pir Fazl Shah of Jalalpur in the Jhelum district, its victories there owed much to the exploitation of wartime grievances. In the Rawalpindi and Jhelum districts the Unionist supporters were either reluctantly swept into the Muslim League by the groundswell of opinion in its favour[54] or were defeated by outside League candidates who in more normal times would have stood little chance because of their lack of personal influence in the constituencies in which they were standing. There were, however, few other areas of the province in which the League similarly acted as an external force which fractured the local political system. In the central and south western districts it in fact entirely owed its success to the capture of the support of the landlords and pirs who controlled the social networks through which votes were always gathered.

By the beginning of 1946 a third of the Unionist Party's elite supporters had deserted it in favour of the Muslim League. In the two districts of Jhang and Sheikhupura of all seven of the Muslim Legislative Assembly members had joined the League.[55] Although in such other areas as Amritsar and Gujrat the local landlords remained steadfastly loyal, the Muslim League had nevertheless made a substantial inroad into the Unionist Party's elite support. Its position in 1946 as a rival to the Unionists in the countryside constituted a radical new dimension in Punjabi politics. Amongst the landlords who had entered its ranks were members of the Hayat, Noon and Daultana families from which the Unionist Party had traditionally drawn its leadership. It had also lost the support of the pirs of Jalalpur, Jahanian Shah, Rajoa and Shah Jiwana who had represented it in the Legislature ever since 1923. The Muslim League had also captured the support of such other pirs as Pir Taunsa, Pir Sial and Pir Golra who had always provided the Unionist Party with valuable tacit support.

A multiplicity of social, economic and religious reasons lay behind the landlords' and pirs' decision to quit the Unionist Party. They were set to the background of the breakup of the party's unity following the death of its leader Sikander Hayat Khan in December 1942.[56] Even more important were such external factors as Jinnah's increased wartime stature in Indian politics and the growing realization that the British would soon be leaving India. Indirectly through their effects on the wavering local faction leaders they were to undermine the Unionist Party's support in the villages. As the war drew to a close it seemed to many leading landlords that the Unionist Party's non communal approach to politics and its loyalist stance had outlived its raison d'être.[57]

Although the first desertions from the Unionist Party occurred in April 1944 over the question of the All-India Muslim League's right to intervene in provincial politics, significantly it was the collapse of the Simla Conference in July 1945 which led to the decisive exodus from its ranks. The landlords and pirs had become involved in politics for two main reasons - to safeguard their local authority and to increase their power and patronage. They sought to achieve these aims through membership of the provincial government and the Assembly, through their control of the district boards and municipal committees and by securing appointments as zaildars and honorary magistrates. They supported the Unionist Party not out of any loyalty but because it gave them access to patronage. The breakdown of the Simla Conference because of Jinnah's demand that all Muslim nominees of the proposed interim government must be Muslim Leaguers, painfully brough home to the Punjabi landlords and pirs that if they did not join the Muslim League they would be excluded in future from office and power. The most notable League convert was Firoz Khan Noon who resigned from the Viceroy's Council in September in order to return to the Punjab and work for the Muslim League's cause. That same month the League gained another influential supporter in Major Mubarik Ali Shah, one of the sajjada nashins of the Shah Jiwana shrine in Jhang. When he joined the League he appealed to all the sajjada nashins of the Punjab to give a right lead to their followers and to strengthen the Muslim League.[58]

The province's pirs were prompted like its landlords to join the Muslim League for a variety of reasons many of which were purely local and had little to do with religious considerations. The cut and thrust of local factional rivalries led for example the Gilani and Qureshi Pir families of Multan to support opposite sides in the conflict between the Unionist Party and the Muslim League. Pir Makhad stood as an independent in the Punjab, whilst he advised his murids in the Kohat district of the North West Frontier Province to support the Congress following the failure of his nominee to secure the Muslim League ticket. The growing power of the All-India Muslim League led many pirs to accommodate themselves with it in an endeavour to safeguard their local influence. Amongst the pirs of the Chishti revivalist shrines however the desire to put politics in the Punjab on a stronger religious footing played the major part in their decision to join the League.

Whether a shrine derived its wealth and status from government patronage or spiritual influence was another important factor in determining its sajjada's response to calls to join the Muslim League. Sajjadas of small shrines who owed their status more to their political loyalty than to their religious influence were far less likely to desert the Unionists than those of large and influential shrines whose reliance on government patronage was much smaller. An interesting example of a pir from the first category was Pir Mian Syed Badr Mohy-ud-Din who was narrowly defeated as the Unionist candidate for the Batala constituency. He was the son of the sajjada nashin of the Qadiri dargah at Batala. The shrine was small. The family's social status stemmed not from its sanctity but rather from its long tradition of loyalty to the British. This dated to before the Mutiny, after which the shrine's sajjada was rewarded by being granted a jagir for life and being made a provincial darbari. The sajjada nashin in 1946, Khan Bahadur Syed Nazar Mohy-ud-Din held a hereditary seat in the darbar, whilst Mian Syed Badr Mohy-ud-Din was himself an honorary magistrate and sub-registrar, besides holding the title of Khan Bahadur.[59] Other Syed families which had a similar tradition of government loyalty but whose status ultimately derived from their religious influence were far more responsive to calls to join the Muslim League. Such was the Pir family of Jahanian Shah. Their Bukhari Syed ancestors had migrated to India about the beginning of the eleventh century. The shrine at Jahanian Shah had large landholdings attached to it, and its spiritual influence was great throughout the west Punjab. The Pirs had loyally supported the British during the First World War for which they were soon afterwards well rewarded. The sajjada in 1946, Pir Ghulum Muhammad Shah, was not only a provincial darbari but also an honorary magistrate, Zaildar of Jahanian Shah and had been a Unionist Legislative Council member. Despite his close links with the Unionist Party he joined the Muslim League along with Major Mubarik Ali Shah of the neighbouring Shah Jiwana Pir family. They both subsequently secured election as its candidates for the Jhang constituencies.[60]

As in previous elections in most of the Punjab's rural constituencies in 1946 the selection of candidates was more important than the electioneering itself. 'The parties have yet to choose their respective candidates and much thought and study will be needed for this important step in electioneering', the Editor of the *Civil and Military Gazette* declared on 4 September 1945, 'the party which chooses a better set of candidates, keeping in view the local alliances and clannish feelings will of course have a tremendous advantage'.[61]

Although it had earlier criticized the Unionist Party for using 'tribalism' and the peasants' superstitious reverence for pirs to win political support, the Muslim League did not quibble about adopting these same methods when it was in the position to do so. Indeed it was so determined to field candidates who possessed personal influence in the villages, that it passed over many of its loyal workers in order to run 'convert' landlords and pirs on its ticket. Sardar Barkat Hayat, Sikander's younger brother, was for example selected as the Muslim League candidate for the North Punjab Labour seat instead of the President of the Rawalpindi Artisans Union who was also Vice President of the Rawalpindi Muslim League.[62] Despite the unpopularity of this policy with its activists, it was vital to the League's success in many of the West Punjab constituencies. Its failure to pursue a similar course of action in the North West Frontier Province was in part responsible for the Muslim League's embarrassing defeats there.[63] In the one area of the N.W.F.P. in which it gained the whole-hearted support of the local Khans, the Hazara district, it significantly won eight of the nine Muslim seats.[64]

The Punjab League's ability to call on its parent body for external support and resources during the elections was of much less importance to its success than the fact that it could field candidates who controlled the traditional networks for mobilizing rural political support. Because of its greater financial stability and control of the machinery of government, the Unionist Party easily matched it in bringing external pressures and resources to the support of its local candidates. Both parties put a large number of workers in the election field[65] and rushed vans fitted with loudspeakers round the villages in order to whip up support. The cost of this kind of electioneering soon badly stretched the Punjab League's resources and it had to apply for a loan of Rs.3 lakhs from the Central Muslim League Election Fund.[66] The situation was, however, even worse in neighbouring Sind, where a party of Aligarh student propagandists found themselves stranded because of the lack of finance to pay for their return trip.[67]

As in the 1937 elections the biraderi played an important part in mobilizing the votes of the peasant proprietors. The Meos' support for the Muslim League throughout the Gurgaon district was assured when it won over the biraderi's two main leaders, Sardar Muhammad and Sapat Khan who openly agitated for the inclusion of Mewat in Pakistan.[68] Just before the elections the Punjab League persuaded Jinnah to remove the ban on Begum Shah Nawaz's membership of the League so that her influence as Vice-President of the Punjab Arain Anjuman could be utilized in those constituencies of the Lahore, Jullundur and Ferozepore districts in which most voters were Arains.[69] Mian Nurullah this time used his influence amongst his fellow Arains in the Lyallpur district on the Muslim League's behalf. He devoted the biggest part of his electioneering effort to the registering of voters rather than popularizing the League's message as he knew that if he increased the number of voters from his biraderi he would almost certainly secure election.[70] Wherever strong biraderis existed the Muslim League endeavoured to choose their leaders as its candidates. An interesting case in point was the Wazirabad constituency in which most of the voters were Jats. The Muslim League parliamentary Board had to choose between two applicants for the League ticket for this seat. One was Mohammad Salah-ud-Din, the son of Mohammad Nasir Din, the sitting Unionist member; their family was one of the most influential Jat families in the district. Mohammad Salah-ud-Din was, however, a very recent convert to the Muslim League in 1946 although he had almost immediately been made its district organizer.

The other applicant was Captain Raja Mohammad Abdullah Khan whose father had been chairman of the Gujranwala District Board and president of the Wazirabad Municipal Committee until his death. Raja Mohammad Abdullah Khan had been active in Muslim League politics ever since 1936, first as president of the Gujranwala District League and then as president of the Wazirabad City League. He was, however, a member of the small Rajput community. The Parliamentary Board could not risk losing the Jat vote, and so gave the ticket to Mohammad Salah-ud-Din despite his rival's longer service in its cause.[71]

The Punjab Muslim League went to considerable lengths to secure the co-operation of the leading biraderis. In January 1946 for example it organized a special Gujar Conference at Lahore which was presided over by Captain Chaudhri Shamsir Ali. It appealed to the Muslim Gujars not only of the Punjab but of the whole of India to 'sacrifice body, heart and wealth for Pakistan'.[72] It condemned Mohammad Shafi who was the Unionist candidate for Ludhiana, and declared that he and his supporters were not really Gujars. 'They were the people who were going to give the biraderi a bad name when Pakistan was formed'.[73] In order to counter the influence of Shafi's paper, the *Gujar Gazette*, it was proposed to start a new pro-League Gujar paper.

The landlords who had joined the League used their influence over their clients and their wealth to win it votes. 'Treating' the electorate bulked as large in the 1946 Indian elections as in any eighteenth century British election. The Governor of the North West Frontier Province wrote to the Viceroy:

> In Bannu where I spent 3 days recently, the results in the voting for the Muslim seats seem likely to be decided by the number of sheep each candidate can kill to feast his supporters .... One was said to have killed 93 sheep already and the general estimate is 10 votes per sheep.[74]

In Sind it was estimated that the average cost to a candidate was around Rs.50,000.[75] In contrast in the Punjab the votes of whole villages were bought up for one or two thousand rupees with, 'a few goats and bottles of country liquor ... thrown in for good luck',[76] although inflation so took its toll during the course of the week's polling that quotations for a vote in some constituencies soared to twenty times the original price.[77]

The Muslim League realized how vital it was to obtain the pirs' support not only in the Punjab but in other Muslim areas of India. It had therefore proposed in 1943 to

> respectfully [request] the Muslim religious heads, pirs and sufis to help the Muslim Nation of India in its present life and death struggle, by their sincere prayers and by exhorting their followers to sacrifice their all in the cause of the attainment of a free and independent Muslim India.[78]

In the period immediately preceding the provincial elections the Punjab League created a committee of men of religious influence known as the Masheikh committee in order to marshall Sufi support behind its cause. As in the North West Frontier province where League propagandists were sent into the countryside disguised as pirs in an attempt to win the Pathans' support,[79] so in the Punjab many landlords adopted the garb of pirs during the course of the elections. Among the members of the Masheikh committee were such unlikely Sufis as Pir Mamdot Sharif (Khan Iftikhar Husain Khan of Mamdot), the sajjada nashin of Wah Sharif (Shaukat Hayat) and sajjada nashin of Darbar Sargodha Sharif (Firoz Khan Noon).[80] The pirs were not easy to organize: few attended the Jamiat-al-Ulama-i-Islam conference which the Muslim League held in the grounds of Islamia College, Lahore, in January 1946, so that most of the League's dealings with them had to take place at local level. It approached individual pirs and asked them to issue 'fatwas' in its support. These were disseminated by means of small leaflets and wall-posters as well as by publication in such newspapers as *Nawa-e-Waqt* and *Inqilab*. Appeals to vote for the Muslim League were couched often almost solely in terms of loyalty to the piri-mureedi relationship. The following 'fatwa' issued by Syed Fazl Ahmed Shah, sajjada nashin of the shrine of Hazrat Shah Nur Jamal is a good illustration of this:

> An announcement from the Dargah of Hazrat Shah Nur Jamal. I command all those people who are in my Silsilah to do everything possible to help the Muslim League and give their votes to it. All those people who do not act according to this message should consider themselves no longer members of my Silsilah.

> Signed Fazal Ahmed Shah, Sajjada Nashin Hazrat Shah Nur Jamal.[81]

Most of the leading Sufi shrines issued similar 'fatwas' on the Muslim League's behalf. Many Pirs were active as League candidates and propagandists. Among the most influential were Pir Fazl Shah of Jalalpur, Pir Mehr Ali Shah and Pir Jamaat Ali Shah. The Muslim League achieved its greatest success in such areas as Jhang, Multan, Jhelum and Karnal where it had obtained the support of the leading local pirs. Khalid Saifullah, the editor of the pro-League *Eastern Times*, did not overstate the case when he wrote immediately after the elections:

> What are the factors that have brought about the revolution in the Pakistani lands? What has made the great change possible? In my view the greatest praise must be lavished, as far as the Punjab is concerned on the Pirs ... who when they saw the Pakistani nation in mortal danger emerged from their cells and enjoined upon their followers to resist evil and vote for the League and Pakistan.[82]

*Conclusion*

This study of the Pakistan movement in the key province of the Punjab has revealed how much more important local social and religious networks may be in mobilizing political support than has been recognized by existing theories.[83] It has also reinforced the point frequently made in studies of national movements in South Asia that they were not usually monolithic in character but drew their strength from local grievances and political needs. Also it has touched on the subject of the interaction of British rule with rural society. It has shown that far from always having a de-stabilizing impact on the Indian countryside as some writers have argued in the past, British rule could also sustain the economic and political influence of the rural elite, provided the latter adapted and took advantage of the new circumstances. The landlords and pirs retained their local influence and acted as brokers between the village communities and the wider world.

Immediately after the 1937 elections the Punjab Muslim League attempted to bypass the rural elite which remained loyal to the Unionist Party by appealing directly to the villagers, but its efforts made little headway. Despite its organizational skills it was unable to mobilize the passive rural population which was either too cowed or felt insufficient grievances against the landlords to oppose them. The outbreak of the Second World War transformed this situation: heavy recruiting demands, high prices and grain-requisitioning provided the League with the opportunity to exploit growing rural discontent. Even so it was only in the areas where the impact of the war was greatest and the landlords' power weakest (the Rawalpindi and Jhelum districts of the north west and the eastern Ambala division of the Punjab) that it was able to put pressure on the rural elite by voicing the villagers' grievances. The landlords in these areas reacted to the groundswell of discontent by leaving the Unionist Ministry's ranks in the effort to maintain their local political influence. Elsewhere in the Punjab the landlords remained firmly in control. The Muslim League found it impossible to create a grass roots organization and desperately needed the landlords and pirs to act as its brokers in vote-gathering. Until a large section of the rural elite deserted the Unionist Party during 1944 and 1945 the prospects of the League's winning power in the Punjab were extremely remote. Its position in 1946 as a rival rural party to the Unionists marked an important turning point in Punjabi politics. The landlords and pirs had deserted the Unionist Party for a myriad of local reasons and interests, most of which had their roots in the belief that it had outlived its usefulness as a vehicle for their interests in the changed political circumstances by the end of the war. The Punjab Muslim League willingly selected convert landlords and pirs as its candidates in 1946 because it recognized the importance of traditional allegiances in mobilizing political support. Its grass-roots organization and its ability to call on the All-India Muslim League for support were very minor factors in its crucial electoral success.

Although the Unionist Party was defeated in 1946 the patron system of politics remained intact. Personal influence rather than party organization still held the key to victory in most of the rural constituencies. The resilience of this type of politics resulted from the encouragement which it had received from the British. Their political and economic policies were designed to secure stability in the Punjab by consolidating the power of the leading local landlords and pirs. It was by utilizing the strengthened ties of kinship, of tenant to landlord, and murid to pir that the Muslim League was able to mobilize the rural voters who held the key to the successful creation of Pakistan.

## *NOTES*

Talbot, 'Muslim political mobilization in rural Punjab 1937-46'

*Abbreviations*

| | |
|---|---|
| NAI | National Archives of India |
| IOL | India Office Library and Records |
| DG | District Gazetteer |
| FR | Fortnightly Report |
| FMA | Freedom Movement Archives, Karachi University |
| SHC | Shamsul Hasan Collection |

1. S.J. Burki, *Pakistan under Bhutto 1971-1977* (London 1980), p.18.
2. The proportion of the total cultivated area farmed by tenants rose from 43 per cent in the eastern Ambala district of the province to nearly 75 per cent in the western Multan district. Some large estates did of course exist in the East Punjab, notably the Mamdot estate in Ferozepore.
3. Z. Bhatty, 'Status and Power in a Muslim Dominated Village in Uttar Pradesh' in I. Ahmad, ed., *Caste and Social Stratification among the Muslims* (Delhi 1973), p.96.
4. Landlords gave the village menials a share of the crop in exchange for labour services. They were for example expected to attend and perform 'caste' services at the time of ceremonial occasions in the landlord's household. The jajmani relationship was not however a modern type of contract but was a permanent and hereditary social relationship.
5. Punjabis still refer to their land today as their *patlaj*, a word which has a similar meaning to izzat: that of power, honour and respect.
6. Jhang DG (Lahore 1930) p.133.
7. Rawalpindi DG (Lahore 1895) p.139.
8. Attock DG (Lahore 1909 p.229.
9. Ibid.
10. There was for example much less risk involved for them in switching to cash-crop production. Moreover they possessed the surplus resources to invest in the new irrigation facilities provided by the British.
11. E. Hodges, 'The Faqir, The Industrialist and the Pirs: Debt, Status and Marriage among Four Punjabi

Muslim Families', unpublished paper presented to the Seminar on Intermediate Linkages (Berkeley, March 1978), p.7.

12. R. Nath, 'Punjab Agrarian Laws and their economic and constitutional bearings', *Modern Review*, 65 (1939), p.28.

13. A. Husain, *Fazl-i-Husain. A Political Biography* (London 1946), p.152.

14. M.K.A. Siddiqi, 'Caste among the Muslims of Calcutta', in Ahmad, op.cit., p.148.

15. In the only constituency in which the Congress fielded a candidate who had strong biraderi backing, it significantly secured its most outstanding victory. At Kasur, Mian Iftikhar-ud-Din, a member of the influential Arain Mian family of Baghbanpura Lahore, defeated the veterin Unionist Sardar Habib Ullah Khan by mobilizing the Arain voters on his behalf.

16. R. Eaton, *Sufis of Bijapur 1300-1700: Social Roles of Sufis in Medieval India* (Princeton 1978), pp. 217 and 241.

17. M.M.H. Nun, 'Assessment Report of the Pakpattan Tehsil of the Montgomery District' (Lahore 1921), p.18, Punjab Proceedings P 11372 April 1922, Part A, IOL.

18. T.G. Singh, *Baba Sheikh Farid* (Delhi 1974), p.43.

19. *Report on the Administration of Estates Under the charge of the Court of Wards for the Year ending 30 September 1921* (Lahore 1922): Statement No.1, L 5 VI (3), Departmental Annual Reports, IOL.

20. G.L. Chopra, *Chiefs and Families of Note in the Punjab* Vol. 2 (Lahore 1940), p.242.

21. M. Milson, trans., *Kitab Adab al-Muridin of Abu al-Najib al-Suhrawardi A Sufi Rule for Novices* (Cambridge, Mass. 1978), p.46.

22. Pirs kept registers of their murids and frequently visited them to bestow their blessings in return for gifts.

23. D. Gilmartin, 'Religious Leadership and the Pakistan Movement in the Punjab', *Modern Asian Studies* 13, 3 (1979), p.504.

24. W. Ahmad, ed., *The Letters of Mian Fazl-i-Husain* (Lahore 1976), pp.592-4.

25. M.R. Afzal, *Malik Barkat Ali: His Life and Writings* (Lahore 1969), p.36.

26. *Civil and Military Gazette* (Lahore), 17 October 1936.

27. Ibid., 15 July 1937.

28. *Tribune* (Ambala), 7 October 1937.

29. This pact, which was agreed at the October 1937

Lucknow Muslim League session, was surrounded by controversy from its inception. Whatever the interpretation of its signatories, its effect was to seal off the Punjab countryside from the Muslim League's influence as the control of the provincial League organization fell into Unionist hands.

30. Muslim League Council Meetings, vol.253, pt.2, p.60, FMA.

31. Muslim League Working Committee Meetings, vol. 142 (1943-7), p.23, FMA.

32. The students who toured the Punjab during December 1945 from the Aligarh Muslim University had attended the League Workers' Training Camp to hear lectures on such topics as the Muslim League in the light of Islam, Islamic History and the religious background to Pakistan.

33. Translation of a pamphlet issued by the election board of the Punjab Muslim Students Federation, FMA.

34. The Unionist Party employed Mirasis to work on its behalf during the elections. *Eastern Times* (Lahore), 30 December 1945.

35. Report of the Punjab Provincial Muslim League's Work for June and July 1944 submitted to the All-India Muslim League Committee of Action, 28 July 1944, SHC, Punjab vol.1, General Correspondence.

36. Ibid.

37. Report of the Organizing Secretary Rawalpindi Division Muslim League, vol.162, pt.7, Punjab Muslim League (1943-44), pp.74 ff., FMA.

38. Punjab FR for the first half of July 1944, L/P&J/5/247, IOL.

39. Punjab FR, 23 August 1944, loc.cit.

40. This by-election took place as a result of the death of Khan Bahadur Muhammad Hasan Khan Gurmani. The Muslim League was unable to find anyone to oppose Sardar Ghaus Bakhsh, a leading member of the Mazari Baluch tribe, which continued its wild, nomadic way of life even into the twentieth century.

41. *Nawa-e-Waqt* (Lahore), 30 April 1945.

42. *Eastern Times* (Lahore), 23 May 1945.

43. Punjab FR, 20 September 1944, L/P&J/5/247, IOL.

44. Punjab Board of Economic Inquiry, No.90, Annual Review of Economic Conditions in the Punjab 1945-6 (Lahore), pp.6 ff.

45. Punjab FR, 2nd half of February 1946, L/P&J/5/249, IOL.

46. The extent of the communists' influence in the Punjab Muslim League was brought home in July 1944 when

a leading communist, Daniel Latifi, became its Office Secretary.

47. Punjab FR, 2nd half of October 1943 and 1st half of November 1943, L/P&J/5/246, IOL.

48. The Jat Minister, Chhotu Ram, was an outspoken critic of the requisitioning of foodgrains and the placing of a price ceiling on them. In October 1944 a deputation from the Punjab led by the Sikh Minister, Baldev Singh, unsuccessfully attempted to get the Central Food Department to lift its ban on the movement of grain between the Punjab and the U.P.

49. See above, note 33.

50. *Eastern Times* (Lahore), 28 December 1945.

51. *Eastern Times* (Lahore), 28 August 1945.

52. The speedy end of the war in Asia had taken the Unionist Government by surprise so that its plans to ease the problem of demobilization by resettling ex-servicement on land in the Canal Colonies were not completed. Even by the end of 1946, less than 20 per cent of the demobilized soldiers registered with employment exchanges had been found work. Punjab FR, 14 December 1946, L/P&J/5/249, IOL.

53. *Eastern Times* (Lahore), 29 September 1945.

54. The Rajput Unionist members for the Rawalpindi East and Gujjar Khan constituencies, Major Farman Ali and Raja Fateh Khan, both joined the League for example after popular pressure from their villagers to do so. Report of Sayed Ghulam Mustafa Shah Gilani, Honorary Secretary Rawalpindi Division Muslim League, vol.162, pt.7, Punjab Muslim League (1943-4), FMA.

55. *Eastern Times* (Lahore), 13 September 1945.

56. The Khattar group led by Sikander Hayat Khan were traditional rivals of the Noon-Tiwana faction. There was considerable disappointment amongst the Khattars that one of their number did not succeed Sikander as Premier. The fact that one of their rivals, Malik Khizr Hayat Khan Tiwana, became Premier only rubbed salt in the wound. Significantly, amongst the Muslim League's earliest landlord converts were such prominent members of the Khattar faction as Shaukat Hayat (Sikander's son), Mr Maqbool Mahmood and Mian Mumtaz Daultana.

57. *Eastern Times* (Lahore), 18 September 1945.

58. *Dawn* (Delhi), 26 September 1945.

59. Information compiled from G.L. Chopra, *Chiefs and Families of Note in the Punjab* vol.2 (Lahore 1940), p.52 and Gurdaspur DG (Lahore 1915), p.74.

60. Pir Ghulum Muhammad Shah was unopposed in the

Jhang East constituency. Mubarik Ali Shah defeated Khan Inayat Ullah by over 7,000 votes in the Jhang Central seat.

61. *Civil and Military Gazette* (Lahore), 4 September 1945.

62. M. Haqil Bukhsh to Jinnah, 14 January 1946, SHC, Punjab vol.1, General Correspondence.

63. *Khyber Mail* (Peshawar), 15 February 1946.

64. N.W.F.P. FR, 27 February 1946, L/P&J/5/223, IOL.

65. Whereas the Muslim League's were mainly student volunteers from Aligarh and the Punjab Muslim Students Federation, the Unionist Party's were paid up to Rs.300 for their work. *Dawn* (Delhi), 23 December 1945.

66. Ibid., 19 January 1946; also *Eastern Times* (Lahore), 23 February 1946.

67. Professor M.B. Mirza to Jinnah, 29 January 1946, SHC, U.P. vol.3.

68. P.C. Aggarwal, 'The Meos of Rajasthan and Haryana' in Ahmed, op.cit.

69. V. Noon to Jinnah, 18 October 1945, SHC, Punjab vol.4.

70. The Unionist candidate Pir Nasir-ud-Din exerted influence mainly over the 'jangli' section of the population. He endeavoured to enroll 10,000 new 'jangli' voters, whilst Mian Nurullah submitted about 8,000 fresh applications from the constituency's Arain community. Abdul Bari, President of Lyallpur District Muslim League, to Jinnah, 23 January 1946, SHC, Punjab vol.1.

71. *Eastern Times* (Lahore), 27 October 1945.

72. *Nawa-e-Waqt* (Lahore), 19 January 1946.

73. Ibid.

74. N.W.F.P. FR, 24 January 1946, L/P&J/5/223, IOL.

75. Sind FR, 5 October 1945, L/P&J/5/261, IOL.

76. *Civil and Military Gazette* (Lahore), 7 February 1946.

77. Ibid.

78. G.F. Ansari to Jinnah, 25 April 1943, Quaid-e-Azam Papers, File 1101/105R, National Archives of Pakistan, Islamabad.

79. *Pioneer* (Lucknow), 24 November 1945.

80. K.B. Sayeed, *Pakistan. The Formative Phase 1857-1948* (London 1968), p.203.

81. *Nawa-e-Waqt* (Lahore), 19 January 1945.

82. *Eastern Times* (Lahore), 15 March 1946.

83. Most existing theories of peasant political activity contain the idea that social mobilization and external leadership are the necessary prerequisites for political mobilization. That is, it is only when

*Note to page 266*

peasants have greater access to the outside world as a result of increased education, improved communications and extended contact with the national market that their political horizons expand beyond the village and it is only with the aid of the organizational skills and resources from outside politicians and parties that they can successfully challenge the rural elite. Lerner suggests that it is contact with a 'superior' culture which drives peasants into external social and political activity. Wolf lays stress on the role of the external agent as a necessity for peasant mobilization. Even Migdal, who maintains that the breakdown of peasant social structures rather than culture contact has led to increased peasant political activity, implies that social mobilization must precede large scale peasant political mobilization. See T. Shahin, ed., *Peasants and Peasant Society* (London 1979), p.269; D. Lerner, *The Passing of Traditional Society* (Glencoe Ill. 1958); and J.S. Migdal, *Peasants, Politics and Revolution: Pressures Towards Political Change in the 3rd World* (Princeton 1974), pp.20 and 229.

# THE RURAL WORLD OF TARASHANKAR BANERJEE: SOCIAL DIVISIONS AND PSYCHOLOGICAL CROSS-CURRENTS

*Rajat K. Ray*

The appropriate categories for the analysis of agrarian social structure have long engaged the attention of rural historians of South Asia. The simplicity of the dual division of society into landlords and tenants no longer carries conviction. It is not clear what has replaced it. Should we - in Leninist terms - further break down the tenant economy into rich, middle and poor peasants? Or should we - following Chayanov and Shamin - think of an integrated peasant economy in which differences of income and property are marginal and patterned on a cyclical order in which a simple peasant family, through multiplication and division, moves within one generation through rich, middle and poor phases?[1] The dangers of imposing alien class categories on a traditional society organized along a caste hierarchy has been emphasized by some leading sociologists.[2] Ronald Inden, for instance, has sought to understand medieval Bengali society in terms of its own cultural categories - lineage and caste - found in the genealogical records of the Rarhi Brahmans and the Rarhi Kayasthas.[3] There are, on the other hand, other sociologists who have emphasized that the rural people themselves have their own indigenous terms and categories by which they divide their society into distinct class strata. Andre Beteille, for one, has demonstrated how important it is to understand the changing content of the Bengali term, *jotedar*, over a period of time and from district to district, in order to track long-term changes in Bengali rural society.[4]

The ongoing debate has thus served to emphasize the importance of trying to understand the changing structure of rural society as perceived by the rural people themselves. The categories of analysis, whether castes, classes or lineages, should take account of the mental categories by which the contemporaneous consciousness conceived of its own society. Sociologists and historians often fall into the trap of imposing ab-extra analytical categories on a rural society which is organized, in the consciousness of the members of that society, on altogether different lines. One means to guard against these dangers is to pay closer attention to the literature specific to the area and the time of study.

In this essay we shall study the social categories in a rural locality of Birbhum district in West Bengal in the first half of the twentieth century through the fiction of a contemporaneous Bengali novelist, Tarashankar Banerjee (1898-1971). Born and bred in the rural locality of Labpur, this novelist settled in Calcutta in middle age and was lionized among its intellectual circles for the 'truly rural' quality of his fiction. Till then he had been a villager, and even in Calcutta he remained, as Suniti Kumar Chatterjee notes in the foreword to his *Collected Works*, something of a rustic.[5] He did not imbibe the urbanized English education of Calcutta to the extent that cut off so many contemporary novelists from the rural roots of the indigenous Bengali culture. His elder contemporary, Rabindranath Tagore, told him when he visited Santiniketan: 'I have never read before stories of village people as yours'.[6] At Tagore's orders, his stories were read out at the evening gathering of the local elders. Tagore's lieutenants in rural reconstruction had misgivings on this score, because peasants did not comprehend modern Bengali literature. But as Tagore had predicted, there was no gap in communication as far as Banerjee's stories were concerned: the old men understood and appreciated them.[7] This was because Banerjee was firmly rooted in his indigenous rural experience, his terms and categories being drawn purely from this native consciousness. The historian who seeks to understand Bengali rural society in its own terms will find in his works a spontaneous expression of cultural categories indigenous to the Rarh social region of which Birbhum forms a part.

One major purpose of this essay is therefore to sift his novels for the indigenous terms and categories in which the rural people of Birbhum understood their own social arrangements. This will throw light on those hotly-debated questions of class and status in South Asian rural societies which have claimed the attention of historians and sociologists. But that is not the only purpose. The use of literature is not merely to answer questions suggested by the preoccupations of the community of scholars. If they can wrench themselves from these preoccupations for a moment and try to absorb the things which preoccupy the artists and writers of the society under study, new questions in their area of investigation will crop up. New ways of looking at society will suggest themselves. This takes us to the second major purpose of this essay.

It is to explore the sexual, mental and cultural differences which contribute, often imperceptibly, to the social differentiation in the countryside. Reading Banerjee's novels, one is struck by the thought that human bodies and human minds interact in markedly different ways at various levels of rural society. It is possible to distinguish the levels of society by paying attention to the differing patterns of mental and physical interaction in the countryside. This is not an area into which the historian or sociologist normally ventures. But the novelist, whose attention is fixed on the inter-personal relationships of men and women, hits at social facts which are not to be laid bare by an abstract preoccupation with notions of class and status. Often, these are facts of vital relevance to the historian or sociologist in understanding the society he investigates. The normal methods of social science or historical enquiry would not reveal these facts. But the historian can in this case rely on the novelist. Banerjee's rural novels make it clear that there are different levels of physical, emotional and mental existence in the countryside. These levels define different strata in rural society and create differing cultural patterns which underpin economic and social differences.

Rural society, unlike urban society, is an organic society. In spite of social and economic differences, it has a synthetic culture sustained by bonds of interdependence and sentiment between people in different stations of life. Banerjee's close study of the Birbhum countryside, however, detects sub-cultures within the composite rural culture. His novels are crowded by three basic categories of people: the gentry, the caste peasants and the untouchable agrarian dependents. There are minute differences within each of these levels of society, but they are clearly marked out from one another. It is not merely ritual and economic differences which create these distinctions. Material and status differences are accompanied and accentuated by differing patterns of inter-personal relationships within and beyond the family. The very quality of life differs from one level of society to another. These differences in the inner life of the gentry, the peasants and the untouchables are the basis of distinct sub-cultures within rural society.

Such psychological and cultural themes, subjective by their very nature, are bound to raise one disturbing question: how authentic is the experience recorded by Tarashankar Banerjee? He came of a lesser landed family in Labpur, and was thus able to see gentry society from within. But would this rural identity necessarily give him an inner view of the mental and emotional life of people in walks of life below his own? Is it possible for a Brahman member of the gentry to penetrate to the centre of the consciousness of a Sadgop peasant, or a Kahar farm servant?

There is no reason to doubt the complete authenticity of his portraits of gentry life. The swadeshi movement stirred gentry society in Ladpur in his boyhood and left a permanent mark on his mental development. He saw from within how profoundly the inner life of the gentry in his own rural locality was transformed by the events of 1905-8. Subsequently his contact with rural society broadened as he became closely involved, as a young man, in rural politics. This, too, was partly a product of his experience of the swadeshi age. The swadeshi movement created a new type of youth in rural Bengal, distinguished by a social conscience which expressed itself through 'volunteering'. A social-service corps was formed in Labpur. Banerjee was involved in it from the start. He carried on this social work during the cholera epidemic of 1925-5, when he visited at least 40 villages around Labpur and attended to stricken people for six months without any rest. These experiences are recorded in his novels, *Dhatridevata* and *Ganadevata*. As an active social worker, Banerjee had wide opportunities for coming into contact with the lower orders of the people. He was helped in this by one fact, as he records in his memoirs: he was not handsome. 'Any pleasant quality of appearance I might have had was destroyed by long exposure to the sun. I learnt their ways of speech and customs just as one of themselves'.[8] For much of the 1920s, before he shot to literary fame, he was an unemployed young man roaming around the country - visiting rural fairs and staying overnight in peasant households. He also went round on official business as he served as the president of the local union board for some time. He travelled on his bicycle throughout the Labpur union in order to carry out rural reconstruction work in his official capacity.[9] He was also an active Congress worker and was involved in rural nationalist activity in Birbhum. He was gaoled for his part in the civil disobedience movement, but thereafter gave up politics and concentrated on writing. His first major novel, which established him as a novelist, was

*Dhatridevata*, published in 1939. *Ganadevata* and *Panchagram*, two successive parts of one single work, were written between 1942 and 1944; and *Hansuli Banker Upakatha*, widely acclaimed by critics, in 1947. After independence, he wrote several volumes of Bengali memoirs which enable us to compare the actualities of his experience with the content of his novels. The most important of these memoirs, *Memories of My Times* (1951) and *My Literary Life* (1966), make it evident that he bodily lifted several real persons and actual events in and around Labpur into his novels. His portraits of peasant and untouchable households are thus filled in by details of solid experience. Nonetheless, there is one danger in his descriptions of their emotions and thought-processes. As a member of the gentry, he was affected by the romantic culture of the swadeshi age and, in spite of his conscious attempt to check it, he is not always successful in checking the projection of romantic gentry notions on to the emotional life of his peasant and untouchable characters.

To understand and to cross-check the social context of his novels, it is necessary to glean some independent information about Birbhum from official sources. The district gazetteer of 1910 and the land settlement report of 1924-32 give much useful information about agrarian relationships in Birbhum during the period covered by Banerjee and his major rural novels. By comparison with these official handbooks it is clear that Banerjee mines information from depths which are beyond the reach of the official machinery. The gazetteer and the settlement report trace correlations between caste rank and economic condition on the basis of the census caste categories, which are broad notional categories, such as Brahman, Muslim or Bauri. Yet reading Banerjee's novels it becomes clear that the real community is always smaller than the census caste category, which lumps together several endogamous units which are for most purposes self-contained social units. The Bauris, for instance, are divided into four subcastes - Kahar, Dului, Sikhure and Gubure.[10] Banerjee examines the inner life of the Kahar community in great depth in *Hansuli Banker Upakatha* and the events of the novel impress on the reader how much closer to reality is the category Kahar than the category Bauri. Furthermore, even within the Kahar community of Hansuli Bank, a real place near Banerjee's native Labpur called Western Kadipur, there were two local divisions, the Beharas and the Atpoures, whose interaction determined much of the action of the novel. The district gazetteer and the settlement report do not achieve this depth of social observation.

The settlement report, however, contains land statistics which are useful for cross-checking Banerjee's detailed descriptions of agrarian relationships. The landlords of the district had little of the land under direct cultivation. Of the total land area of the district 77 per cent was cultivated under direct possession by raiyats who were recorded under the settlement. Predominantly, then, the cultivation of the rice lands of Birbhum was carried on by a peasantry with recorded rights to the soil. Below this peasant economy was a lower level of the rural economy, consisting of share-croppers and farm servants, who loom large in Banerjee's novels but do not figure in the settlement statistics. Bonded cultivators (*krishans*) and farm servants (*mahindars*) were not recorded under the settlement's record of rights, so there is no means of knowing exactly how much of the land was cultivated by tied agricultural workers under the control of raiyats. The experience of contemporaries like Tarashankar Banerjee suggests that it was a substantial area, an assumption strengthened by the census evidence of the number of untouchable agriculturists in Birbhum. Curiously, the settlement operations recorded 2.2 per cent of the land as under the occupation of under-tenants, of which again only 0.2 per cent was found to be cultivated by share-croppers with no right of occupancy.[11] Yet, *bhagjotedars*, as the share-croppers were locally known, occupy so large an area in the consciousness of keen rural observers like Tarashankar Banerjee that no reliance can be placed on the settlement statistics in this respect. The settlement statistics do, however, give us some hard information regarding the degree of differentiation within the economy of the recognized tenants. The tenancies in the district were classified in the settlement report under the following grades:[12]

| | *Percentage of total interests* | *Percentage of total area* |
|---|---|---|
| 1 acre or less | 66.8 | 15.2 |
| 1 - 2 acres | 14.9 | 16.6 |
| 2 - 3 acres | 7.1 | 13.5 |
| 4 - 5 acres | 2.3 | 8.1 |
| 5 - 15 acres | 4.5 | 26.8 |
| 15 - 25 acres | 0.3 | 4.7 |
| Over 25 acres | 0.1 | 4.9 |

This information puts it beyond doubt that the peasant economy was predominantly a small-tenant economy and not one controlled by a small group of large capitalistic farmers. To summarize this statistical evidence in static economic categories (categories which, as we shall see, may mislead us), nine-tenths of the tenantry held less than one-half of the land and one-twentieth of the tenants held over one-third of the land, while in between them a middle group, 2.3 per cent of the total, held the rest, about eight per cent. Thus nine-tenths of the tenants, holding below four acres, constituted a dwarf-holding economy, almost permanently indebted and shading off into the untouchable landless category. At the top was a surplus agricultural economy which was not predominant in terms of the land under its control (a little over one-third), but which supplied the credit and the surplus lands that enabled the dwarf-holding and landless economies to go on functioning. This would imply that the richer villagers had not succeeded in concentrating the entire economy in their own hands, but enjoyed extensive influence because the agricultural economy was a small-tenant economy which could not survive without small parcels of land and small amounts of seed and grain taken from other villagers on extremely adverse terms. Exploitation, small and dispersed in terms of the people benefiting from it, was massive in terms of the number of people exploited. The peasant economy was undoubtedly going through a process of internal differentiation. But it was still predominantly a small-peasant economy in which income differences were fluid. Thus the peasant economy as a whole could be viewed as an integral economy vis à vis other broad economic categories, such as the landlords above or the untouchable below.

Birbhum's agrarian economy was closely related to its caste hierarchy. At the top of this hierarchy were the gentry castes, mostly Brahmans in this district. A sample survey showed that the Brahmans held as much as 72 per cent of the proprietary interests in the land. By comparison the great agricultural communities of the district, the Sadgops and the Muslims, held only two per cent and five per cent of the proprietary interests respectively, and the untouchable castes, the Bagdis and the Doms, nothing at all. So far as tenancies were concerned, however, the sample survey showed a different pattern of the distribution of the raiyati land among the various castes: Brahmans 17 per cent, Muslims 24 per cent, Sadgops 23 per cent, and Bagdis,

Bauris and Doms less than one per cent each.[13] The high-caste gentry held something like a sixth of the tenancies in the district, which they cultivated through share-croppers, under-tenants and bonded labourers. But nearly half of the raiyati land in the district was in the possession of the two principal agricultural communities, the Muslims (21 per cent of the population) and the Sadgops (ten per cent of the population). Even at this lower level of interests in the land, the untouchable castes hardly appeared, their role in agriculture being practically restricted to that of landless agrarian dependents. Yet the untouchables and the tribals together formed something like 30 per cent of the population of the district in 1931.[14] The landless untouchable economy was depressed even below the dwarf-holding peasant economy.

Tarashankar Banerjee's novels dealt with all these different levels of the rural economy. In this essay we shall concentrate on three of his major novels: *Dhatridevata*,[15] *Ganadevata* (including *Panchagram*)[16] and *Hansuli Banker Upakatha*.[17] Published between 1939 and 1948, these novels cover a more or less continuous time span from 1905 to 1943: *Dhatridevata* the period 1905 to 1921, *Ganadevata* the period 1922 to 1933 and *Hansuli Banker Upakatha* the years 1939 to 1943. East of these novels descends to a successively lower stratum of rural society. *Dhatridevata* focuses on a Brahman family of small landlords - in fact Tarashankar Banerjee's own family, with the names of his mother, his wife and himself changed, but that of his paternal aunt, Shailaja Devi, unchanged. *Ganadevata* portrays the whole rural community but focuses principally on the dominant Sadgop peasants of Birbhum. *Hansuli Banker Upakatha*, as already noted, deals with an untouchable community of bonded agricultural workers, the Kahars. Read together, these three novels give us glimpses of all three levels of the rural economy: the landed society, the peasant economy and the servile classes. They also make us aware that each of these levels supports a distinct subculture within the rural community - a sub-culture with its own family structure, sexual mores and emotional life.

## 2

Tarashankar Banerjee viewed his own society in terms of three distinct strata: the high caste gentry, the caste peasants (including Muslims) and the untouchable agrarian dependents. The artisans of the clean Nabasakha castes of Birbhum, among whom the dominant agricultural caste of the Sadgops figured, belonged in his view to peasant society. Various artisan groups, such as the blacksmiths, the potters and the carpenters, were engaged in rural crafts which were closely integrated with the agricultural cycle. Usually they held agricultural lands themselves.[18] Through the common panchayat of the Nabasakha castes, peasants and artisans came under the same collective social control regarding ritual and social offences.[19] Peasant society was thus wider than the peasantry and comprised those villagers of roughly the same caste status who were engaged in respectable rural crafts and village professions. It would include the artisans, the serving castes of clean status (for instance, the barbers) and rural literate persons from peasant households such as the village pedagogues (for example Debu pundit of *Ganadevata*), the quack doctors (for example 'Doctor' Jagan of *Ganadevata*) and the cultivating clergy (for example Irshad Maulvi and Haren Ghoshal of *Ganadevata*, both of them tenants, the one a maulvi and the other a Brahman). But Tarashankar Banerjee hesitates to include the large number of untouchable cultivating people, who contributed substantially to the agricultural work force of the district, within peasant society. He sometimes calls them *chashis* (peasants) but qualifies the term by a two-word formula, *shramik chashi* or *chashi majur* (peasant worker).[20] In the village sanctum (*chandimandap*), where the peasants assemble to judge the actions of the disobedient village blacksmith and carpenter, the untouchables stand to one side, while the peasants and the artisans sit down on the carpet spread out on the floor. Clearly the harijans are not full members of the community. A peasant enjoys the status within the village community which enables him to sit on the floor of the village sanctum while discussing village disputes in the assembled panchayat. Interestingly, the Brahmans sit at one corner, maintaining a certain distance from the rest of the peasants.[21]

These sitting arrangements reveal the mental categories in which the rural people unconsciously classify themselves: the Brahman gentry in a separate corner, the caste peasants on the floor and the untouchables standing at one side. The mental constructs of the rural people are by no means accidental: they are derived straight from the physical and social geography of the rural locality. The countryside is dotted with settlements which are socially distinct: large gentry villages, villages of the caste peasants, and attached hamlets for untouchables. Each of these settlements has important internal differences. The households in a gentry village belong to widely varying levels of income, wealth and honour, and the competition for precedence is keen among them. A process of internal differentiation is going on in the peasant village as well. Even the untouchable hamlet is not altogether without some inner differences as regards material possessions. But for all these differences within each of these worlds, the gentry world is sharply distinct from the peasant world, and the peasant world from the untouchable world.

The pattern of geographical settlements ensures these fundamental distinctions. The rural locality of Labpur, on which Banerjee modelled the imaginary natural and social setting of *Hansuli Banker Upakatha*, consisted of several villages related to each other by unequal interdependence. From this actual setting he drew mauza Bansbadi, popularly known as the Hansuli Bank or the Hairpin Bend, because the river Mayurakshi takes a double turn at this spot. On this real geographical spot, Western Kadipur, Banerjee placed the imaginary Kahar settlement of Bansbadi or Hansuli Bank. Bansbadi mauza is a hamlet, a small Kahar settlement, appended to the 'lot' Janal, a larger peasant village inhabited by the Sadgops. These prosperous agriculturists are employers and patrons to the landless Kahars. There was an actual Sadgop village near Labpur, called Mastali, where Tarashankar Banerjee used to go in order to supervise the cultivation of his agricultural land. He modelled Janal on this real village. The gentry village of Chandanpur, which lies further north of Janal in the story, is Banerjee's native Labpur, identified by the fact that it appears as a railway junction.[22] The Sadgops of Janal, big men in the eyes of their Kahar servants, are themselves tenants of the Chandanpur babus. The Kahars of Bansbadi understand that the 'babus' of Chandanpur - Brahman gentry, of great wealth and honour - are far bigger men than the 'mandals' of Janal, and accordingly they keep themselves at a fearful distance. They feel more comfortable in the company of the Sadgop masters of Janal, who have ceased to hold the plough themselves but are still men of the soil.

These social distances are measured by degrees of material and cultural proximity to the railway junction.

The rural town around the junction station plays a critical role in Tarashankar Banerjee's novels. It represents the external dimension to the rural locality, the point through which contact is made with the outside world. The closer your life is to the junction, the higher your station in rural society. Accordingly, Bansbadi, Janal and Chandanpur appear in ascending order. Chandanpur, once a big village of the Brahman gentry, is now practically a rural town on account of the railway junction and factory which have come up there since the turn of this century. The life of the Brahman gentry of the village was transformed beyond recognition. As it became closely integrated with the wider educational, professional and business world to which the junction station gave access, the Brahmans ceased to be 'thakurs' (priests) and became 'babus' (bourgeois gentlemen) in the eyes of the Kahars. The bara-babus of Chandanpur, originally Brahman landowners, made millions in the coal business; and the lesser gentry families of the town got access through English education to Calcutta and beyond.[23] The Sadgop agriculturists of Janal also reaped some benefits from this external connection. During the first world war, they became prosperous by selling rice, jaggery and oil seeds in the war market. They then became adha-babus (half gentlemen) by ceasing to hold the plough and by employing Kahar servants to plough their lands.[24] The Kahars were not affected by these changes in price levels during the first world war. They neither sold anything, nor did they buy (except a few clothes a year). Their life was almost completely outside the orbit of the market.[25] Their way of life depended on isolation from Chandanpur and the world beyond. This isolation was, however, violently broken during the second world war, when the war supply office set up a camp in Bansbadi to take away all the bamboo and wood from the sacred woods of the Kahars. The Kahars were uprooted from their native habitat and became a labour gang at the railway factory of Chandanpur.[26]

Access to the external world, and the opportunities and dangers it may bring, thus vary from Chandanpur to Janal, and from Janal to Bansbadi. This social fact is reflected in the communication system of the locality. Thus Chandanpur is an important rural market town, served by a junction of several railways and a railway bridge across the river Kopai. From Chandanpur a cartway moves to Janal. It is along this street that the Sadgop peasants dispatch their grain for the market on bullock-drawn carts. The street does not, however, stretch from Janal to Bansbadi, which is reached by an embanked track on which no wheels can move. The Kahars do not sell rice and they have no need of bullock carts.[27] In the final act, however, their isolated way of life is shattered when the war office builds a straight metalled road from Chandanpur to Bansbadi to dispatch the bamboos.[28]

The junction town, the symbol of the external dimension in rural life in Banerjee's novels, steadily increases its magnetic pull on the village. But to understand the nature of this pull, especially its differential character, it is necessary to look at an intermediate dimension in the relationship between the junction town and the village. It appears in Tarashankar Banerjee's novels as the rural locality. Rural settlements in any area form a closely-knit circle within which a complex set of inter-dependent relationships subordinates one village to another. The impact of the junction town on the village is mediated and differentiated by these inter-village relationships within the locality. Reduced to its simplest form, the model of the rural locality that one can deduce from Banerjee's fiction consists of the following elements: an untouchable hamlet behind the peasant village; beyond the peasant village a richer and larger village inhabited by the local gentry; and further on a railway junction - a rural town - which represents to the stratified rural locality the world beyond.

In the novel *Ganadevata* Banerjee fills in with overwhelming detail the complex social geography of an imaginary rural locality named Panchagram (five villages), modelled on his native Labpur and its environs. Five villages, lying in a semi-circle along the river Mayurakshi, form here a distinct social unit, which interacts, across the railway bridge over the river, with the junction town on the opposite bank. The five villages are named Kankana (pseudonym for Labpur), Mahagram (an actual village near Labpur), Kusumpur (pseudonym for Kusumgaria near Labpur), Sibkalipur and Dekhuria.[29] Kankana is the rich gentry village that dominates the Panchagram rural locality economically. Mahagram is the seat of the Nyayaratna family, the traditional legislators for the five villages. Sibkalipur and Kusumpur are peasant villages, one dominated by the Sadgops, the other by the Shaikhs. Dekhuria is a settlement of the Bhalla Bagdis, who make a living out of share-cropping, agricultural labour and crime. Beyond the five villages is the railway junction across the river (but in fact situated at one end of Labpur itself), a rural town with a police station and several shops, grain storage centres and rice mills, where rural industrialization was going on at full swing in the inter-war period. It was the rice-mill owners who encouraged the peasants of the five villages to resort to a rent strike against the landlords in 1928. The Kankana gentry had long prevented the rural poor of the locality from going to work in the rice mills and the mill owners took this opportunity for revenge by financing the rent strike with loans to the peasants. As the Kankana gentry ceased to be the only patrons in the locality and the mill owners emerged as an alternative source of patronage, the traditional structure of rural control began to break down. However, it was the traditional social unity of the five villages which enabled the peasants of the different villages to combine against the landlords.

This unity, a product of the historical memory that the five villages formed at one time organically-related units of the local Hindu society, had been much attenuated over time, especially after Kusumpur became a Muslim village. But still there is a real bond between them - the minimum bond without which the agricultural cycle would come to a halt. Hindu and Muslim peasants go for implements of cultivation to the same artisans. They pay rent simultaneously at the zamindar's 'cutcherry' and discuss the question of rent reduction in bad harvests. An occasion for such consultation is provided by the Amuti festival, where peasants from both communities participate in wrestling. For the Hindu peasants, a focal point is provided by the Ratha festival at the house of the Nyayaratna. The rent strike is decided on at the gathering of the Hindu peasants from the five villages at his house on this occasion. It is directed against the Kankana babus, and rich peasants allied with them, such as Srihari Ghosh of Sibkalipur and Daulat Shaikh of Kusumpur.

These two grain-lending peasants, who use their surplus stores of grain to give rice and seed loans to their poorer neighbours, are amassing lands, at the cost of their debtors, though on a smaller scale than the Kankana babus. The concentration of village produce in the hands of Srihari Ghosh and Daulat Shaikh indicates a process of internal differentiation among the Hindu and Muslim peasantries of Sibkalipur and Kusumpur. However, in spite of this the two villages are peasant settlements with a distinctive peasant culture, which marks them out from the gentry settlement of Kankana on the one hand and the Bhalla settlement of Dekhuria on the other. The Brahman landlords, who live in Kankana, do not supervise cultivation as the peasant households, which employ bonded labourers, do in Kusumpur or Sibkalipur. The tendency of the Kankana babus is to let out land to share-croppers, usually Sadgop or Muslim peasants, who in turn may employ the Bhalla Bagdis on that land as day labourers or farm servants. For instance, Raham Shaikh, the leading Muslim peasant of Kusumpur, has land on share-crop basis from the rich Mukherjee babus of Kankana, and employs labourers on that land to improve it.[30] Even the richest peasant of Sibkalipur, Srihari Ghosh, who has his land cultivated by agrarian dependents, is a mere tenant to the elder Mukherjee, though of course an honoured and trusted tenant with whom he confers as to how to break the rent strike. The houses in Kankana - white, yellow and red - are built of brick and cement, unlike the thatched houses of Sibkalipur and Kusumpur. Situated on an open ground are the school, the theatre and the hospital, things of wonder to any peasant visiting Kankana. Even old man Chaudhury from Sibkalipur is impressed, though he is a respectable tenant who does not cultivate himself.[31] But then the peasants of Sibkalipur and Kusumpur are themselves socially rather distant from the Bhalla labourers of Dekhuria. There are some Sadgop households in Dekhuria. But the Bhalla Bagdis are the majority there. They cultivate the land, but seldom have a title to it. As so few among them are raiyats, their stake in the no-rent movement of the raiyats against the zamindars is but marginal. However, the excitement caused by the rent strike arouses their criminal tendencies. Ram Bhalla, leader of a band of Bhalla dacoits in Dekhuria, plans an abortive raid on the house of Srihari Ghosh, whose surplus store of grain attracts his notice at a time when starvation stares the Bhallas in the face and the village is in a commotion on account of the rent strike. He intends to 'finish' Srihari off; and to push the rent strike to a successful conclusion - not that he has any sympathy for the peasant householders. He is a dangerous man, as householders appreciate instinctively: a man whose laugh, careless and raucous, is like the lightning of a stormy night. They fear him, oppress him, give evidence against him to the police. 'So in their direst straits he does not look back. Their misfortune is his great delight. He laughs heartily'.[32]

Rural distinctions are thus clearly etched out by the social pattern of settlements in the countryside, and the differing links of these settlements with the junction town. The rural people perceive two basic distinctions in their society: the distinction between the gentry and the peasantry, and the distinction between the peasantry and the agrarian dependents. The divisions are not absolute. In the first place, a series of patron-client linkages and relationships of unequal interdependence fuse these divisions into an organic rural community. Secondly, the rural people perceive more minute divisions in their society in terms of technical agrarian categories which do not fit neatly into these broad divisions. The terms which occur most frequently in Banerjee's novels are, in descending order of rank, zamindar, patnidar, raiyat, bhagjotedar (share-cropper), *krishan* (bonded labourer paid in one third of the produce), *munish* (day labourer) and *mahindar* (farm servant). As will be seen in the chart below, these technical categories roughly coincide with certain broad ritual and economic divisions in rural society, but not in every detail. The high-caste gentry include raiyats in their lower ranks, but predominate among zamindars and patnidars. The caste peasantry are raiyats and bhagjotedars, but many bhagjotedars are untouchables. Below the level of bhagjotedar a man ceases to be a peasant. The krishan, the munish and the mahindar are untouchable agrarian dependents, but these lowest members of rural society shade off into the peasantry above them because many untouchables are share-croppers too. The bhagjotedar has an uncertain station in rural society, poised between peasant and agrarian dependent. Whether he is a peasant or an agrarian dependent seems to depend on whether he is a clean (or semi-clean) Sudra or an untouchable. This is because a share-cropper of clean Sudra caste is not unlikely to have a small strip of raiyati land, the inadequate income from which he has to supplement by share-cropping, whereas it is extremely unlikely that an untouchable would have a title even to the smallest strip. (These rural hierarchies are illustrated schematically on page 290.)

In view of these over-lappings, how do the rural people make out between gentry society and peasant society, and between peasant society and the stratum of agrarian dependents? Styles of consumption are as important as tenurial rights in making out the first distinction. The second distinction turns on differences in the possession of material means, such as land, implements of cultivation and homesteads; these differences are strengthened by varying degrees of ritual impurity of the body and of social habits.

*Rural Hierarchy*

| | | |
|---|---|---|
| Pure Castes | Zamindar<br>Patnidar | Gentry |
| Nabasakha | Raiyat<br>Bhagjotedar | Peasantry |
| Untouchables | Krishan<br>Munish<br>Mahindar | Agrarian Dependents |

The distinction between gentry and peasantry is not based solely on superior and inferior land rights, or higher and lower levels of wealth. The rich peasant may be far richer than the poor but genteel landlord. Sibnath Banerjee, the petty landlord hero of *Dhatri-devata*, seems to be perpetually in debt, while Srihari Ghosh, the rich peasant of *Ganadevata*, is a creditor and a grain monopolist who has the zamindar in his debt. The annual income of Sibnath Banerjee's estate does not exceed Rs.4000, but his house contains the buildings and installations essential to maintaining the state of a zamindar: a residence, an office, a household temple, an orchard, a flower garden, and a large tank. The same lordly style is reflected in the number of employees and dependents who fill these buildings. The Banerjee house is a small zamindar family and cannot afford to maintain hundreds of drones, widows and servants. But the house does maintain several servants, footmen and educated estate officials and has service lands assigned to palanquin bearers, priests, a drummer, a gardener and a hairdresser.[33] The house makes its power and authority felt among the subordinates. There is no hesitation in this - the gentry are the masters of the land. The disobedient headman of a mahal is promptly put in his place by Sibnath's formidable aunt, but when he makes a present of five rupees on a red silk handkerchief to the boy zamindar, he is sent off by his aunt with a pair of cloths, a scarf and a heavy meal, as befits the hospitality of the master's house.[34] The exercise of power is accompanied by a certain refinement which is considered necessary to the 'style'.

As Srihari Ghosh's wealth increases, he awakens to the importance of acquiring a style. But it is not a style that would identify him with the Kankana babus. His house undergoes improvements, but it is still not a 'pucca' building like those in Kankana. True, he gets two outcasted girls as mistresses, but they are employed in his own household as cooks. There is no question of keeping them in a garden house as dancing girls. The peasant fair that he organizes in connection with the Gajan festival is far removed in spirit from the theatre of the Kankana gentry. The rich peasant may acquire something else - a different type of education, culture and living style. Patterns of consumption are as important in establishing social distinctions in the countryside as levels of wealth.

To turn to the distinction between peasants and agrarian dependents, three crucial criteria - land, implements of cultivation, and homestead - emerge from Banerjee's novels. Differing rights over these material means coincide with varying degrees of ritual pollution to mark out the caste peasantry from the landless untouchables. The peasant proper is a raiyat, with an occupancy which is recorded in the zamindar's rent-roll. Ordinarily he would be a Sadgop or a Shaikh, and if he aspires to gentility he would employ a bhagjotedar, krishan, munish, or mahindar to plough his land. These are categories of agrarian dependents, except - as already noted - the bhagjotedar, who has an uncertain position at the lower edge of peasant society as a landless peasant. But he is still a peasant, albeit landless. Why? Because the bhagjotedar, unlike the krishan, the munish or the mahindar, owns the implements of cultivation. Since he supplies the plough, bullocks and seeds he takes autonomous decisions regarding cultivation, which is the essential characteristic of a peasant. The krishan, the munish and the mahindar are supplied the means of cultivation by the master, and the master therefore decides how much to plough, what to sow and which manure to apply. The untouchables supply the bulk of these categories of agrarian dependents, because few among them own the complete unit of two bullocks and a plough which would enable them to take land on share (*bhag*) from a master and to cultivate it in the manner they choose. In the whole of the Harijan hamlet of Sibkalipur, there are only five ploughs and four bullocks, out of which Satish Bauri has a complete unit of two bullocks and a plough. The other Bauris, who own incomplete units, enter into a crop-sharing arrangement with him known as *bhagato*, under which they can make use of his implements of cultivation to till other strips of land. Satish is thus an 'elder' within the Harijan community, a patron to other Bauris.[35] The crop-sharing arrangements, variously known as bhagato, *ganto*, etc., by which the rural poor pool their meagre implements of cultivation, ensure leadership within the community for the slightly privileged individual who owns more implements than his neighbours. He is, after all, a sort of peasant, while his kinsmen are bonded labourers.

But even such a fortunate untouchable is not a full member of the peasant community. A peasant (*chashi*), as Banerjee makes it clear, is a householder (*grihastha*), with a solid title to his homestead. Before the settlement operations in Birbhum, no untouchable had a title to the flimsy shack in which he lived. The householder used to assign living space on his own land to Bauri, Dom and Muchi families. The latter were endlessly grateful for this and became hereditary servants in the master's household. The settlement of 1924-32 gave them for the first time written documents conferring a right to the homestead. Before this - comments Tarashankar Banerjee - 'these men generation after generation simply could not conceive that they could own a piece of land on earth'.[36] Naturally such psychology deters the untouchables from claiming full membership of the community of cultivators. The peasants want their agrarian dependents to be in a state of mental subjection; and are alarmed when the untouchables propose, with the consent of their Sadgop leader Debu Ghosh, to go off to the junction town as mill hands. 'Don't do this son', the peasant elder, Harish Mandal, pleads with Debu Ghosh. 'No *munish*, no *mahindar*, will be available in the village. People will suffer greatly. We shall have to go, basketfuls of cowdung on our heads, to the field ourselves. Prevent them from going'.[37] The following scene, of untouchables and peasants going to the field, reveals almost unconsciously the distinctions in the community of cultivators.[38]

> The *krishans* are going to the field - bands of Bauri, Dom, Muchi and such other *shramik chashis*. They have only one cloth wrapped around their bodies. They are smoking the hookah and are carrying their

> scythes on the other hand. This is the season of harvesting. Most of the *chashi grihasthas* [peasant householders] of the village, who cultivate along side the *krishans* with their own hands, are also proceeding scythe in hand. They still obey the saying - 'works, makes others work, gets double' - this is to mean, those who work in the field themselves and work their *chashi majurs* get twice the ordinary crop in their cultivation. Only three or four people do not take physical part in the cultivation. Harenra Ghoshal is a Brahman, Jagan Ghosh is not only a Kayastha but also a doctor, Debu Ghosh is the pundit of the primary school; Srihari Ghosh has recently become a high born Sadgop and is the owner of many properties. Only these men do not work with their own hands in the process of cultivation.

The peasant householders, a group apart from the untouchables while proceeding to the field of cultivation, themselves fall into several categories. These types cannot even be called categories in the full sense, because differences are individual rather than anything else. By exploring these individual types, Banerjee reveals the diversity of the peasant world. It is not a world that can be neatly classified into rich, middle and poor peasants. Banerjee's peasant world is more complex, peopled by all sorts of cultivators: dominant grain-lending peasants such as Srihari Ghosh and Daulat Shaikh, who eventually establish control over much of the production, storage and lending and marketing of grain in their respective villages; substantial peasant elders, such as Harish Mandal and Bhabesh Pal, who submit to these grain monopolists in the end; sturdy independent yeomen, such as Raham Shaikh and Tinkari Pal, who are finally broken by their richer grain-lending neighbours of the same peasant caste; genteel tenants, such as Debu Ghosh, Jagan Ghosh and Haren Ghoshal, who do not hold the plough, who have some education in a largely illiterate society and who naturally spring to leadership of the tenant movement against the Kankana babus and their peasant allies; and under-tenants and share-croppers, such as Gadai and Satish, who shade off into the lowest category of agrarian dependents. Central to Banerjee's conception of rural change is the growing concentration of village produce in the hands of grain-lending mahajans, and the emergence of a popular rural movement against this tendency towards growing indebtedness and land transfer. But the tenant movement is riven from within by communal tensions between Hindus and Muslims, and by the divergent interests of different categories of tenants. Gadai, the share-cropper, moved by rumours of new tenancy legislation, asks at a meeting of the Praja Samiti: 'Is it true that the *korfa* (undertenancy) will become a right? Even the *thika bhag* (contract share-cropping)' - Jagan Ghosh, the quack doctor who leads the Praja Samiti, interrupts him rudely, 'Come on. What will be left to men if *korfa* and *bhag* are recognized as rights? Go dream about it. All share-cropping land will become yours'.[39]

Economic distinctions are thus extremely minute in rural society. Cultural differences play a major role in consolidating these numerous economic divisions into the triple classification of rural society which appears in Tarashankar Banerjee's works. His fiction, moreover, shows that at the base of the cultural gulf separating gentry, peasants and untouchables lie divergent sexual mores and family structures. Gentry culture is to be distinguished from peasant culture, and peasant culture from untouchable culture, by a wide range of factors among which the organization of relationships between men and women is the most fundamental.

## 3

The rural economy is integrated by a series of lateral relationships between individuals belonging to the same position in the productive organization, and by a series of vertical relationships between individuals belonging to different levels of that organization. Peasants form by their mutual relationships a community among themselves, and are related in a particular way to the gentry above and the untouchables below. Complementing this system of economic relationships is a parallel system of relations between men and women which may be classified on the same lines - lateral and vertical. At different levels of society as defined in terms of property and income, men and women relate to each other in different ways. Again, across these levels they relate to each other in ways which help define an entire social system of relations between men and women. The availability of material means, of property and income, helps define at different levels the range and characteristics of inter-sex relationships, and also structures these relationships across the levels along certain predictable lines. Not that the spontaneous impulses of men and women can ever be 'structured' in a ridgidly deterministic fashion. It is a sphere of human relationships in which individuality is extremely important. But to a certain extent, the boundaries of possibilities in the relations between men and women can be traced in Tarashankar Banerjee's fiction along those lateral and vertical lines. By carefully tracing these lines, the reader comes to discover a criss-crossing pattern of inter-sex relationships which knits the entire rural community into a single social system. At the top of this system is the enforced deprivation of gentry women, bound by countless restrictions which govern their physical and emotional lives; and at the bottom, the ferocious exploitation of untouchable women by the higher castes, and the decreasing force of artificially-fostered inhibitions down the caste hierarchy.

The varying pattern of relations between men and women fosters at different levels of rural society distinct sub-cultures; and these in turn consolidate the more minute economic divisions into three consolidated social strata. Gentry culture, peasant culture and untouchable culture are integrating social phenomena which impose uniformities over the minute divisions and innumerable differences within the diverse worlds of the gentry, the peasantry and the agrarian dependents. Economic survival and sexual reproduction, the two fundamental instincts of humanity, govern the actions of Banerjee's characters at different levels of rural society. But the reproductive instinct, which he uncovers beneath the formation of different rural sub-cultures, must not be interpreted narrowly. Libido, in the wider Freudian sense of the vitality and life force inspiring creative human endeavours, incorporates a whole range of human relations and human emotions, including, for instance, its logical corollary, the human response to the inevitable fact of death. Banerjee shows that the distinct sub-cultures within rural society are under-pinned by myths, religions and superstitions that vary widely. The supernatural orders conceived by men and women change along with the material orders at successive levels of the caste hierarchy. The rural culture and the associated human emotions portrayed by Tarashankar Banerjee have many dimensions. Even so, in a caste society so profoundly dominated by notions of ritual pollution, rules governing contact between bodies and objects, and men and women, exercise a pervasive influence. The emotional and daily lives of Banerjee's rural characters are profoundly affected by these rules of touch.

To illustrate these rural cultural and emotional themes, let us first look at the characteristics of gentry culture - depicted in detail in *Dhatridevata* - and trace it to its emotional and physical roots. The gentry, as we have seen, are distinguished from the rest of rural society by their living style. At the root of the style lies a notion which governs their behaviour within and outside the home: honour. The life of a gentry family is geared to maintain this notional thing because its entire position in rural society - the respect it claims - rests on its ability to preserve it. Those who cannot retain it are degraded. The rural poor have no honour to maintain. The richer members of the peasantry, fired by social ambition, aspire to it, but not being able to achieve quite the same style, look on with envious admiration. Daulat Shaikh, a rich peasant of Kusumpur who aspired to higher social status, is full of admiration for the Mukherjee babus of Kankana, who, having made their pile in trade, have risen to the top social position at the expense of other Kankana families:

> At one time they saluted the Roy babus and the Banerjee babus, took the dust of their feet. Then again we saw them earning lakhs of rupees. The head of the Mukherjee family became the principal man. He then used to sit in the chair, and seated the Roy babus on the cot! One has to maintain one's prestige.[40]

Keen competition for honour and precedence divide gentry families, and paradoxically it is this very rivalry - the fight over points of precedence in a narrow rural setting - which unites them as a class. But the gentry, by virtue of their education and responsiveness to the new ideals that stir nationalist Bengal at the turn of the century, are capable of lifting over these petty rivalries for precedence and of uniting in the defence of a highly romanticized notion of their country conceived as the Mother. A new notion of honour, a new notion of manhood, make themselves felt in the life of the rural gentry during the period of the swadeshi movement, when the action of *Dhatridevata* begins.

A struggle between two contending notions of 'honour' imparts social significance to the emotional conflicts in *Dhatridevata*. The aunt and the estate manager want to see the young Sibnath grow up as a powerful zamindar who would uphold the prestige of the family. His mother, on the other hand, wants him to be a highly-educated and patriotic young man who would make sacrifices for the nation and for the poor. She is careful to see that he does not inherit the faults which run in the typical landlord tradition of the family - pride, harshness, dissipation and love of luxury.[41] The new patriotism is a romantic patriotism; and the new notion of manhood - of the young patriotic who would brave all dangers and walk on alone when everybody has abandoned him - is a romantic notion of manhood.

*Dhatridevata* conveys the power of the romantic urge, so natural to adolescents waking to manhood, among the new youth of Bengal which the gentry create out of their younger generation in course of the anti-partition agitation. The psychological aspects of this urge become clearer as Banerjee explores the motivations behind Sibnath's patriotic actions. One begins to appreciate the critical importance of adolescence, of awakening manhood, behind the romantic patriotism of the swadeshi youth. The tensions that pull young Sibnath and his wife apart drive him on to a dangerous course of revolutionary terrorism. In love of woman and in love of country, Banerjee sees the same restless, unsatisfied, romantic urge. Romanticism permeates the culture of the Bengali gentry at the turn of the century and makes them emotionally a community apart from the broader mass of the uneducated rural population, who do not respond to those romantic sentiments and aspirations that come to constitute the new patriotism. The following passage,[42] in which Sibnath pictures to himself a future of glory and self-sacrifice, gives an insight into the romantic mentality which fused love and patriotism to create a new type of young man from the ranks of the rural Bengali gentry:

> In his imagination, his aunt cries for him, his mother gazes with tearful eyes at the road, Gouri is left behind with a sea of tears locked inside her heart - and he walks ahead: the road is dangerous, the sky overcast, the light fading, the darkness profound, on two sides a thick forest, the way so enveloped by darkness that he cannot feel himself, has no sense of front or back, yet he moves on. At the end of the dark lies the illuminated cremating ground where stands Kali the Mother - 'What Mother has become'.[43]

The inter-personal relationships within Sibnath's family show some of the unique characteristics of the social structure of the gentry. The preservation of gentry status requires the acceptance by their women of a kind of deprivation which is not enforced at the lower levels of rural society. Highly restrictive rules of behaviour between men and women add to the complexity of their emotional life. At the turn of the century, child marriage is universally practised among the gentry to bring up women in a proper state of meekness and submission. An extensive code of prohibitions limits interaction between young husbands and their wives during daytime. Ideas and aspirations regarding fidelity play a vital role in structuring gentry society. There is no escape from widowhood for gentry women, either by law or by social custom; and widows form an element in gentry families which impart to them an unusual structure, giving rise to a type of emotional conflict which is not to be seen at the lower levels of rural life.

The uncompromising struggle between aunt and wife over the possession of Sibnath - the theme on which the dramatic action of *Dhatridevata* turns - contains revealing insights into this type of emotional conflict. Sibnath's aunt, Shailaja Devi, is a widowed gentlewoman, who depends for emotional sustenance on the boy. Her deprivation expresses itself through a sexual jealousy which poisons Sibnath's relationship with his wife. To save the honour of his aunt, he cuts off relations with his wife. As Sibnath grows up, his yearning for his wife increases, but for the sake of his aunt he does nothing to bring her back. It is inconceivable in a peasant family that a young man should banish his wife to defend the honour of his widowed aunt. The readiness to accept sexual deprivation in deferance to claims of honour and gentility give a distinct colour to the inner life of the gentry family. Sibnath is so hurt by his aunt's jealousy that he imagines he would withdraw entirely from wordly life. 'Let Gouri live as a nun, he too would spend his life as an ascetic'.[44] Only the young member of a gentry family would feel and think like this. He would also tend to expect the strict adherence of his wife to the same ideal. When the estate manager urges him to bring Gouri back, he replies: 'It's her fault. She went away from our house of her own motion. Did anyone drive her away? When Rama went to the forest, Sita accompanied him of her own free will. Many people tried to dissuade her, was she dissuaded?' The elderly manager cannot check his smile, and the young man says with dignity: 'You are laughing, but that is the ideal of a Hindu girl'.[45]

His 'ideal of a Hindu girl', however, is the ideal of the gentry - a means by which the gentry distinguish themselves from the rest of society; the lower levels of Hindu society follow different standards of sexual conduct. There is something new in the conception of the relationship between man and wife that Sibnath expresses. Even one generation back, nothing would have been thought of a landlord maintaining a mistress in his garden house.[46] The new conception expressed by Sibnath - the notion of purity - distinguishes the gentry still further from the lower classes, for the latter are not affected by the underlying notions behind the changing standards of gentry behaviour. The notions of purity, self-denial and honour are tinged with the romanticism of the age.

Romanticism is fostered by the inner structure of the gentry family, by the physical deprivation that the gentry adopt voluntarily under their code of restrictions to maintain honour. But there is more to the inner life of the gentry than romanticism. Sexual jealousy plays a dominating role amongst men and women who act under so many restrictions. Contending disappointments are numerous, and each relationship is charged with an explosive sensitivity which usually - but not always - manages to cloak with good taste the fundamental conflict of wills over material points which assume so naked and crude a shape in non-genteel families. When sexual jealousy is added to these ingredients - and it is bound to arise in a society bound by so many rules - the family, usually so tight in its structure, begins to disintegrate. To maintain the honour of their family and the purity of their lineage, the gentry, especially their women, pay a price. Peasant communities aspiring to social responsibility seek to adopt some of the sexual prohibitions of the gentry, especially child marriage and the instituion of widowhood. But the peasant family is so structured by its work cycle as to preclude dependents who do not contribute to its income, and thus widowhood, when enforced, is invested with a structurally-different role. Hence a widowed aunt of the type of Shailaja Devi does not appear among the peasant families portrayed by Taranshankar Banerjee in *Ganadevata*. Ranga-didi, the typical old widow in *Ganadevata*, lives on her own. She supports herself by selling milk and by lending small amounts of money to neighbours. The very existence of the concept of widowhood, however, distinguishes the Nabasakha castes of Sibkalipur from the Bauris and the Muchis living in the hamlet below the main village. Lax as the morality of peasant women might seem to the gentry, there is a world of difference between them and untouchable women. Compare, for instance, two young women of the village: the blacksmith's wife, Padma, and the tanner's daughter, Durga. The comparison makes it evident that the emotional and physical role of womanhood undergoes important changes from peasant society to untouchable society.

Padma is childless. Not having dealt with the mess made by babies, she suffers from the mental disorder known as the touch complex (*suchibayu*), an abnormal state in which a woman is compulsively preoccupied with how to remain ritually clean. Such a disorder is unknown among the untouchables, who are by definition unclean from birth. Widows in gentry households are the most vulnerable to this disease, which in their case is most commonly the reaction to the suppression of bodily desires which cannot be fulfilled. In this type of psychology, things and persons pollute at touch, and the desire to avoid touch is compulsive. It is a disease which can appear only among the ritually-clean castes of Hindu society. Padma is a woman of the Kamar caste, which belongs to the Nabasakha group, whose water is acceptable to the higher castes. She suffers acutely from the touch complex and at the slightest touch with a polluting object, takes a dip in the pond.

Implicit in this abnormal sensitivity to touch, bred by a society profoundly affected by notions of ritual purity governing the bodily existence, is a stricter mode of sexual conduct. By observing it a woman of clean caste prevents her descent to all the degrading things to which untouchable girls are habitually subjected. At the root of the rift between the blacksmith and his wife, and his liaison with the tanner's daughter, is his physically less-satisfying relationship with Padma, caused by her touch complex. The novelist, who is explicit on this point, sets out in the following passage the nuances which distinguish Padma's sexual behaviour from that of her rival:

> Padma, even with her healthy young body, could not give him the satisfaction which Durga had given him. She had a load of metal amulets on her bosom. It always caused him pain. In her absorption with

> ritual performances, she kept him off like an untouchable. The excess of maternal care in her love for him caused him frustration. She never sprang to his breast with the wild abandon of Durga. Having worked before the fire all day, he would drink a bit in the evening on coming home. But his pleasant intoxication evaporated as soon as he stood before his wife in that state of body and mind.[47]

The touch complex, by inhibiting Padma's sexual behaviour, makes her less attractive than her untouchable rival who has no such complex. But in a paradoxical way it makes Padma Kamrani more attractive to other men than Durga Muchini. The touch complex implies less easy access; and this inflames the desire of Srihari Ghosh. His newly-won respectability precludes a continuation of his 'low' association with the tanner's daughter, but a blacksmith's wife - as his patron Das snidely points out - is not low association. Durga is to be had for money by any one, and with his new fastidiousness the ennobled peasant wants something less easily accessible. Significantly the mental image that Srihari has of the blacksmith's wife is that of a tall woman with a sharp axe on her hand and a cruel smile playing on her lips. The weapon stands as an actual as well as symbolic barrier between him and the object of his desire, its steel reflecting the sunlight and blinding him for a moment. The blacksmith's wife keeps it by her side after being abandoned by her husband, because she is afraid of being reduced to the state of the tanner's daughter - the proverbial 'fate of the Hari and misfortune of the Dom'.

True she is driven one night by her subconscious desire to the house of Debu Ghosh. But her love for him is nursed in secret, whereas Durga proclaims it openly. When Srihari Ghosh proposes to assemble the Nabasakha panchayat to excommunicate Debu Ghosh for his alleged misconduct with both women, their reactions show characteristic differences. 'What will happen to you?' Padma asks Durga. 'Me?' Durga burst out laughing, 'I shall beat a drum and dance at the centre of the assembly. I shall recount all my affairs with men. I shall have a song composed by brother Satish. I shall not spare the name of Brahman or Kayastha, of zamindar or mahajan. Srihari Ghosh's activities will be the refrain of the song'. Seeing Durga laugh, Padma wishes she could be as wildly abandoned before the panchayat.

But such conduct is out of the question for a peasant woman of the Nabasakha group, and she therefore imagines herself going to the assembly, removing the veil from her face and saying in a clear voice: 'The pundit is a good man, not like you. His eyes are not so full of the dark smudge of desire as yours. Don't go into a huddle about me. I shall go away - no, I am leaving the village right now. I shall not live on anyone's charity'.[48] The last is a reference to her material dependence on Debu Ghosh. She hates being dependent on him and would rather that he take her. The peasant woman has her pride. The same pride which makes her body inaccessible to other men makes physical rejection so unbearable that she goes to Srihari immediately after being rejected by Debu. Debu does not allow Durga to come any closer, but she has no grouse on this score, because she has given her body to too many men to feel like Padma. When a woman, who by social training is acutely conscious of the inviolability of her body, breaks the inhibitions to go to a man and is rejected by him, vengeance at whatever cost is her natural reaction.

The two women differ markedly in one other respect: the desire for child and family. Both are childless. Durga has no desire for a child, whereas Padma is obsessed with it. The structure of living conditions and social possibilities is so differnt for the two women that even supposedly fundamental instincts are altered from one person to another. Durga has no desire for a child because at her level in society conditions are so fluid as to smother the emotional need for a stable family life. But the peasant woman knows, and desires, a 'household'. The maternal instinct develops when a woman has a household. The childless Padma picks up any child that she meets in the street. Durga, who is also childless, rebukes her for this: 'Why do you add to the trouble when you have no child of your own?'[49] A child is a burden to a woman who cannot conceive of a stable family life. But for one who experiences and desires family life, lack of a child disturbs the mental balance.

Padma's austerities are fundamentally an attempt to repress the unfulfilled desires of her barren life. Her desires take the form of a dream which no untouchable woman is able to entertain. Padma wants not merely food and sexual satisfaction - she wants to be an Annapurna, a bounteous goddess who fills the plate with rice. She wants to serve it plentifully on the plate of a man, and her child by him.[50] These dreams are denied to a tanner's daughter degraded to the lowest level of rural life. At the end of the novel, the peasant woman's dreams are fulfilled. Coming back from gaol after the civil disobedience movement, Debu encounters her in a railway station with her second husband - a Christian - and a three-year-old child. Material opportunities for peasant women are such as to permit the fulfilment of their simple dream of household, husband and child. But not for the women of the untouchable castes. Women at all levels of society are deprived. But there are different levels of deprivation for women in different levels of life.

It would, however, be misleading to think that Banerjee paints the life of rural degraded exclusively in the dark colours of deprivation. They have an inner life within their community which is not governed by the untouchability which characterizes their relationship with the higher castes. Banerjee's insight into the life of untouchable men and women within their community is revealed in his chronicle of the Kahar community of Hansuli Bank. In this novel he does not ignore the economic subjection of the Kahars, and the sexual exploitation of their women. But he also shows that Kahar men and Kahar women enjoy compensations in their mutual relations within the community. Living close to nature, they enjoy greater freedom in relation to each other than men and women in the Sadgop village of Janal, or in the rural town of Chandanpur. In Banerjee's portrait of Kahar life and love, a certain romantic nostalgia characteristic of the gentry attitude to more 'natural' forms of existence can be easily detected. But he has an eye for detail which makes it a valuable chronicle of life of an isolated rural community, degraded in relation to their Sadgop masters but free among themselves.

The world of the gentry includes the high school and the college, and a widespread network of education, service, professions, business and landed property. Even the narrower world of the peasantry includes the village *pathsala* or *maktab*, which imparts the rudimentary knowledge of arithmetic and alphabet essential to the grain-lending and grain-marketing carried on by the righer peasants who control a produce surplus. But the hamlet of the Kahars under the dark shadows of the bamboo forest knows no form of instruction. Kahar culture is an illiterate culture. It is dominated by ignorance, superstition and an inability to trace the connections between physical phenomena by means of reasoning. The supernatural world of the Kahars extends far and wide. Ghosts and spirits lurk at every corner. The Chandanpur babus, and even the Janal Sadgops, laugh at their beliefs and superstitions.[51] Their community god, Baba Thakur, has no place in the Hindu pantheon. But the Hindu divine order integrates them by assigning a place at the bottom to the Kahar worshippers of Kala Rudra, a form of Shiva whom the untouchables are allowed to worship at the Charak festival. There is a clear hierarchy in the divine order conceived by the Kahars: their own community god, Baba Thakur, is a disciple of Kala Rudra, a god of the Hindu pantheon honoured by their Sadgop masters at Janal. Beyond a point, however, their entry into the Hindu divine order is forbidden. The gods and goddesses worshipped by the Chandanpur babus do not accept the homage of the Kahars. Even their gaze from a distance pollutes the offerings to these highest members of the divine community, and they fearfully avoid the temples which house the gods at Chandanpur.[52]

But while Baba Thakur is undoubtedly degraded in the company of these high gods and goddesses, he is free to savour joys denied to them. The characteristics of this community god offer a clue to the life of the Kahars within their own community. He eats meat and drinks wine, a habit inconceivable among the gods and goddesses of Chandanpur, or even for the less respectable Kala Rudra. When the Kahars hold a funeral service for a killed viper which has since been identified as the Baba's mount, they offer him a lamb, two goats, several ducks and several jars of liquor in order to propitiate him. At the end of the service, the headman distributes the sanctified meat and the sanctified liquor among the Kahars. The men and women sit down to drink together. The old woman who has identified the snake as Baba's mount dances and sings after having drunk three cups of liquor. A young married woman resolves, under the 'combined intoxication of love and drink', to leave her asthmatic husband and to move into her lover's house.[53] Kahar religious festivities are directly linked to physical enjoyments. Men and women drink, dance and move off in pairs on festival nights, stressing the physical aspects of the festivities with a frankness which is not to be found in the religious festivals of the gentry, who carefully push this element out of sight in their complex ceremonies. It is not that the Brahman gentry of Chandanpur or the Sadgop peasants of Janal are not attracted by the joys of drinking with women and dancing with them. But they have to purchase these delights from the women of Hansuli Bank. There is no question of drinking and dancing with their own women, which would pollute the latter and destroy the purity of their lineages.

Degraded though they are to the bottom of their society, the Kahars of Hansuli Bank are partially compensated by their freer and more natural living style. The highly-complicated arrangements and elaborate rules by which the Chandanpur babus and the Janal Sadgops control the expression of natural instincts, do not operate among the Kahars. Divorce and remarriage, known as Sanga, are commonly practised. Women who escape from their homes think nothing of leaving their children behind. Families dissolve at a stroke. There is no property to inherit, and therefore no lineage to maintain. The community lives perpetually on the edge of natural disaster - of flood, fire and famine. In such insecure and fluid conditions, family relationships do not get a chance to coalesce into tightly-knit structures. Legend - as recounted by the old woman Suchand - has it that in the great flood that engulfed the Kahars two generations ago, the young wife of an old man plunged straight into the flood water from the tree on which she had taken shelter at night with her husband and swam to the next tree and her lover, with whom she was discovered in the morning.[54]

But that is not to say that the Kahars are a lawless community in these matters, as the Chandanpur babus and the mandals of Janal would assume. They have their own rules of pollution and it is forbidden for their women to go and work in the railway factory of Chandanpur. The headman, Banwari, refuses to shelter the women defiled by the line mechanics and the construction workers.

> If there is an affair with kinsmen or with the Janal Sadgops or the Chandanpur babus, it is tolerated. Among kinsmen one man eats another man's left-over, and vice versa. They have, moreover, always eaten the left-overs of the Janal Sadgops and the Chandanpur babus. But one must draw the line at aliens of uncertain caste. Those girls who escape with them are the left-overs of the trash can.[55]

Such restrictions are essential for the maintenance of the identity of the community. It is the reason why the headman is so strict in enforcing the prohibition against work on the railway line, though girls are permitted to work in the households of the Chandanpur gentry. When the Kahar community is uprooted from Hansuli Bank and reduced to a labour gang at Chandanpur, these restrictions disappear and the Kahars loose their traditional identity.

The name given by these rural folk to the human emotion of love is *rang*, which in its literal sense means colour. The manifestation of this emotion among the Kahars, as implied in the name they have given to it, is characterized by certain features which distinguish their social and psychological behaviour from that of the Janal peasants and the Chandanpur gentry. In the first place, it is marked by a certain directness of expression. Nayan's wife, Pakhi, protests instinctively when the old woman of the community recommends that the young and handsome dare-devil, Karali, should be punished for his violation of the community norms.

> They feel no shame in these matters. If they love, they cannot conceal it for anything - shame, fear, or the disapproval of neighbours. The Kahars do not have it in them, they cannot do it. It is for this reason that from time to time a possessed young girl of the Kahars leaves her home to take to the way, like the flooded Kapai.[56]

When Karali turns his attention to the young wife of the headman, Pakhi turns violent, and after hitting him on the head with a sharp instrument, goes and hangs herself. Violence of passion and violence of jealousy mark the affair from start to finish. Kahar men and women are not trained, like the Chandanpur babus, to conceal their passions. Banwari, the headman of the community, is amazed to see the Mukherjee babus and the Chatterjee babus, rivals and enemies in Chandanpur for more than a generation, exchange social visits and participate in functions. Karali, who has acquired the psychological characteristic of concealment as a railway worker in Chandanpur, invites Banwari for a drink. Untrained in the school of hypocrisy, the headman brushes aside the invitation and rushes out to kill the young man when he finds proof of the latter's involvement with his wife.

A second feature of the manifestation of love among the Kahars is the predominance of physical force that arises from the violence of passion and jealousy. Nayan tries to bite Pakhi's nose off and gets a thrashing from

Karali which might well have been fatal but for Banwari's intervention. The women stand round and watch the fight with dilated pupils. Banwari himself is involved with Kaloshashi, the wife of the Atpoure headman, Param. When the headman of the Atpoures challenges the headman of the Beharas and suffers defeat in battle, the bloody victor goes straight to his lover.

> Kalo Bou put her hand on his body, and started. 'What is this? Blood?
> 'Yes, he is lying in the field'.
> Kalo Bou showed no sign of disturbance. She gazed for some time in silent admiration, then she said,
> 'But wait, wash away the blood first'.[57]

Banwari is not so fortunate in his second, and mortal, encounter with Karali. The younger man not only takes the defeated and dying headman's wife, but also the headship of the Kahar community. Physical strength, sexual conquest and headship of the community are closely inter-related in the action of the novel.

It also highlights a third feature of the red colour of fun, as the Kahars characterize love. It is the absence of the romantic longing and spiritual abstractions that we have noted in the manifestation of gentry love in *Dhatridevata*. The Kahars live too close to the soil to develop abstractions meant to divert natural instincts through artificial channels to sustain a complex culture based on 'honour'. Physical passion expresses itself overtly in the red colour of fun, and there is no far-reaching system of rules of interpersonal behaviour to sublimate or suppress the sexual instinct. In these conditions of interaction between men and women, love does not develop the form of romantic attachment, though undoubtedly the novelist himself looks on it from a romantic angle. There is no question of physical deprivation in their case, and it is this that sharpens the emotional and romantic longing which the gentry emphasize in their notions of love. That is not to say that the Kahar way of love lacks an emotional content. Banwari's affair with Kaloshashi is the finest portrayal of love in the novel. But the emotional intensity of the affair derives from the physical deprivation imposed on the couple by Banwari's self-imposed duty, as a headman, to keep off the wife of another man. The occasions for sexual union between the two are rare and overshadowed by a sense of sin which sharpens its emotional content. The affair is, however, unusual. More typical is the violent passion of Pakhi for Karali.

The relatively free love among the Kahars is accompanied by the sexual servitude of their women to men of higher castes. The two aspects are organically related in a caste-bound rural society. Having no honour to maintain at the cost of their women, the Kahars have no need of the artificial sexual restraints by which the gentry preserve the purity of their lineage. By the same logic, however, their dishonoured women are exposed to sexual exploitation by the men of the higher castes. The Kahar community have lived under economic and sexual servility from the very time they settled in Hansuli Bank under the patronage of the indigo planters. The planter sahibs took their women - a fact still attested to by the grey eyes that many Kahars have. The sahibs were succeeded by the Janal Sadgops and, subsequently, the Chandanpur babus and their footmen. Prostitution - euphemistically known as 'income of wife' or 'income of daughter' - is a recognized means of livelihood within the Kahar community. At night young men come from Janal and Chandanpur, whistling at the windows of the Kahar girls and throwing clods of earth to draw their attention. Mothers do not object, nor even mothers-in-law. But a furore breaks out when a husband catches on to what is happening. But the Kahars hold their own women guilty, especially if they 'defile' Brahmans. The young men of Chandanpur are Brahmans. 'How could Kahar women absorb their touch? They burst apart under their own sin'.[58] The divine order of Hinduism, and its complex system of rules governing touch, instil into them a passive acceptance of their servile economic and sexual status.

## 4

The three major novels of rural life by Tarashankar Banerjee which we have analysed above span vertically all the levels of society in a rural locality of the Rarh area in the period stretching from the swadeshi movement to the second world war. The innumerable sketches of human relationships scattered through the pages of these long novels add up slowly to a total historical view of the social divisions within this rural locality, and at the same time provide a connected picture of the vertical ties of interest and sentiment which fuse these divisions into an organic rural-local community. Banerjee proceeds in his analysis by instinct and observation - using the spontaneous mental categories of the people of the locality - and, fortunately for the historian who looks in his novels for source material, is not unduly preoccupied with the 'scientific' identification and use of rural categories. While proceeding in this manner, the creative novelist and observer of human relationships throws light on obscure psychological and cultural dimensions of rural distinctions which would not be uncovered by an exclusive preoccupation with patterns of land ownership and land use. He leads his readers into areas of the mind - and of fundamental human instincts - which are ordinarily beyond the reach of the scientific investigator of social and historical phenomena.

The highly complex but unitary pattern of rural culture is traced back by the novelist to variations of two basic motifs - survival and reproduction - which manifest themselves through a series of economic and sexual relationships demarcating different levels of culture within his rural locality. Relations between producers and consumers, and between men and women, combine to create an inter-dependent, hierarchical social order which is unequal but tightly knit at the same time. The fundamental lines of demarcation, in the eyes of the constituent members of the social order themselves, run between the high-caste gentry and the caste peasants, and between the caste peasants and the untouchable agrarian dependents. The specific terms and categories by which these broad classifications are indicated include, in top rank, Brahmans, Kayasthas, zamindars, patnidars and babus; in the middle rank, Nabasakha, Sadgops, Shaikhs, mandals, chashis and bhagjotedars; in the lowest rank, Bagdis, Bauris, Muchis, Doms, harijans, munishes, mahindars, krishans and chashi majurs. These terms themselves indicate a wide range of differences within each category. But each category is knit by a certain cultural uniformity and distinction. Each has a culture of its own, or rather, a sub-culture subsumed within an over-arching rural culture. The pattern of physical settlements in the countryside mark out these distinctions. The basic constituent elements of a rural locality, as viewed by the novelist, are the large and prosperous gentry village, the village inhabited by the caste peasantry and the untouchable hamlet, with a junction town on the periphery of the locality, mediating between it and the outside world. The gentry, peasant and untouchable settlements, however wide their cultural gap, form in relation to the external world a rural-local unit in the novels under discussion. Chandanpur, Janal and Bansbadi form a distinct unit in *Hansuli Banker Upakatha*, so do Kankana, Mahagram, Siokalipur, Kusumpur and Dekhuria in *Ganadevata*. Differences of property and income as amongst these distinct settlements within the rural locality - and of access through the junction town to educational and market opportunities - define a highly-differentiated material order which is integrated by ties of inter-dependence and patron-client linkages among people at different stations of life.

On reading Banerjee's novels, however, one is struck by how many more dimensions there are to these distinctions and gradations. The very quality of the life experience seems to vary from one level of society to another. What the historian and the social scientist tend to overlook in their preoccupation with abstract notions like class and status, the novelist - by the very nature of his art - cannot miss: that men and women are not just reference points in a system of abstract notions, but are made of flesh and blood, experience physical joys and mental sufferings and are deeply involved in the manner their bodies and minds interact with one another. The nature of this involvement expresses itself in markedly different ways at different levels of society, defining a sexual and cultural hierarchy that underpins the differentiated material order. The bodily and emotional existence of men and women possesses characteristics unique to each settlement within the rural locality. These differences in the inner life of each group - especially in the structure of the family at each level - define particular ways in which the higher and lower ranks of the rural-local community relate to one another. Sexual deprivation at the top and sexual exploitation at the bottom - aspects logically related to each other - integrate an entire social system based on hierarchy, complementing and buttressing the material differences arising from the production and distribution of crops. The more complicated its rules governing the outward expression of the basic physical impulses, the higher is the position of a social group on the caste scale of ritual purity. The more deprived its women, the greater its 'honour'. Conversely, the wider the gap between the laid-down rules of ritual pollution and the actual conditions of interaction between men and women, the lower the position of the group down the caste scale, and the greater the exposure of its women to sexual aggression of men from the 'cleaner' ranks.

## *NOTES*

Ray, 'The rural world of Tarashankar Banerjee: social divisions and psychological cross-currents'

Comments by Ashin Dasgupta, Lakshmi Subramanian, Suranjan Das and Ranjit and Kumkum Bhattacharya helped me greatly in writing this essay.

1. For a summary of the debate, Neil Charlesworth, 'The Russian Stratification Debate and India', *Modern Asian Studies*, February 1979; also Eric Stokes, *The Peasant and the Raj* (Delhi 1978).
2. See Louis Dumont, *Homo Hierarchicus* (Chicago 1970).
3. Ronald B. Inden, *Marriage and Rank in Bengali Culture* (California 1976).
4. Andre Beteille, *Studies in Agrarian Social Structure* (Delhi 1974).
5. Tarashankar Banerjee, *Tarashankar Rachanavali*, vol.I, Foreword by Suniti Kumar Chatterjee.
6. Tarashankar Banerjee, *Amar Sahitya Jivana*, 1st book (Calcutta V.S. 1360), p.126.
7. Ibid., pp.129-30.
8. Ibid., pp.27-8.
9. Ibid., pp.18-50.
10. Government of Bengal, *Final Report on the Survey and Settlement Operations in the District of Birbhum 1924-42* by Rai Bijay Behari Mukharji Bahadur (Alipore 1937), p.18.
11. Ibid., p.59.
12. Ibid., p.67.
13. Ibid., p.71.
14. Ibid., p.13.
15. I have used the 13th printing of the 1st edition (Calcutta 1939).
16. *Ganadevata*, a single work, has two parts: *Chandimandap* and *Panchagram*, but it is the first which has come to be known more specifically as *Ganadevata*. *Chandimandap*'s first edition is dated Calcutta 1943. I have used the following editions: *Ganadevata*, 2nd ed., 1943, and *Panchagram*, 2nd ed., undated.
17. The first edition of *Hansuli Banker Upakatha* is dated Calcutta 1948. I have used the second edition, also dated 1948. The title means 'The Tale of the Hairpin Bend'.

18. Thus Aniruddha Karmakar (blacksmith) holds 13 bighas of land which he cultivates through a *bhagjotedar* and sometimes himself. *Ganadevata*, pp.167,256.
19. *Panchagram*, p.167.
20. Ibid., pp.106.174.
21. *Ganadevata*, pp.2-4.
22. These identifications were provided by Tarashankar Banerjee's brother Parvati Shankar Banerjee, at an interview he kindly gave me at Labpur on 16 August 1980.
23. *Hansuli Banker Upakatha*, pp.135,232-3.
24. Ibid., p.135.
25. Ibid., pp.134-5.
26. Ibid., pp.431-53.
27. Ibid., pp.26,94-5.
28. Ibid., p.438.
29. These identifications are based on my visit to Labpur on 16 August 1980, as well as incidental references in Banerjee's *My Literary Life* and *Memories of My Times*.
30. *Panchagram*, pp.66,73,109.
31. *Ganadevata*, p.27.
32. *Panchagram*, pp.70.90.
33. *Dhatridevata*, pp.1,6-8,18,25,33,37,39,43,117.
34. Ibid., pp.14-15.
35. *Panchagram*, pp.277-8,285-7.
36. Ibid., p.289.
37. Ibid., p.288.
38. *Ganadevata*, p.138.
39. Ibid., p.287.
40. *Panchagram*, pp.29-30.
41. *Dhatridevata*, p.22.
42. Ibid., pp.119-20.
43. A reference to the image of Kali, embodying the motherland, in the secret monastery of the sannyasis in Bankim Chandra Chatterjee's novel, *Anandamath*.
44. *Dhatridevata*, p.127.
45. Ibid., p.129.
46. Ibid., p.153.
47. *Ganadevata*, pp.251-2.
48. *Panchagram*, pp.101-2.
49. *Ganadevata*, p.130.
50. *Panchagram*, p.197.
51. *Hansuli Banker Upakatha*, pp.128,152,296,298, 359-60, 364.
52. Ibid., pp.178,205,206,231.
53. Ibid., pp.65-76.
54. Ibid., pp.78-9.
55. Ibid., pp.113-14.

56. Ibid., p.17.
57. Ibid., p.267.
58. Ibid., p.233.